BENGHAZI!

BENGHAZI!

*A New History of the Fiasco That
Pushed America and Its World
to the Brink*

ETHAN CHORIN

NEW YORK

Hachette Books
Hachette Book Group
1290 Avenue of the Americas
New York, NY 10104
HachetteBooks.com
Twitter.com/HachetteBooks
Instagram.com/HachetteBooks

First Edition: September 2022

Published by Hachette Books, an imprint of Perseus Books, LLC, a subsidiary of Hachette Book Group, Inc. The Hachette Books name and logo is a trademark of the Hachette Book Group.

The Hachette Speakers Bureau provides a wide range of authors for speaking events.

To find out more, go to www.hachettespeakersbureau.com or call (866) 376-6591.

The publisher is not responsible for websites (or their content) that are not owned by the publisher.

Library of Congress Control Number: 2022940622

ISBNs: 978-0-306-82972-7 (hardcover), 978-0-306-82974-1 (ebook)

Printed in the United States of America

LSC-C

Printing 1, 2022

For my parents

Contents

PART I
Pieces of a Puzzle

PART II
Risky Business

PART III

The Attack and the Scandal

PART IV

The World Benghazi Made

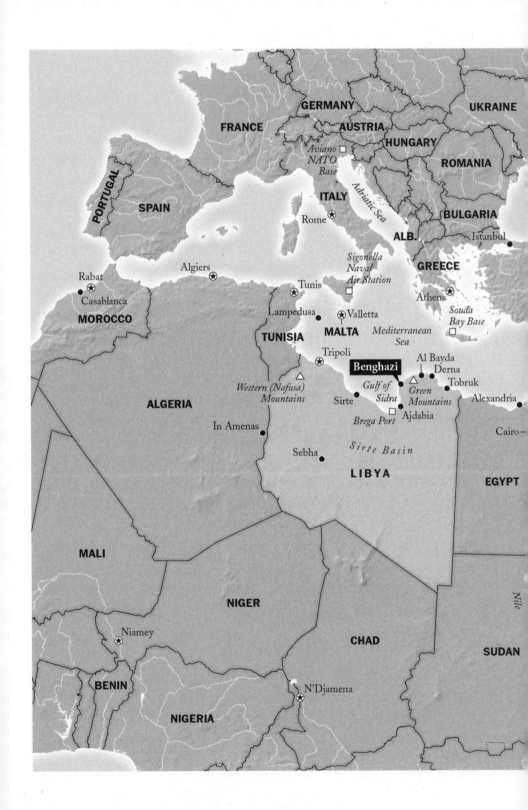

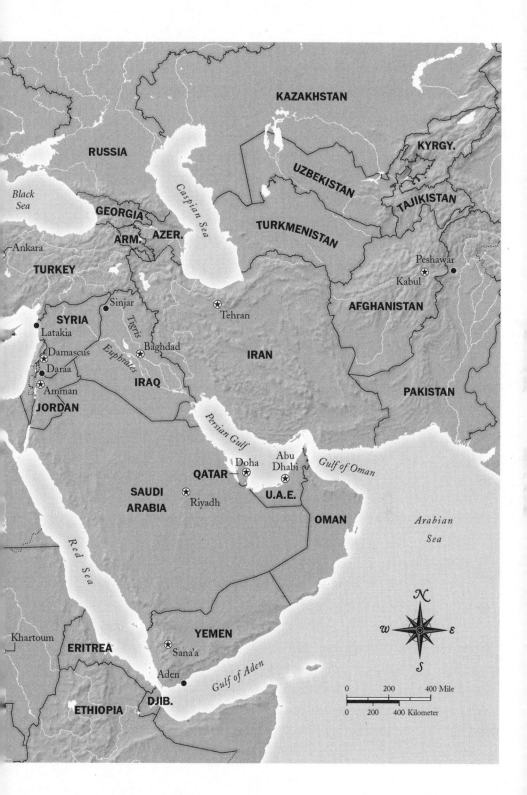

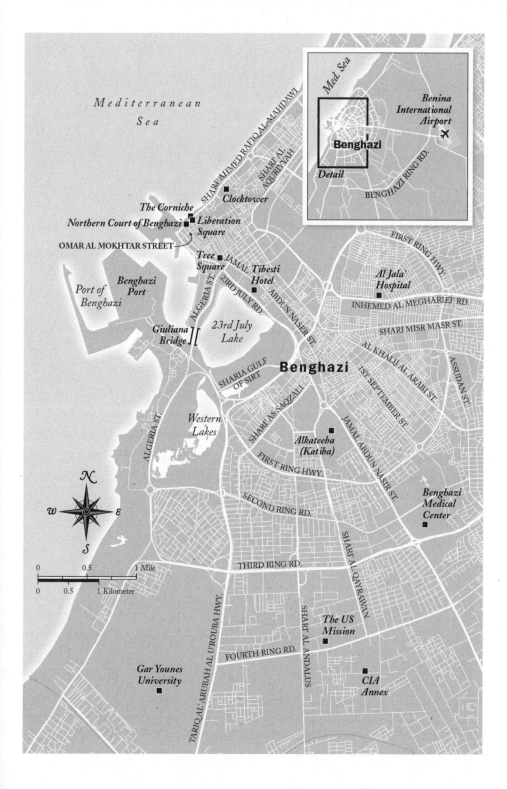

Mediterranean Sea

SHARI' AHMED RAFIQ AL-MAHDAWI

SHARI' AL AQURIYAH

Clocktower

The Corniche

Northern Court of Benghazi

Liberation Square

OMAR AL MOKHTAR STREET

Tree Square

JAMAL

Tibesti Hotel

Port of Benghazi

Benghazi Port

ALGERIA ST.

23RD JULY RD.

ABDUN NASER ST.

Al Jala' Hospital

FIRST RING HWY.

INHEMED AL MEGHARIEF RD.

SHARI MISR MASR ST.

Giuliana Bridge

23rd July Lake

SHARIA GULF OF SIRT

Benghazi

AL KHALIJ AL ARABI ST.

ASSUDAN ST.

1ST SEPTEMBER ST.

ALGERIA ST.

Western Lakes

SHARI' AS SAQZALI

Alkateeba (Katiba)

JAMAL ABDUN NASIR ST.

FIRST RING HWY.

SECOND RING RD.

Benghazi Medical Center

𝒩
W — E
S

0   0.5   1 Mile
0   0.5   1 Kilometer

THIRD RING RD.

SHARI AL QAYRAWAN

TARIQ AL 'ARUBAH AL UROUBA HWY.

FOURTH RING RD.

SHARI AL ANDALUS

The US Mission

Gar Younes University

CIA Annex

Med. Sea

Benina International Airport

Benghazi

Detail

FIRST RING HWY.

BENGHAZI RING RD.

Principal Characters

AMERICANS

US Officials in Tripoli or Benghazi at the Time of the Attack

Glen Doherty: Member of the Global Response Staff, former Navy SEAL, killed in Benghazi on September 12, 2012

Gregory Hicks: Deputy Chief of Mission (DCM) at US Embassy Tripoli in 2012

Brian Linvill: Lieutenant Colonel in the US Army, Defense Attaché at US Embassy Tripoli, 2008–2012

David McFarland: Foreign Service Officer and Acting Principal Officer at the Benghazi Mission just prior to the attack

Sean Smith: State Department Communications/Information Officer, Air Force veteran, on temporary duty to US Embassy Tripoli, killed in Benghazi on September 11, 2012

John Christopher (Chris) Stevens: US Ambassador to Libya from May 22, 2012, to September 11, 2012

Scott Wickland: Stevens's assigned personal diplomatic security agent in Benghazi

Tyrone S. Woods: Member of the Global Response Staff, former Navy SEAL, killed in Benghazi on September 12, 2012

Obama Administration Officials

Joseph Biden: Vice President of the United States, 2009–2016; forty-sixth President of the United States, 2021–

Derek Chollet: Lawyer, Senior Director for Strategic Planning at the National Security Council

James Clapper: Director of National Intelligence, 2010–2017

Hillary Rodham Clinton: Secretary of State, 2009–2012; Democratic Senator from New York, 2000–2008; Democratic presidential candidate in 2016

James Comey: Director of the FBI, 2013–2017

Robert Gates: Secretary of Defense, 2006–2011

Mike Morrell: Deputy Director of the CIA, 2010–2013; acting director in 2011 and 2012–2013

Barack Obama: Forty-fourth President of the United States, 2009–2016

Leon Panetta: Secretary of Defense, 2011–2013; CIA Director, 2009–2011

David Petraeus: CIA Director from September 6, 2011, to November 9, 2012; Commander of the US forces in Afghanistan, 2010–2011

Samantha Power: Special Assistant to the President, National Security Council, 2009–2013; author of *A Problem from Hell: America and the Age of Genocide*

Ben Rhodes: Deputy National Security Advisor for Strategic Communications and Speechwriting in the Obama administration, 2009–2017

Susan Rice: Ambassador to the United Nations at the time of the US intervention in Libya

Jake Sullivan: Director of Policy Planning at the State Department from February 2011 to February 2013

Republican Officials

John McCain: Senator from Arizona, who supported Obama's intervention in Libya; Republican presidential nominee in 2008

Mitt Romney: Governor of Massachusetts (2003–2007); Republican presidential candidate in 2012

Republican Politicians Connected to Benghazi Hearings

Trey Gowdy: Representative from South Carolina, Chair of the House Select Committee on Benghazi from May 8, 2014, to July 8, 2016

Darrell Issa: Representative from California, Chair of the House Oversight Committee, 2011–2015

Ron Johnson: Senator from Wisconsin

Mike Pompeo: Representative from Kansas, member of Republican majority on the Benghazi Committee

Donald Trump: Forty-fifth President of the United States, 2017–2021

US Ambassadors

Prudence Bushnell: Ambassador to Kenya, 1996–1999

Gene Cretz: First post-reconciliation Ambassador to Libya, 2008–2012

Gerald Feierstein: Ambassador to Yemen, 2010–2013

Deborah Jones: Ambassador to Libya, 2013–2014

Anne Patterson: Ambassador to Egypt, 2011–2013; Assistant Secretary of State for Near Eastern Affairs, 2013–2017

Jacob Walles: Ambassador to Tunisia, 2012–2015

LIBYANS

Islamists*

Ahmed Abu Khattala: Convicted of lesser terrorism charges in a US court in connection to the September 11, 2012, attack

Mohammed Al Gharabli: Head of the Rafallah al-Sahati Brigade at the time of the Benghazi US Mission attack

Abu Anas Al Libi: A.k.a. Nazih Abdul-Hamed al-Ruqai'i, former member of the LIFG, indicted in the United States in connection with the 1998 East Africa US embassy bombings

Abu Laith al-Libi: A.k.a. Ali Ammar Ashur al-Rufayi, Al Qaeda's number three under Osama bin Laden

Ibn al-Sheikh al-Libi: Libyan Al Qaeda operative whose remarks under torture were used to help make the case for the US war on Iraq

---

* NOTE: Most Salafi jihadi fighters go by their nom de guerre or *kunya,* which may be formed from the name of their oldest son. The suffix "Al Libi" ("The Libyan") indicates someone who identifies as Libyan.

Abdel Wahab Al Qaid: A.k.a. Abu Idris Al Libi, the LIFG's political counselor and strategist

Mohammed Hassan Al Qaid: A.k.a. Abu Yahya Al Libi, Al Qaeda's number two under Ayman Al-Zawahiri, brother of Abdel Wahab Al Qaid

Sami al-Saadi: A.k.a. Abu Munthir, LIFG's expert on Islamic law

Khalid al-Sherif: A.k.a. Abu Hazim al-Libi, LIFG's number two, rendered to Libya by the CIA in April 2005, participated in the *Corrections*

Mohammed al-Zahawi: Leader of Ansar al-Sharia Libya

Abdulhakim Belhaj: A.k.a. Abu Abdullah al-Sadiq, Emir of the Libyan Islamic Fighting Group (LIFG) since 1995; Head of the Tripoli Military Council after the fall of Tripoli

Wissam Bin Hamid: Head of Libya Shield One militia

Abu Sufian Bin Qumu: Former driver of bin Laden in Sudan, Guantanamo prisoner, LIFG member, head of Ansar al-Sharia Derna

Mahdi Harati: Ex-co-commander of the Tripoli Brigade and commander of Syrian fighting group Liwa al Ummah

Ali Sallabi: Significant figure in the Libyan Muslim Brotherhood, mediator of the *Corrections*

Ismail Sallabi: Early leader of Rafallah al-Sahati Brigade, brother of Ali Sallabi

Politicians and Public Figures

Mustafa Abdel Jalil: Chairman of the National Transitional Council from March 2011 to August 2012, former Minister of Justice under Gaddafi

Abdurrahim El Keib: Interim Prime Minister of Libya from November 2011 to November 2012

Bubaker Habib: Chris Stevens's Benghazi-based assistant, former US Liaison Office Tripoli employee

Khalifa Heftar: Former Gaddafi general, launched Karama movement and the Libyan National Army in 2014

Mahmoud Jibril: Interim Prime Minister for the National Transitional Council (2011), head of National Forces Alliance party

Aref Nayed: Islamic scholar, former Libyan Ambassador to the United Arab Emirates and head of the Stabilization Committee during the revolution

Abdel Fattah Younes: Former Gaddafi Interior Minister and commander of the Al-Saiqa special forces, subsequent rebel forces commander

Gaddafi Regime

Muammar Gaddafi: Leader of Libya

Saif Gaddafi: Second-oldest son of Gaddafi, de facto head of Libya's reform program, heir apparent to Gaddafi

Abdullah Senussi: Gaddafi's Head of Internal Security and brother-in-law, linked to the Abu Salim massacre of 1996

INTERNATIONAL ISLAMIST FIGURES

Ayman Al-Zawahiri: Cofounder of Al Qaeda, founder of Egyptian Islamic Jihad, successor to bin Laden

Muhammed Al-Zawahiri: Brother of Ayman Al-Zawahiri, allegedly helped plan protests at US Embassy Cairo on September 11, 2012

Osama bin Laden: Leader of Al Qaeda, killed in Obama-ordered US raid in 2011

LIBYAN AND SYRIAN GROUPS, MILITIAS, AND POLITICAL PARTIES

Al Qaeda in the Islamic Maghreb (AQIM): Leading formal Al Qaeda franchise in North Africa, allied with Ansar al-Sharia Libya

Ansar al-Sharia Derna: Affiliate of Ansar al-Sharia Libya, headed by former Guantanamo detainee Abu Sufian Bin Qumu

Ansar al-Sharia Libya: Salafis-jihadi group headed by Mohammed al-Zahawi, accused of masterminding the Benghazi attack; pledged allegiance to the Islamic State in October 2014

February 17 Martyrs Brigade (Feb 17): Umbrella group for a mix of Islamist militias, contracted by the US Embassy to provide security to the Benghazi Mission

Free Syrian Army (FSA): Military alliance founded July 2001 by defected officers of the Syrian Army, with the goal of taking down Assad; eroded by late 2012 with influx of Islamist groups

General National Congress (GNC): First post-revolution elected parliament, July 7, 2012, to June 25, 2014

Government of National Accord (GNA): Product of the Libyan Political Agreement (LPA), 2016–2021

House of Representatives (HOR): Second elected Libyan parliament, 2014–

Libyan Islamic Fighting Group (LIFG): Libyan jihadist affiliate of Al Qaeda, most active in Libya in the mid-1990s, disbanded as part of the *Corrections*; also known as *muqatila* for short

Libyan Islamic Movement for Change (LIMC): Successor to the LIFG, thought to have been created February 2011; changed its name to Islamic Movement for Reform in November 2011, with many of the same LIFG members as advisors

Libyan National Army: Military force that emerged from General Khalifa Heftar's Karama movement of May 2014, later reported to the parliament (HOR), elected in 2014

Libya Shields: Government-sanctioned armed groups formed in 2012 to manage regional security following the fall of the regime. The most visible was Libya Shield One, based in Benghazi

Liwa' al Ummah: Libyan-led militia in Syria fighting Bashar al-Assad, founded by Mahdi Harati in 2011

Muslim Brotherhood: Muslim Revivalist organization founded by Hassan al-Banna in Egypt in 1928

National Forces Alliance (NFA): Coalition of progressive parties founded by Mahmoud Jibril, won plurality in the 2012 elections

National Transitional Council (NTC): The Libyan transitional government following the US–NATO intervention in March 2011

Rafallah al-Sahati Brigade: Libyan militia established in Benghazi, linked to the killing of Abdel Fattah Younes

Syrian National Council (SNC): Syria's government in exile, formed in 2011 and located in Istanbul

Note on Arabic Transliterations

In most instances I use the most common English spellings for Arabic proper nouns.

Timeline

1928: Founding of the Muslim Brotherhood

1951: Libyan independence as federated constitutional monarchy under King Idris

1959: Discovery of oil in commercial quantities in Libya

1969: September 1: Military coup headed by Muammar Gaddafi overthrows King Idris

1979

December: Soviet invasion of Afghanistan
December 2: Mob attacks and burns the US Embassy in Tripoli
December 22: United States designates Libya a state sponsor of terrorism

1980: February 15: US Embassy in Tripoli closes

1986

April 5: A bomb explodes in the La Belle discotheque in West Berlin, killing three (two Americans) and wounding 230
April 15: United States attacks targets in Tripoli and Benghazi

1988

Key members of future LIFG leadership travel to Afghanistan to join the mujahideen
Osama bin Laden and Ayman Al-Zawahiri establish Al Qaeda
General Khalifa Heftar captured in Chad
December 21: Bombing of Pan Am Flight 103 over Lockerbie, Scotland, kills 270

1989: Gaddafi bombs French airliner, Union de Transports Aériens (UTA) Flight 772, over Niger

1992

Al Qaeda moves to Sudan

March 31: UN Security Council resolution demands Libya turn over suspects in Pan Am and UTA bombings

1993: UN Resolution 883 escalates sanctions on Libya and freezes Libya's foreign assets abroad

1994: LIFG assassination attempt on Gaddafi in Sebha fails

1995: Belhaj becomes emir of LIFG, which announces its presence in Libya

1996

February or March: UK-backed LIFG assassination attempt on Gaddafi in Sirte fails

Summer: Massacre of approximately 1,250 prisoners at Abu Salim prison in Tripoli

November 1: Qatar launches Al Jazeera channel

Bin Laden and Al Qaeda kicked out of Sudan; Al Qaeda and LIFG members return to Afghanistan

1998

August 7: East Africa bombing of US Embassies in Kenya and Tanzania by Al Qaeda

LIFG broken as a force in Libya

2000

October 12: Bombing of USS *Cole* in Aden, Yemen, by Al Qaeda

LIFG announces unilateral cease-fire in Libya

2001

September 11: Al Qaeda terrorist attacks in United States

Gaddafi offers condolences to United States in wake of 9/11 attacks

October 6: UN resolution designates LIFG a terrorist group

2003

March 20: United States invades Iraq

May: Libya indicates willingness to resolve outstanding issues with United States and United Kingdom

May: Casablanca, Morocco, bombings kill forty; Moroccan Islamic Combatant Group and LIFG implicated

September 12: UN Security Council adopts Resolution 1506 lifting sanctions on Libya

December 19: Libya announces its intention to dismantle its Weapons of Mass Destruction

2004

United States begins returning LIFG leadership to Libya as part of "extraordinary renditions" (2004–2005)

February 8: Resumption of a direct diplomatic presence in Libya occurs with the arrival of US personnel at the US Interests Section in Tripoli

June 28: The US Liaison Office (USLO) in Tripoli officially opens

First work on opening an "American Corner" in Benghazi (2004–2005)

2005: Unofficial start of the *Corrections* process of rehabilitating the LIFG

2006

February 17: Anti-Gaddafi riots in Benghazi and eastern cities, superficially linked to Danish cartoon controversy

May 15: The United States begins the process of rescinding Libya's designation as a state sponsor of terrorism, announces its intention to upgrade the US diplomatic presence in Tripoli to an embassy, and certifies that Libya is cooperating fully with USG anti-terrorism efforts

2007

June: Christopher Stevens arrives in Tripoli as Deputy Chief of Mission

October: Sinjar Records found along Iraq's Syrian border, indicating a startling number of Libyan recruits to Al Qaeda, coming from Benghazi and Derna

November 3: Al Qaeda leader Ayman Al-Zawahiri and Abu Laith al-Libi each proclaim merger of LIFG and Al Qaeda in two separate videos

2008

April 19: *Newsweek* publishes "The Jihadist Riddle" cover story about the Sinjar Records

Late May: Christopher Stevens sends "Die Hard in Derna" cable to Washington

November 4: Obama elected forty-fourth president of United States

2009

June 4: Obama's "New Beginning" speech in Cairo

August 20: Convicted Lockerbie bomber Abdelbaset al-Megrahi released from Scottish prison; Saif Gaddafi accompanies him back to Tripoli to hero's welcome

December 25: Underwear Bomber nearly blows up Northwest Airlines flight over Detroit

2010

March 23: Saif officiates a readout ceremony for the *Corrections*, attended by some Western diplomats and nongovernmental organizations; LIFG leaders Abdulhakim Belhaj, Sami al-Saadi, and Khalid al-Sherif released from Abu Salim prison

December 17: Jasmine Revolution starts in Tunisia, marking the start of the Arab Spring

2011

January 13: First demonstrations in Libya

January 25: Egyptian Revolution begins

January 27: Yemeni Revolution begins

February 15: Gaddafi regime arrests Abu Salim families' lawyer Fathi Terbil

February 17: Libyan Revolution officially begins

February 20: Mahdi Ziu detonates a car bomb outside the Katiba, allowing it to be stormed by rebels

LIFG rebrands itself the Libyan Islamic Movement for Change (LIMC)

March 6: Start of Syrian Revolution

March: Obama administration gives Qatar and other countries green light for covert aid to Libyan rebels

February 21: Saif's "rivers of blood" speech

February 22: Gaddafi's "zenga zenga" speech; Interior Minister Abdel Fattah Younes defects to the rebel side

February 27: Libyan National Transitional Council (NTC) announced in Benghazi

March 14: Secretary of State Clinton meets in Paris with Jibril and Essawi

March 17: UN Resolution 1973 authorizes "all necessary measures" to protect civilians in Benghazi

March 19: US-led NATO air campaign in Libya begins (US code name Operation Odyssey Dawn)

April 5: Stevens arrives in Benghazi on Greek freighter *Aegean Pearl* as US Envoy to the Libyan transitional government

March 21: American F-15 ditches in Libya, pilots rescued

July 15: NTC recognized by United States

July 28: Rebel Commander Younes killed in Benghazi by Islamists

August 23: Bab Al Aziziya taken; Belhaj declares Tripoli liberation

October 20: Gaddafi killed in Sirte by rebel mob

October 23: NTC declares liberation of Libya

Late November: Belhaj and Mahdi Harati travel to Syria; Belhaj meets with members of the Free Syrian Army in Istanbul

November 19: Saif captured in southern Libya by rebel forces from Zintan

Wissam Bin Hamid becomes commander of Libya Shield One

2012

April 6: IED tossed over US Mission wall in Benghazi

May 22: Stevens assumes US Ambassadorship to Libya; Red Cross
   building in Benghazi hit by two RPGs

June 4: Mohammed Hassan Al Qaid killed by a drone strike in northwestern Pakistan by US drone

June 6: Bomb explodes outside wall of US Mission in Benghazi

July 7: National elections held in Libya; "progressives" win officially,
   affiliation of independents not known

August 15: At meeting in Tripoli, regional security officer expresses
   concern that the Benghazi Mission could not withstand an attack

Summer: Clinton–Petraeus plan for arming Syrian opposition
   rebuffed by President Obama

September 9: David McFarland and Bubaker Habib meet with militia leaders Wissam Bin Hamid and Mohammed Al Gharabli in
   Benghazi

September 10: Al Qaeda Leader Ayman Al-Zawahiri urges followers
   to avenge death of Al Qaeda's number two, Abu Yahya Al Libi

September 11: Attack on US Mission in Benghazi kills Ambassador
   Christopher Stevens and Sean Smith

September 12: Attack on CIA Annex in Benghazi kills Tyrone Woods
   and Glen Doherty

September 12: Libyan Parliament votes on Prime Minister in Tripoli;
   cargo ship *Al Intisar* leaves Benghazi for Turkey, suspected to be
   carrying weapons for Syrian rebels

September 16: UN Ambassador Susan Rice appears on Sunday talk
   shows with incorrect Benghazi talking points

September 19: Director of National Counterterrorism Center is first
   Obama administration official to use the phrase "terrorist attack"
   in reference to the events of September 11, 2012

September 20: FBI shares results of eyewitness interviews within the
   US government; FBI director of National Intelligence James Clapper says attack had "all earmarks of a premeditated attack"

September 21: Secretary Clinton says "what happened in Benghazi
   was a terrorist attack"

September 25: President Obama's UN General Assembly speech eulogizes Ambassador Stevens, emphasizes the impact of the *Innocence of Muslims* video on the region

December 20: Accountability Review Board releases its findings on the Benghazi attack

2013

May 5: Libya's General National Congress passes the Political Isolation Law

August 21: Ghouta chemical attack on civilians in Damascus, Syria

December 28: *New York Times* publishes David Kirkpatrick's "A Deadly Mix in Benghazi"

2014

January 15: US Senate Select Committee on Intelligence releases its investigation of Benghazi attack

March 2: *New York Times* publishes story about Hillary Clinton's use of private email server for official emails

May 2: House Speaker John Boehner announces intention to create House Select Committee on Benghazi

May: Heftar announces Karama (Dignity) campaign to take Libya back from Islamists

June 25: Second national elections in Libya held, resulting in election of the House of Representatives and a political loss for Islamists

July 26: US Embassy evacuation in face of post-election fighting in Tripoli

House of Representatives moves to Tobruk in eastern Libya

2015

October 22: Clinton testifies before Benghazi Committee

December 17: Libyan Political Agreement signed in Libya, paving way for Government of National Accord (GNA)

December 9: LIFG removed from the US State Department list of terrorist organizations

2016

July 5: FBI Director James Comey announces no grounds for criminal prosecution of Hillary Clinton on email issue

July 19: Trump wins Republican presidential nomination

October 28: Director Comey announces FBI will reopen investigation into Clinton's emails

November 9: Trump elected forty-fifth president of the United States

2017

June 7: Heftar declares Benghazi liberated

2019

April 4: Heftar orders forces to move on Tripoli and attempt to overthrow the GNA

September: First known support by Russia of the Libyan National Army and General Khalifa Heftar

2020

January: Turkey intervenes against Heftar's forces

November 7: Joseph Biden elected forty-sixth president of the United States

Prologue

The Attack, Part I

Istanbul, September 10, 2012

I did what by this point had become routine: woke up early, stuffed my suitcase into the Hotel Ibrahim Pasha's lilliputian elevator, and climbed into a waiting cab for the forty-minute ride to the Istanbul airport. I hadn't slept well. Through groggy eyes, I navigated a busy airport stuffed with passengers waiting to cram their suitcases and jury-rigged boxes through an X-ray scanner. I stood in a long security line, which ultimately deposited me in a waiting area, from which a bus took me to a plane bound for Benghazi. Looking around at my fellow passengers, I realized that the in-flight demographic was very different than a year before. Then, the passengers consisted mostly of refugees, families, and war-wounded; now, the crowd was overwhelmingly twenty- and thirty-year-old males. Some wore casts and used crutches, suggesting they'd been treated in Turkey for injuries sustained in Libya (or Syria, where some Libyans were fighting the regime of Bashar al-Assad).

The plane took off, and I fell asleep. Three hours later, I was jostled awake by the tug of gravity as the pilot cut the engines back for the descent. Often, the final descent into Benghazi affords a stunning view of the Jebel Akhdar, or Green Mountains, an unspoiled wilderness ringed with white sandy beaches and mottled turquoise waters. Not a cloud in sight. It promised to be a gorgeous day.

What had I been so worried about? I asked myself, with a hint of conscious self-deception, as I stepped off the plane and headed for customs. The customs process changed every month, a symptom of the fact that the Libyan rebels who'd taken over the country from Muammar Gaddafi the year before were still learning their way around running a country. But the bearded young men in front of me seemed to know where to go. I followed them through dark corridors and up to a group of men in full-body camouflage. They directed some travelers to sit, others to pass.

Typically, this would be when my fixer, the local contact who made sure bad things didn't happen, would appear. But fifteen minutes . . . half an hour . . . nearly an hour went by, and no one came to fetch me, and now my cell phone wasn't working. This was the kind of unscripted moment when anything could happen. If I were to be abducted, no one would know for hours.

"*Anta liwahdak* (You're alone)?" one of the men in camouflage asked me, highlighting the obvious. This was both the first time I was traveling alone into Benghazi and the first time someone wasn't waiting. The general atmosphere seemed strained, more impersonal than previous trips. But I reminded myself, again, that by themselves, these emotional samples were just noise. Trying to decipher a pattern would be counterproductive.

This trip had its origins two years earlier. In the summer of 2010, I had left the US State Department and was in Dubai working for a multinational company. In that role, I spent time in places like Djibouti and Mozambique, trying to understand the unique developmental challenges facing communities in port cities. One day I received an email from someone I had never met. "Ahmed" (not his real name) had read a book I had written a few years before—translations of Libyan short stories mixed with travelogue. He said that reading the stories brought back memories from his youth in Benghazi—a period that felt to him increasingly distant, as he'd now spent more than half his life in Texas. His wife had urged him to reach out. We spoke a few times on the phone and became fast friends. When I took a trip back to the United States, we arranged to meet in person.

A few months later, the Arab Spring revolutions started in Tunisia and spread to Egypt and then Libya in February 2011. Throughout the Arab world, demonstrations were leading to the ousting of leaders.

For two years, from 2004 to 2006, I had been one of a small number of American diplomats posted to Libya, following an unusual American rapprochement with Libya's flamboyant, iron-fisted dictator, Muammar Gaddafi. Libya had been effectively off limits for Americans for nearly a quarter century. Due to my position as the liaison between American businesses looking to capitalize on the opening of an oil state, and Libyans looking to partner with Americans, I developed a deep community of professional contacts, some of whom would become dear friends. It was an exciting, chaotic time: I felt as if I lived a period of ten years in the space of two. And in the process, I felt I had absorbed many of the hopes and aspirations of those Libyans with whom I interacted on a daily basis.

And seven years later, they'd done it—Libyans had risen up against their omnipresent dictator. Suddenly, I was getting text messages from acquaintances and friends alike, some fearing they would be arrested, others trying desperately to get out of the country. Then the United States intervened militarily, ostensibly to protect Benghazi from a massacre. And soon after, I heard that a former colleague, Chris Stevens, had been named the US envoy to Libya's nascent rebel government in Benghazi.

I called Chris and told him that I really wanted in. I wanted to be back in Libya, working for him. His response wasn't what I hoped to hear: "You've got a good job out there in Dubai, Ethan. And you know how the US government works. By the time you're back in the system, things in Libya will be very different. And you might wind up in

Venezuela . . . not Libya. I wish I could hire you directly, but you know that's not possible."

I felt dampened by Chris's reaction. The sudden and dramatic reappearance in my life of Libya and the connections I had made there—many of them assuming I was still working for the State Department and asking for help in ways that might make the difference between life and death—upset me, energized me, and got me wondering again whether I had made the right decision to leave the Foreign Service after four years. But Chris was right. There were practical reasons behind my decision to leave State, and I needed to follow my own path for a while.

Still, I couldn't leave Libya behind. Ahmed, who had made his own decision to leave the country years earlier, felt the same. We both started talking about how and if we might contribute on a humanitarian level to this chaotic uprising. We quickly settled on medical support. As I had seen firsthand, medical services had never been a priority for Gaddafi, and the war had pushed Libya's shabby medical infrastructure to the breaking point.

Ahmed and I were an odd pair: the fifty-six-year-old Libyan with a Texan accent and a gray goatee and the forty-two-year-old former American diplomat. But we had complementary skills, and we worked well together. Neither of us were doctors or conventional public health professionals, but we had experience getting things done in tough environments and had a wealth of contacts in both Libya and the United States. Over the following months, Ahmed and I formed a small nonprofit focused on wartime trauma, emergency medicine, and diabetes, and we registered it with the United Nations. We were interested in emergency medicine for its immediate relevance to war, but also because the field was increasingly seen as a cornerstone of efforts to build broader health infrastructure in developing and fragile states. The theory was that if you get emergency medicine right, you have a chance of building everything else on top of it correctly.

Quickly, Ahmed was able to make contact, through family connections, with the directors of Benghazi Medical Center (BMC), a 1,200-bed facility that nearly twenty years after its construction was still operating at a fraction of its capacity due to government corruption and neglect. While Ahmed worked his connections in the Benghazi medical community, I reached out to American institutions with experience operating in developing countries. In my conversations with internationally focused physicians and health workers, I found a surprisingly strong interest in Libya. It was at the higher, administrative level that things got complicated: Libya wasn't a normal operating environment—it was still a war zone. These institutions needed time to consider what we were proposing—but given the pace of change in Libya, time was not on anyone's side.

BMC's director, Fathi Al-Jehani, was in his forties, lanky and unusually tall for a Libyan, with a neatly manicured beard. I rarely saw him without his white surgical jacket. He was one of those people who preferred to listen and spoke only when necessary. Dr. Laila Bugaighis was his codirector, and the more vocal and demonstrative of the two. Against Fathi's reserve, she was a flash of color, literally and figuratively; Laila typically wore sharp pantsuits with a scarf that could double as a face covering outside the hospital. She was self-assured and vocal about the dangers she saw facing Benghazi and Libya from all sides: former Gaddafi regime thugs, violent Islamists, general chaos. But she was also optimistic, envisioning rich possibilities if the country managed its transition from dictatorship to democracy. She was determined not to squander the opportunity to make up for the decades of what she proclaimed as "lost time" under Gaddafi.

It didn't take long for Ahmed and me to become very impressed with both Fathi and Laila and their personal commitments to Libya and the revolution underway. Fathi had been working in the Arabian Gulf as a specialist and returned immediately after the liberation of Benghazi in March 2011. For his troubles, he had been targeted by local militias, who one day ambushed him outside the hospital, shooting him in the arm before he managed to drive his SUV to a safer area of town. The next day, he was back at work. Laila, also in her early forties, came from one of eastern Libya's most visible families and was one of several in her family to make deep sacrifices. Her cousin Salwa would be murdered in 2014 for her outspoken positions in support of progress.

For Fathi and Laila, my and Ahmed's backgrounds were clearly both an attraction and a source of concern: Why exactly were a former US diplomat and a member of another of Benghazi's distinguished local families, long living in the States, suddenly here, seemingly alone, offering help? What kind of help could these two provide? And what strings were attached? One evening during our second trip to Benghazi, Laila expressed some of these thoughts openly as she prepared a fish tagine. This kind of invitation, into a woman's home, in the conservative social environment of Benghazi, could only be interpreted as an expression of unusual confidence—even as she ran through a litany of possibilities including that we were sent by some US government agency to keep tabs on them. She concluded with a touch of fatalism, if not light-hearted sarcasm: "What other choice do we have—we asked for help from the Americans, and you two showed up. *Alhamdulillah* (Praise be to God)," Laila said.

In one of our subsequent meetings, Laila said with a laugh, "Maybe the next thing we'll hear is that you've brought us Harvard. But seriously," she added, "we can't tell you how much we appreciate your efforts."

A month or so later, I was sitting in a quiet teahouse in my hometown of Berkeley, California, working on a draft of a book on the Libyan Revolution, when I overheard two men discussing a project to create emergency medical capacity in South Sudan, which had recently become Africa's newest independent state. South Sudan had a vaguely similar profile to Libya. It had just emerged from its own long and bloody civil war, needed international support, and yet was so rich with oil that it could contribute its own money to pay for reconstruction. I apologized for eavesdropping and chatted them up, telling them about our work in Benghazi and our quest for institutional partners. It was a fateful meeting, as it turned out they were connected to a professor of emergency medicine at Harvard, Dr. Thomas Burke, who didn't seem fazed by the security challenges in Benghazi. He saw an opportunity in getting in on the ground floor of this kind of project.

When we told Laila about this development, I'm certain both her hopes and her fears were confirmed—there was no way that Ahmed and I could be working alone. We had to be a front for someone. The State Department. The CIA. Both. After all, she was joking when she implored us to connect them with Harvard.

Over the next few months, Ahmed and I introduced Dr. Burke and his colleagues to Laila and Fathi, and helped his team iron out the skeleton of a program promising to meet some of BMC's and eastern Libya's immediate and longer-term needs. The initial emphasis was on mentoring and training of staff by American counterparts. Other American universities were interested, but to their credit, Burke and his staff were able to mobilize quickly. We arranged an introductory trip to Benghazi for Burke and one of his colleagues, during which they were treated as VIPs. Things looked promising.

Over the following year, I remained in touch with Chris Stevens, who had since been confirmed at the first post-revolution US ambassador to Libya. His colleagues were thrilled with this news, as Chris had a reputation for being a consummate professional, someone who preferred the field to Washington and did not calculate his every career move based on its political value.

Since we hadn't spoken in a few months, I thought it would be wise to meet with him in person at the US Embassy in the Libyan capital of Tripoli following our next trip to Benghazi. I wanted to explain where Ahmed and I had gotten with our medical efforts, as I knew Chris was trying to move the State Department to invest more time and assistance in the city.

Initially, we suggested the eleventh of September. But as the date approached, I felt that stopping in Tripoli added a level of complexity to our movements that made me uncomfortable. I told Chris I was very sorry not to see him on the trip, but we were going to do just a quick in-and-out in Benghazi to help structure an agreement between BMC and Harvard.

From the start of the BMC collaboration, I watched the security situation in Benghazi very carefully. I was admittedly adventurous, but I wasn't into taking unnecessary risks, especially when I felt responsible for others. Even at the time of our previous trip to Benghazi, in June, I didn't like what I was seeing. Since April of 2012, there had been a substantial uptick in targeted attacks on local journalists, civil society figures, and Western diplomats. On June 6, an improvised explosive device (IED) was dropped outside the gate of the US Mission, damaging the exterior wall. And the following month, a group of Red Crescent workers were kidnapped.

A week before the September trip, I decided after reading some particularly alarming local Facebook posts that the level of risk had become too high for me to sanction our group's travel to Benghazi. I told Ahmed that I thought we should cancel our trip immediately— and indefinitely. Technically, because Ahmed and I had brought the parties together, and had been entrusted with making decisions related to project scope and safety, it was our call. But Burke and his colleague declared that they were going, no matter what. It was clear they'd established a bond with Laila and Fathi, and I got the strong sense that they felt they no longer needed us.

"Impossible to cancel now," Burke said, curtly, on a conference call. "We're already under pressure from our administration to get this moving or close it down—if we pull out, we won't get another chance." And he was right about that.

Of course, BMC also felt highly vested in the trip and, in their own way, also downplayed the risks.

"We live these risks daily," Laila would often remind us.

I was torn between the gut feeling that something really bad was about to happen and an awareness that this might be our last chance to get the projects Ahmed and I had been working on for the last year into higher gear. The more American attention on Benghazi, the better. Each success enabled others. I knew that Ambassador Stevens was pushing for a permanent official US presence in Benghazi; all of us were working toward the same basic goal, from different ends.

Burke and his group dug in. And I couldn't blame BMC for encouraging them. Fathi and Laila came to see Harvard as a crucial political lifeline, even though at that point very few people back in Washington even knew that this project existed. The Harvard brand was desirable, but it also represented some guarantee that someone in Washington would be paying attention to Benghazi. It was the same with Stevens—his presence in the city was comforting to many because it seemed to be a physical manifestation that the United States hadn't abandoned Benghazi. Chris understood this, and I'm certain that this was a factor in his own decision to travel to Benghazi.

Ahmed and I conferred—we couldn't prevent the Harvard group from going, and we also knew there was something bigger here at stake. If the meeting was going forward, Ahmed and I felt it was important to have someone from our team there overseeing the proceedings, both because it was our defined role in structuring the original agreement and, second, because we had an increasing feeling that corporate interests were trying to edge us out of any future participation. We trusted Laila and Fathi but also knew they were under their own sets of pressures. I agreed to go for three days, September 10 to 12. Ahmed wanted to stay longer.

Back at the customs checkpoint, one of the men in blue fatigues—tall, with an air of authority, but probably no older than twenty—flared his nostrils at me. I was suddenly intensely aware of the fact that Benghazi was no longer the sleepy backwater that I was used to. It was a war zone. I told the man about my work at the hospital and gave him Fathi's name. He barked a response, "*Istana shwai* (Wait a second)." He pointed to a plastic seat in the corner, then disappeared. I sat down, and the anxiety returned with a vengeance. Had I made a serious error in not listening to my instinct? Yes or no, I was now committed to be in Benghazi for the next three days.

A few minutes later, the man returned. I saw his phone light up with a call, revealing his background image: the rugged mien of the rebel commander Abdel Fattah Younes. This was another clue. Younes had been a former Gaddafi minister who disobeyed his direct orders to crush the Benghazi uprising long enough to give the rebels time to regroup. But he was an early casualty of a growing ideological battle, assassinated in July 2011 by what were widely presumed to be Islamist forces. There were rumors that Younes was a traitor, a double agent working for Gaddafi and the rebels both. But for many of the people of Benghazi, Younes remained a hero. If these guys were affiliated with Younes's tribe and his militias, I was probably going to be okay.

As he perfunctorily flipped through my passport, my cell connection returned just long enough for me to text Ahmed. I was irritated. "I'm all alone out here," I wrote.

Finally, the man in fatigues waved me through. That wasn't necessarily for the better. I was now out, but alone and unprotected. I pushed my way through a raucous crowd toward a car that looked like it might be a taxi.

Sitting in the back of a derelict cab, I hurtled across a maze of overpasses into the city's industrial zone, dominated by sand-colored apartment buildings and warehouses built by Turkish or Korean contractors, who priced their work high and built as cheaply as possible. The city had been completely destroyed in fighting between Allied and Axis forces during World War II, clearing the way for a concrete jungle in the 1960s and 1970s. From this angle, Benghazi looked more like the chaotic, impoverished slums of Cairo—but the view got better as the cab came closer to the traditional city center, where the architectural influence of the Italian colonizers dominated: wide boulevards and stately, wedge-shaped apartments with high ceilings.

I had the cab wait while I checked in to the Tibesti Hotel, then left my bags in my room. I knew this room. It was one of a handful regularly assigned to foreign diplomats in the early 2000s, almost certainly because it was bugged. The room smelled of mothballs and mildew. The bed was rock-hard and shrink-wrapped in thickly starched sheets that took some effort to peel back. There was an old TV in one corner and, as always, nothing in the minibar. I didn't dally. I left my bags and took the cab to BMC, a sprawling complex halfway between the hotel and the airport.

At the entrance, water bubbled up from a small fountain into a shallow, ornamental pool. On our first post-revolution visit to the hospital a year before, the basin of the fountain was clogged with foul-smelling muck. Ever fastidious, Ahmed took one of the junior administrators aside and gently pointed out that the patients' impressions of the facility would be far improved if the first thing they saw when they entered looked hygienic—and worked.

It seemed they listened.

I found Ahmed, Burke, Fathi, and the rest of the team in a conference room on the third floor, sitting in oversized swivel chairs under intense fluorescent lights, poring over a draft of the contract. Twenty million dollars was the price tag for Phase One. But it still wasn't clear where the money was going to come from—Libya had the resources, but many of its assets were still frozen, and there was no national budget.

I had half a mind to express my frustration that I'd been forgotten at the airport. But I was distracted by a question from one of the hospital staff, asking me if I knew that the US ambassador was in town.

Word of Chris's presence in Benghazi caught me off guard. Because we were no longer going to Tripoli, I hadn't expected to see him on this trip. My first reaction was that it was a nice turn of luck. Then I wondered what he was doing here, now. *Had Chris*, I wondered, *made progress in convincing the State Department to support his idea of a more formal diplomatic presence in Benghazi?* A few hours later, after our meetings wrapped up, I emailed Chris from the hospital.

"I heard you were in town. Do you have time to meet?" I wrote.

"We'll make it work," he answered.

Back at the hotel, I spent some time pulling the sheets off the bed, then crawled onto the odd-smelling cot, exhausted. That evening, the night of September 10, Fathi and the other BMC staff had arranged a dinner for us at a local restaurant. The energy was high; there were various heartfelt speeches by the Libyan doctors and administrators, who told us how grateful they were for the collaboration and for our presence. It was a heady moment, but I had enough experience with these kinds of projects in cities emerging from conflict to know that you had to hold your breath—there would undoubtedly be more obstacles ahead. I was, however, relieved that things seemed to be going well.

On the side, one of Ahmed's cousins, a doctor at BMC, told Ahmed that he had flown in from Tripoli that morning, on the same flight as Ambassador Stevens. Fatima Hamroush, Libya's newly appointed minister of health, was also on the flight, and she told Ahmed's cousin that she would not stay overnight in Benghazi because the situation was "far too dangerous." But she had the impression that Stevens was going to stay for a few days. Ahmed later recalled wondering what was so important that Stevens would stay for a few days when a Libyan minister herself thought it too dangerous.

In the early afternoon of the eleventh, Ahmed and I took a cab from BMC back to the Tibesti, where we sat at a table in the first-floor café to wait for Chris's call. My phone had stopped working at some point during the previous day, so I had given Chris Ahmed's cell number.

I stayed at the Tibesti on my trips to Benghazi during the years 2004–2006. It was also Chris's base on his trips to the city in 2007 and 2008, and where he set up a makeshift diplomatic post just after the US-backed military intervention in 2011. Named after the mountains along Libya's border with Chad, the hotel is an architectural oddity and one of the most recognizable features of the city's skyline. It looks like the front grille of Darth Vader's helmet, shrouded in obsidian-black glass. The café consists of a series of tables, arranged single file on a raised platform. Every so often, someone would push his or her chair a bit too far back and topple onto the floor below.

In front of me, a single, circular cake sat on the third tier of a glass display case. That cake puzzled me. Years before, when I was a diplomat visiting Benghazi, I used to write up my day's reporting notes in this café. I'd often take a table near a rotating display case and watch the cake as it turned counterclockwise. I remember the beads of humidity that accumulated on the hard, chocolate shell. There was never a slice cut from it. Was this, now, the very same cake? Was it made of plastic?

Behind us, armed men passed through a security scanner, setting off alarms as the machine's chain-smoking attendants waved them through.

Ahmed's phone rang.

"Ambassador Stevens for you," Ahmed smiled as he handed the phone to me.

"Ambassador—Chris," I said, satisfying my preference for formality with his for informality.

I stepped away from potential eavesdroppers to an area up a few stairs, the spot where French philosopher Bernard-Henri Lévy, on a fact-finding mission regarding the Benghazi rebels more than a year and a half before, claimed to have called President Nicolas Sarkozy to plead for France to support the Libyan rebels, lest "the blood of the people of Benghazi [stain] the flag of France."[1]

Chris sounded distracted, agitated even. But when I told him that the Libyans and the Americans had just signed a high-priced memorandum to revamp Benghazi's medical infrastructure, there was a clear shift in his tone. This was big news. From the pauses in the conversation, I could sense his mental calculations, similar to the one Fathi and his colleagues had made months ago. Harvard's presence in Benghazi would be useful in getting the resources Chris desperately wanted from the State Department and the appropriations committees in Congress.

"I had no idea you'd gotten so far with this—this is amazing news, congratulations!" he said.

Chris first suggested that Ahmed, Burke, Fathi, Laila, and I come over for dinner or coffee that evening at the Mission, the State Department's compound in Benghazi.

"I'd come to you," Chris said, "but I can't leave the compound today."

I understood why. It was September 11, and this would be an expected precaution for US diplomats. I knew from past experience that outside visitors to US missions often attract more attention than those inside. A voice in my head was repeating what I felt but couldn't bring myself to say out loud: "Chris, do you want to get us killed?" He had protection, I reasoned. We had none.

Stevens picked up on my reaction and suggested we meet the next day at the hospital instead. "That'll give me an opportunity to give the US government imprimatur to this project. I'm so happy to hear this," Chris effused, in a tone that sounded almost like relief.

Days later, I'd have a chance to reflect on this conversation, with some horror. Had I said yes, we all might have been at the compound during the attack.

"One of my security detail will call you this afternoon to go over the mechanics of how we will get in and out of BMC tomorrow," Chris said. "Things are tricky these days, as you know." He asked me to make sure that the head of BMC—Fathi—was aware that his team would be carrying concealed weapons. *Wasn't everyone in Benghazi carrying weapons?* I asked myself. I didn't ask Chris for clarification.

Around 4:00 PM, I got a call from someone calling himself "Jack." I had enough experience with diplomatic security (DS) and the US intelligence community to tell by the tone of his voice that this wasn't his real name. An unwritten code existed between those who'd been in governmental foreign postings, an implicit swagger that some used to broadcast information that couldn't be stated openly.

He told me that the ambassador and three or four of his people would be coming through a side entrance to the hospital. Jack and his team had the building's floor plans.

"I know you're former State Department," he said to me, "but I must repeat: do not tell anyone about the ambassador's movements, except for your immediate colleagues."

Once again, I felt a bit reassured. But it started to seem like everyone was relying on everyone else for reassurance, as if peace of mind were a giant Ponzi scheme.

Ahmed and I ate dinner together in the hotel dining room, which doubled as a soldiers' mess hall attached to a billeting station for rebel soldiers. If it's not home-cooked, Libyan food is rarely something to write home about, but this was far worse than usual—tuna sandwiches on stale bread spread with rancid mayo. These were military rations, for a city under siege.

It was about 8:00 PM, and it was dark outside. As we walked out of the dining area, I glanced up at a flat-screen TV. Under Gaddafi, Libyan news was laughable, diatribes delivered in a monotone over a floating symbol of the national broadcasting company, which Libyans called the *qunfuz* (hedgehog) for its resemblance to that creature. Now, it had received a complete makeover, thanks to the Qataris, who broadcast news favorable to their perspective from the capital of Doha 2,400 miles away. I called Fathi again to talk to him about tomorrow's plans.

There was no answer.

I tried again about an hour later. Still no answer.

Just before 9:30 PM, Fathi rang Ahmed's phone and I spoke with him. It was a brief conversation, punctuated by silence. Something felt off. I sensed he had something to tell me but didn't know how to phrase it.

"Have you spoken to Chris in the last half hour?" Fathi asked.

"No, why?" I said.

"Something's happening at the Mission." I could tell by his tone that this "something" spelled trouble.

I heard voices around him in the background.

"I'll call you back," he said rapidly and hung up.

I felt a dull sensation in the pit of my stomach and walked purposefully down the corridor toward Ahmed's room, trying to suppress a feeling of panic and the slight urge to vomit. My gut had been trying to tell me something these last few weeks, and I had ignored it.

I became aware of details around me that had long ago faded into the background. I remember thinking, *My god, after all this time in this hotel, I never noticed the wall-to-wall carpet was such a disgusting shade of orange.*

As I rounded a corner in the hallway, I encountered a woman, kneeling on the floor, her long blonde hair covering her face. She was crying. I asked what was wrong, but she didn't answer. "Can I help?" I asked. More crying. Was this related to what was going on outside? What did this woman know that I didn't? I couldn't stay, so I moved on, my thoughts racing.

I knocked on Ahmed's door, and he let me in. I walked over to the window behind the bed and peeled back the curtain a few inches to see what was happening on the back side of the hotel. There were no streetlamps, and it was too dark to see anything clearly.

Ahmed sat down on the edge of the bed while I pulled up a chair across from him. Suddenly, an explosion pierced the silence. If this noise was connected to the conversation I just had, this was some serious firepower, as the US Mission was nearly three miles away. For an explosion to be that loud, it must have been large. I wasn't a military person, and I didn't know what heavy artillery sounded like, but the explosion sounded devastating.

Ahmed and I stared at each other.

"Well, that doesn't certainly sound good," Ahmed said, his deadpan voice contradicting the eyes nearly popping out of his head.

His face said what I was thinking. We'd been through some scary incidents since we started this unlikely adventure, but this had entered a whole new level of frightening.

As Ahmed and I debated what to do, my previously inert cell phone sprang to life. Someone was texting me, and I jumped at it like a lifeline.

It was a friend back in California who didn't know I was in Libya, asking if I wanted to join him for a beer. I read the text to Ahmed, who laughed, maybe a little too loudly. "I think you should take him up on it." Together we clutched at the brief moment of levity.

I thought perhaps we should try to get out of the hotel, track down some of Ahmed's cousins, and ask for sanctuary, so to speak. But the hotel had our passports, and trying to fetch them would be problematic.

Ahmed urged me to call Jack back on the grounds that whatever was happening at the Mission, it was relevant to our own safety.

"Our lives might depend on it," he insisted.

I couldn't argue with that. I dialed the number and waited. Then I heard a voice, which didn't sound much like the guy I spoke to earlier.

"We're under fucking attack!" the voice said, with a hesitation that sounded like it was trying to verify whether I was someone who could be helpful. I wasn't, clearly. The call hung in the air for a few seconds before the line cut. In the background, I heard what sounded like gunfire. After a few minutes, Ahmed and I came up with a simple plan. We'd stay put until something changed. Fathi seemed to have some influence on our safety from wherever he was, but he would need to know where we were in order to help.

I realized that neither I nor Ahmed had seen Burke since before dinner. I walked the few paces down the hall to his door and knocked. No answer. I knocked again. I thought I heard some movement. Burke opened the door. I gave a quick summary of what had happened the last hour, but he appeared unperturbed.

When I went back to my room, I was wondering how Ahmed was. I didn't want to disturb him if he'd managed finally to get to sleep, nor was I keen on leaving my room. Ahmed would, much later, confess that at the time he was grappling with thoughts that disturbed him deeply.

"My fear," he explained, "was not so much of being killed, but not knowing what I would do if I were asked to identify myself as an American or a Libyan. In a moment of life and death, would I stand with you, my colleague and friend, or claim to be Libyan and try to melt into the surroundings?" I didn't begrudge Ahmed the thought—he had that option. I didn't.

"Ahmed," I told him, "if that situation came up, in all likelihood your standing with me would only have compromised you. It wouldn't have helped me."

I went back to my room. I assumed no one on street level could see into windows five floors up, but I didn't want to take any chances. I switched the light off and stared out into the night, looking for any clues about what was happening. The side of the room that faced the street and the front of the hotel was one giant window above bed level. Whatever was happening at the front of the hotel was obscured by a large awning. In the center of my view, there was a parking lot, partially illuminated by streetlamps. At one end was a lone police car, its intense blue lights flashing. Just beyond was a two-lane highway, usually one of Benghazi's busiest; now, the only vehicles coming and going were military. On the far side of the highway was a wide shoulder that edged up to the side of the lagoon. There was a lot of activity over there. Dozens of men in fatigues with machine guns milled around. There was a row of pairs of pickup trucks positioned hood-to-hood with their bed-mounted machine guns pointed at one another. To me it looked like a diabolical ant farm, or a giant beehive, whose members were each carrying out some mysterious task known only to the queen—whoever she was. *Who are these people outside, and what are they waiting for?* I asked myself.

At around 10:30 PM, the police car disappeared. I went across the hall to tell Ahmed, who relayed it to Fathi. Ahmed told me then that Fathi was in contact with the head of Benghazi's municipal security, run by defected members of Gaddafi's special forces. I told Ahmed I was going downstairs to the lobby to try to get a better idea of what was happening outside.

"Don't go out there!" Ahmed pleaded. "You'll get yourself killed!"

The sounds of battle in the distance continued, echoed by bursts of gunfire in our vicinity.

"And keep away from the windows in case bullets shatter the glass," Ahmed said.

Twenty minutes later, the police car was back. It was obvious that one car wasn't going to save us from anything, but for me, psychologically, it was a lifeline, in the same way Stevens's presence was a comfort to anxious citizens of Benghazi, desperate to believe someone was watching over them. As the night wore on, the hive continued to buzz at a higher frequency. Militiamen crossed the road from the pickup trucks to confer with other figures in the parking lot and at the front of the hotel. The pickup trucks were joined by personnel carriers with canvas tops.

There was clearly some logic to these movements, but heck if I could figure out what it was. Was the Tibesti—a watering hole for foreigners—the next target? I sat there for hours, frozen in an awkward and painful crouch, my face partially covered by the corner of a velour curtain.

As dawn approached, the noise of gunfire in the distance tapered off. I was dead tired. I could no longer keep watching the hive to see what else might crawl out of it. The adrenaline that had been flowing for hours now must have been depleted. I fell, fully dressed, on top of the hard cot and drifted in and out of consciousness to the sound of gunfire, interspersed with long periods of silence.

At daybreak, I opened my eyes and stared at the ceiling, trying to sense what might be happening outside and guessing how long I'd been asleep. I rolled over toward the window, but I had to get up to see anything below. I was afraid of what I might find. The dawn sky was mottled gray and purple, bisected by the contrail of a jet passing overhead. A high-altitude cloud looked like it had caught a bit of fire from the rising sun. Then my eyes fell on where I expected the hive to be. Nothing. I was baffled. Every trace of what had happened here when I fell asleep was gone. The dozens of pickup trucks, the roadblocks, the crates of unidentified materiel, the hundreds of men in fatigues—gone. The streets were empty.

The two-lane road that crossed in front of the hotel (July 23rd Street during Gaddafi's time) should have been packed with morning rush hour traffic. But there was nothing, not a single car. I poked my head into the corridor and walked tentatively down to the breakfast area. Something told me perhaps I'd find Ahmed there.

Another surreal scene unfolded in front of me. On the other side of the high-ceilinged dining area was a long buffet, fitted out carefully with containers of dry cereal, jugs of juice, and piping hot, rubbery chicken sausage. Someone had taken the trouble to get up this morning, prepare this spread, and painstakingly lay it out. But the normally bustling dining area was empty—with one bizarre exception. At a single table in the back sat a young couple with an infant. They spoke English and laughed as if they were on holiday in the Azores, ready to head out for a beach walk. *What the hell?* They barely acknowledged my presence and seeing neither Ahmed, who hadn't responded to a knock on his door, nor Burke, I continued down to the ground floor.

I had a feeling Fathi would come look for us, so I parked myself on a large black leather couch under a staircase that shielded me from the line of sight of anyone entering the hotel. After about twenty minutes, I saw Fathi's tall, thin frame pass a few steps in front of me, headed for the stairwell.

I called out to him.

He came over and sat down facing me for about half an hour. He didn't initially say much. *Was he trying to decide what he could tell me, or was he shell-shocked himself?* Hours earlier, Fathi had told us on a call that there had been casualties—at least one, on the American side. The idea that Chris was one of them didn't figure into any of the scenarios that I had played out in my mind.

The first inkling I got that my assumptions were wrong came when Fathi referred to Stevens in the past tense.

"Wait . . ." I said, holding my breath. "Chris—?"

Fathi looked at me and said nothing.

"Holy shit," I said.

I can't remember what I thought at that moment. After what had transpired, I was prepared for bad, even catastrophic, news, but I found this very difficult to process. I was shocked. But as I tried to connect to a number of different feelings, including profound sadness, I felt the emotional content of my thoughts drop out entirely. It felt as if someone or something else was clearing out of my brain anything that didn't assist in resolving the obvious problem: How were we going to get out of Benghazi?

"Where are the other Americans?" I asked.

"They've been evacuated—"

"And what about us?" I asked.

"I spoke with the Americans earlier this morning," he said, referring presumably to the Embassy in Tripoli. "It was decided—*we* decided," Fathi corrected himself, "that it would be less stressful for you to remain with us, so you're my responsibility now."

It took me a minute to process the implications of this, including the fact that the US government had chosen to leave me, Burke, and Ahmed behind. I felt another wave of anxiety wash over me. And from Fathi's expression, more things were clear: First, our care was a responsibility he would really rather not have on his shoulders. Second, we were about to have one hell of a day.

Introduction

Benghazi was a tragedy: four Americans were killed as a result of a situation that investigations later agreed was preventable. But the tragedy goes far beyond the deaths of these four individuals—Ambassador Chris Stevens, Sean Smith, Glen Doherty, and Tyrone Woods. The events that Americans collectively came to call just "Benghazi" triggered events within and outside the United States that affected the lives of millions, in the Middle East and at home. These events left a massive impact on US policy in the Middle East and triggered one of the most polarizing periods of American politics since the American Civil War.[1]

For most Americans, many of the events for which Benghazi was a hinge—particularly anything that dealt with US policy in the Middle East—flew under the radar. What we collectively remember of Benghazi, if anything at this point, was the political shouting match, bordering on hysteria. Meanwhile, the origins and details of this political brawl and media circus seemed baffling, if not incomprehensible. It began with a giant media frenzy over whether the attack on the US Mission in Benghazi was the result of a repulsive anti-Islamic video posted to YouTube or a premeditated attack by Islamist radicals. Then the attention shifted to what and when the Obama administration knew about the nature of the attack, and whether it was trying to cover up details for political reasons. On the fringes, there was wild speculation about whether something else might be lurking under the surface—possibly a covert operation gone wrong? Iran–Contra redux? The event morphed into a rationality-devouring creature that grew conspiracy theories for arms and eventually loomed in terror over the entire American sociopolitical landscape.

The controversy turned into a heat-seeking political missile, which first landed on the US ambassador to the United Nations, Susan Rice, after a series of talking points she used on national Sunday morning talk shows proved inaccurate. And instead of petering out after the election, as many expected, the controversy grew, veering its focus toward former Secretary of State Hillary Clinton. Republicans accused Democrats of covering up critical information and withholding assistance that might have saved the four victims. Democrats insisted Republicans had gone mad—there was no cover-up, no lie. All of it was drama manufactured by Republicans.

For a time, it felt like the whole country was screaming "Benghazi!" Memes proliferated. Ten congressional investigations, including six House committees, were convened. Fox News featured Benghazi in more than 1,000 broadcasts.[2] Indeed, that one word—Benghazi, the name of a city most Americans had never heard before—became a symbol of what people of different political persuasions felt passionately was absolutely and completely wrong with America. The controversy became inextricably political, branched in seemingly endless directions, and even began to fold back in on itself. Regardless of their credentials, all these congressional investigations had partisan elements to them, and they focused on different things—including one another. By late 2015, 59 percent of Americans said they were sick of talking about Hillary Clinton's emails, and three out of four felt the House Select Committee on Benghazi was politically motivated.[3]

So, it wasn't such a surprise that four years after the attack, Democrats and Republicans were further apart in their mindsets and trust in each other than they had been when the event occurred. Benghazi mania had lit other fires, notably the controversy over Clinton's use of a private email server for her work emails. The Russians saw weakness in America's internal fights and an opportunity to deepen the controversy using new and more powerful social media tools. All the while,

Benghazi trailed behind like a tin can attached to a pickup truck, rattling away in the background.

Within this free-for-all, Donald Trump—real estate mogul, reality TV host, World Wrestling Federation referee, political chameleon, and lawsuit magnet—emerged as the unexpected Republican nominee. Dismissed as a joke or an impossible candidate at first, Trump exploited the zeitgeist and the Benghazi controversy to land first the Republican nomination and then the White House.

By 2017, Benghazi was left on the side of the road, dismissed as a regrettable but ultimately inconsequential artifact of a country gone mad. And yet, it wasn't. To a degree, its consequences were (and still are) all around us. Emerging from decades of American history as well as a very particular moment, it helped create America as it is today: divided at home, increasingly absent abroad, the extent of its global influence in question. Benghazi was a symptom of long-standing political divide, as well as an accelerator of it. It conditioned the way America responded to Libya but also to farther-flung conflicts involving Syria, Yemen, and Iran. Traces of Benghazi abound if you look carefully.

Benghazi was a perfect political storm. Its subject, its timing, its symbolism, its connection to past events . . . everything about it spoke directly to grievances on both sides of American society. As such it was easy to manipulate for political gain.

Given how the controversy played out, Americans—mostly the Left—have an instinctive aversion to the topic. Democrats exhibit a kind of collective trauma response to the word, as if the mere mention of it might trigger the rhetorical equivalent of a blow to the head. For the Right, Benghazi has become a catch-all trigger for a range of outrage and anger at what it feels has been an assault by the Left on its vision of traditional America, in which strength and safety come from strength and homogeneity, not vulnerability and diversity. But sticking to these very general descriptions of Benghazi's impact misses the significance of the event and what it can tell us about where America is now, where it's headed, and what can be done to cope with increasing internal division and a marked decline in global influence.

Today, so much about Benghazi remains muddled or unclear. Where did the attack itself come from? Where did the partisan animosity come from? What exactly was it about the event and the interaction between politicians on both sides of the aisle that made it so toxic? What other factors were at play? Was the controversy inevitable, or might something have contained it? After living on the edge of this scandal for so long, I have been driven to try to answer these questions, and more.

Benghazi wasn't the cause of any of America's political dysfunctions, obviously. But it was both a symptom and an accelerator of them. This is why understanding the context of the attack, and the resulting partisan war, is so important. With that information, we can try to create strategies to identify and manage or disable similar dynamics before they become instruments of self-harm on a national scale. But understanding how and why Benghazi became a scandal is critically important. These dynamics aren't going away. And failing to understand their nature means leaving ourselves exposed to other kinds of blowouts that have the potential for even more harm.

I have been connected to Libya, and by extension the city of Benghazi, for nearly seventeen years. During that time, I have witnessed the honeymoon phase of the US–Libyan rapprochement with the regime of Muammar Gaddafi, the subsequent tension and decline in relations, the Libyan Revolution from start to chaotic aftermath, the attack on the US Mission in Benghazi, and the violence that followed. I saw some of the internal dynamics of the State Department and other agencies during this time. For over thirty years, I have witnessed pieces of the American foreign-policy-making and -delivery process, and have seen the effects of those policies on the ground, in hot spots across the Middle East.

America's future matters to me, as it does to the vast majority of Americans, including the diplomats, journalists, politicians, businesspeople, and others whom I interviewed for this book—regardless of whether we agree on specific issues. Libya also matters to me—my time there was the formative experience of my career, and it's a country in which I had some of the happiest, fascinating, and challenging moments of my life. As a diplomat, I had experiences in Libya that I couldn't replicate under any other circumstances. It allowed me the opportunity to appreciate America's capacity for positive change and to understand some of the dynamics that have rapidly eroded that influence. Once America stops being able to lay claim to an exceptionality in global affairs, that status will be very difficult to regain.

It took me a while to realize how deep an impact the Benghazi attack had on me. As with many who have gone through such traumatic experiences, I was convinced that the periods of intense anger, anxiety, and hopelessness were transitory. But as I learned, it's generally not a good idea to try to repress such feelings, as they'll just return, or show up in different forms. And I didn't completely repress them. From the moment I left Libya, I was driven to try to make sense of the attack itself and the loss of a colleague and friend, whose feelings about Libya were so close to mine and with whom I shared the experience of being the first American a large number of Libyans had ever met. I've never stopped thinking about how lucky my colleagues and I were to get out of Benghazi, and that we weren't at the compound during the attack. And there are some feelings of guilt there as well: that we made it, and others didn't.

Writing this book and talking with policy makers and other witnesses—many of whom, particularly non-Americans, had never testified or spoken to the media before—was a part of my process of coping. Many of those I spoke with told me that it was therapeutic for them as well. So I've seen firsthand what happens when Benghazi becomes unexamined trauma, and by extension, I've come to see the Benghazi phenomenon as a kind of unexamined trauma for America as a whole. Coming to terms with what the event did to the country requires reexamining it—with the benefit of hindsight, and without the partisan fervor that made a more clear-eyed assessment impossible at the time.

With time comes perspective. Given the frenetic pace of American politics, there often isn't time to see the bigger picture—which, in turn, is essential to learning and applying lessons. Not every scandal or controversy is worth a second, let alone a third, look. Benghazi is different.

As you'll see, there are some very good reasons why Benghazi was confusing. It wasn't just because of media distortions or an abundance of caution. Some questions are genuinely puzzling. In some cases the information is missing; in others the accounts have become distorted. The intentions of specific individuals and groups remain unclear. There are some questions to which we will never have answers.

In writing this book, I set out to push the boundaries of what we know about Benghazi, its causes, and its impact—to see if my own personal experience in Libya and the region, and as a witness to the attack, could help create some closure and situate Benghazi in the broader context of a very real American dilemma. Part of this means looking at events in Libya. Part of this means looking at America and showing that the fight over "Benghazi" could not have reached the pitch it did, or had the consequences it did, without the existence of a mutually reinforcing, dysfunctional relationship between the American Right and Left. My hope is that by examining the dynamics that turned Benghazi into a massive exercise in self-harm, this will encourage changes that assure that Benghazi was a black swan, and not the new norm.

At the end of the day, this is my version of events, based on new interviews and countless pages of history, news, testimony, and analysis across multiple languages, and my testimony concerning a place and a time that I believe at some point will be recognized as a significant and consequential period in American history. Not just a partisan red herring that cost a few millions of dollars of taxpayers' money to investigate.

Part I

PIECES OF A PUZZLE

1

Setting Up Blowback

Over the course of four years and the ten congressional committees that investigated the Benghazi attack and the Obama administration's response, rarely did public attention stray much beyond the immediate circumstances of the attack. The popular book by Mitchell Zuckoff, *13 Hours*, an account of the attack from the perspective of American security officers at the US Mission and CIA Annex, is the epitome of that focus. But in order to understand where the attack came from, we need to back up and see the forest for what it is. That, in turn, requires a quick tour through the regime of Muammar Gaddafi and his war with individuals who would help grow Al Qaeda: the Libyan Islamic Fighting Group.

The Benghazi attack—and the scandal it produced—are intimately tied up with the concept of political Islam and America's inconsistent relationship with it.

Political Islam, also often referred to in the West as Islamism, is a catchall phrase used to denote organizations, parties, and movements that invoke the religion of Islam to accomplish political ends. There may be differences in the ideologies and tactics of these groups, but ultimately they share the vision of creating a society governed by Islamic law, or Sharia.

The phenomenon of political Islam started to gel in the late nineteenth and early twentieth centuries with Muslim reformist thinkers like

Jamal al-Din al-Afghani, Muhammed Abduh, and Abul A'la Maududi, all of whom sought ways to reclaim a Muslim identity they believed had been deeply harmed by Western colonialism, as well as secular ideologies like communism and nationalism.

A large step forward in the so-called Islamic Revival came in 1928 when Hassan al-Banna, a charismatic schoolteacher, created the Muslim Brotherhood, a group that operated (and still operates) more like a secret society than a political party—with different levels of initiates and an opaque leadership structure. Though the exact number of members is unknown, the Brotherhood has attracted many millions of followers globally, and its political epicenter has always been Egypt.

Through the 1940s, the State Department didn't recognize the Brotherhood as a major factor in local Egyptian politics, and when American diplomats did offer an opinion on the group, they assessed it as a "fanatical," "anti-Western" society that had some potential to become violent.[1] That changed with the rise of Egyptian nationalist leader Gamal Abdel Nasser.

When Nasser came to power in 1954, the United States worried about his connections with the Soviet Union. And when the Muslim Brotherhood's relationship with Nasser soured dramatically, America started to entertain the idea that the Muslim Brotherhood might be a potential ally. Nasser's violent crackdown on the Brotherhood in the 1960s produced activist leaders that brought the movement into greater conflict with regional regimes.[2]

While the Brotherhood was evolving in Egypt, the United States had become interested in Afghanistan, where the *mujahideen* (those who wage jihad, or holy war) were fighting a Soviet-backed regime, following the Soviet invasion in 1979. The Cold War was at a high pitch, and the United States saw an opportunity to draw the Kremlin into its own Vietnam War, by providing arms, training, and supplies to the mujahideen—and even helped fund recruitment schemes.[3]

The mujahideen were made up of native Afghan fighters (many of whom would join the ultraconservative Taliban when it was formed in 1994) and groups of so-called Afghan Arabs—Muslims from Arab countries who were drawn to the conflict for a range of reasons, but mainly their collective desire to fight back against the forces they saw as responsible for decades, if not centuries, of exploitation and the rise of ruthless strongmen.

The Muslim Brotherhood was present in Afghanistan and, due to its proximity to Islamists of all flavors and its focus on global Islamic solidarity, played an essential role in keeping various radical groups focused on the task at hand—defeating the Soviets—and not on fighting one another, which still happened frequently.[4] This is an early example of the importance of the Muslim Brotherhood as a source of Islamist identity and a common reference across Islamist groups. This was one of the qualities that later attracted the United States to the Brotherhood as a candidate for co-optation: if the United States could engage the Brotherhood, or so the thought went, perhaps it could pull the entire Islamist movement away from its most extreme edges, and temper organizations like Al Qaeda in the process.

The American assistance plan for the mujahideen, heavily advocated by President Jimmy Carter's National Security Advisor Zbigniew Brzezinski, worked—at least to the degree it helped speed the collapse of the Soviet Union in 1991. But there was a longer-term price to be paid, as these battle-hardened fighters coalesced around figures like Osama bin Laden and Egyptian radical Ayman Al-Zawahiri, who together founded Al Qaeda in 1986. With one of the two world superpowers gone, America was the next obvious target.

The US intelligence community calls unintended consequences of working with groups whose core ideologies and interests are different from ours *blowback*. Though some senior officials at the CIA would later express strong reservations about backing the mujahideen, President Carter's former National Security Advisor Brzezinski remained unapologetic: "This secret operation was an excellent idea. Its effect was to draw the Russians in to the Afghan trap. You want me to regret that?"[5]

In his now-classic book on the Afghan war, John Cooley offers a general lesson from the conflict, which America has somehow continued to fail to learn, twenty and thirty years later: "When you decide to go to war against your current main enemy, take a good, long look at the people behind you whom you choose as your friends, allies or mercenary fighters. Look well to see whether these allies already have unsheathed their daggers—and are pointing them at your back."[6]

The Afghan Arabs were primarily made up of Saudis, Egyptians, Algerians, Syrians, Jordanians, and Iraqis.[7] The Libyan Arabs were a much smaller number, but they grew to be some of Al Qaeda's smartest, best, and most committed. By September 11, 2001, as a group, they were probably the most influential members of Al Qaeda. What was it about Libya that made these individuals so keen and able to outperform their counterparts from other Arab countries? The answer to that question lies in the evolution of Islamism in Libya, a tragic history wrapped up in the dark psychological universe of one man: Muammar Gaddafi.

A large country in the center of North Africa, at the crossroads of Africa and Europe, Libya has been invaded and occupied numerous times over the centuries, by Arabs, Greeks, Romans, Byzantines, and Italians. During World War II, the Allied and Axis powers collided at Benghazi, which was shelled completely beyond recognition. Libya was so poor at the time that its main source of income for years was the sale of livestock and scrap metal left over from the war. With assistance from the newly formed United Nations, Libya became independent as a federated constitutional monarchy in 1951 under King Idris al-Senussi, the leader of Libya's dominant Sufi order. Sufism was considered by most of the Islamist Revival groups as a heresy, deviating from true Islam by incorporating superstition and saint worship—but it was woven deeply into the conservative religious and intellectual fabric of Libya.

With the possibility that Libya might become a major oil producer still just that—a possibility—Libya's government appealed to the United States for development and financial assistance to help deepen and stabilize its fragile political and economic systems. But the United States was focused on Nasser's move toward its nemesis, the Soviet Union. To try to get America's attention, Libya's prime minister Mustafa Ben-Halim flirted with the Soviets—which angered, rather than engaged, the Americans.[8] The British were inclined to help but wanted the United States to shoulder the burden of "state-building" in Libya. Without outside help, and with many Libyans complaining that their king was too sympathetic to a growing, oil-fed commercial elite, the young Libyan state was fertile territory for a coup, which came on September 1, 1969.

While King Idris was convalescing from an illness at a resort in Turkey, a strikingly handsome twenty-seven-year-old army officer announced from the Benghazi radio station that he and his Free Officers (a term borrowed from Nasser) were now in control in Libya. His name was Muammar Gaddafi. Practically no one in Libya had ever heard of him.

In his early years in power, Gaddafi presented himself as an informal kind of leader, a guide who would shepherd not only Libyans but Arabs into a brighter, unified future, in service to a "third way" between capitalism and socialism. He drove across the country in a powder-blue VW Bug, preaching something he called "direct democracy"—something not too far from hippie flower power—that he said would be achieved through a system of People's Committees and Congresses. But Gaddafi's revolutionary agenda was no more than what one Libyan writer later called a "collection of high school ideas."[9] What Gaddafi was actually building was a classic rentier state, one in which power and revenue derive from the distribution of the proceeds of a single resource, in this case oil.

Everything about Gaddafi screamed showman, from his flowing, theatrical robes and headgear to his cadre of Amazonian female revolutionary guards. His promises of utopia were very transparent fictions, however, as Libya quickly became a police state, and very little happened in Libya without Gaddafi's personal approval.

Gaddafi worked systematically to eliminate all potential sources of competition, starting with his coconspirators. Next he went after wealthy businessmen, nationalizing their assets and replacing most commercial activity with state-run factories. Last, but not least, Gaddafi tried to cut off any path for local religious leaders to mobilize against him under the banner of Islam.[10] By doing this, he shut down the traditional Libyan religious establishment and opened the door to clandestine, puritanical movements. Gaddafi had observed carefully how his idol Nasser had initially tried to co-opt, and then wound up in a fight to the death with, the Muslim Brotherhood. He was determined that they would not establish a foothold in Libya and jailed anyone suspected of Brotherhood ties. He wasn't so effective in this, as the Brotherhood managed to maintain a limited clandestine presence, particularly in eastern Libya, where there was a flow of communication with Egypt and the Brotherhood home office.

Failing to find a message that would sustain Libyans' enthusiasm for his revolutionary posture, Gaddafi increasingly turned to repression, intimidation, and selective acts of brutality—such as the hanging of dissidents in public spaces—and to something for which he had innate and significant talent: being ringmaster for intrigues designed to distract and intimidate anyone who might try to topple him. But this was itself a kind of trap, for as Libyans adapted to his methods, Gaddafi had to constantly add more acts, which required more juggling and made the whole system gradually more unstable.

Meanwhile, just as Gaddafi demanded adulation from Libyans, he exhibited an insatiable need to be recognized and courted by the international community—particularly the United States. But when the Arab world failed to embrace his ideas (including a unified Palestinian–Israeli state he called "Isratine"), he resorted to more low-intensity chaos sowing, backing revolutionary groups like the Popular Front for the Liberation of Palestine (PFLP) and the Irish Republican Army. Gaddafi's personal affect and appearance, and statements, became theatrical. He taunted President Ronald Reagan as "mad," "foolish," and an "Israeli dog."[11] If Gaddafi had had a clearer sense of limits, he might have stayed under the radar. But he pushed on and chose more visible targets, financing the parallel Rome and Vienna airport commando attacks in 1985, which killed nineteen people and injured more than a hundred, and the bombing in 1986 of a disco in West Berlin, which killed three US servicemen and injured 230. Reagan upped the ante, ordering US jets to bomb Tripoli and Benghazi in 1986, narrowly missing Gaddafi, who is widely believed to have been a target.[12] Some Libyans were said to have cheered the attack, thinking the United States had finally come to deliver them from their nightmare. That event seemed to have deepened Gaddafi's paranoia and desire for revenge.

Two years later, in 1988, a bomb exploded on Pan Am Flight 103 bound for New York as it flew over the town of Lockerbie, Scotland. The plane was full of young American students returning home for Christmas break. The explosion killed 270 passengers and people on the ground, and set off a multiyear investigation that first focused on Iran but ultimately pointed the finger at Libya.[13] The motive was assumed to have been revenge for Reagan's 1986 attacks on Tripoli and Benghazi. The following year, French airline Union de Transports Aériens (UTA) Flight 772 exploded over the desert in Niger, killing 170, including the wife of the US ambassador to Chad. The explosive device used was nearly identical to that used in Lockerbie, weakening early theories that Lockerbie was the exclusive work of Iranian- or Syrian-linked groups. Gaddafi's former foreign minister and defector to the rebels, Abdel Rahman Shalgam, claimed in a 2011 interview that the UTA blast was an attempt to assassinate Mohammed Megaryaf, the former head of Libya's largest opposition group abroad, who either was tipped off to the plot beforehand or missed the flight.[14] But it was the Pan Am bombing, above any other act, that triggered international sanctions on Libya and made Gaddafi an international pariah.

By the late 1980s, Libyans had been suffering for more than a decade. Despite Libya's wealth, unemployment was rampant, personal aspirations were subverted to Gaddafi's outlandish political visions, and

productive investment had nearly ground to a halt. Gaddafi spent tens
of billions of dollars on white-elephant projects, like the Great Man-
Made River, a scheme of massive pipes siphoning off what the regime
called a bottomless resource of underground water to develop Libya's
cities and green the Sahara Desert. He also sent exorbitant subsidies to
revolutionary movements in far-flung parts of the world—part of his
campaign to build alliances with future revolutionary leaders.

Gaddafi did some positive things for Libya. In his first years in
power, he built schools and clinics across Libya, in places that had no
access to education or basic medical care. He also emphasized women's
education and inclusion in the workforce. By mixing populations and
encouraging migration to the cities, Gaddafi reduced the pull of tribalism. He also singlehandedly reshaped the economics of oil production,
by pressuring independent American oil companies to break industry
convention and give a greater share of revenue to the producing countries.[15] But these advances would be judged harshly compared to what
could have been done with Libya's oil wealth. Gaddafi created what
British historian Fred Halliday called a grand "kleptocracy"—a system
powered by corruption, where Gaddafi's allies and cronies were able to
enrich themselves almost without limit.[16]

This was the environment that pushed young Libyans to find ways
out of their hell and led a number to join the Afghan jihad against the
Soviets. At first, Gaddafi was glad to see them go, thinking they'd be
caught up in the Afghan war and never come home. But soon enough,
they were back—and out for his hide.

Neither tall nor short, with a high forehead and penetrating eyes,
Abdulhakim Belhaj rarely smiles in photographs. Over the course of
thirty years, he would become one of the most charismatic, influential,
and visible of Libya's Afghan Arabs.

Belhaj was born in 1966 in the Souq Al Jum'aa neighborhood of
Tripoli, the fourth of nine children and the son of a ranking manager
at a state company. If there was a middle class in Libya in the 1980s,

he was part of it. But he also grew to detest the Gaddafi regime. Like the other Libyan Islamic Fighting Group members, he linked his antipathy to the regime's repression of religious practices. But he also had a personal grudge: Gaddafi had imprisoned his father for nearly five years after an accident at the factory where he was manager. Belhaj was twelve.[17]

In 1983, Belhaj passed his university entrance exam to Tripoli University, where he had planned to study architecture.[18] Gaddafi was then at war with Libya's southern neighbor, Chad, over a uranium-rich region called the Aouzou Strip. As a result, Belhaj's good marks won him an unwelcome direction from the regime to become a fighter pilot, like his older brother, in a war that was going extremely badly, under the management of someone who would become one of Belhaj's future nemeses, General Khalifa Heftar. Despite Libya's great wealth, Gaddafi's fear of a countercoup against him caused him to deprive his military of needed training and equipment. As a result, his forces were being beaten by those of a country with far less resources.[19]

Rather than enter pilot training, Belhaj started reading up on Islamic law and going to local mosques and study groups—*halaqaat.* Belhaj joined an Islamist cell, where he was introduced to the recorded speeches of Palestinian jihadist Abdallah Azzam, an associate of Osama bin Laden, who spread bin Laden's call to jihad in Afghanistan.[20] Belhaj also listened to the speeches of Iran's Ayatollah Khomeini, whom many Arab Islamists admired for leading the revolution that toppled the US-backed shah of Iran. For Libyans imagining an end to the Gaddafi regime, these examples were inspirational and offered a practical map to overthrowing Gaddafi. And if they joined the Afghan jihad, they might acquire the fighting skills that would enable them to face Gaddafi at home.

Belhaj's closest associates included Khalid al-Sherif, a pharmacology student, also from Tripoli, and Sami al-Saadi, then an engineering student at the University of Tripoli. Determined to bring the fight back to Gaddafi one day, the three set off in 1988, via Saudi Arabia

and Pakistan, to join Osama bin Laden and the mujahideen.[21] Belhaj
described his feelings at the time to *Le Monde* correspondent Christophe Ayad: "I was forced into exile, I didn't have a choice! In Libya
we were living under a dictatorial regime that did not permit any sort
of freedom of thought or expression. . . . The Gaddafi regime wanted
to destroy us."[22]

   In Afghanistan, Belhaj met other Libyan fighters, including Abdel
Wahab Al Qaid (whose nom de guerre, or *kunya* in Arabic, was Abu
Idris Al Libi), his brother Mohammed Hassan Al Qaid (a.k.a. Abu
Yahya Al Libi), and Abu Sufian Bin Qumu, a thin man with a long
beard tinted red with henna and wild brown eyes that hid behind circular spectacles. Bin Qumu was originally from Derna, a town of less
than 50,000 people situated 182 miles northeast of Benghazi. Over the
1990s, Derna was often mentioned with Benghazi as one of the hotbeds
of armed, Islamist resistance to Gaddafi. But it hadn't always been that
way. For much of its history, Derna, like Benghazi, was known for producing many of Libya's intellectuals and writers.[23] The transformation
from a focus on secular learning to intolerance and rage was sealed by
a generation of young men deprived of dignity and the opportunity to
make a living or have a family. That all these people and places would
become relevant in the context of the attack in Benghazi twenty years
later is no mere coincidence.

   With the Soviets defeated, the local Afghan resistance worried
about a standing army of Arab fighters in their midst and encouraged
their former allies to return to their home countries.[24] Bin Laden and
Al-Zawahiri needed a new base to lie low and plan their next moves,
because they were in a highly unstable environment: President Najibul-
lah's Soviet client state of Afghanistan had collapsed, and infighting
between sects of the mujahideen had skyrocketed. They found sanctuary in Sudan, whose president, Omar al-Bashir, had cozied up to the
local Islamist movements, which he used to put down an insurrection
in the country's Christian-majority south. Al Qaeda and its allies and
affiliates decamped to Sudan's riverine capital of Khartoum, where bin

Laden and Al-Zawahiri shifted Al Qaeda's focus from overthrowing local and regional regimes to advocating global jihad against the West.

Al Qaeda's declaration of war against the West came on February 23, 1998, with a fatwa against "Jews and Crusaders."[25] In the language of political Islam, this was called taking jihad from the near enemy to the far enemy, shifting the priority from toppling local despotic regimes to undermining (in Al Qaeda's view, defensively) the power that fed and supported those regimes—the United States. For bin Laden, a seminal event leading in this direction had been the presence of American military forces in Saudi Arabia following the start of the Gulf War. That, in bin Laden's mind, was an affront to Islam and its two holiest cities, Mecca and Medina.

With Al Qaeda's target now reset, disparate operational strands came together in Khartoum. There, in 1995, Abdulhakim Belhaj formalized the Libyan Islamic Fighting Group, or LIFG, with himself as its leader, or emir.[26] The LIFG's relationship with Al Qaeda was never explicit—the organization didn't advertise itself as a part of Al Qaeda, and to the extent it communicated its goals and ideology, it stressed that its sole purpose was to overthrow Gaddafi (and, by extension, to create an Islamic state in Libya). But from the beginning, the LIFG's broader circle served as a kind of elite recruiting ground for senior Al Qaeda leadership. The LIFG leadership mixed with other Libyan Islamists in Sudan who would become important to their story in years to come, like Ali Sallabi, one of three Libyan brothers strongly connected to the Muslim Brotherhood and based in the Arabian Gulf emirate of Qatar.

For the LIFG, Al Qaeda's move to Sudan was highly welcome, as it brought them back from the wilds of Afghanistan to a country on Libya's southern border—a much better place from which to execute its plan to kill Gaddafi. From Sudan, the LIFG set about, with the utmost secrecy, to infiltrate Libya. It would take a bit of time to set up cells capable of pulling off a successful attack, especially as Gaddafi's spies and informants were everywhere and he had already been tipped off to the identities of some of the LIFG leaders. While bin Laden and

Al-Zawahiri were plotting to attack New York and Washington, D.C., the LIFG was focused on Gaddafi and Libya.

One of the LIFG's first attempts to assassinate Gaddafi took place in 1994 in the perpetually dusty southern Libyan city of Sebha, on the main north-south desert artery linking West Africa to the Mediterranean coast.[27] Belhaj reportedly helped train the suicide bomber who was to approach Gaddafi's motorcade carrying a placard on which was written one of Gaddafi's many inane slogans—and then blow himself up as Gaddafi came into range.[28] But the device malfunctioned, and the plan was scrapped.

What Gaddafi didn't know was how extensive a network his enemies had managed to create. What followed were reciprocal *Spy vs. Spy* operations, with each side—Belhaj's men and Gaddafi's agents—setting up traps and paramilitary operations against one another; the LIFG aiming to kill, and Gaddafi, at first, trying to gauge their capabilities. At one point Gaddafi allegedly brought Belhaj's parents to Khartoum and drove them around the capital as bait, to lure Belhaj into the open. It didn't work.

Other tactics were equally outlandish, some worthy of tales of the *1001 Nights*. In 1994, a lavish residence suddenly appeared along one of the access roads to Benghazi.[29] It was rumored to be financed by a local businessman and was known as the "palace." It housed a mosque and offered a resting place for travelers. Local Islamists, including members of the LIFG, began to frequent the place, unaware that it was surveilled by the regime. One day, Gaddafi's intelligence moved in, arrested everyone, and burned the complex to the ground.[30]

A year later, in 1995, a group of LIFG operatives dressed as members of the Libyan security forces walked into a Benghazi military hospital to rescue a member who had been wounded in a firefight with government forces.[31] The regime tracked the fugitives to a farmhouse in the Benghazi suburbs, where it found weapons and documents that revealed that there were now hundreds of LIFG members within Libya, mostly in the east, which had long since established itself as the seat of resistance to the Tripoli-centered regime. Gaddafi ordered large swathes of the Green Mountains outside Benghazi napalmed to destroy and expose LIFG hideouts. He also summoned Abdullah Senussi, his brother-in-law and head of internal security, and Abdel Fattah Younes, his minister of interior, and charged them with leading his counter-jihadist operations.

During Bill Clinton's administration, the US and British governments started paying more attention to political Islam, in the broader context of increased terrorist activity by the Afghan Arabs and Al Qaeda.[32] But there was far from any clear policy. In 1995, the British intelligence community seemed to be more focused on what they saw as the threat from Gaddafi. In addition to involvement in the Pan Am Flight 103 bombing and the killing of a female British constable outside the Libyan Embassy in London in 1984, Gaddafi had been backing the Irish Republican Army, which London considered a terrorist group. Here, MI6 saw common cause with the Libyan Afghans. Over the following few years, a British MI6 agent allegedly gave LIFG operatives weapons and several installments of about 40,000 British pounds to finance an attack, which involved putting a bomb on Gaddafi's motorcade as it passed through his hometown of Sirte.[33] MI6 envisioned the assassination as part of a larger coup in which five former Gaddafi generals would secure the country, form a provisional government, and set a timetable for national elections. It's still unclear how high up in the British government this plot to assassinate the Libyan leader went, and if, as the British government has claimed, it was the action of a rogue cell within MI6. The plan went off in March 1996, but the bomb was placed under the wrong vehicle. Three LIFG members were killed.[34] Gaddafi emerged unscathed but more alert to the plots against him. There were more attacks: a few months later, in November, an LIFG member threw a grenade at Gaddafi in the town of Brak, but it didn't go off.[35]

It's likely that the British government was so aware of the LIFG's activities in Libya in part because they were monitoring the group's activities in England, where a number of senior LIFG members had found asylum and lived mainly in London and Manchester, part of which is known as Little Tripoli for its large Libyan population.[36] Sami al-Saadi, who left Libya for Afghanistan around the same time as Belhaj and Khalid al-Sherif, says he left Afghanistan after the Soviet-backed government fell in 1992—and applied for and received asylum in the United Kingdom, where he lived from 1994 to 1997. He says he worked there to plot against Gaddafi.[37] Camille Tawil, a journalist focused on North African jihadists, claims that British intelligence's relationship with the LIFG was at least partly motivated by the fear that it might ultimately start planning attacks in London.[38] Engagement, then, might help create a kind of immunity. But as becomes clear time and again in the larger story of Benghazi, these kinds of back-room accommodations, while they might yield short-term gains, are highly risky and rarely turn out well. In 1998, two distinguished American and British diplomats, former US Assistant Secretary Richard Murphy and British Ambassador Basil Eastwood, drew some notice with op-eds making the case that the West should engage with the Brotherhood, not only because diplomacy is about keeping doors open, but also because dialogue could provide valuable intelligence about the organization and its intentions—and, presumably, the nature of its ties to overtly radical groups like Al Qaeda.[39] A few years later, the United States started meeting—quietly—with Brotherhood representatives at the US Embassy in Cairo.[40]

While the British were secretly collaborating with the LIFG to try to get rid of Gaddafi, the CIA was also plotting to remove the Libyan dictator. But there was little interest in Washington at this time in joining with Islamists, who were hated by many of America's friends in the region (including Israel). The Americans found their anti-Gaddafi collaborator in a very different personality, that of former Gaddafi general Khalifa Heftar. A strapping figure always pictured expressionless, in uniform, wearing a black mustache, Heftar had been captured in the late 1980s during Gaddafi's disastrous war with Libya's southern neighbor Chad. It's then that the CIA allegedly recruited Heftar and brought him to the United States to work on a contingency plan to topple Gaddafi.

It's notable that the United States and the United Kingdom recruited Heftar and the LIFG, respectively, to power their plans to get rid of Gaddafi, as these would be the two groups that fought each other for control over Libya after Gaddafi's death while the United States and the United Kingdom stood aside.

Meanwhile, the United States was starting to see blowback from American support for the Afghan mujahideen in the 1980s. In the summer of 1998, the CIA discovered an Islamist cell in Tirana, Albania, connected to Ayman Al-Zawahiri's Egyptian group Islamic Jihad. The group was suspected of plotting to blow up the US Embassy in Albania. In July 1998, the CIA and Albanian intelligence kidnapped four of Al-Zawahiri's operatives and handed them over to Egypt. This was one of the first of a few early incidences of what would come to be known as extraordinary rendition—the covert kidnapping and delivery of suspects to a third country, for interrogation in ways that ran counter to American law (i.e., torture).[41]

Weeks later, on August 7, 1998, two explosive-laden trucks simultaneously drove into the US embassies in Kenya and Tanzania, killing 224 people and injuring thousands. These deadly terrorist attacks on American interests abroad were matched in recent history only by the 1983 bombing of the US Marine Barracks in Beirut and the Pan Am Lockerbie bombing in 1988.

The embassy attacks were not only a display of Al Qaeda's increasing operational capacities and its determination to strike American interests, they were also a kind of blueprint for future attacks on US diplomats. Several details are particularly notable, due to parallels with the attack in Benghazi fourteen years later.

On August 4, 1998, three days before the attack, the organization Al-Zawahiri founded in Egypt, Islamic Jihad, issued a statement linking what it said was a pending attack to the abduction and extradition of Al-Zawahiri's colleagues in Albania.

Prudence Bushnell, US ambassador to Kenya at the time of the US embassy attacks, wrote that Al-Zawahiri "took the kidnappings personally."[42]

Perhaps most tragically, senior US diplomats in Nairobi were acutely aware of the danger they were in. Bushnell had written a number of cables to Washington over the previous year highlighting the precariousness of the Embassy's security position. And there were warnings—while Bushnell was in Washington pleading the case for more security, a man approached the US Embassy in Nairobi about a plan to plant a bomb in the Embassy's parking garage.[43] There had also been a surveillance event, undetected, in which at least one senior Libyan Afghan participated: Nazih Al-Ruqai'i (a.k.a. Abu Anas Al Libi).[44]

The State Department deferred Ambassador Bushnell's requests for major changes in the Embassy's preparedness level—and a new Embassy building—on the grounds that Nairobi had been classified as a "medium" threat location and didn't warrant more resources.[45] Bushnell took the unusual step of passing a message to then–Secretary of State Madeleine Albright directly, saying she felt the "the chancery [Embassy] remains vulnerable, and I remain nervous."[46] Albright would later tell Bushnell that her communications were delayed in reaching her.[47]

As expected, after the embassy attacks Secretary Albright called an Accountability Review Board (ARB), which found that while a general pattern of violence preceded the attack, there had been no tactical intelligence that could be construed as a direct threat.[48] State Department officials suggested that Bushnell was a security-obsessed "nuisance."[49] Other investigations into the bombing revealed that the US government actually had quite a bit of information on the groups and individuals behind the attack—but the agencies with that information didn't coordinate or share information, due to long-standing rivalries and suspicions. As Bushnell noted in 2018, "the three organizations with capabilities to intercept information—the FBI, the CIA and the NSA—each had their own wall of secrecy, and no agency would fully share data with the others."[50] The embassy bombings didn't change that situation.

In October 2000, Al Qaeda struck again. This time in the port of Aden, Yemen, the southernmost point on the Arabian Peninsula. There, on a second attempt, Al Qaeda blew up a US Navy destroyer using an explosive-laden fiberglass boat. Once again, the United States had the information to foil that attack, but the information wasn't shared between the National Security Agency (NSA) and the CIA.[51] The attack killed seventeen US service members, injured thirty-seven, and triggered a huge investigation by the FBI, whose agents descended upon Aden in droves, looking for clues and pressing the enormously corrupt regime of President Ali Abdullah Saleh to crack down on Al Qaeda. Saleh was an inveterate opportunist, who discovered he could use Al Qaeda as a bogeyman to catch America's attention and lavish financial assistance, which in turn kept his enemies at bay and the Yemeni people at heel. This situation would become a prime example of the self-reinforcing loop that was America's growing conflict with radical Islam: Yemen's domestic political problems and America's indiscriminate war on Yemeni terrorists turned the country into a sanctuary for one of Al Qaeda's most powerful affiliates.

While these events were unfolding, the US government unwittingly allowed itself to be drawn deeper into relationships with states and organizations that supported Islamist causes—principally the immensely wealthy Arabian Gulf state of Qatar, an emirate with under a million people that shares borders with the United Arab Emirates and Saudi Arabia.

The Qatari royal family had been patrons of the Muslim Brotherhood since the late 1940s—before Qatar gained its independence.[52] The relationship with the Brotherhood wasn't born out of any strict ideological affinity, as the Qataris, like Saudi Arabia's leaders at the time, were rooted in the ultraconservative Wahhabi interpretation of Sunni Islam, which looked on the Brotherhood as a kind of heresy. What the Qataris saw in the Brotherhood was a potentially powerful political tool: Though Qatar was small and vulnerable to the bullying of its neighbors, the Brotherhood's membership was growing, particularly in some of the countries that either posed threats to Qatar or where Qatar had commercial interests. The Brotherhood's regional ambitions and influence might be very helpful, as long as Qatar remained immune to its undermining.

In 1995, Qatar's Crown Prince Hamad bin Khalifa Al Thani staged a velvet coup against his father, Khalifa bin Hamad Al Thani. Sheikh Hamad pursued a much more aggressive regional foreign policy than his father. One of his first projects was to launch the region's first pan-Arab media channel, Al Jazeera, in November 1996. Al Jazeera offered the region something new: uncensored news footage of every Middle East regime's dirty laundry—Qatar excluded—and every uneven and violent confrontation between Israel and the Palestinians. By creating the ability to shape regional public opinion, Qatar gained a one-up on many of its rivals, many of which suspected—or accused—the Brotherhood of trying to topple them.[53]

In parallel with its media empire, Qatar donated large amounts of money to American think tanks to underwrite a range of research including material supportive of the Muslim Brotherhood.[54] Qatar wasn't the only Arabian Gulf country to cultivate such soft power in Washington and the European capitals—practically all of them did.

As strange as it seems given this long ramp-up of Al Qaeda activity, when 9/11 hit, the United States still knew painfully little about Al Qaeda—or the Muslim Brotherhood, or how the two organizations influenced, and diverged from, one another.[55] The fact that Libyan Islamists played significant roles in Al Qaeda would be, not surprisingly, another revelation.

2

Flipping a Rogue

Al Qaeda's next attack would alter the trajectory of global politics for decades to come. The fact that America's response to it was heavily determined by chance should offer no comfort to those worried about the future of American democracy.

Texas Governor George W. Bush won the presidency in 2000 over Vice President Al Gore by the narrowest of margins, as a result of winning the popular vote in the battleground state of Florida by just 537 votes. A questionable decision in *Bush v. Gore* by the Supreme Court to stay a recount of so-called "undervotes" in Florida effectively confirmed Bush's win. Though it's impossible to say what might have happened had Gore been elected president, it's hard to see how the Iraq War would have taken place, as this was a plan that resulted from a resonance between a small group of ideologues known as Neoconservatives (or Neocons, for short) and President George W. Bush, both of whom had strong and long-standing interest in toppling Saddam Hussein. The Neoconservatives saw the fall of Saddam Hussein as the start of a domino effect of falling dictatorships hostile to Israel, which would assure American hegemony in the Middle East. George W. Bush was known to hold a grudge against Saddam Hussein for conspiring to assassinate his father, President George H. W. Bush.[1]

Despite the fact that Saddam Hussein was a secular dictator, the Neocons had built their argument for regime change (not just Saddam's but those of many regional governments) on the idea that the West and

Islam were doomed to a period of increasing conflict. The academic and policy props already existed, in the form of writing by academics like Samuel Huntington, who coined the term "Clash of Civilizations" in a 1993 article for *Foreign Affairs*. Huntington's argument amplified the work of Middle East policy hawks like Princeton professor Bernard Lewis, whose 1990 piece in *The Atlantic*, "The Roots of Muslim Rage," was frequently cited by the Neocons.

But still, a war against Hussein required a link to 9/11 and Al Qaeda, and that link simply didn't exist in reality. As Muhammed Ahmad, author of *The Road to Iraq: The Making of a Neoconservative War*, notes, in order to sell their case for war, the Neocons needed to bend agencies like the CIA and the State Department to their own will—as the agencies' reservations "could potentially derail the campaign."[2] That would require creating shadow agencies like the Office of Special Plans (OSP), whose main job was to fast-track information supporting the argument that Iraq was developing Weapons of Mass Destruction, or WMDs, and had ties to Al Qaeda. Centralizing power in the executive branch was supported by other administrative shunts, like the hiring of huge numbers of external contractors, who weren't part of the formal bureaucracy, which blurred the divide between government and private industry.[3] Thus began an accelerated campaign to bypass and neutralize dissenting voices within the government—a process that would have significant long-term effects, as the CIA, Department of Defense, State Department, and FBI were pitted against one another, malleable officials were promoted, and, at least anecdotally, a large number of knowledgeable experts either left or were effectively driven out of government.

One of the critical pieces of information the administration used to justify its claims of a link between Saddam Hussein and Al Qaeda was a forced confession produced by one of the Libyan Afghans and senior Al Qaeda operative, Ibn al-Sheikh al-Libi, whom the Americans captured in Afghanistan and turned over to Egypt for interrogation. Al-Libi told interrogators that the Iraqis had taught two Al Qaeda agents how to use chemical and biological weapons.[4] US intelligence officials thought this was baloney, but it was critical to Bush's own perceptions of the truthfulness of the claim that Al Qaeda and Iraq were linked, and it was used (among other dubious intelligence) to convince Secretary of State Colin Powell, who didn't know the origins of the information, to deliver the speech to the United Nations making the case for war—a speech journalist Robert Draper, in his history of the Iraq War, calls a "meticulous brief of institutionalized deception and murderous intent."[5]

Literally hundreds of books have been written on the Iraq War's impact on American power and influence. But, oddly, virtually no attention has been paid to one of its stranger, but highly consequential, by-products: America's remaking of the man Ronald Reagan once called the "Mad Dog of the Middle East"—Muammar Gaddafi.

A few days after 9/11, Gaddafi did something seemingly out of character: he sent his condolences to the American people and publicly urged Libyans to donate blood to help the victims.[6] The outreach wasn't exactly selfless—Gaddafi had plenty of reason to worry that he might be blamed for 9/11 and find himself next on America's list of regimes to overthrow. Gaddafi also had reason to be if not sympathetic, then concerned about Al Qaeda's operational strength, given that the LIFG had nearly killed him on several occasions.

At first, the Bush administration was not interested in Gaddafi's overtures. Nor were they interested in wasting resources on toppling him. The consensus inside the Beltway was that sanctions had sealed Gaddafi off from the outside world, leaving him exactly where Washington wanted him. But as the magnitude of the problems facing America and American forces in Iraq started to become clear a few years later, some in Bush's circle got the idea that Gaddafi's overture could be useful. First, Libya could—at least on paper—offer some of the prizes Bush promised Americans in Iraq: Gaddafi had a nuclear program, which, though primitive and far from producing a nuclear warhead, could be described as a threat. If the United States were to cart it away, along with materials that could be used as chemical weapons precursors, it could claim a success in halting the spread of WMDs—a victory that was proving still elusive in Iraq. Second, Gaddafi could offer lucrative deals to American companies—another payoff that wasn't coming to fruition in Iraq. Third, if Gaddafi were willing to agree to a program of political reform, this could signal that the Iraq War was working toward the Bush administration's stated plan to democratize the region, the positive domino effect that was supposed to start with the removal of Saddam Hussein.

If there was one major stumbling block to the American plan to flip Gaddafi, it was how to make the story of Gaddafi's conversion from evil dictator to quirky ally seem somewhat credible and organic. Relations between the United States and Libya had been horrible for decades, and Gaddafi was the poster child for unstable, violent Middle East dictators. It made sense to highlight someone else in his inner circle as a facilitator of change. And there was really only one obvious candidate: Gaddafi's stylish, bald, London-educated, second-eldest son, Saif. Gaddafi had groomed Saif to be his Western-facing alter ego and had already deployed him in initial talks with the international community around the lifting of UN sanctions. So Saif emerged, debutante-like, as the face of the new, gentler, on-its-way-to-something-like-democracy Libya, supported by a gaggle of highly paid British and American consultants. They pulled together strategy papers, held conferences on reform, and helped with Saif's PhD thesis on civil society at the London School of Economics, all of which were meant to bolster Saif's credibility as a young, progressive leader. Saif operated from the quasi-official perch of the Gaddafi International Charity and Development Foundation. Officially, he held no government position, nor Gaddafi's official endorsement as heir apparent, which kept outsiders guessing as to how much influence he actually had, or if his father still called all the shots.

In the end, the eagerness with which the United States pursued the handshake with Muammar Gaddafi was its—and Gaddafi's—undoing. Each side had its list of wants, but there was no road map, no formal treaty, no agreed-upon order of actions, and only a laundry list of points on which misunderstandings could and would likely be easily made.

In 2003, Gaddafi agreed to pay out 2.7 billion dollars to the families of the victims of the Lockerbie bombing, in exchange for the lifting of international sanctions and the normalization of relations with the United States. The first step on this road was the opening of a diplomatic mission in Tripoli in February 2004.

Back in the United States, 9/11 created a short-lived moment of partisan unity. For a time, the State Department and other US government agencies saw a spike in applications. It was a Kennedy-esque, "ask not what your country can do for you" moment. If the United States could be the target of such a horrific act, many Americans felt that something must be wrong, and maybe it was a time that called for personal sacrifice. I was one of these applicants.

I was thirty-five at the time. I had spent the previous ten years living and studying across the Middle East, in places like Yemen, Jordan, and Tunisia—mostly on US government fellowships. I had been working for an international oil company in Texas, hoping that this would expedite my transfer back to the region, but that wasn't going as planned. It seemed the right time and place to make a jump.

The application process for the Foreign Service was long and cumbersome, but I was offered an appointment in early 2004 and spent three months in a sprawling complex in Virginia going through the training program with a hundred other diplomats-to-be.

During breaks and meals, new hires mingled with more seasoned diplomats returning for home leave or briefings and trainings between assignments. It was clear that the Iraq War was highly unpopular within the Service, across the board. The staunchest opponents were those who had spent careers in the Middle East learning local languages and doing the hard work of understanding local political dynamics. They saw the Iraq War not only as a repudiation of their expertise and advice—a "dumbing-down" and marginalization of the State Department's role in America's foreign affairs—but also as evidence of a moral failure on the part of the United States, particularly as the more unsavory aspects of the war came to light: falsified evidence of WMDs in Iraq and rumors that the United States was involved in the torture of prisoners. And now, nearly a year into the war, many diplomats were openly questioning whether to take posts in Iraq or be conscientious objectors.

The State Department tried to induce their diplomats to work in Baghdad with various perks and pay incentives. Then it turned to directives: either you served in Iraq, or your career would suffer. The Bush administration took advantage of what was anecdotally a huge exodus of talent from the State Department, to introduce noncareer diplomats and to promote people who were felt to be politically malleable and would back up its agenda. This bureaucratic engineering and wave of departures would have a huge impact on the Foreign Service over the following years, weakening its talent pool and conveying the message that politics was more important than competence. The Iraq War's ability to vacuum up resources was particularly devastating for so-called hardship posts (of which a large percentage were in Africa and the Middle East) where even under the best of circumstances it was hard to recruit officers—even in places like Libya, where suddenly there was a new, high-profile mission. These deficiencies would only get worse, and would contribute to the bottleneck that emerged from the Arab Spring revolutions in 2010, which were in part triggered by the Iraq debacle.

At the end of three months of training in Washington, D.C., I was assigned to be a vice consul in Kuwait—a standard job for newly minted American diplomats. This wasn't my first choice—there were nine other posts ahead of it on my list of preferences, starting with Khartoum and Djibouti. My first reaction was to see if I could volunteer for a position in Iraq. While I had been vehemently against the Iraq War from the start, I figured that it would be an environment in which, at the very least, I could learn something new. But with a new policy that made Iraq suddenly off-limits to first-tour officers, I resigned myself to an uneventful two years in Kuwait City, processing visas and doing undefined support work for Iraq operations.

But a couple of weeks before I was set to ship out, a call came out for volunteers willing to serve in the newest American diplomatic post: Tripoli. I immediately asked if I could put myself forward for one of the advertised positions: commercial and economic officer. I understood there were two parts to the job: I'd have to report, as a kind of internal foreign correspondent, to the US government on all economic developments in the country, and I'd be responsible for representing the US Department of Commerce to American companies seeking to set up operations in Libya—and to promote those deals.

My background was very well suited to the work: apart from speaking and reading Arabic, I had a PhD in resource economics and had worked for a major oil company. Coincidentally, it was clear to me at the time that without the Iraq War raging, I probably would not have been sent to Libya—that kind of assignment would have gone to someone with a higher rank in the Service.

It's striking, to a degree, that despite Gaddafi's past atrocities, his record of transcontinental troublemaking, and his relationships with the A-list of international gangsters and terrorists, not to mention the fact that Libya sat on top of the largest oil reserves in Africa, the country had basically fallen off the US government's list of active interests. But isolation and enmity breed more of the same.

And though, as we saw, the United States and the United Kingdom had various plans to try to topple Gaddafi, there wasn't any real urgency, particularly after UN sanctions triggered by the Lockerbie bombing kicked in. Gaddafi was behind a wall, and as long as he sat there, it seemed the damage he could cause was limited. Then there was the fact that—because of the harsh, intrusive nature of the Libyan regime, the sanctions, the difficulty getting access to the

country, and Libya's overall perceived irrelevance to the big-ticket
political problems of the region (the Palestinian–Israeli issue, Iran,
Syria, etc.)—few American journalists or scholars made the effort to
get there.

One notable exception was Dartmouth professor Dirk Vandewalle,
whose Belgian citizenship and focus on far-flung oil states allowed him
access. Dirk and I had been roommates at the American Institute for
Yemeni Studies in Sana'a for a summer, when I had plenty of time to
hear about his work, which piqued my interest and created a bookmark
in my mind—there was a lot more behind Libya's wacky exterior than
I had thought. And I wanted to get there.

"New posts can be a curse for new officers," one of my assigned State
Department mentors cautioned me before I agreed to the assignment.
"There are few rules in these posts, and one can easily cross the bureaucracy without knowing it—and shoot your career in the foot before it
gets started—and not even know why." As much as I noted and appreciated the warning, I hadn't joined the Foreign Service seeking a cushy
assignment or a life-long career. I joined to be useful, and to have an
experience I wouldn't have otherwise. How often did one have a chance
to look under the hood of a country that had been off-limits to Americans for more than twenty years, and whose politics and personalities
were as bizarre as Libya's?

Despite my excitement, it wasn't as if I had no qualms about working for the US government in Libya. One rather obvious concern was
the morality of rehabilitating the Gaddafi regime. I was in college
when the Pan Am Flight 103 bombing happened, and the images
from the news stuck with me for some time. It was a flight I had
been on before, and there were many students my age on it. On the
other hand, was it just for the world to keep punishing the population of a country for the crimes of their leadership? What was really
motivating this shift in direction, and how did it relate to the Iraq
War? How dangerous was this assignment? I didn't know the answers
to these questions, but I settled on the feeling that it was better to

try to understand what was going on than not. And working for the American government in this context was not the same as supporting an unjust war. Had I known more at the time, I would probably have felt differently.

It was August 2004 when I stepped off a flight from London to Tripoli into a hot, dry heat. I almost didn't make the flight. There was one European airline with regular flights into Tripoli, and it hadn't been informed that Americans could now travel to Libya. From the airport, my new colleagues drove me through a patchwork of red-earth farms, their borders marked with palm trees, to a British diplomatic residence, where a party was being held in honor of a British diplomat's departure after a two-year tour. Holding what was to be my last can of beer for some time, I looked out on an enormous harvest moon hanging over the horizon and wondered what on earth was in store for me in this country, whose contours were still set by my imagination.

The next day, I participated in something that had become a rite of passage for new arrivals to the US Mission: a tour of the remains of the last US Embassy, ransacked by the regime after the 1980 departure.[7] As Gaddafi minders led us through the rubble, I stepped on a broken picture frame, but the photo inside wasn't of Ronald Reagan (US president at that time), it was Richard Nixon. A crack in the illusion. I had a feeling that most of what we had just seen was fake—one of the many staged productions and veiled threats to come. This one seemed to be "Behave or you know what's waiting for you."

There were two American government presences in Tripoli at the time. One was the US Liaison Office (USLO), opened in June 2004. USLO was neither an embassy nor a consulate, and as such, it was led by a chargé d'affaires, not an ambassador. It was housed in the only business-class hotel in Libya, the Corinthia Bab Africa Hotel, jointly built and managed with a Maltese investor (some locals claimed Gaddafi had it built on the grounds of a Jewish cemetery—which was credible if only because Gaddafi did things like that). All the American diplomats worked and lived in the hotel.

The other American presence in Tripoli at the time was a CIA Annex, much like the structure that would be attacked in Benghazi a few years later. Like its analog in Benghazi, it was supposed to be a well-kept secret, but like its future analog, many Libyan civilians and officials knew about it.[8]

The USLO was no Club Med. It was an unaccompanied post, meaning no spouses or families. There were none of the perks of being a diplomat in a developed country: no elaborate cocktail parties, no state dinners, few conventional diversions. The quarters were cramped, and twelve- to fourteen-hour workdays were the norm—mainly because there were too few people to do the work that was expected from Washington. Gaddafi made Libya a dry country, though a crisp 100-dollar bill could get you a bottle of wine or whiskey from guards at one of the African embassies.

Even as I arrived, the twenty-odd person mission had developed a reputation back in the State Department as a problem post: low morale and constant staffing issues. The reasons were pretty obvious to me, as they were some of the same reasons I found Libya fascinating—and why I was chosen for the job. Bureaucracies like the State Department promote a certain kind of risk aversion: It takes a decade and a half typically from entry to be on the cusp of the senior Foreign Service. In the years following 9/11 and the Iraq War, diplomats made names for themselves in Baghdad, Kabul, Moscow, and Washington, D.C., not places that were marginal—or safe. Libya was assumed to be a bit of both.

I think it's fair to say that a certain percentage of diplomats are drawn to the career because of its potential for predictability, not volatility: a stable, long-term job with regular hours and, often, an interesting and comfortable social setting. Though I was open to a career, at the time I was looking for a way to make a difference, and to get a perspective on the Middle East that I might not get otherwise.

Perspective I got. But it wasn't easy, and I got it in ways that would

have been hard to fully anticipate or prepare for. One of the most drain-
ing aspects of the job was the constant surveillance—Libyan intelligence, or *mukhabarat*, signaled their presence through various tricks of
the trade, such as small changes to your living space done to make you
feel more acutely that your movements were being observed: a reshuf-
fling of business cards, books out of place. When walking through
town, you could often tell you were being tailed. Once or twice someone randomly came up to me and repeated something I had said to
someone earlier in the day—just to make it clear someone was listening.
At one point, I took a vacation in Malaysia. On the flight I was flanked
by two middle-aged Libyans in suits, who made a point of chatting
me up and telling me of their upcoming beach holidays. Years after I
left Libya, I found that some of the infectious paranoia and heightened
vigilance I had developed there stayed with me. For a long time, I would
question coincidences that I otherwise would have never given a second
thought. To distract myself from the claustrophobic work environment
in the hotel, I swam laps in the hotel pool, which looked out over a series of jagged rocks that created a large pool at high tide. There, locals
washed their horses. For all its stunning beauty, the view of the sea in
front of the hotel always struck me as somewhat sad—partly because
I never saw anyone other than the horses enjoying the water. Though
you could swim along the capital's corniche in places, there were no
sailboats, parasails, or motorboats in Gaddafi's Libya. Many of the best
beaches were contaminated by sewage mains pouring directly into the
water. Gaddafi made it very hard for his people to enjoy themselves
and the natural beauty around them. Yet, paradoxically, or by necessity,
Libyans were some of the most good-humored people I had met, anywhere. They had developed an elaborate language with which to lament
their situation while keeping within the regime's red lines of acceptable
dissent. But the Americans, at least at first, brought hope that maybe
things would start to change.

Over my first months in Libya, one of the things that surprised me
most was how little the US government knew about what was going

on in Libya—and how few resources were expended on supporting
the rehabilitation of the regime and developing US–Libyan commercial ties. I was responsible for reporting on the Libyan economy and
reform process. But I was also charged with briefing representatives
of US companies, from Boeing to Exxon, who were flying in to scout
out commercial opportunities. It was mostly I and my assistant who
handled these tasks, which included answering thousands of emails,
attending government auctions, meeting with Libyan lawyers and businessmen (and -women), and trying to make heads or tails of Gaddafi's many inconsistent edicts regarding how business could be done
in Libya.

By comparison, any other country with comparable economic opportunities for American companies would have had a group of four or five
US diplomats, and as many local assistants, just to cover the trade part
of the relationship. But once again, the Iraq War had drained all other
resources.

I assumed that the United States had continued, through whatever
means, to accrete a fat file on the Libyan leader. I was wrong: We
didn't know much about Gaddafi or the subterranean opposition to his
regime. Back in Washington, D.C., most foreign policy people thought
Gaddafi was simply a lunatic, or an idiot, or both. We certainly didn't
know much about the Gaddafi family dynamics, at a time when several
of his seven children were now grown and jockeying for commercial
and political influence. A few times over the course of my two years
there, these fraternal fights spilled out into the public, as Gaddafi's
older sons pit their private militias against one another to lay claim to
the control of well-known American brands, like Coca-Cola, Pepsi, and
Caterpillar. Once I had to debrief one CEO who had been abducted
and driven around Tripoli in the trunk of a car as a result of one of
these spats.

It seemed like the rolling tape of what was going on here had ceased
when the last American diplomats had left in 1980. Countries with

which the United States doesn't have diplomatic relations tend to get less attention almost by definition—there's no regular stream of diplomatic activity and working in these countries doesn't tend to lead to promotions. Further, North Africa had a limited budget at the State Department and the CIA, and the Algerian civil war took up the lion's share of intelligence resources in the 1990s. Wayne White, former deputy director for the Near East and at the State Department's Bureau of Intelligence and Research (INR), estimated that from 1992 to 1997, the State Department had a fraction of one man-year devoted to Libya while the CIA had perhaps three full-time employees on the country. He said further that from 2002 to 2003, "90 percent of my own efforts had been thrown into coverage of Iraq . . . keeping fully abreast of what was transpiring on the Libyan domestic political scene, in parallel, was highly problematic."[9]

Having people on the ground could perhaps finally change that, though. Without question, the most valuable information I gained in Libya I got in the field, watching, listening, and interacting with people. And it was often in the mundane bureaucratic tasks that I found the most insight into how Libya worked, how American diplomacy worked, and where the two sides were not understanding one another.

Given how much the chargé d'affaires had on his plate, I was often asked to stand in for him at Gaddafi's speeches, command performances that often took place in his birthplace of Sirte, where in a few years he would meet his ugly end. This production invariably left a pool of ambassadors (or occasionally, as was the case with me, their assistants) sitting for hours on a blistering-hot runway, waiting for one of the first Boeing 727s ever made to ferry them from Tripoli across 300 miles of Mediterranean Sea to Sirte. Once there, our minders would shove us on a bus sealed with curtains, which would drive around in circles before depositing us in front of Gaddafi's Italian-made, onyx marble complex, Ouagadougou Hall.

We'd wait for hours for Gaddafi to emerge and sit in a chair facing the audience.

Gaddafi's speeches were long and unstructured, with his mumble at times almost inaudible. Gaddafi's chief of protocol, dressed in a garish marching band outfit, roamed the hall wielding a seven-foot-long whip, which he cracked whenever the crowd failed to express its enthusiasm sufficiently. The muffled screams made it hard to concentrate on what Gaddafi was saying. The vast majority of the diplomats present couldn't understand Arabic, anyway.

Gaddafi's speeches, while interminable, were often more interesting than I expected. His themes tended to be conspiratorial (the idea that the CIA was spreading genetically modified organisms [GMOs] to control the world's food supply was one), but his references suggested someone who, even if disturbed, was intelligent and well-read. Though I wasn't qualified to make psychological evaluations, I thought there was enough material in these events to build a better model of who this person was and what motivated him. But with perhaps two people in the mission who spoke Arabic, this didn't seem likely to happen.

Visitors from Washington seemed convinced that Libyans, as a group, were anti-American. Sure, there were Libyans who didn't like Americans—or at least, had a very negative view of the US government. But I never experienced any of the overt hostility to America that I had in so many other Arab countries during the 1990s. All the same, I imagine much of this had to do with the fact that, due to Gaddafi's censorship, Libyans weren't bombarded with satellite TV images of wars and conflicts in which America or Israel were implicated. Gaddafi's control over religious affairs and public gatherings also limited some of the most virulent anti-American and anti-Western language. When I lived in Yemen in the late 1990s, you could tell the mood on the street from the *khutbahs* (Friday sermons) that were broadcast via loudspeakers onto the street. Not so in Libya's main cities.

I was confident that there were opportunities to improve America's image in Libya. I saw an easy one in the Tripoli International Fair, where foreign firms came to display their products and make deals, many related to the oil industry. The United States had been absent from this event since 1979, and the question came up in the summer of 2005 whether we should participate, on short notice. I argued strongly, yes—and was put in charge of managing the procurement of a pavilion and recruiting US companies to participate. There was a tension here, though, as we had to strike a balance between doing something appropriate to the fresh—and uncertain—nature of the US–Libyan relationship, and something suitable to the stature of the United States. Those issues were solved, but the trickier one was what kind of cultural display we would put on for the fairgoers, who were expected to number in the hundreds of thousands over the course of a month. The State Department had a list of available international entertainers, but they seemed to me too drab and not quite suitable for the event. So I called up a friend, a rising musical talent in the Bay Area, and asked if he might be interested in bringing his jazz band to Libya. He had other commitments but recommended a group called Luna Angel, which turned out to be a reggae band. The question was whether Libyans would associate reggae with America.

I didn't realize just how popular reggae was in Libya. The band was a huge hit, even if the show created a few moments of panic, as tens of thousands of Libyans rushed the stage, cheering and waving American flags that the mission had handed out to the crowd. It was a stunning sight. Colleagues and I looked at each other and asked, "My god, where else in the Middle East would you see such a scene?" There was going to be no overnight democracy here, but Libyans were palpably eager for change, and the US government seemed basically unaware of the degree to which Libyans were looking for the possibility that the United States might help change their lives for the better—by opening up opportunities to study, to travel, and to work.

The other thing that struck me was that, despite all the chaos and deprivation of the previous thirty-five years, there were many professionals—lawyers, writers, doctors, scientists, and engineers, many educated abroad—who seemed to have reached an accommodation with the regime that allowed them to keep practicing their chosen fields with integrity. They may have been a minority, but many of them were among those who later rose up against the regime and worked, tirelessly, to try to build a working state that served the needs of its people. They may not have had access to the latest research or training, or opportunities to market their work, but they were proud of remaining uncorrupted by the regime. Unlike in many other Arab countries, the group included a good number of professional women, like BMC's Dr. Bugaighis, who had also been able to get a first-class education abroad. And these people by and large had children, who were young and smart and were pushing for the government to give them the same opportunities and taking advantage of every minor concession Gaddafi made that might allow them to start new companies or enroll in schools abroad. Libya was mismanaged, and its people traumatized by Gaddafi's regime, but one couldn't go far without running into some sign of Libyans' general attachment to the United States and American culture.

For all these reasons, I came to see Libya as something like the Jurassic Park of America's Middle East—Gaddafi's tight grip on the media had shielded many Libyans from the most gruesome images of American-backed wars in the Middle East, allowing a number of older Libyans to hang on to an image of America from the 1960s and 1970s, when America had a significant military base in Libya, American companies ran Libyan oil, and American products and companies were seen to be a mark of quality. In a more open Libya, these favorable stereotypes would inevitably fall.

In 2005, at the middle of my tour, former Assistant Secretary for Near Eastern Affairs Richard Murphy introduced me to Chris Stevens, a fellow diplomat doing a tour with the Senate Foreign Relations Committee.[10] Chris had put in for the position of number two in the soon-to-be US Embassy in Tripoli, a job he'd start a year and a half later, in 2007, after I finished my tour.[11] In a few years, he'd be tapped to advise the Obama administration on how to cope with Libya's meltdown during the Arab Spring. Somewhat incredibly, in a short time, Stevens would be the US government's foremost expert on Libya, which speaks both to Stevens's aptitude for communication, as well as our low starting level of knowledge about Libya.

Murphy thought I could give Chris a sense of what working at the US Mission in Tripoli was like. Chris had good reason to investigate what he was getting into, as Tripoli's USLO had the poor distinction of being the American diplomatic post with the highest rate of curtailments—or broken assignments. As I heard it, Chris had been tapped to try to change that dynamic. I told Chris how I saw it: I didn't have his years of diplomatic experience—fifteen years spent in places like Israel, Egypt, and Saudi Arabia—but I could tell that the mission was dysfunctional. I also told him that I found myself completely in my element in Libya. I loved being able to get out and talk to Libyans, in their language, and to not be tied to a desk. This was the kind of experience I hoped to get when I joined the Foreign Service. I had a sense that Chris was similarly motivated—that he saw Libya's oddities and mysteries as insights waiting to be had, and that this was a corner of the world where a skillful first contact would make a bigger difference than in other places. In other words, we shared an idealistic streak.

I thought to tell Chris about my worries about security. Generally, I felt quite safe in Libya, out on the street at night, for example. But we had been living and working in the hotel for a year, and increasingly it felt like we were sitting ducks. As Gaddafi's relationship with the West deepened, the hotel became a prime meeting place for businesspeople and diplomats, and it housed the offices of several major oil companies. If someone wanted to pick a place to attack, to drive a wedge between

Libya and the West, this was it. The regime seemed to have a strong incentive to protect us, but just how good were Gaddafi's intelligence services? And could his intelligence thwart determined attackers? The Corinthia Bab Africa Hotel had no Marine Security Guards or security contractors. The local guards posted outside our residential and work floors were unarmed and prone to taking naps.

Chris wasn't arriving to fill his post for another year, though. I assumed things would be a lot different by then. A month later, I moved into a residence outside the hotel, but even so, I felt a constant nagging that we were all exposed. Clearly the post management felt the same and wrote several cables back to Washington alerting Main State to the security situation and requesting assistance. The general sense back in Washington was that Gaddafi's interests lay in keeping American diplomats safe. But our Regional Security Officer (RSO), Dan Meehan, would describe our security situation then, from the perspective of the 2012 Benghazi attack, as woefully inadequate: "the local police that protected the hotel were unarmed and wore torn sandals, even though the terrorist's threat to the hotel from the Libyan Islamic Fighting Group was very real."[12]

When I finished my tour and left Libya after two years, I wasn't sure what to think of the efforts to flip Gaddafi, and where they might lead. It was obvious that, for the most part, the regime's reform effort was a sham. The United States and particularly Europe were too interested in the potential economic gains of the relationship to be honest advocates for and enforcers of the reform process—as demonstrated later by numerous bribery scandals involving senior UK and French officials and several international companies. It was clear Saif Gaddafi had a shaky future as his father's heir, and relations between the United States and Libya were deteriorating, not improving.

But all this didn't mean that the opening of international relations didn't have promise, and impact. Libyans got a new look at the outside world and found hope—something that had been missing for decades. And that may well have been the biggest threat to Gaddafi's ability to keep his juggling game going. For it is a well-known observation— a phenomenon known as the Tocqueville effect, for the philosopher's observations on the French Revolution—that revolutions tend to happen not when things are getting worse, but when things are looking up and people realize that there are other realities. But I was missing much of what was going on behind the scenes, details that would have made me feel much less hopeful both about Libya's future and the future of American foreign policy.

3

The Dark Side of the Moon

We also have to work, through, sort of the dark side, if you will . . .
if we're going to be successful. That's the world these folks operate in.

—US VICE PRESIDENT DICK CHENEY,
SEPTEMBER 16, 2001

On the outside, America's shotgun relationship with Gaddafi was supposed to be about political and economic reform—adding another feather to America's newfound campaign to promote democracy through "transformational diplomacy."[1] But promoting democracy was never what the Iraq invasion was about. In the Neocons' calculus, Iraq was about making the Arab-Muslim world respect and fear American power. Democracy promotion was tacked on after the fact to make that idea sound more noble. Behind the scenes, the US relationship with Gaddafi reflected that dissonance.

Following 9/11, any group with suspected connections to Al Qaeda was immediately flagged as an enemy of the United States. And the LIFG was no exception. Two weeks after 9/11, President Bush signed an order freezing LIFG assets in the United States.[2]

By 2000, the LIFG had become the most significant of Al Qaeda's allies. Its immediate network constituted an elite pool from which bin Laden, and then his successor, Ayman Al-Zawahiri, chose many of their closest aides. The CIA and certainly British intelligence, to its past collaboration with the LIFG, were aware of both Gaddafi's war with the LIFG and the LIFG's connections to Al Qaeda. The United States wanted Gaddafi's help in identifying those linkages and obtaining information from them about Al Qaeda's structure, and possible next moves. So, a deal within a deal was struck: Gaddafi would provide the United States with a list of his most wanted Islamist enemies—essentially a Who's Who of the LIFG leadership. The US and UK intelligence services would track them down and deliver them back to Libya for interrogation and torture, with the objective of getting information on bin Laden and Al Qaeda. This program, carried out in the shadows via "black sites" and unmarked Learjets, would become the most widespread application of a process known as extraordinary rendition. And of those in the US government who knew about it, not everyone was happy. A turf battle quickly erupted between the FBI, which wanted to retain oversight of the rendition process, and the CIA, which drove the practice deeper into the shadows.

So while the United States was framing the deal with Libya as a step toward reform and democracy promotion, behind the scenes it was violating the basic human rights of suspected terrorists in pursuit of information on bin Laden's future plans. These relationships would eventually come to light in documents found in the office of Gaddafi's spymaster Moussa Koussa after the regime was toppled.[3] And with these details, it became clearer why USLO's regional security officer was so concerned about the LIFG, starting in 2004, as the group certainly had strong reason to want to disrupt the US–Libyan relationship.

Abdulhakim Belhaj stands at the heart of the Libyan rendition story, its most prominent victim—and, ultimately, perhaps its most prominent beneficiary.

In memoirs partly dictated to *Le Monde* correspondent Isabelle

Mandraud, Belhaj describes a meeting he had with Osama bin Laden and Ayman Al-Zawahiri shortly before 9/11, at bin Laden's base in Kandahar, Afghanistan, with his deputy Khalid al-Sherif in tow. Belhaj says he told bin Laden that he felt he had gone too far with his global jihad against "Jews and Crusaders." The LIFG was not concerned with global jihad, Belhaj apparently said; it was solely focused on freeing Libya from the grasp of Gaddafi, and Al Qaeda's escalation with America was a distraction. As Belhaj tells it, bin Laden said little, and that was the end of the conversation.[4] Others say that this—and most of what Belhaj and his LIFG colleagues said after their release—was an extremely useful fiction, to facilitate the LIFG's claim to have traded violence for the ballot box.

Belhaj told his biographer that he watched in shock with the rest of the world as the twin towers of the World Trade Center in New York collapsed.[5] Given Belhaj's proximity to bin Laden and many of the most senior Al Qaeda leadership, it seems hard to believe that he didn't know something big was in the works. But there is no firm evidence that bin Laden brought the LIFG leaders into the circle of "need to know."

Belhaj says that as soon as he grasped the magnitude of what had happened, he told his LIFG colleagues, "Prepare to flee, you won't find anywhere to hide."[6]

As a fugitive in the wake of 9/11, Belhaj crossed the border from Afghanistan to Iran, where he thought he might get some support from the Iranian mullahs, or Sunni Muslim mosque leaders.[7] However, while Belhaj admired the Iranian Islamic Revolution, it wasn't the 1970s anymore, and the deep split in doctrine between the Sunni and Shi'a Islamic fundamentalists meant that while the Iranian mullahs would occasionally make common cause with the Afghan Arabs, it wasn't a stable relationship. And it certainly wasn't a friendship.

Iranian intelligence arrested and tortured many of the LIFG members arriving from Afghanistan and Pakistan around that time. Belhaj was detained but apparently got off relatively easy and was released after a couple of months. From Iran, he went to Iraq, where he thought he might be able to maintain a low profile. He quickly realized his miscalculation: Iraq in 2003 was now an American target. From Iraq, Belhaj traveled to China and then Malaysia, from which he hoped to apply for asylum in Britain. This sounds counterintuitive—to seek shelter from the United States in a country that was its close ally—but it seemed that Belhaj hoped that the past rules held. But the game had changed 180 degrees: after 9/11, MI6 was working hand and glove with the Americans and the Gaddafi regime, which it had once been so hard-pressed to overthrow with LIFG help.

When boarding a flight from the Malaysian capital Kuala Lumpur to London, Belhaj was stopped by the Malaysian authorities, who offered him a false choice: They could turn him directly over to the CIA, or send him back to Libya. Ultimately, the Malaysians opted to put Belhaj and his wife, Fatima Boudchar, on a flight to Bangkok, Thailand, where they were ensnared in a joint CIA–MI6 operation. Upon arrival in Bangkok, Belhaj says he was separated from his wife, put in a cell, pistol-whipped, and beaten "with great force" while interrogated about his connections to Al Qaeda.[8] He says he was then stripped naked, covered in ice, and beaten so hard that the binding on his hands broke.[9] In a report on rendition, Human Rights Watch confirmed that Belhaj's pregnant wife was also stripped and subjected to degrading treatment, after which both were placed on a C-130 transport and flown to an unknown destination while further interrogated about Al Qaeda's plans.[10] When Belhaj arrived at their final destination, he heard Libyan voices. He was back in Tripoli.

The other senior members of the LIFG had similar experiences, though their paths back to Libya have not been documented in as much detail. The United States would render at least eleven more LIFG members back to Libya in 2004 and 2005. Khalid al-Sherif, who went to Afghanistan with Belhaj in 1988 and became his deputy, was arrested in Peshawar, Pakistan, in 2003 by Pakistani intelligence and detained for two years in Afghanistan, where he says he was subject to similarly horrifying torture, which he described to Human Rights Watch as including

> being chained to walls naked—sometimes while diapered—in pitch black, windowless cells, for weeks or months at a time; being restrained in painful stress positions for long periods of time, being forced into cramped spaces; being beaten and slammed into walls; being kept inside for nearly five months without the ability to bathe; being denied food; being denied sleep by continuous, deafeningly loud Western music; and being subjected to different forms of water torture.[11]

What the United States did to the LIFG leaders was, by the standard of any liberal democracy, unconscionable. But it didn't mean that the LIFG wasn't a threat. While the LIFG's collective post-9/11 narrative is one of trying to find refuge from America's wrath, there are indications that LIFG members had time after 9/11, and before their capture, to help their non-Libyan North African Islamist allies with anti-Western operations: authorities in Spain and Morocco say that between September 9, 2001, and 2004, the LIFG was in contact with Al Qaeda affiliates planning major terrorist attacks. The Moroccan government linked the LIFG to terrorist bombings in Casablanca in 2003, in which forty-five people were killed. Spanish authorities linked the LIFG—and Abdulhakim Belhaj specifically—to the March 11, 2004, Madrid train bombings, which killed 193 and injured over 2,000.[12] This supports the idea that the LIFG was, as Belhaj's biographer describes it, "the jihadist group closest to Al Qaeda" and a resource for other groups in the region that were also advancing Al Qaeda's agenda.[13]

The terrorist attacks of 9/11 instantly created a new enemy for the United States, to replace the one that it had lost with the collapse of its previous adversary, the Soviet Union. Radical Islam wasn't a perfect substitute for the Soviet Union—far from it—but it had some of the key elements of a suitable enemy: ruthless and uncompromising, just like the totalitarians and fascists of World War I and II. But stateless movements were problematic adversaries, as they were resistant to conventional tactics and warfare—and indeed the more conventional war you threw at it, the more powerful it tended to become. Nor was democracy the antidote: when given the chance, political Islam was adept at using elections to its own advantage.

Unfortunately, there were no Jeffersonian democracies in the Middle East that the United States could enlist as allies. This was the legacy of colonialism and of past US support for dictatorships that satisfied America's priorities of opposing the Soviet Union, assuring America's access to energy, and support for the State of Israel. It is in this muddle that the Bush administration seemed to have determined that it would look for an imperfect ally to help advance freedom until real democracy took hold. In this situation, the Muslim Brotherhood started to look like the best of a thin pool of options. And there had been a precedent: the United States had met—quietly—with Brotherhood representatives in Egypt in the early 1990s but then backed off in the second half of the decade, due to a combination of increasing concern in Washington about "fundamentalist Islam" and the strong objections of Egyptian President Hosni Mubarak.

The Bush administration had no immediate plan to topple longtime allies like Hosni Mubarak, but it used substantial economic assistance as a lever to encourage reform. Accordingly, the United States instructed Mubarak to lighten up on its persecution of the Muslim Brotherhood during the 2005 parliamentary elections. In response, Mubarak overcompensated, thinking this would scare the United States into a realization that his regime was the last thing standing between Egypt and an Islamic government hostile to Israel and various other things the United States held dear. Hazem Kandil, one of the few scholars of the Brotherhood with access to the group's leadership, relates a telling exchange:

"Asked . . . if he expected a comparable success in the next elections, the Brotherhood's general guide [leader] said he was not sure, because last time 'State Security gave us a list of districts to run in, and promised to let us win in most. They have not contacted us so far about next year.' "[14]

Despite the somewhat farcical nature of this three-way interaction, many in Washington, either out of ignorance or willfully, chose to misinterpret what was happening: to them, the results were further evidence of the Brotherhood's inevitable rise, and its compatibility with democracy.

Overnight, the Muslim Brotherhood, long a near-taboo subject in Washington, became almost trendy, with a number of opinion pieces arguing that it was time to dispense with preconceptions and to listen to the organization.[15] In the summer of 2007, the US State Department's internal intelligence bureau, INR, hosted a meeting of US intelligence officials to discuss the pros and cons of new overtures to the Brotherhood, which in turn led to informal meetings between US diplomats and senior Muslim Brotherhood members at the US Embassy in Cairo later that year.

The newfound influence of the Brotherhood had something to do with another development: the United States' deepening relationship with the Arabian Gulf emirate of Qatar, arguably the Brotherhood's most influential state backer. In 2003, Qatar offered to host US forward military facilities in the region, absorbing forces withdrawn from Saudi Arabia. This approach was a masterstroke on Qatar's part, as it generated goodwill within the US government, provided Qatar with an American military umbrella with which to repel any regional attack, à la Saddam Hussein's invasion of Kuwait, and gave Qatar free rein to further develop its international soft power campaigns, predicated on a more visible role for the Muslim Brotherhood in regional politics.

These two developments—America's resort to wide-scale kidnapping and torture of the LIFG and its incautious (or not fully considered) alliance with the Muslim Brotherhood—are rarely mentioned in the context of America's continuing misadventures in the Middle East. And yet they are two sides of the same coin. They mark a distinct and dangerous breach with past US policy—and perhaps more than anything else, the absence of strong, coordinated institutional analytic capacity. In the case of Libya, they are at the heart of why the 2011 intervention in Libya failed so miserably, and why the US Mission in Benghazi was attacked in 2012.

4

City of Light and Darkness

Nestled into the eastern shore of the Mediterranean, Benghazi is Libya's second-largest city, home to about a million people. In normal times, a quarter or so of the population are expatriate workers, mostly Egyptian. The city is flat and low, with few structures rising above five stories. Approaching Benghazi from the sea, a once-bustling port dominates the view; from the landward side, the city is oriented around a lagoon, which connects to a jungle of concrete apartment buildings, warehouses, garages, and single-story grocery stores. No one is completely sure where the name "Benghazi" came from, but the accepted story is that it was named for an itinerant Sufi, ibn Ghazi, or "son of Ghazi," whose shrine used to stand in the foothills of the Green Mountains until Muammar Gaddafi had it destroyed.

How Benghazi looked in the early 2000s was a testament to the Italian colonization that started in 1911 and ended in 1943, which produced a formal city plan, wide boulevards, and distinctive architecture. During World War II, the Allied and Axis forces faced each other over Benghazi, destroying much of the old city and forcing new pulverized, though distinctive, buildings and city squares. Add to that the striking, layer-cake lighthouse, built in 1928, an art deco theater, and the waterfront courthouse, which became the epicenter of the rebellion in 2011.

When Libya won its independence in 1951 as a constitutional monarchy, Benghazi became the first among three regional capitals, and the seat of government. The discovery of oil in commercial quantities in

1959 resulted in an economic boom that pushed the limits of the city outward in a somewhat disorganized fashion.

Some of the most cheerful images of Benghazi are from the late 1950s and 1960s, the decade that linked the discovery of oil to Gaddafi's revolution. Postcards and tourist photos from the time depict Libyans out and about, sipping espresso in cafés, wearing the latest Italian fashion, and sailing on the lagoon. A cosmopolitan, Mediterranean city in full bloom, Benghazi had established itself as the cultural capital of Libya, fed by the energy of Cairo and Alexandria, two of the leading centers of Arab arts and letters, along with Beirut, Damascus, and Baghdad.

But Gaddafi's coup changed everything. Over the next years, Gaddafi grew to detest the city of Benghazi and directly and indirectly tried to undermine it. It's not clear when, exactly, his antipathy started, but it was rooted in some fundamental differences. Benghazi and its new, Westernized elites and bohemians were the antithesis of the revolutionary *Jamahiriya* (a neologism meaning "state of the masses") Gaddafi sought to cultivate.

Easterners resented having to relocate to Tripoli for jobs and felt that their resources were being siphoned off to feed Gaddafi's collection of self-aggrandizing monuments and Arab unification efforts. Add to this the fact that eastern Libya had a historical reputation of defying centralized authority—and the trajectory was clear.

One of these Easterners, Sadiq Neihoum, was a native of Benghazi and an iconoclast who wrote lengthy philosophical texts that played with the ideologies of the day: Marxism, Arab nationalism, etc. Despite his allegiance to Benghazi, he had Gaddafi's ear for a time. And Neihoum's newspaper columns may have been an inspiration for Gaddafi's *The Green Book*—a collection of ruling aphorisms, stripped of Neihoum's deeper philosophical arguments.

While posted to Libya, I became fascinated with Neihoum's work, in particular his essays and fables, many of which were set in Benghazi and spelled out the roots of Islamist rage, as well as Gaddafi's discomfort with the city. In one story, titled "The Good-Hearted

Salt Seller," Neihoum portrays Benghazi as an eternal battleground between the forces of light and darkness.[1] The story's protagonist is a dark-skinned salt seller dedicated to a life of honest, hard labor. The Devil appears one day and challenges him to a wrestling match, which continues over the course of days. It's an allegory loosely built on the Old Testament story of Job. In another, called "The Sultan's Flotilla," a paranoid, deluded leader is haunted by dreams of a black dog, which every year smashes down one of seven sets of his palace's outer walls. A soothsayer interprets the dream to mean that the Sultan has seven years to prepare for an epic flood. So the Sultan orders an ark built.[2] The flood comes as predicted, but carries away not only the kingdom but the Sultan as well—a transparent observation that dictatorships don't often end well, and a ruler's paranoia only gets deeper with time.

As Gaddafi's political and economic policies got more and more outlandish, his behavior toward eastern Libya became more violent, and many who dared stand against him were "disappeared"—never to be heard from again. Others were hanged at university campuses.

Throughout the 1980s, soccer games—the only sanctioned public gatherings—were a kind of preprogrammed steam venting, until they became the scenes of open riots and were canceled. Benghazi was, increasingly, a city in a low-level state of revolt—a situation that fed the Islamist infiltration, which, as we saw, was in full swing by the early 1990s.

Despite Benghazi's opposition to Gaddafi, not all of its people hated Gaddafi for the same reasons, or to the same degree. Two events in the late 1990s helped create a common cause.

In 1998, more than 400 infants at several Benghazi-area hospitals contracted HIV, the virus that causes AIDS, under mysterious circumstances. Attempting to calm popular anger, in 1999 the regime arrested five Bulgarian nurses and one Palestinian medical intern and charged them with a conspiracy to murder Libyan children. A Libyan court subsequently sentenced them to death. Epidemiological data strongly suggested the medics were innocent. The regime was under tremendous pressure to hold someone accountable.

At the same time, the verdict and incarceration of the medics became an obstacle to the West's full normalization with Libya. Gaddafi needed this normalization to release domestic pressure, which was mounting as rumors spread of another atrocity, this one committed two years before, in 1996. A riot had broken out at Gaddafi's notorious Tripoli Abu Salim prison, where inmates were demanding better living conditions. What ensued was a standoff between inmates and guards that ended hours later with an alleged order by Gaddafi's then head of internal security, Abdullah Senussi, to systematically gun down about 1,250 people in under two hours. It seems Gaddafi had decided to use the protest as a pretext for getting rid of many of his Islamist adversaries, including many LIFG members, in one fell swoop. A large fraction of Abu Salim inmates were from eastern Libya, and Benghazi and Derna in particular. These two events were highly significant for their ability to bond a large percentage of Benghazi residents together in common rage, not just Islamists, but ordinary people caught in the middle: virtually no family was unaffected by one or both of these tragedies, through a father, cousin, son, or close friend.

When I began work in Tripoli in 2004, I had only the most rudimentary idea of the smoldering Benghazi backstory, and its relevance for the regime's longevity. Nevertheless, it was clear to me after a couple of months that Tripoli, though the center of Gaddafi's world, was only a part of the Libya dynamic—to understand Libya, the United States needed to understand what was going on in Benghazi, too. Many of the European embassies had set up consulates a couple of years before the Americans arrived to gather intelligence and lay the foundation for commercial deals. But the small American staff was already stretched dangerously thin.

The Public Diplomacy section, charged with explaining American policy abroad and setting up academic and cultural exchanges, consisted of one experienced career diplomat and a couple of Libyan assistants. This small group started to work on setting up something called an "American Corner" in Benghazi—a small public cultural space with English-language books on American history and culture, as well as information on educational programs and fellowships, as a kind of placeholder for an eventual larger presence. Though modest, it would be a means of making contact with the population of Benghazi and setting the path for an eventual consulate. But the bureaucratic obstacles on both the US side and the Libyan side were enormous. When I left Libya in 2006, there was still no progress in setting this up. It wasn't until Chris Stevens's last trip to Benghazi in 2012 that the plan looked like it would finally see the light of day.

When I arrived in Libya, I was keen to get out to Benghazi as soon as I could. From the outside, and from the perspective of someone already deeply interested in the Middle East, as I was, Benghazi was almost a phantom city. It rarely appeared in the media, and one didn't often meet people who had just been there, for somewhat obvious reasons. Long before I thought of joining the Foreign Service, I had heard stories from a family friend about growing up in Benghazi, which at the time sounded very exotic to me. She described memories of a warm, tight-knit community in a city with beautiful gardens and the ever-present Mediterranean Sea. She spoke of growing up Jewish and attending an Italian Catholic school in an observant Muslim country. Benghazi had been a melting pot then, a place without conflict and without much overt religious discrimination. That harmony would change with the 1967 Arab–Israeli War, which sparked violence that forced Libya's Jews to emigrate. It would never have occurred to me, listening to her then, that in a few years I'd be one of the first Americans back to Libya.

In October 2004, I flew with a Libyan colleague to Benghazi for a weekend—an hour flight on another antique 727. After landing, the plane's door popped open, letting in a stiff breeze heavy with the scent of pine and salt. We walked down the stairs to the tarmac and past a line of screaming families, waving at their loved ones. We took a cab from the airport down the long, straight road into the city, whose modern orientation and shape took form under the Italians.

This was my introduction to an environment significantly different from the one I'd gotten to know in Tripoli. In Tripoli, evidence of Gaddafi was everywhere, in billboards proclaiming his "Libya's heart beats for you," on signposts bearing inane aphorisms from *The Green Book*, and in the constant surveillance. Here, there was none of that. Gaddafi may have had his ominous, windowless barracks in the center of town to remind the people of Benghazi who was in charge, but the regime knew not to push itself in peoples' faces, lest it provoke a conflict it couldn't contain.

The city had seen better times—that was obvious. Public monuments were corroded with rust; garbage piled up. The Benghazi Lake, the centerpiece of Benghazi leisure in the 1960s, was devoid of signs of life. No sailboats or swimmers here either. And for good reason: as early as 1995, as one of Gaddafi's endless provocations, the effluence from a slaughterhouse was diverted into the lake, creating a noxious stench that many residents blamed for migraines. But still, surveying the damage done to the city by decades of neglect, you could easily imagine how it had been—and how it might be, with a bit more attention. And there were signs of new life—with Gaddafi's latest lifting of restrictions on business, there were, among the concrete monstrosities, coffeehouses and boutiques that clearly hadn't been there a year before. On my trips to Benghazi, I got to know the traditional downtown, "Old Benghazi," much better than the rest of the city, partly because it was within walking distance of the Tibesti Hotel, where I stayed, and a quick drive to most of my meetings.

After exiting the Tibesti, I'd walk along 23rd of July Street, past Maydan al-Shajara (Tree Square), Maydan At-Tahrir (Liberation Square), and the Benghazi courthouse, to Omar Al Mukhtar Street. There, on the left, was a bookstore. A small sign above the door read

Qureena (a reference to the ancient Greek city of Cyrene, not far from Derna). In the front window were carefully placed Arabic translations of books from Italian and English. Inside, it was a long, narrow space filled with bookshelves. Piles of books blocked the aisles, making movement through the store difficult.

My colleague introduced me to the owner, a distant cousin (everyone seemed related to everyone else in this city). He looked to be in his seventies, tall, thin, and bespectacled, with thin white hair. He was clearly highly educated and spoke English well. I wasn't surprised to learn that he had been a member of Parliament in the 1960s, during the rule of King Idris. I rarely saw anyone actually purchase a book there, yet the gentleman seemed to maintain a receiving line of people of all ages—but only men—who filtered in to pay their respects. My colleague introduced us, and told him about a hobby I was pursuing that involved collecting and translating short stories set in different places in Libya, and then going to visit those places.[3] The owner waded into stacks of books reaching shoulder height and pulled out a collection of stories by Wahbi Bouri, considered one of Benghazi's literary greats. Over several visits, the bookshop owner schooled me in Benghazi's main contemporary writers and life in the city before Gaddafi's catastrophic policies. He was so outspoken on this later topic that I was concerned, lest someone overhear what he was saying and report him to the authorities. But I was quite sure I wasn't the first person to hear his tirade.

"I'm an old man," he'd say, without a trace of fear. "What are they going to do to me?"

When I listened to him, his passionate defense of Benghazi, his love of books, and his references to forces of light and darkness, it reminded me of Neihoum and his good-hearted salt seller. So in my own thoughts, I nicknamed him the Good-Hearted Bookseller.

My investment in building relationships in Benghazi paid off, in a sense, when contacts there and elsewhere in eastern Libya provided me with early news and details of a dramatic event that took place in Benghazi on February 17, 2006. A crowd had gathered in Benghazi near the Italian Consulate to protest the publication of cartoons insulting to the Prophet Mohammed in a Danish newspaper. The broader "Danish cartoon controversy," as it was known at the time, sparked protests across the Muslim world—just as an anti-Islamic hate video would generate a wave of protests in the Arab world in 2011. The 2006 protests got out of hand, setting the Italian Consulate on fire, and morphed into an attack on the Gaddafi regime, spreading across parts of Benghazi and into the towns of the Green Mountains.

Ostensibly, the immediate trigger for the Benghazi protests was the appearance of an Italian minister in public wearing a T-shirt emblazoned with the same offending Danish cartoons. But contacts within Libya and at the Italian Mission said no, the protests were only superficially related to the cartoons, and that the Gaddafi regime, which had been pressuring the Italian government to pay five billion dollars in reparations for the damage done by the Italian colonial occupation, had organized the protests to put pressure on the Italian government—and it backfired. Others said that Islamists or Islamist sympathizers either were behind the protest or hijacked popular anger at the Italians to fire shots at the regime. Whatever the case, the event signaled to Gaddafi and Libyans that the initial hopes for reform and a better life were wearing thin. The regime was vulnerable, and Benghazi was still a powder keg.

Even in 2006, there was a growing awareness that to understand the Islamist phenomenon and its link to eastern Libya, Americans would have to put in a lot more time and manpower. And it would take further warnings, and two more years, for that to even begin to happen, with the arrival of Chris Stevens.

5

Die Hard in Derna

After fifteen years as an American diplomat, Chris Stevens had established himself as one of the State Department's career Arabists: He had served embassies and consulates around the region, including Saudi Arabia and Jerusalem, and he was conversant in Arabic and French. He had absolutely no interest in serving in Iraq, which he considered condoning an unjustifiable war.[1] At least one of his colleagues thought his stubbornness on this point was counterproductive, as most paths to promotion went through Baghdad. Stevens was much more interested in a possible exception to that rule, Libya, which some colleagues had already started calling during my tour "just like Iraq without the shooting—yet." Because of its unpublicized link to US policy in Iraq and the post's continued low morale, a Tripoli tour might now be considered by the promotion boards as a substitute for Baghdad. In his conversations with me, it was clear that Chris liked the idea of a posting to Libya, which brought him back to his experience teaching English with the Peace Corps in Morocco in the mid-1980s. The challenge would be making sure that the US Embassy didn't become a flash point for an international diplomatic incident.

If Chris had any initial qualms about the Libya assignment, they seemed to be around whether engagement with Libya could be construed as giving Gaddafi a pass for his involvement in the Lockerbie bombing. Another principled stance.[2] It's unlikely that Chris knew about extraordinary rendition at this point, as it was almost certainly exclusively a CIA operation.[3] By the end of my own tour in 2006, US relations with Libya had been fully normalized, leading to the establishment of a formal Embassy, which, by the time Chris arrived, would soon be housed in a compound with a full contingent of marines (which US diplomats would frequently be reminded were not there to protect them, but classified documents). But the staffing gaps persisted because still few diplomats wanted to go to Libya, and those who might be most interested and useful were in Iraq. Most of the US personnel were temporary: people came for a few months on TDYs (temporary duty assignments) and stayed for barely enough time to acquire much new information or insight, let alone pass it on to others.

Things didn't look to be improving in the big picture, either. By the end of 2007, the Western relationship with Gaddafi had exited the honeymoon phase. Gaddafi was now regularly complaining that he hadn't been adequately compensated by the United States for his sacrifices— by which he meant giving up his Weapons of Mass Destruction (such as they were). The United States and Europe, for their part, were still waiting for Gaddafi's promised commercial benefits to materialize, in the form of oil and infrastructure concessions. And the reform process seemed to be slowing to a crawl. Saif, Gaddafi's son, was feeling increasingly insecure in his position as heir apparent and in 2010 would run off to London briefly, proclaiming that he was retiring from politics.[4]

It was against that background that Secretary of State Condoleezza Rice visited Libya in early September 2008, to fulfill a Bush administration commitment to send a senior representative to mark full normalization of relations. But the trip had a grudging, placeholder quality to it, as if Washington had already decided that the relationship had reached the limits of its potential. Secretary Rice's visit would be the first by a sitting US secretary of state since John Foster Dulles arrived in Tripoli in 1953. Chris was asked to comment on what Rice should expect in her meeting with Gaddafi. There wasn't much to say, other than be prepared for something odd, as meetings with Gaddafi were *always* odd. But with Rice, whom he referred to as "my African princess," Gaddafi reportedly outdid himself. He made her wait for hours, as he did most important guests, refused to shake her hand, and presented her with a music video he had commissioned in her honor, entitled "Black Flower in the White House."[5] Stevens was present for much of the encounter. Rice seems to have come away from the meeting further convinced that Gaddafi was a lunatic, and as such, the trip seemed to have marked a further chill in US–Libyan relations.

But Libya's continued relevance to American policy in the region would suddenly become a bit clearer, at least to those who were paying attention. Rice's visit came a few months after *Newsweek* ran a cover story on the Sinjar Records, a collection of 700 digitized IDs seized by the US military at an Al Qaeda safehouse on the Iraqi side of the Syrian–Iraqi border.[6] The records belonged to Al Qaeda recruits entering Iraq between August 2006 and August 2007. The Combating Terrorism Center at West Point published a detailed analysis of the Sinjar Records, which showed a much greater rate of participation by Libyan radicals in Al Qaeda than anyone suspected. After Saudi Arabia, the highest number of represented nationals came from two cities in Libya: Benghazi and the nearby much smaller settlement of Derna.[7] A footnote to the West Point report mentioned that members of the Libyan Islamic Fighting Group were "providing logistical support to the Islamic State of Iraq"—even while its leadership was in Gaddafi's jails.[8]

In late May, a month after the *Newsweek* story appeared, Stevens filed the necessary paperwork with the Libyan regime to fly from Tripoli to visit Benghazi and the Greco-Roman site at Cyrene, the oldest of five ancient Greek cities founded in Libya in the seventh century BCE and known as the Pentapolis. Though Chris would have been interested in Cyrene on its historical merits, the timing of his visit, its location, and his own role as a political reporting officer suggested that the ruins weren't his main interest. He wanted to go to Derna, about an hour and twenty minutes' drive farther east. The *Newsweek* article had aroused public interest back in the United States, including in Congress, which would be querying the Embassy staff for more information. Why, US officials wanted to know, were nationals from a country with which the United States had just normalized relations sending recruits to Al Qaeda to fight Americans?

Stevens told the whole story of the trip in a cable he wrote afterward.[9] He was able to tack on a trip to Derna, he explained, due to an "apparent lapse in coordination between security officials in Tripoli and Benghazi," which had led to a gap in surveillance—which in this case would have doubled as regime-provided protection. Stevens rented a car and driver in Benghazi to take him to Cyrene; the driver happened to speak English and happened to have a relative living in Derna—who also spoke English. The plan was to go speak with him, and anyone else he could find.

According to Chris, when he got to Derna, the driver introduced him to his relative, a man I'll call Z, who, when he found out that Chris was American, threw up his hands and said, "There goes my evening"— meaning he believed he would be interrogated later by Libyan intelligence for meeting with an American. Chris posed the million-dollar question raised by the Sinjar Records: Why Derna? Z said it was because Derna's youth had no economic opportunities, they'd been oppressed and discriminated against by the regime, and so they were radicalized by those seeking to exploit that anger for political purposes. He added that the United States brought the problem on itself by reconciling with Gaddafi. "Fighting against U.S. and coalition forces in Iraq represented a way for frustrated young radicals to strike a blow against both Qadhafi and against his perceived American backers," he said (in Stevens's paraphrase).[10]

In their conversation, Z implies that the United States has selfishly chosen oil deals and Gaddafi's support in the War on Terror over the legitimate interests and economic needs of Libyans, and the exodus of young people to Iraq was the natural result. It's a plausible explanation of what was going on, and a scathing rebuke of the Bush administration's policy toward Libya. Z treads a fine line on the subject of the young men leaving to fight in Iraq, saying that many people in Derna were "uncomfortable with the town's increasingly conservative Islamist bent," but that they sympathized with the fighters' grievances and immediate goals. He compares them to Bruce Willis in *Die Hard*, "who stubbornly refused to die quietly," calling their choice to fight "an important last act of defiance." He adds with pride that "most Libyans" felt the same, but those from Derna were uniquely willing to act on it. From this exchange, Stevens titled his cable "Die Hard in Derna."[11]

Though it's possible Stevens was describing the sequence of events exactly as it happened, it seems to me he may have taken some editorial license, in order to give voice to a reasoned, middle-of-the-road view of what was going on in Derna, delivered by someone with apparent sympathies to both sides: fluent in English and American cultural references, but also integrated into Derna society (as in many places in the Middle East, American culture was consumed voraciously and could exist side by side with a deep resentment of American policies). Whether or not Z was really one person, or a composite of several whom Stevens met in Derna that day, is unclear.

Chris writes that he repeated to his interlocutors (Z and his driver, at least) the official US position on Gaddafi, i.e., that it was pressuring the dictator to make good on his promises with regard to human rights. But Z interrupted to argue that if that were the case, the United States might have easily demonstrated such concern by pressuring the regime to release Libya's best-known dissident, Fathi el-Jahmi, first arrested in 2002 for criticizing Gaddafi, and rearrested in 2004 for calling Gaddafi a dictator on an American-backed cable channel.[12]

Chris's reporting cables have a sphinxlike quality to them. As a good reporter should, he lets his interlocutors speak. But reading between the lines, and knowing something of Chris's views of the Iraq War, the Muslim Brotherhood, and the Gaddafi regime, it seems that Chris is trying to make a point back to Washington that the problems bubbling up in Libya are a direct result of an American betrayal of its public narrative on Libya, the one in which the United States is supposed to be helping spread democracy and prosperity, not enabling repression.[13] Chris hadn't lost his idealism and was acknowledging that America's position in Libya was morally fraught.

When I read this cable six years after it was sent, in 2014, two years after Chris's death, I couldn't help but be reminded of a conversation that I had on Christmas Eve in 2005 with a cab driver in Tripoli. As soon as I got in the cab, he surprised me with a "Merry Christmas!" as if he had been waiting all afternoon to find someone to whom he could flaunt his new, quasi-civil liberties. As the cab hurtled from the mission to my new residence in the Gargaresh area of Tripoli, I listened to a long, but powerful, soliloquy about America's power to enable Libyans to breathe again, to speak freely. That attitude of hope would sour before it blossomed.

6

The Corrections

Though the exact origins of the US–Libyan renditions plan are still unclear, the 2003 US–Libyan "understanding" opened the door for a series of unconventional side deals. The first was the capture and delivery of the LIFG leadership-in-exile to Gaddafi for torture (although much of the torture seems to have been done by the United States, not the Libyans). The second installment in this saga was even more bizarre, as it involved the Libyans, apparently with US support, spending years trying to "flip" the LIFG away from violent jihad, somewhat in the same way that the United States tried to turn Gaddafi away from his own brand of secular terrorism. Once again, little thought seems to have been given to the potential for blowback.

From the moment the LIFG victims of extraordinary rendition arrived back in Libya, there were hints that Gaddafi had something more than simple revenge in mind. LIFG rendees say they were approached by senior regime figures soon after their arrival in Libya about a possible deal, the essence of which was the formal dissolution of the LIFG and an apology, in return for their freedom. At some level, Gaddafi must have realized that in order to survive a loosening of societal restrictions at home, he had to do something about the Islamists, and he may have seen a deal with the LIFG as a means to a potentially lasting truce. He had tried negotiating with the Islamists before, sending his head of internal security Abdullah Senussi to debate with them the futility of jihad. The difference this time was that Gaddafi now had the backing of the United States—as would have been obvious to Belhaj and the others from their renditions by the CIA and MI6.

It might have seemed implausible to some that the regime would negotiate with their archenemies like this, but from Gaddafi's standpoint, this latest outreach wasn't so crazy. It was a piece of the regime's effort to reach out, via Saif Gaddafi, to the families of the victims of the Abu Salim massacre—many of whom were LIFG—offering them some confirmation of what had happened back in 1996 and offering monetary compensation for their losses (some families accepted, some didn't). It was also consistent with Gaddafi's past strategies for dealing with his non-Islamist opposition, by offering a heavy stick followed by a carrot.

The operational obstacle to the plan was obvious: Gaddafi and the United States had together kidnapped and brutalized the LIFG leadership. The idea that they would be so easily convinced after this, and close to two decades of violent struggle to make peace with the man and the regime they had sworn to destroy, seemed far-fetched. And even if Gaddafi did manage to get them to go along with some kind of a truce, what possible assurance could either side offer the other that they would stick to the deal?

The US–Libya deal came into play once again. First, Gaddafi may have been convinced that the consequences of a reneging weren't so great. He now had a counterterror partnership with the Americans, who were also interested in stopping the spread of Al Qaeda and their allies. He didn't see the United States investing such energy in his own so-called rehabilitation only to abandon him to the mercies of the Islamists. Second, one of the benefits of the new relationship with the United States and Europe was the lifting of remaining arms sanctions. So he bought large quantities of small arms and high-tech surveillance equipment—whatever he thought he would need to put down an insurrection and watch his citizens closely.

And it's possible the Americans had their own logic in supporting Gaddafi's outreach to the LIFG. At the time, there were several so-called deradicalization programs being put into play with American support across the region, with the hope of bringing the radicals back from the dark side. It fit with the evolving ethos that would find expression in the "firewall thesis" (see Chapter 8), and some in the US government felt it was worth a try.

But there was another twist in the story. According to Saif's erstwhile advisor Mohammed al-Houni, Saif had a direct interest in this deal with the LIFG. The outside world saw Saif as Gaddafi's heir apparent, but three years after his debut as the face of a New Libya, Saif still had no formal claim to succession, and several of his younger siblings were starting to court their father's favor. In this climate there were no firm guarantees that Saif would ultimately succeed his father. At one point, frustrated with increasing challenges to his unwritten status, Saif briefly fled to Britain, claiming he was leaving Libyan politics altogether.[1]

Al-Houni claims that the leaders of Qatar and Turkey convinced Saif that the Muslim Brotherhood could help solve two of his biggest problems: they could help assure his succession and take care of the problem of Islamic radicalism. All he had to do was to help create a space for the Muslim Brotherhood and the LIFG within Libya. "Saif didn't know what was going on in the corridors of leadership between Libya and Qatar," al-Houni wrote, "but he believed that this was the one channel that could help him contain and domesticate the Islamist organizations."[2]

For several years the ball remained in the LIFG's court. The last renditions were completed in 2005. Many if not all members rejected Saif's initial approaches. Abdulhakim Belhaj seems to have viewed any kind of deal with Gaddafi as a complete nonstarter. As time went by, the regime put the LIFG leaders on trial, and they were variously sentenced to either death (Abdulhakim Belhaj and Khalid al-Sherif received death sentences) or long prison terms. Finally, during Chris Stevens's first tour in Libya, there was a breakthrough.

Whether on his own or via Qatar's good offices, Saif Gaddafi contacted Ali Sallabi, Libya's most visible Muslim Brotherhood–linked figure, then living in Qatar. Sallabi seems never to have been a formal member of the LIFG, but he knew their leadership from their overlapping time in Khartoum. Saif's proposal involved a joint mediation between the regime and the LIFG, conducted by himself and Sallabi.

The LIFG leaders, many of whom had been in solitary confinement, requested to meet together as a group to consider the outlines of the proposal. They agreed to meet with Sallabi. From there, the idea of a public accommodation between the LIFG and its archenemy, the Gaddafi regime, started to take shape. Around this time, in November 2007, Al Qaeda's number two, Ayman Al-Zawahiri, and Abu Laith al-Libi, Al Qaeda's Afghanistan commander, announced the formal merger of the LIFG with Al Qaeda—an indication that LIFG members outside Libya and in the orbit of Al Qaeda knew about Gaddafi's overtures and were trying to nip discussions in the bud.[3]

Back in Libya the LIFG leaders in custody were given a certain amount of time to contemplate their past actions, with a view to offering a public rejection of their formal positions: that is, they would lay down their weapons and abandon the cause of jihad, not only against Gaddafi, but also all regional leaders. The proof of conversion was to take the form of a book, written together by six of the senior members of the LIFG: Belhaj, Sami al-Saadi, Khalid al-Sherif, Abdel Wahab Al Qaid, Mitfah al-Duwdi, and Mustafa Qanaifid.[4]

True to form, Gaddafi tried to gild the lily by demanding from the LIFG, in addition to a formal apology, a statement that he was a "good Muslim." Belhaj reportedly scoffed at that.[5] But while Belhaj and the others rejected Gaddafi's religious absolution, the LIFG did later agree to issue a weak apology to Gaddafi for trying to kill him.[6] All of this was very useful to the Brotherhood, as they could demonstrate to the Americans that talking to them paid big dividends in terms of their ability to help deradicalize Al Qaeda allies. The same went for Qatar and Turkey, who were also presenting themselves as forces of moderation who could speak to all sides: the radicals, the moderates, and the West. In 2008, the Gaddafi regime released hundreds of Muslim Brotherhood and LIFG members from prison as an act of good faith.

By 2010, the 417-page *Corrective Studies in Understanding Jihad, Accountability, and the Judgment of the People*, or the *Corrections* for short (*muraja'at* in Arabic), was done. On March 23, Saif convened a small press conference attended by members of the foreign diplomatic community to announce the results. He held up the book and referred to it as a "very important document."[7] In these pages, the LIFG rejected the use of violence against Arab and Muslim regimes and, without referring to Al Qaeda directly, distanced itself from bin Laden's organization.[8] The LIFG leaders said they had made a "mistake" in trying to overthrow Gaddafi, and that it was not an acceptable interpretation of jihad to overthrow Middle East Arab regimes, or to kill foreigners in Arab states, or to kill civilians.[9] Saif made two unusual remarks: he referenced the 1996 Abu Salim massacre (a regime taboo), and he thanked Ali Sallabi for his support in the mediation process.[10] On the same day, the regime released LIFG leaders Abdulhakim Belhaj, Sami al-Saadi, and Khalid al-Sherif from Abu Salim prison; 170 more Muslim Brotherhood prisoners were released the same year.[11]

Ambassador Gene Cretz doesn't recall the event specifically—and it's unclear if Chris Stevens was present—but he takes a skeptical tone toward the *Corrections*, calling it "just another of Seif's 'forward looking' proposals to show that he could be a reformist and lead Libya into the 21st century."[12] But his presence was read in analyst circles as a sign of at least tacit US approval of the process. But Cretz was State Department. If other agencies were involved, once again the State Department wouldn't necessarily know. And the LIFG had a long history with foreign intelligence services. Was the United States just a spectator to the *Corrections*, or was it one of the architects? And if a participant, to what end?

A 2010 report written by Arab journalist Camille Tawil, an expert on Al Qaeda and its North African franchises, argued that the *Corrections* constituted a truly milestone agreement and potentially the beginning of the end for Al Qaeda "because they come from leaders who are widely respected by the jihadists themselves across North Africa . . .

[and] because they challenge the ideas and ideology of al-Qaeda and similar organizations."[13] Was this the ultimate goal of the renditions and *Corrections*, to create a self-destructive, ideological inconsistency within Al Qaeda?

But the basic question that hovered over the *Corrections*, and would continue to linger for years to come, was simple, and was the same that lingered over the US deal with Gaddafi: Had the LIFG truly changed its spots, or was it all a well-orchestrated act?

Tawil suggested that the real measure of the impact of the LIFG's formal disbanding would be seen in the response from Al Qaeda. If bin Laden and Ayman Al-Zawahiri felt threatened by these events, the world would hear from them, publicly, through organized rebuttal, based on the organization's interpretation of Islamic law. Tawil seemed to think that the challenge was so great that Al Qaeda had to respond as it had to previous, similar challenges, or lose credibility with its following.

The result was less conclusive. Al Qaeda issued no formal refutation of the *Corrections'* arguments. But back in 2007 Ayman Al-Zawahiri had already insisted that the LIFG had not actually changed its ideology or its mission, and that the LIFG and Al Qaeda were in fact the same thing. In that communication, he called out Abdulhakim Belhaj specifically as a committed leader in jihad.[14] The participants in the *Corrections*, led by Belhaj, all insisted that their conversions were very real and concluded in good faith. They maintained that they were pragmatists, changing with the times and the interests of the Libyan people. Both Belhaj and Abdel Wahab Al Qaid made public statements to the effect that their participation in the *Corrections* was the result of a maturation process and an observation that other jihadists had made mistakes.[15]

But there were still skeptics and a number of unanswered questions about the *Corrections* process itself. Christopher Boucek, an expert on Middle East deradicalization programs, wrote that even Gaddafi regime officials couldn't describe what the program involved.[16] The record of success for state-sponsored deradicalization wasn't good, and for this reason, most of the programs tended to focus on disengagement, rather than deradicalization, because it was easier to get radicals to refrain from acting on their beliefs than to change those beliefs.[17]

In the following years, neither the renditions nor the *Corrections* got much attention. Generally, coverage of the rendition campaign took a back seat to other human rights abuses committed by the United States in the context of the War on Terror, such as waterboarding, the humiliation of prisoners at Abu Ghraib prison in Iraq, and detainment at Guantanamo Bay. The *Corrections* program was substantially more obscure, remaining unknown even to most Libyans. But anyone thinking these two linked and seemingly self-canceling events—the renditions and the *Corrections*—were footnotes to the US–Libyan relationship would be very wrong. They are at the heart of why the US intervention in Libya failed, and part of why and how the US Mission was attacked on September 11, 2012.

Part II

RISKY BUSINESS

7

Fear and Loathing in Washington

"Don't run," I said. "They'd like an excuse to shoot us." He nodded,
seeming to understand.

—HUNTER S. THOMPSON, *Fear and Loathing in Las Vegas*

Hillary Clinton, not Barack Obama, had been the early favorite to win the 2008 Democratic nomination for US president. By 2008, she was an experienced stateswoman, following eight years in the Senate, four more than Obama. Though Clinton had been a magnet for Republican attacks for decades, within the Left she had an admiring, energized constituency, keen to see her break the gender glass ceiling on the nation's highest office. And the country seemed ready for a woman president.

At the same time, 2008 was shaping up to be a referendum on the Iraq War. Bush had won reelection in 2004 as a war president, but by 2008 the country saw Iraq for what it was: an unmitigated disaster. And Clinton's 2002 Senate vote authorizing Bush to declare war on Iraq would return to haunt her. Clinton would explain that her vote was not for war, but supported President Bush's argument that the authorization would provide leverage to get UN weapons inspectors back into Iraq to verify whether or not Saddam Hussein had Weapons of Mass Destruction. In her view, Bush went back on his word. But as Scott Beauchamp, writing in *The Atlantic*, noted, if the 2002 vote didn't "outright disqualify her in the eyes of voters, [it] at least breathe[d] oxygen into then-Senator Barack Obama's outsider campaign."[1] This, and an exceptional grassroots mobilization effort by the Obama campaign, pushed the Illinois senator past the finish line. While Hillary was promising pragmatism and experience, Obama's message of hope and change offered a better fit for the mood of a country tired of war and rising partisan division.

But to many, Obama's victory had the quality of a setup. The challenges facing his presidency seemed almost insurmountable: in addition to two wars in Iraq and Afghanistan, the country was going into the worst recession since 1930. Writer Ta-Nehisi Coates recalls his father telling him: "Son . . . you know the country got to be messed up for them folks to give him the job."[2] Coates was conveying a widespread sense, particularly within the African American community, that Obama's election might ultimately help entrench predominantly white establishment interests.[3]

Conservative attacks on Barack Obama started early, framing him as alien to their core beliefs and values, to American-ness itself. The undertones of these attacks were clearly racial, but Obama's broader life story offered more socially acceptable targets. For example, the fact that his father was a Muslim of Kenyan origin was used to question his loyalties and his religious beliefs: Was he a Muslim? Had he been born in the United States, and thus was he qualified to serve as president? This doubt sowing fed the so-called "birtherism" movement. Not far behind were accusations that Obama favored opening the door for mass immigration (though in reality his immigration policies were quite tough). All these themes could be tied together to create a fantasy that spoke to the Right's deepest fears. And his victory didn't dissuade the Right from the effectiveness of this line of attack, as clearly shown in the way Donald Trump kept hammering these points during Obama's second term. They were also, not coincidentally, themes that could be readily mapped onto the Benghazi attack.

Obama's campaign was aware of the ways that this web of chatter could be weaponized. A number of Obama administration memoirs highlight the campaign's panic when reading a glowing March 6, 2007, profile of then Senator Obama by *New York Times* columnist Nicholas Kristof, in which Obama, reflecting on his childhood in Indonesia, describes the Arabic call to prayer as "one of the prettiest sounds on Earth at sunset."[4] The reflexive worry—Kristof wrote in the same piece that this remark would "give Alabama voters heart attacks"—was that this would immediately spark claims from the right-wing media that Obama was a terrorist sympathizer.[5]

But the Obama administration wasn't just worried about the Right. There were concerns about fellow Democrats as well. Obama and Clinton's relationship before the campaign was described as cordial, but the primaries turned nasty. Both sides lobbed grenades at the other. Sidney Blumenthal, whose name would come up in context of the Benghazi investigations, was alleged to have distributed negative information about Obama while Obama's advisor Samantha Power at one point called Hillary Clinton a "monster" in an interview with *The Scotsman*.[6] Many of Obama's close political advisors were not fond of Clinton and were worried, reasonably or not, that she might undermine Obama from the Senate.

Obama decided it was better to bring Clinton into the fold rather than leave her on the outside, so he offered her the position of secretary of state. It was a substantive enough role to be tempting to Clinton, who was demonstrably more interested in foreign affairs than Obama was. If there was one thing Obama seemed to admire in Clinton, it was her demonstrated loyalty. And he recognized that her foreign policy expertise would help compensate for both his lack of experience in that area and his relative disinterest compared to domestic policy.

Clinton's first reaction was no. As Bob Woodward wrote, "She was a Clinton. She was not an Obama acolyte. It was a matter of retaining her identity." "There wasn't exactly a reservoir of trust between her camp and his. She might find it difficult, if not impossible, to operate."[7] Clinton must have looked back on that moment later, years after

Benghazi, with some regret. But for its significant risks, at the time the offer had a tantalizing upside. A success as secretary of state would not only make her very visible during the Obama presidency, but it would also seal her claim to being the most qualified presidential candidate in history come 2016.[8] Clinton's 2008 campaign strategist and pollster Mark Penn pressed the point that accepting the job would also show that Clinton didn't "carry a grudge."[9] It seemed as though, if all went well for her, it would make her next presidential run even more potentially successful.[10]

In order to capitalize on the opportunity, Clinton would need to avoid traps and look out for opportunities to showcase her crisis management skills. And at all times, she would have to demonstrate her loyalty. She would be counting on Obama's active support in 2016 if she ran—which most expected she would.

Clinton requested to bring a number of staff members with her to the State Department, which meant she had trusted allies around her. Clinton enjoyed good access to the president. But many within the Obama team never seemed to trust Clinton fully and watched her closely. These dynamics helped create mutually reinforcing, and at times frictional, bubbles, with the president's advisors on the NSC taking the lead on shaping foreign policy. Clinton responded by developing her own signature issues within State (many of them related to reform and increased accountability) and deepening relationships with her foreign counterparts.

Congress created the National Security Council in 1947 to assist decision-making within the executive branch, by streamlining and coordinating input across all agencies with responsibilities for security and foreign policy, including the Department of Defense, the State Department, the National Security Agency, and the CIA. This efficiency was felt to be of utmost importance in the climate of the Cold War.[11]

With the end of the Cold War, the NSC's mission started to drift, and it grew in size. Under President Carter, the NSC was just 15 members; under George H. W. Bush, it was 50; under Clinton, 100; under George W. Bush, 200; and under Obama, rising to an estimated 270.[12]

During the George W. Bush administration, senior State Department officials started to complain that they were receiving policy directives from junior NSC staffers—a sign that the White House was perfectly comfortable subverting the State Department chain of command, deepening levels of distrust between the politically loyal NSC and ostensibly less political departments with whom they worked.[13] Thus, quite quickly, the NSC became, in the description of NSC veteran Richard Hooker, a kind of "mini State Department."[14]

These changes were driven by a number of factors, which were overwhelmingly political. For one, the increasing cost of political campaigns deepened donors' demand for perks and access. Further, as the professional bureaucracies grew in size and became slower, innovations in technology and media created opposing pressures, driving shorter and shorter news cycles. There was a direct mismatch in terms of demand and supply of information. The president needed a team that could make decisions and produce those answers on the fly, in a manner that took the president's political interests directly into consideration. The NSC was particularly well suited to these tasks, as its members are not subject to the requirement of Senate confirmation, which makes it "among the most influential entities in the federal bureaucracy that are not subject to direct Congressional oversight," as described by journalist David Rothkopf in his book on the NSC.[15]

Given the number of political knives drawn in Washington, it's easy to see why the Obama administration would rely on the NSC as a bulwark against political attacks. In a 2016 congressional hearing on the drift of the NSC's mission, former NSC senior director for strategic planning Derek Chollet defended the council's enlarged role, saying, "without more control by the NSC, the President would be exposed . . . to the whims of the capricious news cycle, supercharged by social media."[16]

The main offensive tool at the NSC's disposal was narrative—a proactive articulation of policy that anticipated and deflected attacks while pushing out the benefits of the president's policies. At the center

of narrative creation for the Obama team was the cerebral wordsmith
Ben Rhodes, who had previously worked for Democratic congressman Lee Hamilton and started working for Obama as a speechwriter
during the 2008 campaign. When Obama was elected, Rhodes, then
thirty-two, joined the NSC as deputy national security advisor for strategic communications, a brand-new position whose existence made
clear the importance of communications for the new administration.
Rhodes worked extremely closely with the president and drafted most
of Obama's major foreign policy speeches. He was referred to as the
president's "amanuensis," and colleagues joked that he and the president
had a "mind meld."[17] In a profile of Rhodes published toward the end
of Obama's second term, bitingly entitled "The Aspiring Novelist Who
Became Obama's Foreign Policy Guru," David Samuels marveled at the
influence Rhodes had over the shape and direction of Obama's foreign
policy, calling Rhodes "the single most influential voice shaping American foreign policy aside from POTUS [the president] himself."[18]

An increasing chorus of officials and journalists pointed out that
along with its increased influence, the NSC, though full of talent,
was remarkably green, particularly in the area of international policy.
"Obama's young foreign policy advisors," wrote Justin Vaïsse of the
Brookings Institution, "manage[d] the essentials of the decision process . . . They did not have experience in power and were not special-
ists in foreign policy (apart from Samantha Power), but were rather
political advisors, attentive to the domestic repercussions of international affairs—the danger of the instrumentalization of the terrorist
menace."[19]

This emphasis undoubtedly had short-term, tactical advantages,
but the risks were substantial. The main danger was that communications and legal concerns would wind up driving policy rather than the
reverse. Also, when policy narratives are fashioned by a small number
of people, they tend to be more resistant to change and effective challenges. And related to this, the more closed the decision-making loop,
the more the president and his senior decision-makers are insulated

from the views of deep policy experts within the wider bureaucracies. In other words, in its attempt to fend off an explosion of political attacks, the Obama administration was also keeping out some of the expertise that was absolutely necessary if the president were to avoid the same kinds of mistakes that his predecessors had made.

This dynamic was perhaps most visible in the White House's relationship with the State Department, where Hillary Clinton, a self-professed policy wonk, now had to pay at least some deference to policies she vehemently disagreed with during the presidential campaign (such as an accelerated drawdown of troops from Iraq, and a more hands-off policy toward the Middle East). Though Clinton understood the limitations of the bureaucracies from her previous roles as a senator and the First Lady, and pushed for greater efficiency and better performance from the State Department, she was doing this at a time when the State Department's gravity in the president's foreign affairs decision-making was waning. This situation certainly did not empower the State Department, as lingering suspicions in both camps, Obama's and Clinton's (if not the president and the secretary themselves), maintained a kind of professional distance that would make it harder to diagnose and treat foreign policy problems, and would also later provide an opening for the partisan attacks it hoped to avoid.

So, in the years leading up to the Benghazi attack, and after nearly eight years of the Bush administration's War on Terror, Al Qaeda may have been on the run, but the United States' ability to deal with complex foreign policy challenges had been greatly reduced. The main reason was that beneath the surface, partisanship was reconfiguring American bureaucracies to fight domestic political battles rather than protect the United States from its adversaries and those who would exploit its weaknesses for their own interests. Given this atmosphere, and the huge domestic policy challenges the Obama administration faced, it's no wonder that it sought to take the Middle East off boil and move it to simmer.

8

Goodwill Hunting

Obama's early approach toward the Middle East resembled that of someone looking to change the channel from a horror movie to something more pleasant—but not too deep or engaging.

When searching to define policy, there were constraints. Obama's commitment to ending the wars in Iraq and Afghanistan had been hardwired into his campaign. Also, domestic issues would have to take precedence over foreign policy: Obama's team had to steer the country through an emerging global economic recession, and his personal agenda included an expansive reform of the national healthcare system. There was also a standing sense in Washington that the Middle East wasn't as important as it used to be: America was theoretically, if not in practice, no longer dependent on Middle East oil, and Asia was seen to be far more important to America's longer-term strategic and economic interests. Overall, Obama was guided by the view that there were practical limits to America's engagement—and its power—and that the White House needed to create a portfolio of interests that took these factors into account. But that didn't stop the administration from searching for policy and messaging bargains, opportunities to reduce tensions and signal that America was the Good Guy, not the Bad Guy, in the region—as long as the benefits exceeded the direct costs.

One of the first visible changes with the Obama administration was in rhetoric and vocabulary. Gone was the Neocon talk of an inevitable Clash of Civilizations between the Muslim world and the West. When speaking about the Middle East, the administration consciously separated the words "Islam" and "Islamic" from terms like "radicalism" and "terrorism," and refrained from calling acts of violence "terrorism" (whether domestic or otherwise) until and unless there was clear proof they were. Jumping to such conclusions, the administration observed, fed anti-Muslim sentiment and served the interests of groups like Al Qaeda. There was also the fact that homegrown, and predominantly white, political violence was becoming a real issue: after events like the Knoxville Unitarian Universalist church shooting, neo-Nazi Keith Luke's shooting spree, and countless school shootings, one couldn't reasonably assume that all acts of terrorism were done by foreigners—or committed in the name of a single cause or religion.

But for all Obama's downplaying of expectations of what the United States could do in the Middle East, there were wish lists and window shopping.

When asked by the *New York Times* during the 2008 campaign whether there were any circumstances in which the United States might actually intervene militarily, again, in the Middle East, Obama emphasized his attachment to the notion of a Responsibility to Protect, or multilateral intervention to prevent genocides like those committed in Rwanda in 1994 and the former Yugoslavia (1992–1995).[1] Recruiting one of its most visible advocates, journalist Samantha Power, to his campaign, Obama signaled his interest in highlighting multilateral humanitarian efforts and placing the United States back on the moral side of international affairs. The president expressed enthusiastic support for restarting the Middle East peace process, and on his second day in office, he appointed former Senator George Mitchell as special envoy for Palestinian–Israeli negotiations. But the enthusiastic support for that effort didn't last much beyond the summer of 2009, as Mitchell resigned in 2011 after failing to make headway.[2]

In parallel with early hopes for Israel and Palestine, Obama caused waves in Washington by saying that he was ready to talk to Iran without preconditions, and invited the country to "unclench its fist."[3] On the

Iranian festival of renewal, Nowruz, March 20, 2009, Obama recorded a video message to the Iranian people, stressing a "new beginning" between the two peoples and a shared humanity.[4] "We seek instead engagement that is honest and grounded in mutual respect," he said. But when wide-scale protests broke out following what many Iranians considered a stolen election, the Obama administration stepped back.[5]

While the administration eyed the Iran prize, it reached out to what it considered model regional states, like Turkey. In an April 6, 2009, speech to the Turkish Parliament, President Obama praised Turkey's "strong, vibrant, secular democracy."[6] Turkey at the time was (and still is) a member of NATO and considered a US ally—but there were some red flags: Erdogan's AKP party, which, though not officially tied to the Muslim Brotherhood, was heavily connected to and influenced by them. And Erdogan had expressed some tendencies toward authoritarianism—which over the following decade would become more than just tendencies, as he turned an alleged 2016 coup attempt into an opportunity to further centralize power.[7] But for now, this was just another sign that the Obama administration and its advisors were reacting to, not leading, events in the region.

When the president praised Erdogan and said things like "America respects the right of all peaceful and law-abiding voices to be heard around the world, even if we disagree with them,"[8] most in the region, regardless of their feelings about Islamism, saw support for the Muslim Brotherhood.

Many saw the speech as superficial and Western-centric, projecting American individualistic freedoms while eliding America's long-term role in curtailing those freedoms: in other words, something designed to make Americans feel good about themselves, but that didn't do much for resolving regional problems.

If Obama's speeches produced mixed reactions in the region, they did the same at home. Liberals applauded Obama's approach. But to many on the Right, Obama's focus on dialogue and respect read as sympathy for Islamic radicals and spineless political correctness. The Republicans framed the "New Beginning" speech in particular as an apology for America. Massachusetts Governor Mitt Romney, who would face off against Obama in the 2012 presidential election, called his campaign the "No Apologies Tour"—a direct reference to the 2009 Cairo speech.

Nevertheless, Obama's uplifting, hopeful communications made him the darling of Europe and attracted the attention of the Norwegian Nobel Committee, which in October 2009 announced that it was awarding him the Nobel Peace Prize for his "extraordinary efforts to strengthen international diplomacy and cooperation between peoples."[9] This was a good-news predicament Obama may have just as soon foregone, as it was sure to aggravate political tensions back home, particularly among Republicans who felt his positivity was selling America down the river. Rather than turn down the award, the president (via Rhodes's writing) took an unorthodox path with the acceptance speech. Obama began by acknowledging that the award had caused controversy at home and, relative to others who had received the prize, that his achievements were "slight." He then proceeded to speak of the role of war, or the threat of war, in keeping the peace:

> I face the world as it is, and cannot stand idle in the face of threats to the American people. For make no mistake: Evil does exist in the world. A non-violent movement could not have halted Hitler's armies. Negotiations cannot convince al Qaeda's leaders to lay down their arms. To say that force may sometimes be necessary is not a call to cynicism—it is a recognition of history; the imperfections of man and the limits of reason.[10]

The combination of these two speeches, the "New Beginning" address in June 2009 and Obama's Nobel Prize acceptance speech in December 2009, illustrated how self-referential American foreign policy was becoming, and how confusing this was to external audiences. The "New Beginning" speech was optimistic but waffly, and open to interpretation—leading the Republicans to label it an apology and the Middle East progressives to see it as a vote against them and in favor of the Muslim Brotherhood. Former Obama officials say it wasn't meant to be either. The main purpose of the Nobel speech was to rebut right-wing domestic criticisms, based on how they read previous speeches; it did little to explain to America's allies and enemies what principles would guide American foreign policy in the coming years. And with its attention focused domestically without a solid foreign policy doctrine to guide it (other than generally, whatever kept the domestic demons at bay), the Obama administration created patterns that would shape its reaction to the Libyan Revolution and, later, the Benghazi attack.

If the Obama administration had any illusions that its framing devices and outreach were robust enough to calm tensions in the region while giving it more space to pursue its domestic agenda, those were shattered in late 2009, with a near-catastrophic Christmas-day terrorist attack by an Al Qaeda franchise.

Northwest Airlines Flight 253 had started its descent to Detroit, Michigan, with 290 passengers on board, when Umar Farouk Abdulmutallab, a Nigerian Al Qaeda member recruited by Anwar al-Awlaki, a leader of the Yemeni Al Qaeda franchise, reached into his underwear to detonate an explosive device. There was a flash, but the chemical mixture failed to ignite, and other passengers tackled Abdulmutallab (subsequently dubbed the "Underwear Bomber") before he could finish the job. As with most attempts of this kind, there had been unheeded warnings: Abdulmutallab's father reported his son's suspicious behavior to the US Embassy in Abuja, Nigeria's capital, months before, but that information didn't prevent Abdulmutallab from boarding a flight to the United States.[11] Al Qaeda in the Arabian Peninsula (AQAP) claimed responsibility for the attempt several days later.

The Obama communications team opted to downplay the Al Qaeda link to the Detroit attack, on grounds that drawing more attention to the event would only serve Al Qaeda's propaganda.[12] But the White House and NSC failed to anticipate the outcry from the Right, as Neo-con rabble-rousers cited what the *New York Times*'s Scott Shane called the "Cheney critique" (after Dick Cheney, vice president under George W. Bush): the idea that "for seven years after 9/11 Bush and Cheney had kept America safe (albeit after ignoring the warning signs before 9/11). Now Obama's feckless weakness had allowed the terrorists to strike again."[13]

Obama gathered many of his senior staff together to share his realization that, had it succeeded, the Detroit attack would likely have meant the end of his presidency. No second term.[14] The political outcry from the Right and accusations that the Democrats were unable to protect America from more 9/11-like attacks would have been merciless. The administration seemed to take two lessons from this. First, it couldn't take the high ground and downplay events like this. They had to lead the messaging, or the Right would gleefully jump in and fill the void. Second, the Democrats would have to find a way to project strength, particularly on terrorism, without getting back into the region with boots on the ground.

This second consideration led, in part, to an escalation of war in Yemen, a country increasingly on America's radar as an Al Qaeda bastion—since the USS *Cole* bombing in 2000, but now even more so with the Detroit attempt and various others attributed to Anwar al-Awlaki, one of the leaders of Al Qaeda in the Arabian Peninsula. Thus, the drone war against Al Qaeda in Yemen—which was started by George W. Bush and was already running at a good clip—escalated under Obama. The president and his national security advisors liked drones, as they could be sold as a tough US response to terrorism that minimized civilian casualties and did not require boots on the ground. Best of all, they polled well with Democrats, of whom almost 80 percent endorsed their use.[15]

However, somewhat like the Middle East speeches, the hopes of a cleaner war in Yemen were an optimistic fantasy. Reports issued later by various human rights organizations would show that the Defense Department and the administration significantly underestimated civilian casualties in Yemen.[16] And as the years went on, the same liberals who had earlier been polled as supportive of drones over other means of intervention were now exercised about the morality of these "fire from the sky" operations. There were other ethical complications with the drone wars insofar as these targeted assassinations were used to kill Al Qaeda operatives who were also US citizens. Anwar al-Awlaki (the originator of the Underwear Bomber plot) and his teenage son, who were killed in separate strikes in 2011, were both Americans.

Gradually, some began to feel that Obama's defense policies were looking disturbingly like Bush's.[17] Obama's oratorical gifts helped get him elected and sell domestic achievements like the Affordable Care Act, but the Middle East required a different approach altogether. Even early on, it was clear his penchant for defensive messaging, positive spin, and "light" interventions was starting to catch up to him.

It was clear that, as much as it wanted to, the Obama administration couldn't escape thinking about political Islam. Motivated by the continued threats from groups like Al Qaeda in the Arabian Peninsula, the president requested a series of policy reviews from his national security staff.

In August 2010, President Obama issued Presidential Study Directive 11 (PSD-11).[18] The question to be answered, broadly, was what the United States should do to manage increasing tension between authoritarian regimes and popular unrest in the Middle East. Specifically, some suspect that PSD-11 requested a strategy for engagement with the Muslim Brotherhood, with the goal of countering Islamic radicalism and transitioning away from undemocratic regimes (possibly involving US-backed regime change).[19]

Dr. Peter Mandaville was one of a few academics who contributed to the Obama administration's stance on Islamism, through the NSC.

Though it's not clear who were the authors of PSD-11, Mandaville told me that his group "was told to address big questions, like what should US policy toward the Brotherhood be?"[20] But the White House also seemed to feel that the Brotherhood itself did not merit a specific policy. "Why," Mandaville asked, "should the US have an 'Islamist policy,' when it doesn't have policy on other ideological or religious groups, whether it be [Europe's] green parties or social democrats?" For those inclined to deep suspicion of the motives of the Brotherhood, or Islamist groups in general, this would seem a naive approach: there are some very deep differences between groups acting in line with an extreme interpretation of religion, and largely secular parties.

Of course there were others outside the US government looking at the question of the nature of the Muslim Brotherhood. One was George Washington University professor Marc Lynch. In 2010, Lynch published a paper meant to highlight unrealistic views of the Brotherhood.[21] On one extreme, Lynch argued, was the idea of the Brotherhood as a "firewall" against Islamic radicalism: It espouses moderation, participates in elections, and follows many of the rules of conventional politics. And as it broadens its political base, it wicks away support from more radical groups and ideologies. On the other extreme is the idea of the Brotherhood as an "escalator": People join with a potentially moderate political outlook but are taken away on a fixed path toward violent extremism. Lynch created these terms to spark debate, but his conclusion was that the Muslim Brotherhood "should be allowed to wage its battles against extremist challengers, but should not be misunderstood as a liberal organization or supported in a short-term convergence of interests."[22]

A couple of years later, in 2014, the UK government of David Cameron commissioned a study on political Islam, known widely as the Cameron Report. According to Sir John Jenkins, who had served in ambassadorial posts across the region, including Libya, and holds a doctorate from Cambridge University in Islamic studies, the report, like PSD-11, was meant to be an internal review of policy and was never meant to be published. But the prime minister summarized the results in a statement to Parliament: "Parts of the Muslim Brotherhood have a highly ambiguous relationship with violent extremism."[23]

In this sea of differing views about the nature of the Muslim Brotherhood and political Islam, the question of whether it was worth talking to groups like the Muslim Brotherhood was never really at issue. The reasons for that, as articulated by Ambassador Richard Murphy back in 1998, remained valid enough: The Brotherhood is a major political actor in the region and can't be ignored. The United States needs to know more about the movement and its factions, as well as its relationships to other political actors and their intentions. The problem arises when engagement becomes an end in and of itself, blocking out a realistic appraisal of the Brotherhood's function within the Islamist universe, and promoting the idea that the group is just like any other civil society organization.

Both the Bush and Obama administrations seem to have been tempted by the idea that there was something definable as moderate political Islam, and that it could be used to build democracy and civil society in the Middle East and related narratives back in Washington. But the Brotherhood weren't a firewall, they were more like an enzyme: Their members were present as conflict mediators among the Afghan Arabs in the 1980s, they were the substrate that enabled the *Corrections*, and the inspiration. For other groups whose views were openly far more radical. When forming policy, the Obama White House needed to be very much aware of this context, or they were going to make mistakes.

9

The 51/49 Decision

Former Secretary of Defense Robert Gates writes in his 2015 memoir that President Obama told him privately that his decision to intervene in Libya was "51/49." That's a bit ambiguous, as it could mean either the choice was razor thin but very carefully made, or that it was essentially a coin toss. Presumably, the former was the impression the White House wanted to give the public: The president was going to war, but this was no repeat of Iraq; he had given it a lot of thought. But in the end, the decision had to have been more instinctive than empirical if only for one reason: as NSC advisor Derek Chollet noted bluntly, "We, the U.S., did not have a particularly good handle on what was going on inside Libya."[1]

With the June 2009 "New Beginning" speech in Cairo, President Obama (with help from Ben Rhodes, who wrote the speech) laid out America's new approach to the Middle East: The United States would no longer try to impose its views on the region but would instead look for opportunities to express its support for popular aspirations. "America is not the crude stereotype of a self-interested empire" was one of the more memorable lines.[2] But there were many in the region who felt that the United States had intervened too deeply to excuse itself so nonchalantly from the region's ongoing upheavals.

As if to prove that point, the Arab Spring revolutions broke out the following year, after a street vendor in Tunisia set himself on fire to protest the despair inflicted by the Tunisian regime on ordinary citizens.

The resulting popular demonstrations led to President Zine al-Abidine Ben Ali's overthrow and triggered protests across the region. Protests broke out in Egypt in January, leaving Libya flanked by two states in turmoil.

Some of those recruited by Saif Gaddafi to help run his reform program told me later that they debated whether revolution could happen in Libya. They concluded, however, that Gaddafi's grip was too strong, particularly given his "understanding" with the United States. But the regional leadership of the Muslim Brotherhood, enervated by the revolutions in two states—Egypt and Tunisia—where it had a strong presence, were watching Libya very carefully. Members of the Brotherhood's international leadership held a meeting in Zurich in late January, in which they concluded that popular upheaval was coming to Libya, and that the regime would respond violently.[3]

It was certainly no surprise that the first protests against the regime began in Benghazi. Smaller gatherings by mothers of Abu Salim victims had been going on for weeks outside the Benghazi courthouse. These became the nucleus for bigger protests. The families' lawyer, Fathi Terbil, joined in while figures like Mahmoud Jibril, who would become the transitional government's de facto prime minister, and Ali Tarhouni, its future oil and finance minister, took steps to create an interim government, the National Transitional Council (NTC). Meanwhile, the Islamists assembled their own competing brain trust, the February 17 Coalition, or *I'tilaf* for short. The contest for power in a post-Gaddafi Libya had begun before Gaddafi had even been deposed.

The Benghazi protestors did not at first call for Muammar Gaddafi's ouster but rather a more definitive and visible commitment to the reforms Saif had been promising for nearly a decade. In the following days, and in line with their *Corrections* commitments, both the Muslim Brotherhood and former LIFG members offered to help the regime calm the protests. This led to some unusual interactions. Abdullah Senussi—the man who ordered the Abu Salim massacre in 1996 that killed so many of the LIFG and Brotherhood members—would later write from prison that the LIFG leadership were in his office "on a daily basis," working to try to put an end to the conflict.[4]

The Islamists knew that the consequences of supporting an abortive revolution would be catastrophic. But instead of engaging with the protestors and trying to calm tensions, as other regional leaders were doing, the Gaddafi regime arrested Fathi Terbil on February 15, 2010. That act led to a chain reaction of protests and violence that shifted the public mood toward confrontation.

Qatar's Al Jazeera channel broadcast news of the Libyan Revolution to the outside world. The Western media soon joined in and accused Gaddafi of mass crimes against protestors in Tripoli. While the regime did respond with force, many of the most urgent accusations, like Viagra-fueled rampages and bombings against protestors, turned out to be, if not completely unfounded, then significant exaggerations.[5]

By February 2011, the Obama administration was taking flak on all sides for not being sufficiently strong in its criticism of the regimes now fighting their own people, particularly in Egypt. Dr. Tamara Wittes was managing democratic transitions at the State Department: "You have to understand," Wittes later said, "within a week in mid-February one had the repression of the protests in Derna, Syria, then Gaddafi's threats to hunt down Libyan rebels street by street. There were the mass protests in Bahrain . . . effectively, the US government was faced with crises on all fronts in the Middle East. We were overwhelmed."[6]

On Sunday, February 20, Mahdi Ziu, a middle manager at a state oil company, loaded his black Kia sedan with propane tanks and drove it into Gaddafi's military complex in Benghazi, known as the Katiba. The impact blew a hole in the outer wall, allowing protestors to swarm into the dark hive of Gaddafi's security forces, a building that had stood for decades as a silent reminder of the consequences of disobedience.[7]

The next day, February 21, Saif Gaddafi appeared on Libyan television in a crumpled black suit and tie, fidgeting, and sporting a five-o'clock shadow. In a desultory speech, he called for an end to the revolution, or else. He said, "Instead of crying over 84 killed people, we will be crying over thousands. Rivers of blood would flow . . . We will have civil war."[8] Many had held out hope that Saif, as the face of Western-backed reform, would show his mettle as a leader and finally challenge his father and put an end to the violence. Instead, in a moment of pathos worthy of a Greek tragedy, he seemed to have abandoned reform to defend his father and the regime to which he was inextricably linked.

Saif's advisor Mohammed al-Houni claimed later that he and Saif had worked together on a very different speech, which was night and day compared to the speech he actually gave. What al-Houni heard instead was "an absolute disaster . . . that challenged the will of the people as they rose up and defended their dignity."[9]

On February 22, Muammar Gaddafi delivered his infamous "zenga zenga" speech, in which he spoke of cleansing the country of traitors, *dar, dar* (house by house), *zenga, zenga* (alley by alley) . . ."[10] Benghazi remained the epicenter of the rebellion, and Gaddafi knew if he was to retain control of the country, he had to put down the revolt in Benghazi. Gaddafi had entrusted Abdel Fattah Younes, the head of the Al-Saiqa special forces, with that task. But Younes was acting slowly (or not at all) and making excuses for it, which gave the rebels time to regroup. And the day of Gaddafi's "zenga zenga" speech, he defected to the rebel side.[11]

Surveying the situation in the Middle East, the White House could see the potential for much bigger trouble looming on the horizon—particularly in Syria. Obama had pledged his support to ordinary Arab people in the "New Beginning" speech, but so far, the United States hadn't done anything to demonstrate its support of the popular revolutions. And now Gaddafi was threatening to hunt down citizens in Benghazi and exterminate them like cockroaches. Secretary Clinton said she was "chilled" by those threats.[12]

When Gaddafi made his peace overtures to Bush after 9/11, he had hoped to keep the United States from overthrowing him. But it was a misread. The United States had no plans for regime change in Libya after 9/11. And at the beginning of the Arab Spring, Gaddafi made the opposite error, apparently believing that the American investment in the US–Libyan relationship meant it wouldn't change its mind. But what Gaddafi didn't realize was that Obama had already discussed military intervention in Middle East regimes making the kinds of genocidal threats Gaddafi had just made—or that the administration was also considering engaging with the Muslim Brotherhood and promoting civil society at the expense of traditional regional dictators. Gaddafi was walking into a trap, largely of his own making.

At the eleventh hour, the president's senior advisors were split down the middle about whether or not to intervene in Libya. The military and security figures, like National Security Advisor Thomas Donilon, Defense Secretary Robert Gates, Chairman of the Joint Chiefs of Staff Admiral Michael Mullen, and counterterrorism chief John Brennan were trending strongly against intervention. Secretary Clinton, UN Ambassador Susan Rice, NSC Advisor Samantha Power, and Ben Rhodes were in favor.

In the against column, the clearest and weightiest voice was that of Robert Gates. As former head of the CIA, and the one cabinet member Obama held over from the Bush administration, Gates had a reputation as a highly experienced, level-headed bureaucrat who was above partisanship. Gates believed that the threat to Benghazi was real—the United States had satellite imagery showing the miles-long armored column headed toward the city. But he was troubled by the fact that US forces in the region were already overextended in Iraq and Afghanistan, and perhaps more to the point, he believed that the United States didn't do interventions well. Further, interventions had a way of inevitably surpassing their initial objectives and entering into mission creep.[13]

Samantha Power was one of the most passionate advocates for intervention. As she was the author of an influential book on genocide, Obama had brought her into the White House in part to advise on issues such as the aspirational humanitarian norm known as the Responsibility to Protect, or R2P, which held that the international community had an obligation to intervene when leaders of a country either committed genocide or were powerless to prevent it. With regard to the threat to Benghazi, Power was said to be beside herself: "He [Gaddafi] massacres civilians," Power argued. "He told us what he was going to do in Benghazi—he'd go house to house, killing people."[14] In Power's view, all million or so residents of Benghazi were in mortal danger.

In the end, Gates credited Clinton's decision to support the intervention with turning Obama to yes.[15] Had both the secretaries of defense and state been against it, intervention would have been politically difficult for Obama.

Clinton was aware that a US intervention in Libya had the potential to define her term as secretary of state, and thus help frame her campaign for president. It was a gamble. But true to form, she was inclined to act rather than dwell on all the things that might go wrong. Clinton focused on two questions: First, was this a genuine popular uprising or an Islamist takeover in the making?[16] Second, were the rebels—the opponents to Gaddafi, the ones camped out in the Benghazi courthouse—reliable?

Of all American diplomats, Chris Stevens was best placed to try to fill in some of the blanks on Libya, despite it having been two years since his last posting in Libya. Stevens was candid about what he—and by extension the United States—knew, and what he didn't. He stressed that the "U.S. team still lacked needed details about Libyan society and politics because of America's four-decade absence."[17] The United States didn't really know where Saif Gaddafi stood with respect to his father, or how much influence he and others in the regime had with Muammar Gaddafi. Many of Obama's advisors' memoirs of the period describe this information void in detail. Chollet expands on his assessment of what the United States didn't know in his memoir, *The Long Game*: "There were few experts on Libya either in or out of government.

We had not grasped how weak its institutions were or appreciated the internal disunity that, as Robert D. Kaplan explains, was the 'underlying cause behind Qaddafi's [sic] unruly tyranny.' "[18]

Ambassador Cretz says that he argued strongly for intervention, and that he and Stevens "were very much listened to during the revolutionary phase."[19] But the circle of expert advisors was still narrow, if not self-referential (meaning it was composed mostly of insiders, the vast majority of whom had no knowledge of Libya). One person whose experience would have been particularly relevant at the time, but who was not consulted, was Dartmouth professor Dirk Vandewalle. Vandewalle had been one of the few Libya-focused academics in and out of the country since the early 1990s, and his 1998 classic, *Libya Since Independence: Oil and State-Building*, laid out exactly how weak Libya's institutions were, and what the United States might expect if Gaddafi were to be overthrown.[20]

Clearly, one of the biggest impediments to any US attempt to resolve the Libya conflict was the lack of understanding of what was happening at the top: Gaddafi's motivations and mental state, and if there was anyone who might be in a position to reason with him. Vandewalle told *Rolling Stone* at the time that he believed that Gaddafi simply didn't understand the danger he was in—that he and Saif truly believed that, despite Gaddafi's vociferous complaints about what the United States hadn't done to live up to its end of the 2003 deal, it still wouldn't overturn the relationship they had built over the previous decade.[21]

"Saif and his father were never really very good at reading accurately where Libya stood in the West. They thought everything was forgiven and forgotten," Vandewalle said.[22] Gaddafi clearly also hadn't quite picked up on the depth of differences between the Bush administration and the Obama administration, which saw the 2003 Libya deal as an unseemly by-product of the Iraq War. Their relationship with the West was not on the stable footing they thought it was.

Further, 2009 had been a very bad year for US–Libyan relations.

Gaddafi and Saif deepened the American government's misgivings with
a number of provocative moves, including welcoming the sole convicted Lockerbie bomber, Abdelbaset al-Megrahi, back to Libya as a
hero (following an unorthodox humanitarian release engineered with
the help of UK Prime Minister Tony Blair).[23] In September, Gaddafi
gave a spectacular speech to the United Nations in which he tore up a
copy of the UN charter, likened the United Nations to Al Qaeda, and
demanded George W. Bush and Tony Blair be put on trial for causing
the Iraq War.[24] The 2009 Wikileaks release of more than 200,000 US
classified cables included an unflattering profile of Gaddafi written by
Ambassador Cretz, in which he referenced Gaddafi's relationship with
his "voluptuous" nurse and described a number of Gaddafi's phobias.
That cable resulted in threats to senior Embassy personnel and resulted
in Cretz's recall back to the States in 2010.[25]

None of this baggage was helpful to Gaddafi's situation, to put it
mildly. But there were those within the regime who recognized Gaddafi's behavior as driving the regime toward an unwinnable war and
tried to intervene. There was Saif's alternate, conciliatory speech, the
one that al-Houni says he and Saif spent hours working on (and Saif
ultimately threw away). Then there was the fact that Saif called the State
Department on March 18, 2011—the day before Obama authorized
US–NATO strikes—seeking to speak with Secretary Clinton. He was
referred to Ambassador Cretz, who relayed the State Department's ulti-
matum that Gaddafi withdraw his troops and step down from power.[26]
Saif's younger brother Saadi seems to have argued desperately with his
father to walk back his threats against Benghazi. Cretz later said that he
doubted there was anyone in the regime with the "gumption" to explain
to Gaddafi how dire his predicament was.[27]

In mid-March, Clinton flew to Paris to rally support for a possible
US-led NATO intervention.[28] She was encouraged by overwhelming
enthusiasm, if not outright pressure, from the US' allies—in particular the United Kingdom and France—and the Arab League, which

gave a rare nod to international military action against a member state. The latter was a testament to how deeply Gaddafi had gotten under the skin of many of his fellow Arab leaders over the years, particularly the Saudis, whose crown prince, Abdullah, he tried to assassinate in 2003.[29]

France and the United Kingdom pressured President Obama to participate in the creation of a no-fly zone over Libya. But Obama also realized that this wasn't going to save Benghazi, as the Libyan leader was sending ground power against the city, not air power. This situation created risk, which the president correctly identified: "As enthusiastic as France and Britain were about the no-fly zone, there was a danger that if we participated the U.S. would own the operation. Because we had the capacity."[30]

After a meeting with the Group of Eight (G8) on March 14 in Paris, Clinton took another meeting at her hotel. French intellectual Bernard-Henri Lévy, who had smuggled himself into Benghazi on a vegetable truck at the beginning of the revolution and allegedly convinced Sarkozy to back the Libyan rebels, facilitated a meeting between Clinton, the interim head of the transitional government, Mahmoud Jibril, and an Islamist member of the council, Ali Essawi, who shared responsibility for the council's foreign affairs.[31] Saif had recruited Jibril—a Libyan with a PhD in political science from the University of Pittsburgh—several years before to lead the Libya National Economic Development Board. Clinton wanted Chris Stevens in the meeting to help her interpret what Jibril was saying.

Over the previous days, Clinton had been leaning toward supporting the US intervention. The encounter with Jibril at the very least solidified her resolve. She expressed her support for American action in Libya to the president shortly after.[32]

I spoke with Jibril a couple of years later, and the pitch he described having made to Clinton was the one I (and Stevens) would have expected him to make: Libya is a large country, with a small population (between 6 and 7 million—the size of the state of Virginia, with the bulk of the population living in a string of cities along a 1,000-mile coastline). Libyans were largely pro-American and had few of the sectarian and ethnic splits that made incipient violence in Syria look so dangerous.[33]

Swung by Clinton's advocacy, Obama instructed UN Ambassador Susan Rice to work to pass a resolution in the United Nations calling for an immediate cease-fire, a no-fly zone over part of the country, and authorization of "all necessary measures" (diplomatic speak for whatever force is required) to protect civilians in Libya. Saif told France-based Euronews on March 16 that none of this mattered: "Military operations are finished. In 48 hours everything will be over. Our forces are close to Benghazi. Whatever decision is taken, it will be too late." Saif also lobbed a public relations grenade at Sarkozy, accusing him of being a traitor for accepting Libyan funds for his reelection campaign.[34]

The moment was one of rare international consensus: Russia and China's abstentions in the United Nations vote were key. Qatar volunteered to participate in sorties against Libya while the United States strongly encouraged other states, such as the United Arab Emirates, to participate in the NATO campaign as well, to broaden Arab support.[35] Resolution 1973 passed on March 17, and President Obama authorized air strikes on March 19.

One of the most insightful views on Obama's decision to intervene comes from Michael Lewis, who shadowed the president for six months in 2011 for a profile of a president at war. Lewis's piece, "Obama's Way," was published in *Vanity Fair* on, ironically, September 11, 2012—the day of the attack that would bracket US involvement in Libya and send the Libyan Revolution into a nosedive.[36]

Lewis describes Obama's polling of advisors, but his main focus is on the factor that most accounts of this deliberation miss, and that colored almost every single Obama foreign policy decision until the 2012 election: politics, and the Obama administration's fear that any false move would bring a Republican incubus crashing down on its head.

Lewis frames his piece with the story of one of two American pilots who were forced to ditch their F-15 jet over eastern Libya on the third day of the US–NATO campaign. The pilot was tracked and rescued quickly, but the weapons systems officer, Tyler Stark, went missing. Obama said, "My first thought was how to find the guy. My next thought was that this is a reminder that something can always go wrong. And there are consequences for things going wrong."[37] Stark was eventually rescued, with the help of Bubaker Habib, my former colleague in Tripoli and Chris Stevens's Benghazi-advisor-to-be. But the episode, viewed from a post-intervention perspective, takes on heavy significance for the president, who sees it as representative of the factors that could determine the political impact of his decision.

If things had turned out differently, Lewis concluded, Stark's story had the potential to wipe out "a complex tale ignored by the American public about how the United States had forged a broad international coalition to help people who claimed to share our values rid themselves of a tyrant." In turn, it might have been replaced with "a much simpler one, ripe for exploitation by his foes: how a president elected to extract us from a war on one Arab country got Americans killed in another." Obama told Lewis that as president he'd been surprised at how little a price the other side would pay for hurting the country just to win the next presidential election.[38] And what Obama appears to be referring to here, prior to the Benghazi attack, is again the idea that a terrorist attack or the death of Americans in combat would cost him a second term.

From the start, any decision on intervention in Libya was bound to be influenced by a jumble of fact, fiction, and emotion. This was a country with which the United States had a highly ambivalent relationship, heavily colored by 9/11, the Iraq War, the rendition process, and American partisan politics (given the relationship's origins in the Bush War on Terror). Libya was also a country whose inner workings we still didn't comprehend, despite having had a diplomatic and rather intimate intelligence cooperation for seven years. Last, the relationship had been under a great deal of stress due to other factors not directly related to the 2011 upheaval. As a result, lines of communication between the United States and Gaddafi were even more indirect than usual.

So though the high-level White House narrative of the US intervention in Libya was focused on operational details and related risks (a tallying of pros and cons), looking under the hood reveals a decision shaped by domestic politics: the ever-present desire by the Democrats, and the Obama administration in particular, to deflect and dodge right-wing political traps; tension between the NSC and the State Department (and, for that matter, between Secretary Clinton and President Obama); a desire by several of Obama's advisors to test and establish a Responsibility to Protect norm; and the ambivalent but increasingly friendly approach to the Muslim Brotherhood, as an agent of democratic change. There's also the possibility that the president and his advisors were taken with the idea that a quick and relatively costless win in Libya might help inoculate the United States from some of the growing pressure to intervene elsewhere in the Arab Spring, in other conflicts like the one bubbling up in Syria.

With all that as background, President Obama's decision to intervene in Libya laid the groundwork for a level of political disorder in the United States and in the region that would have been very difficult to imagine at the time.

10

Expeditionary Diplomat

When the revolution broke out in Libya, I asked Chris to travel to Benghazi. And he did so on a Greek cargo ship, like a nineteenth century envoy.

—HILLARY CLINTON, IN HER SPEECH AT
THE COMMON GROUND AWARDS

The George W. Bush administration coined the term "expeditionary diplomacy" to refer to short-term diplomatic missions in support of US military operations in Iraq and Afghanistan. These were often tied to conflict mitigation, economic development, and civil society initiatives—things that might come under the umbrella of post-conflict state-building. Expeditionary missions might include American officials' serving as a temporary administrator in a far-flung province, mediating a dispute between rival clans over scarce water resources, or negotiating the construction of a new dam. The situations were varied and unique to the time and place.[1]

As secretary of state, Clinton came to see these activities as the future of diplomacy. In her eyes, though, they had to be separated from overt military actions and focused primarily on building partnerships with local development actors and governments. She wanted it to be used not just in response to conflict, but as a means of preventing it. Clinton

called it "smart power," and she envisioned it transforming and rein-
vigorating the State Department in the twenty-first century.

In her proposals for updating and reshaping the way the State Department operated, Clinton argued that forward deployments of diplomatic
expertise would pay off in the longer term, resulting in fewer and shorter
conflicts—hence "smart" power. But for this to be realized, there would
need to be a strategy for developing a more efficient, more responsive State
Department. As part of this effort, Clinton set up the Bureau of Conflict
and Stabilization Operations, known as CSO, in 2011. As the name suggests, CSO was meant to be the operations center for smart power, an
internal brain trust that worked in real time to design strategies and tools
for dealing with localized security challenges, from failed local diplomacy
to disaster relief and refugee logistics, all with relatively modest resources.[2]

The biggest obstacle to the application of smart power in the Obama
administration was the politics of risk. This is a subject that speaks to
Secretary Clinton on a deeper level.

> You can't separate diplomacy from risk. It's part of the job.
> People don't realize this, but our diplomats take huge risks all
> the time—you look at someone like Ambassador Ryan Crocker,
> who received the Department's first expeditionary diplomacy
> award—he's been in more situations as a diplomat than you
> can count in which he was at risk of being killed, in Beirut,
> Kabul, Iraq. There are few riskless professions, but this certainly
> isn't one of them. And the rewards of it are that you have the
> potential to have a great impact on people's lives and welfare.[3]

Certainly Chris Stevens's experiences in Libya exemplified this trade-
off between high risk and diplomatic reward.

I asked Clinton how Stevens entered into the Libya story. "I reached
out to Chris Stevens as soon as the Libya conflict started to escalate,"
Clinton explained. "There wasn't anyone else in the Department who
had his level of experience in Libya, on the street level; he was adaptable,

had been posted all around the region, spoke the language. He was the right man for the job."[4]

Though Clinton was right about Stevens's capabilities, about the inseparability of risk from the job and the need for expeditionary diplomacy, one can't help juxtapose Stevens's intrepid engagement in the field with the White House's multiple political filters, and ask if any of this—the intervention and the expeditionary diplomacy—should ever have been attempted without a clear commitment by the White House to assume the responsibilities that came with the decision to intervene.

Operation Odyssey Dawn was the code name given to the American role in the NATO response to UN Resolution 1973, which authorized the use of "all necessary measures" to protect civilians from Gaddafi's looming assault on Benghazi.[5] The operation started on March 19, in accordance with Obama's instructions that US command of the operation be limited in time and scope, passing to NATO within weeks; America's strategic coordination role ended on March 31.

The first objective was to institute a no-fly zone, which required destroying Gaddafi's air defenses and much of his offensive flight capacity. Sarkozy jumped the gun, ordering his Rafale jets to strike targets in Libya before the official commencement of the campaign—this displeased Clinton, but there wasn't much to be done, as the United States would suffer any consequences of ordering them back. And in fact, at the time of the strikes, Gaddafi's miles-long convoy had already breached the western perimeter of Benghazi. The convoy was turned to cinder, and Benghazi was quickly under the control of the nascent NTC and its rebel forces, led by General Abdel Fattah Younes.

Republican members of Congress quickly objected to what they called Obama's "unconstitutional" intervention in Libya. The Obama administration stood by its decision not to consult Congress before (or after) taking military action, on the grounds that Libya was a limited, multilateral humanitarian endeavor, not actual hostilities. The Obama administration would later be accused of anticipating regime change from the start.

Two weeks after the start of the US–NATO intervention, in early April, with much of eastern Libya under rebel control, Chris Stevens set off on what became one of the most storied American diplomatic adventures of the last half century: He hitched a ride on a Greek freighter departing Valetta, Malta, for Benghazi, along with a small contingent of DS officers and a junior political assistant—none of whom had been to Benghazi before. Libya's airports were closed, and the State Department wanted to effect as low-key an entrance as possible.

Stevens would be doing exactly the kind of work Clinton envisioned for her State Department. "My mandate," he later told an interviewer, "was to go out and meet as many members of the leadership as I could in the Transitional National Council. I've gone around with our small team and tried to get to know other people in the society there."[6]

While there is no evidence Stevens answered to anyone outside the State Department (and the president), he had a vital informant role all the same. Former CIA officer Robert Baer explained this nuance just after the Benghazi attack:

> Never forget that ambassadors are also intelligence collectors. By wading in among the Libyans, from going to dinners at the homes of Libyan leaders to talking with ordinary people in the streets, [Stevens] was gathering both important opinions and intelligence minutiae. It's that daily immersion into the dynamics of a society that has always made the U.S. ambassador's personal take on a situation as important as the judgment of any intelligence agency.[7]

After reaching Benghazi on April 5, Stevens and his team spent the first night on the ship, then the following days looking for accommodation, before winding up at the Tibesti Hotel, where Libya's NTC announced its formation the month before. In the following weeks, they distributed nonlethal aid to the people of Benghazi and established a project to try to collect, buy back, and destroy weapons looted from Gaddafi's arms depots, so as to take them out of the conflict.[8]

As difficult as the situation was, it didn't break Stevens's morale or determination. Shortly after returning to Benghazi, Stevens was reacquainted with Italy's Benghazi consul general, Guido De Sanctis, whom both of us had known from our postings to Tripoli, when he was working at the Italian Embassy as the economic officer. De Sanctis recalls that their interactions in Benghazi were always enhanced by Chris's wry humor: "At one meeting with the NTC . . . the cell phone of the NTC representative chairing the session started ringing with the 'Godfather' tone: Chris was sitting in front of me and he immediately opened his eyes wide, staring at me, and raised eyebrows. It was difficult not to laugh." De Sanctis says that "Chris was inspiring for all of us . . . in May 2012, he was often mentioned in Libyan circles as the ideal representative of what Libya needed (and still needs) from the US and from the world: people-to-people relations, easy access, honest confrontation, and the will to understand each other and grow together."[9]

This period of Stevens's tenure in Libya would be largely overlooked later in the dissection of the Benghazi attack and discussions of what constituted a so-called reasonable level of risk. But it is highly relevant because it's hard to imagine a situation that was more dangerous than his role as envoy. DS agents would do what they could, but anyone hellbent on harming Stevens or his team would face little real resistance. Benghazi was saturated with weapons and fighters. And while the people of Benghazi were on the whole very friendly to the Americans, there were certainly those who were not. It was widely assumed that the biggest danger was fifth-column Gaddafi agents, looking to overturn the revolution from within Benghazi. But Al Qaeda flags had also been seen raised at public gatherings.

As Secretary Clinton explained, "After the Benghazi attack, the media completely ignored the fact that Chris Stevens had, at least by any measure available at the time, confronted far higher levels of risk as Envoy than as Ambassador, and for greater periods of time."[10] Ambassador Cretz seconded this sentiment: "Chris's main contributions were his courageous reporting on the ground while in Benghazi, starting in March 2011."[11] Secretary Clinton and Ambassador Cretz both said that they believed that Chris Stevens was focused on Benghazi because he "felt [it] was very important for America to be present, and to have an ear to the ground."[12]

Later, Stevens would confess to Bubaker Habib, his Benghazi fixer, that he felt an enormous responsibility for making sure the intervention had a positive outcome. "I had a role in getting rid of Qaddafi [sic] and now my mission is to rebuild the country," he said.[13] A member of Stevens's team echoed this view in an account of this period: "The Americans who had arrived in April were already looking ahead to the moment when Libya would start rebuilding."[14] These statements accord with Stevens's demonstrated integrity and idealism and Clinton's own map for "smart diplomacy." But it conflicted sharply with the president's clear concern with limits to intervention.

Jake Sullivan, then head of policy planning at the State Department (effectively Clinton's policy advisor), advised the NSC that "post-conflict stabilization in Libya, while clearly a worthy undertaking at the right level of investment, cannot be counted on as one of our highest priorities."[15] In another email, Sullivan was more blunt: "Libya must not," he wrote, "be a state-building exercise."[16] Clearly the White House, the State Department, and its anointed Libya expert were on different pages with regard to what Libya required.

Stevens's experiences in Libya were notable in their own right. But for those versed in early American history, the US intervention in Libya and Stevens's mission evoked a series of uncanny parallels with events from more than 200 years earlier, when the newly independent United

States found itself in its first war—with a group of pirate emirs who were launching attacks on American shipping from their perches in North Africa.

When Stevens met De Sanctis in the nearby city of Al Bayda shortly after arriving in Benghazi in April 2011, De Sanctis asked Stevens if he felt like the American Consul William Eaton marching on Derna in 1805.[17] Stevens laughed at that. But the reference must have pleased him no end, not only because it came from a foreign diplomat, but because it was a story Stevens had been familiar with at least since he had been a Peace Corps volunteer in Morocco in the mid-1980s. (Stevens worked on a project at the US Consulate in Tangiers, "helping inventory documents and other artifacts . . . including ransom notes from Barbary pirates.")[18]

Because the United States in the early 1800s had no real navy, as well as no federal budget that could pay for one, it was caught flat-footed by the Barbary pirates and resorted to paying protection money to assure the safety of American ships. This situation enraged the American public and ultimately resulted in an order from President Jefferson, who had been against "foreign entanglements," to build new warships, which, without a declaration of war, he promptly sent to blockade Tripoli harbor. In 1803, one of these frigates, the USS *Philadelphia*, ran aground on an unmarked shoal. The pasha of Tripoli, Yusuf Karamanli, suddenly had 308 American hostages, whom he locked up in the former US Consulate, in what is today Libya's old city.[19]

Enter William Eaton, Revolutionary privateer-turned-adventurer-spy, who—in one of many parallels with Stevens—was one of America's few, or only, "Libya" experts. Eaton had started learning Arabic as a student at Dartmouth College and picked up the local dialect while posted as consul general in neighboring Tunis—a position he specifically asked for in reward for unspecified intelligence services rendered to President Adams. In Tunis, the gregarious Eaton befriended the Libyan pasha's kinder, less ambitious brother Ahmed ("Hamet" in historical records) and hatched a scheme to overthrow the pasha and install the malleable Hamet in his place. It was America's first attempt at regime change, a habit still going strong by 2011.

Eaton's plan to handle the hostage situation required him to travel from Valletta, Malta, to Cairo, where he had to first find the pasha's brother Hamet and then convince him to march with him on foot across the Egyptian desert, where he hoped to raise more recruits to march on Tripoli. Amazingly, Eaton made all this happen on sheer guts, bluffs, and self-confidence. He took Derna and was ready to continue on to Tripoli when he was summoned onto a frigate by the head of the US Mediterranean command, thanked for his service, and told to go home. Faced with Eaton's threat, the pasha had sued for peace, and the Americans accepted, leaving Hamet and his followers to the wrath of the pasha's forces (in the end, the pasha spared his brother). Eaton himself returned home an angry and broken man, arguing that Washington had been cautious to its own detriment and that the Barbary pirates would rise again (which they did).

It's easy to read too much into the parallel—for one, Eaton and Stevens were very different personalities. The historical contexts were also very different. But for Clinton and Stevens, his entry into Benghazi "like a nineteenth century envoy" seemed a very apt symbol for America's fight for a just cause and the ability to get things done. But that historical reference also contained a caution regarding American hesitancy and associated short-term horizons when dealing with the Middle East, a trend that hadn't really changed in the intervening two centuries.

11

Arming the Radicals

As soon as Benghazi was liberated, the novice politicos on the ground, the ones whom the West loosely labeled "progressives"—technocrats who had emerged as the public front people for a plausible post-intervention government—and the "Islamists"—those who wanted to steer Libya toward a state governed according to Islamic law—both turned their attention to the looming fight against Gaddafi.

There would be a lot of second-guessing (much of it from *liberal* pundits in the United States, many of whom had never been to Libya) about the danger Gaddafi's forces posed to Benghazi and its citizens. But of the scores of contacts and people I met in Benghazi, not a one has expressed anything but certainty that the United States and its allies prevented a bloodbath. As some of them told me, Gaddafi always did what he said he'd do, and the West always brushed it off as an empty threat. Not this time. Regardless, even with Benghazi secured, this was just the beginning of the latest Libya story. Gaddafi may have suffered a significant loss, but he held western Libya, and was putting up a strong fight.

Once the rebels got to the edge of the eastern oil fields, about 500 miles east of Tripoli, the front became a game of tug-of-war, with the rope moving back and forth over a line that split the country longitudinally from the port of Brega to the town of Ajdabiya.

The United States had no real plan at this point—in part due to the limits that Obama had placed on the intervention. The president didn't seek Congressional approval to go to war, in part because he planned to turn over the operations to NATO within ten days of the start of hostilities, in a maneuver that became known, much to the Obama administration's irritation, as "leading from behind."[1]

Mahmoud Jibril, the man who had pled the case for intervention and demonstrated the rebels' liberal credentials to Secretary Clinton just weeks before in Paris, was now the chair of the NTC's executive board and de facto prime minister of the rebel government. But very quickly, it became clear that there were several groups vying for power and influence.

The progressives had grouped around Jibril and the leading regime defectors. The Islamists quickly coalesced around the LIFG and Muslim Brotherhood figures that had dominated the negotiations with Gaddafi over the previous years. There were revolutionary figures with political aspirations of their own, such as Khalifa Heftar, Gaddafi's former general and the commander of his war on Chad.[2] And there were still Gaddafi loyalists whose fervor suggested they believed Gaddafi might reappear like some kind of messiah.

The striking thing about all these groups was that they had each, at one point or another, been the focus of American attention or attempts at co-optation. For the moment they had a common cause: ending the Gaddafi regime. But the opposition didn't exactly wait until Gaddafi had fallen to fracture.

The Islamists' first reaction to the NTC was to call it "some kind of coup" against them, even as they pushed for representation on it.[3] Early on, the Islamist leadership had determined that the NTC "should not be in the driving seat once the regime was toppled."[4] To that end, they held meetings in regional hubs like Tunis, Istanbul, and Doha, and they lobbied the Qatari government for military support. They also focused their attention on building relationships and a presence on local councils in Benghazi and eastern Libya.

As soon as Benghazi was out of regime control, former LIFG emir Abdulhakim Belhaj flew from Tripoli to Benghazi to survey the landscape and meet with other regional Islamist leaders. With him was the ideological leader of the LIFG, Abdel Wahab Al Qaid. In Benghazi, they met with Ali Sallabi, the Muslim Brotherhood member who served as a mediator during the *Corrections*, and Fawzi Bukatif, another of Libya's exiled, gray-haired Islamists, who had, like several other leading rebels, until recently been living in the United States. Like Ali Sallabi and most of the LIFG, Bukatif spent years incarcerated at Abu Salim prison in Tripoli. Bukatif had recently started to form the Muslim Brotherhood–affiliated February 17 Martyrs Brigade with assistance from the LIFG (which, though disbanded by the *Corrections*, was replaced by the Libyan Islamic Movement for Change).[5] The United States would later hire the February 17 Martyrs Brigade to protect American diplomats while they were in Benghazi.[6] Abu Sufian Bin Qumu moved back to the eastern Libyan town of Derna, where he organized a group of radicals while giving interviews in which he said he couldn't forgive the United States for what it did to him.[7]

The Libyan Revolution was underway, and while the United States hoped they'd enabled the progressives like Jibril, there was no guarantee who would emerge in the subsequent struggles for power. And there must have been some in the CIA and other agencies who were hoping that those they'd beaten and shackled weren't the ones.

By the time Chris Stevens arrived in Benghazi as US envoy to the NTC in early April, the council had grown to fifty-one members, ten of whom were not publicly named. Some said it was because they had family members in Tripoli who were subject to Gaddafi's reprisals; others said it was because they had ties to Al Qaeda.[8] Among the Libyan Afghans joining the NTC were Abdul Razzaq al-Aradi, a businessman and member of the Muslim Brotherhood and the LIFG, and Alamin Belhaj (no relation to Abdulhakim Belhaj).[9]

At first, the council had run into a series of existential crises: They needed money, as most of Libya's funds were still frozen by the West, and they had no official recognition by the international community as Libya's legitimate government. They also lacked sufficient weapons to break the stalemate with Gaddafi. Turkey expressed its willingness to support the council with loans while the Qataris offered to provide supplementary arms to the rebels, including anti-tank weapons.[10] Soon after Benghazi's liberation, the Obama administration gave its blessing to outside powers to arm the rebels and the fighters under the command of Abdel Fattah Younes.

President Obama met in early April with Qatar's leader, Emir Sheikh Hamad bin Khalifa Al Thani, in the Oval Office, where he praised the emir for being an essential part of the coalition that prevented blood-letting in Benghazi: "We would not have been able, I think, to shape the kind of broad-based international coalition that includes not only our NATO members but also includes Arab states, without the emir's leadership," Obama told reporters afterward.[11] Part of the president's appreciation stemmed from the fact that the United States had very few assets on the ground to help facilitate or monitor weapons shipments.

But within weeks, there were reports that Qatari weapons were going to unauthorized recipients, some of whom had ties to radical Islamist groups. Qatar had shifted its supply routes from the NTC and its representatives to Abdulhakim Belhaj, through Muslim Brotherhood intermediaries. French weapons, part of a consignment of more than 20,000 tons of arms, were also funneled to the NTC through Qatar.[12] Meanwhile, an international team of counterterrorism experts, led by two French research outfits, was on the ground in Libya collecting information for a report released in May, which argued that the Western intervention in Libya, and heavily arming radical Islamists in Benghazi, strongly risked "destabilizing all of North Africa and the Sahel, lending itself to the creation of a new home for radical Islam, and terrorism."[13]

Awkwardly, Mahmoud Jibril, in addition to the Muslim Brotherhood and the LIFG, had sought Qatar's support and used the Qatari capital as a kind of commuter hub from which to shuttle back and forth to Libya, where he felt he couldn't maintain a secure bubble. Jibril described the moment he says he realized what was going on:

Our men were waiting for [a shipment of] Qatari weapons at Benina [Benghazi airport], when they saw a representative of the Brotherhood, Ahmed Majberi, who was cooperating with the Defense Minister and the Deputy Defense Minister, Ashraf Bin Ismail, in charge of the distribution of weapons to the rebels. [Majberi] went up to the weapons and covered up the "ship to" tags with duct tape. The weapons were then taken to the farm of Ismail Sallabi [the brother of Libya's Muslim Brotherhood figurehead Ali Sallabi], and from there to Abdulhakim Belhaj in the Nafusa Mountains.[14]

The State Department knew about, and was alarmed at, the fact that Qatar appeared to be focusing their weapons shipments not on the NTC, but on their friends' militias from Misrata and their associated Islamist groups—including the LIFG.[15] Secretary Clinton's conclusion was that the United States had to get more involved and start arming the NTC directly if it wanted to retain its influence. "If not," the Secretary is said to have argued, "whatever happened, your options would shrink, your influence would shrink, therefore your ability to affect anything there [in Libya] would also shrink."[16]

There was also growing concern, supported by sightings of Al Qaeda flags at anti-Gaddafi rallies, that Al Qaeda had a bigger presence in Libya than the United States had realized—or was infiltrating fast.

In the first two weeks of March, Obama signed a presidential finding that enabled a covert operation in which "Humvees, counterbattery radar, TOW missiles" and other equipment were provided to approved end users through the port of Benghazi.[17]

"We were definitely giving them [the rebels] lethal assistance," a State Department official was quoted as saying. "We'd crossed that line." This in turn motivated an accelerated timeline for officially recognizing the NTC as the legitimate government of Libya, on July 15, 2011.[18]

By the summer, the situation had become dire, as the front hadn't moved: Younes's men were still held back at the Ajdabiya line. The West was deeply worried that Gaddafi would manage to regroup, overwhelm eastern Libya, and retake Benghazi. Or that the country would split, leaving a stung Gaddafi in the west and a weak government in the east. In retrospect, the Obama administration had limited its room to maneuver by pre-committing itself to a specific strategy (as it would in Syria), before understanding what was needed on the ground. In this case, as the United States' control over funds and weapons migrated to nominal allies Turkey and Qatar, the Libyan Revolution was being hijacked—even before Gaddafi had been toppled.

12

The Good-Hearted Bookseller

In the months after the intervention, the main way to get into Benghazi was by land, in a car or taxi. You'd come in from Egypt, across the eastern border at Sallum. From there, you had an eight-hour drive to Benghazi across long stretches of desert and into the Green Mountains. This was a treacherous route, along roads that were subject to blockades and random roadblocks set up by the various militias fighting Gaddafi. Wealthy Libyans hitched rides into Benghazi on each other's Learjets. The United Nations had started up a relief air service, which was meant to facilitate the movement of UN and relief workers into eastern Libya. You had to be a member of a registered humanitarian organization to get a seat.

The paperwork for Ahmed's and my small medical nonprofit was ready by mid-July. We named the organization Avicenna, after the tenth-century Arabic-speaking Persian physician. And we managed to make bookings on a UN humanitarian relief flight from Cairo to Benghazi, which some said were worth their weight in gold, for the difficulty in obtaining one.

I met Ahmed in Cairo on July 27, 2011. We ate dinner together, went over plans for the trip, and then went to sleep early so we could get up to catch a cab to the airport. On the way, our cab got lost in the maze of ramps and side roads surrounding the airport, and we had to call the Cairo-based flight dispatch office for the United Nations Humanitarian Assistance Service (UNHAS) for directions. That call would be fateful, as it established a connection with someone who would shortly be in a position to help us when we needed it.

We finally found the terminal and were about to pass through a metal turnstile leading into a cavernous hangar when Ahmed's phone pinged. It was a text message from a Libyan relative in the United States.

Ahmed read the relevant part of the text out loud: Abdel Fattah Younes, the commander of the Libyan revolutionary forces, had been assassinated in Benghazi.

Ahmed and I looked at one another. We knew instantly that the risks of our trip had just skyrocketed. Younes had served as both a senior figure in the Libyan Army and as interior minister, and his defection to the rebel side in February was a stunning reversal for Gaddafi, as well as a threat to the Islamists, against whom he had fought. He was also seen to be the glue holding at least part of the revolution together. At the same time, many in the Islamist camp had seen him as the main obstacle to their gaining political control once this phase of the revolution was over.[1]

With his death, Benghazi could quickly turn into an unstable, violent mess. Or maybe we would be fine. One of the attendants pressed us to hurry; the plane was leaving—no time for conversation. Ahmed turned to me and said: "It's your decision."

I looked at him and felt the turnstile move with the pressure I slowly applied to it. Suddenly, we were on the other side, in a line to board a turboprop with about twenty other people, mostly UN personnel.

The plane was light enough that the takeoff roll lasted only seconds before we shot up through a hole in the cloud cover and hugged the Mediterranean coast, from Cairo to Alexandria and Tobruk, before flying over the Green Mountains and into Benghazi from the west. In all, the flight took about an hour and twenty minutes.

It had been five years since I had last been in Benghazi. For Ahmed, it had been thirty-five years. I wondered what he was feeling, but I'd have to wait to ask as he was sitting several rows away on the opposite side of the plane. Next to him, I noticed a man wearing a gold-embroidered farmala—a traditional Libyan vest—and fez. The man had caught my attention during the flight, with his first-class luggage tags and distinctively Libyan attire.

As the plane taxied toward the terminal, a large white billboard came into view, in front of a row of flags of the countries backing the NTC, proclaiming "Welcome to a Free Libya." As Ahmed and I disembarked, an Italian flight attendant in a dark blue suit and cap gave a perfunctory little wave before matter-of-factly pulling up the retractable stairs and leaving us to our own devices. These flights weren't going to spend any more time than necessary on the ground. As the passengers walked from the plane to the arrivals area, I noticed Ahmed talking with the man in the farmala.

There were no taxis outside the airport, but Ahmed and I were able to find a lone car and driver who was willing to take us to the Tibesti Hotel, where I had stayed many times while a diplomat and where Chris Stevens had been based as envoy during the first few months of the revolution. On the road out from the airport, we passed a huge and rather inspired billboard, dominated by an image of an elderly Libyan man standing in a field, holding at arm's length a daisy, which he seemed to offer to those passing by. Under the image were the words: "A free Libya, we will not budge, we will not falter."

I asked Ahmed about his conversation with the man in the farmala. Ahmed said he asked the man if he knew anything about Abdel Fattah Younes's assassination the day before, and what he thought of it. Ahmed said the man looked at him and said, coolly, "*Kan min al mutaqwaqa'a* (It was to be expected)" and continued to walk forward.

We found out later that he was none other than Ali Sallabi.

When we arrived at the Tibesti, the man who checked us in described the scene less than twenty-four hours before, after the Younes killing: "It was chaos, a militia attacked the hotel, the facade was shot up. Guests climbed up to the mezzanine level, trying to get out the back way." I found that oddly comforting, as it meant that perhaps the shock waves from the Younes killing had been fast, and the worst was over. At least for now things had returned to quiet. You could see where bullets shattered the glass panes above the entrance, but the shards had been cleaned up. Like a narcoleptic dragon, Benghazi had released a puff of fire and gone back to sleep.

While Ahmed met with his BMC contact, I set out to reconnoiter the downtown, walking near the courthouse and the epicenter of the revolution, hoping to track down any of my regular contacts from six or seven years before. As I set out, I noticed a large sign in Arabic in the Tibesti lobby, announcing a conference for the Ikhwan—the Libyan Muslim Brotherhood. This was probably the first time in more than forty-two years that the group had a chance to assemble openly in Libya.

In particular, I wanted to seek out the Good-Hearted Bookseller. I had thought of him many times during the previous six months, particularly when Gaddafi's tanks were rolling toward Benghazi. I walked down Omar Al Mukhtar Street and found the shop, which was still there, untouched by the violence of the preceding months. It looked closed, but when I pushed on the door, it moved. And when I walked in, there was the Good-Hearted Bookseller, in the last pose I left him, leaning over the counter talking to a group of young people. One of them was showing him a newspaper, with great pride. Apparently, this young man was editor of a new political broadsheet—one of dozens that had sprung up after the revolution, some of them excellent. Part of a brief literary bloom.

But the Good-Hearted Bookseller looked sullen. He didn't recognize me at first—after all, it had been seven years since I'd last seen him, and the context was very different. But after I reminded him, he perked up. I asked him what he made of recent events. As usual, he was brutally candid.

"I understand the Americans have their interests," he said, without much preface, knowing of course that I was American. "And that Libya may not be at the top of those interests. But to leave things like this, in disorder—they mustn't. Something dark is brewing in Benghazi now, and it's different from what was in the past. It's evil. Soon it will be too late."

He whispered something to one of his assistants who came back a minute later with a copy of *Translating Libya*, my collection of translations of short stories, many of which he helped me source. *"Alf mabrouk* (Congratulations)!"* he said.

I pressed him to be more specific about the nature of the darkness, but he did not wish to. The man who defiantly criticized Gaddafi while he was still in power, in front of a US diplomat, was now deeply afraid of something. And it wasn't the attack that the city had faced a few months before, from Gaddafi's thugs. I asked him about that. What did he think would have happened if the United States hadn't intervened?

"We'd be dead," he replied, matter-of-factly. "Those who could fled the city to the neighboring towns—or Egypt, if they could. But I am old. I was waiting here, in this shop, fully prepared to die defending it."

This metaphor of darkness was something I heard repeated several times in Benghazi, and later. Aref Nayed, future head of the NTC's stabilization team, used some of the same imagery and the word "darkness" about Benghazi at that time, with reference to the local militias.[2]

Ahmed joined me about an hour into my conversation with the Good-Hearted Bookseller, and they did the usual recitation of family connections. Perhaps a half hour later, Ahmed and I exited the shop and walked down Omar Al Mukhtar Street, toward the corniche, past buildings whose sides had been blown out by mortars and RPGs. There were few people about, but the atmosphere spoke volumes—literally, in the graffiti and glue-backed posters that were affixed to every pole and vertical slab of concrete. It was a visual outpouring of hate and subversiveness, and the images were phantasmagorical: "Topple Qaddafi and his hangers-on" read one piece of black scrawl; "Game Over" and "Fuck

Gaddafi!" (the latter two, presumably for the benefit of Westerners, in English). Benghazi had some fantastic graphic talent, and their productions were vivid: Gaddafi and his most recognizable sons in various grotesque poses, surrounded by swastikas and attached to the bodies of pigs and water buffalo. Granted, this was my first time wandering around the freshly expressed sentiments of a violent revolution, but I too could tell there was something darker in the drawings, the swastikas, and the language of Jews and Crusaders. I had seen it before, only in pictures. This was the language of Al Qaeda.

I took a moment to take a picture of one piece of graffiti on a concrete wall, when I heard a shout, and suddenly I was face-to-face with three armed men, yelling at me to get away from the wall, then asking me who I was, then arguing with each other. Ahmed had gone ahead by this point, and when the shouting reached him, he came back with our driver. Hearing a Libyan accent, the young men yelled at Ahmed but backed away. The immediate danger gone, the driver left Ahmed and me to walk toward the corniche alone, where a macabre, carnivalesque atmosphere prevailed—every few paces there were booths set up, around which were placards bearing the faces of the missing and the martyrs—*shuhada*—of the revolution, most of them barely in their twenties.

Turning back toward the hotel, we found ourselves face-to-face with a rail-thin boy, perhaps in his early teens. He stuck his arm out as if to greet us, then formed his hand slowly, deliberately, into the shape of a pistol.

"Bang, bang," the kid said, listlessly, forming his middle and index fingers into the shape of a gun. "*Aftan* (Watch out); there are snipers on the rooves." Then he turned and walked away.

It took me some time to unwind from all of this.

That night, before we had dinner at the Tibesti, Ahmed and I watched the nightly television broadcast from Qatar. Following the assassination of Younes two days before, Mustafa Abdel Jalil, head of the NTC, had called on all militias in the city to lay down their arms or face drastic consequences.

The next day, July 31, Ahmed and I woke to a tense atmosphere in the hotel. Staff were furtively sharing news plucked from the sporadically working Internet. I asked to see some of these posts, which predicted a military showdown between those forces loyal to the NTC and those (mostly Islamist) that opposed them. Most of the people we'd spoken to over the previous twenty-four hours, including members of well-respected families, were convinced that Islamists were behind the Younes killing, to facilitate a takeover.

It would take many more weeks for details to come out. On the afternoon of July 28, 2011, Younes was summoned, under murky circumstances, from the rebel front line at Ajdabiya—a dusty old caravan stop south of Benghazi—to answer questions from the executive team of the transitional government.[3]

Younes was driven to a location where he was allegedly met, according to Libyan intelligence sources, by one Ahmed Abu Khattala—whose name would become very visible later, in the context of the attack on the US Mission in Benghazi. Abu Khattala had formed the Obeida Ibn Al Jarrah militia, which would also be implicated in the Benghazi attack a year later. Abu Khattala seems to have had only a bit part in Younes's killing—he was quickly relieved of his prisoner by unknown others, who killed Younes and his deputy. Younes's tribe accused three people of conspiring to kill him—one of whom was Ali Al Issawi, one of the council members whom Clinton met in Paris just before deciding to back the Libyan rebels. Abdel Jalil, the chairman of the NTC, was forced to fire the entire executive committee of the council as a result.[4]

At the time, Chris Stevens was back in Washington briefing the White House on the progress of the Libyan Revolution. I hadn't planned on making contact with the US Mission—which had since moved from the Tibesti Hotel to a rented villa in an upscale area of the city—if

Chris wasn't there. But Chris had urged me to contact his colleague, Nathaniel Tek, if I needed anything. Tek was the young foreign service officer who had accompanied Chris on the ship from Malta and was holding down the Mission, basically alone. Cell phones were nearly useless in Benghazi, so to make a call at the Tibesti, you had to use one of two antiquated phone booths in the back of a bank of elevators facing the reception area.

On the second try, I got through to the US Mission. I wanted to know if they had any information that could be useful, and whether they could offer us any help if all hell broke loose. I knew some of the answers already: Without Chris to vouch for us, we were just foolish Americans who had ignored State Department travel warnings. But I went through the motions anyway.

Tek was curt: "The city's under lockdown—the Mission, the UN compound. You're on your own."

When I repeated this to Ahmed, it sent him into a brief rant. His Libyan side was talking now: "Since when are the Americans ever useful?"

I knew we had to get to the airport, and fast. My next call was to the local UNHAS representative, to see if he could get us onto that day's flight to Cairo. The first response was negative. The rules said that one had to book flights at least four days in advance. I referenced the situation unfolding now and emphasized that we'd be left behind in a highly volatile situation. The representative said he would consider the request but not to get our hopes up. At the time, Ahmed and I were waiting for a third member of our group to arrive on the next flight in. I had texted him the previous day to tell him to cancel his flight in from Cairo. I managed to get a fleeting Wi-Fi signal, long enough to text him the name of the UNHAS official in Cairo, with whom Ahmed and I had spoken when we were trying to find the right departure gate. "Please call and ask if they can make an exception to get us out on today's flight at noon," I wrote.

I had no idea if the email had gotten through—but Ahmed and I needed to get to the airport. The combination of what I had read in the morning's paper, the Internet postings, the UN and US Mission lockdowns—it all pointed to a possible meltdown, with the pro- and anti-Younes militias turning Benghazi into ground zero for a very nasty fight.

It was 11:30 AM already—if the plane was on time arriving from Cairo, we were too late. But this was Libya. Nothing worked according to plan—and perhaps this would work in our favor.

The hotel lobby was deserted, with one exception: a man in glasses sitting on one of the massive leather couches in the lobby, writing in a notebook. It looked like David Kirkpatrick, the *New York Times* correspondent who had been covering the Libyan Revolution out of Cairo.

"We need to grab our passports and go," I exhorted Ahmed while trying to call the taxi driver we had been using the previous few days. We drove in and out of thick midday traffic, through a few checkpoints, and finally emerged onto the airport road forty minutes later. Mercifully, the inbound flight was an hour late. And though the entire foreign aid contingent seemed to be there, there were a few more seats.

An hour later, the plane touched down at Heraklion International Airport in Crete. Ahmed and I got up from the narrow, metal-framed seats and pushed our way out.

Suddenly, Ahmed and I found ourselves in a visa line, each carrying a small bag with a change of clothes—we'd had to leave our suitcases in the rush—just behind a group of Australian and Israeli tourists in T-shirts and sandals. The distance between Crete and Benghazi is only 300 miles—but it might as well have been 3,000. Few here were the least bit concerned with, or probably even aware of, what was happening in Libya. We found a hotel, and I set to work writing up what I had just seen for an article in *Foreign Policy* titled "Benghazi Blues." A few days later, I received an email from Chris:

> Ethan—Congrats on a very well-written piece. Balanced and detailed. You captured the mood and the issues very well. Sorry to miss your visit. See you next time, inshallah.[5]

That was a typical State Department understatement. Chris knew as well as I did that the Younes killing was a huge event. Effectively, the Islamists had just declared war on the NTC. That might now split the rebel camp, which could spell the end of the revolution—or its radicalization. If there was a wake-up call for Washington to pay more attention to what was going on in Libya, this was it.

13

The Fall

Within days of Younes's assassination, the impasse at the Oil Crescent was broken, and the rebels were now lurching toward Tripoli.

Younes's opponents cited this as proof that Younes had been the problem: a double agent holding up the rebel advance on Gaddafi. More likely, the speed of the advance was due to increased Western-backed military support, much of which wound up in the hands of the Islamists.

Within three short weeks, the Libyan rebels—Islamists, non-Islamists, fighters from the central coastal city of Misrata and from the Jebel Nafusa Mountains—were in sight of the Libyan capital. The Islamists, under the leadership of Abdulhakim Belhaj, other former LIFG members, and the Sallabi brothers, had their plan for taking Tripoli. Mahmoud Jibril's groups had theirs and increasingly looked to the United Arab Emirates to counterbalance Qatar's support to the Islamists.

The Battle for Tripoli began on August 20, 2011, and NATO cruise missiles hit military infrastructure targets in and around the capital. Gaddafi's defenses collapsed far more quickly than expected, leaving fighters from outside Tripoli scrambling to get to their predetermined positions.

Ultimately, much of the credit for Gaddafi's fall went not to the eastern or Misuratan militias, but to the residents of Tripoli themselves, who rose up against the regime en masse. Gaddafi's elite forces surrendered quickly, allowing the rebels to enter the capital without much resistance.[1]

On August 23, the day after Gaddafi and his family fled, an ambulance delivered Belhaj to the front of Gaddafi's Bab Al Aziziya (Beloved Gate) compound, where Belhaj made a statement before a bank of Al Jazeera TV cameras, in the same spot that Gaddafi had issued his infamous "zenga zenga" speech.

"The tyrant has fled, and we are chasing him," Belhaj proclaimed.[2] It was a shrewd move. Belhaj's performance elicited an immediate backlash from many of his adversaries and allies, including the Misrata militias, who felt he'd upstaged them and taken credit for their work.

At just that moment, Mahmoud Jibril, Libya's de facto prime minister, was in Doha, meeting with the Qatari crown prince, Sheikh Hamad.

"I'll never forget it," Jibril said. "I was sitting with His Highness, talking about how we could initiate a meeting with different forces to do coalition work and avert conflict. All of a sudden the chairman of Al Jazeera whispered in His Highness's ear. The Crown Prince disengaged and swiveled his chair 180 degrees to face a large flat-screen TV. There was Belhaj, in front of Gaddafi's compound, claiming to have liberated Tripoli. I was shocked. The Crown Prince and his entourage left the room. That moment I knew the hijacking of the revolution was underway."[3]

By the time the rebels moved on Gaddafi's compound, Bab Al Aziziya, on August 22, Gaddafi and his sons Mutassim and Saif were already en route by car to Sirte, where the family could count on the support of the local tribes.

This must have been a supremely disorienting experience for Gaddafi, suddenly thrust into a Hobbesian world with a cadre of his closest aides, moving from safe house to safe house while his people foraged for food and the Misrata militias closed in. Gaddafi was eventually found by one of these militias, crouching in a drainage pipe. He looked up at his captors and asked, "What's this? What's this, my sons? What are you doing?"[4]

Gaddafi's tormentors sodomized, then killed him, then put his and his son Mutassim's bodies on gruesome display in a Misratan meat locker. This was an early, visible, and disturbing sign of the raw rage and regional tensions that had the potential to tear Libya apart if something wasn't done to establish order, quickly.

While Gaddafi faced a gruesome end in Sirte, Saif was headed due south in an all-terrain vehicle toward the picture-perfect Saharan oases of Ubari, whose dunes' high iron content produces a striking shade of red. His destination was Libya's southern border with Niger, but his two-car convoy was intercepted by fighters from the northwestern town of Zintan, who had been tipped off by Saif's guide.

On October 18, less than a month after the fall of Tripoli, Secretary of State Clinton flew in a military plane from Malta to Tripoli, to meet with Jibril and other representatives of the new transitional government, which had just relocated from Benghazi. She pledged more political and economic help, following a commitment of 135 million dollars in aid, 40 million of which was earmarked to track down as many as possible of an estimated 20,000 shoulder-launched antiaircraft missiles— MANPADS—that had been looted from Gaddafi's stockpiles in the wake of the intervention. Many were believed to be defective, but a working device is capable of taking down a commercial airliner. These weapons posed an immediate threat to the international community.

Clinton explained to Jibril that the amount of assistance was low because the political mood in Washington was not generous. And, the secretary warned, the rebels needed to get a grip on the militias.[5] Two days later, in Kabul, Afghanistan, Clinton got the news that Gaddafi had been killed in Sirte. "We came, we saw, he died," the secretary quipped (referencing a line attributed to Julius Caesar, following a quick victory in the Roman provinces).[6]

Though the end of the Gaddafi rule may have brought some closure, it didn't bring stability. Over the course of the following year, from October 2011 to September 2012, the struggle between the "progressives" and the "Islamists" continued. The NTC moved from Benghazi to Tripoli—along with militias from all over the country, and others that formed on the spot, all looking to use their armed status as *thuwwar* (revolutionaries) to extort money from the government, against the backdrop of preparations for national elections. Fighters from the coastal city of Misrata, which had suffered sustained and ruthless shelling by Gaddafi's forces, had allied with Islamist militias while various other regional militias staked out their positions to feed on the spoils of war. Abdulhakim Belhaj was named head of the Tripoli Military Council, responsible for security in the capital.

It didn't take long for the Islamists' and the militias' influence to be felt visibly within the interim Libyan government's policy. Mustafa Abdel Jalil, the chairman of the NTC, was widely known to be a devout Muslim, but he apparently wasn't a member of the Muslim Brotherhood and didn't have any known sympathies with the more extreme groups, many of which saw him as an enemy—a liberal—not an ally. But with the growth of the Islamist militias, and increasing death threats against him (as there were against Jibril), he was under enormous pressure to comply with the militias' demands, which included proclaiming that the New Libya was on its way to being an Islamic state. In his liberation speech on October 23, Abdel Jalil told a flag-waving crowd in Benghazi that Libya would be democratic but more strictly Islamic, in its laws and practices.[7] Among other things, polygamy would now be legal. This created an uproar among many Libyans, who felt that this was an attempt by Islamists from outside Libya to impose their own brand of fundamentalist Islam on them. "We're all Muslims" was the public refrain.[8]

On November 24, Abdurrahim El Keib, a professor of engineering, became Libya's interim prime minister. Around the same time, Belhaj traveled to Syria, via Istanbul, to meet with representatives from the Free Libyan Army.[9] With him was his deputy, Mahdi Harati, an Irish-Libyan Islamist commander. (Harati would later draw attention when he claimed in an interview that the CIA had given him suitcases of cash to assist with the Libyan Revolution.[10]) The Libyan rebels—but particularly the Islamists—had expressed strong solidarity with the Syrian Revolution and sought to project some of the momentum they had helped generate in Libya to oust Syrian President Bashar al-Assad. This was a relatively unnoticed, but important, development, as it marked the beginning of a revolving door for fighters going back and forth from Libya to Syria. Harati, who had created his own fighting battalion in Libya, set about forming a Syria-based militia called Liwa' al Ummah (Banner of the Islamic Community).

London-based journalist Tam Hussein, who collaborated with Algerian Islamist leader Abdullah Anas on an autobiography of Anas, interviewed Harati in Malta several years later. Hussein says he couldn't quite place Harati, or his beliefs: Was he a jihadist or a moderate Islamist? It wasn't clear.[11] Harati and Belhaj both described Liwa' al Ummah as a moderate Islamist militia. Syria analyst Charles Lister refers to Liwa' al Ummah and Harati as "not extremist by any means, but perhaps more ideologically aligned with the thinking of the Muslim Brotherhood."[12] Others saw the Harati–Belhaj relationship in a less forgiving way. Sir John Jenkins, Arabic-speaking UK ambassador to Libya from October to November 2011, and the author of the never-released UK government report on the Muslim Brotherhood, says that: "In Libya, Belhaj and Harati were among the worst of the Islamists . . . They presented as moderates, but they were hard-core jihadis."[13] Regardless of what Harati's exact ideological flavor was, this expedition would mark the start of a deep association between Libyan and Syrian Islamist rebels.

After some months, a video surfaced of Saif's dazed arrival in Zintan. With his head wrapped in a headdress of the semi-nomadic Tuareg, he winced from the pain of two severed fingers on his right hand. In the second half of the spliced video, Saif is heard warning his captors about his former Islamist allies: "You're in the valley I was in, climbing to the top of the mountain, where you will see the bigger picture—they'll betray you as they betrayed me."[14] This was the Gaddafi line at that point: that the revolution was incited by jihadists, criminals, and drug dealers. But Saif was the point man for nearly all regime reconciliation initiatives with the Islamists. He had been convinced, for a time, of their mutual interests if not goodwill, and so his expressions of feelings of betrayal were likely genuine.

Luckily for Saif, it wasn't the Islamists who captured him. If he were going to be captured by anyone in Libya, the Zintanis were among the better options. Though not sympathetic to the Gaddafi regime, they were suspicious of foreign influence in the evolving conflict, and Qatar in particular, and held Saif under house arrest for several years, shielding him from the Islamists, as well as extradition to the International Criminal Court (ICC). In November 2011, the ICC issued a warrant for Saif's arrest, linked to charges that Saif had participated in war crimes at the start of the revolution.[15]

Through all the years of the LIFG's underground warfare against Gaddafi, few people in Libya knew who the LIFG leaders were or what they looked like. In the months following Gaddafi's fall, many of them became public figures—particularly Belhaj, whose fame was sealed by his Al Jazeera TV appearance in front of Gaddafi's compound, just after Gaddafi had fled. More media attention followed the revelation of details about the extraordinary rendition program. A letter had been discovered in the rubble of Bab Al Aziziya that Mark Allen, head of MI6's counterterrorism unit, had written to Gaddafi's spymaster Moussa Koussa on the rendition of Belhaj and his wife: "I congratulate you on the safe arrival of [Belhaj] . . . It was the least we could do for you."[16]

Predictably, this made for juicy copy, as the media bathed in the irony of Western intelligence agencies having to digest the idea that they now might have to collaborate with their former victims.

"In Libya, Former Enemy Is Recast in the Role of Ally" read the headline of a *New York Times* piece published on September 1. "Subjected to extraordinary rendition on behalf of the United States," the copy read, "[Albdulhakim Belhaj] is in charge of the military committee responsible for keeping order in Tripoli, and, he says, is a grateful ally of the United States and NATO."[17]

Some Western journalists attempted to tease out of the former LIFG leaders more about their conversion from Al Qaeda affiliates to self-professed democrats and architects of a post-Gaddafi order. Belhaj had a tendency to laugh off any concerns. He had "no Islamic agenda," he said, and would transfer his men to the formal police and military after the end of the revolution.[18] His French-language biography carried the change-affirming title *From Jihad to the Polls*.

In 2014 Belhaj won the right to sue the former UK foreign secretary and the ex-head of counterterrorism at the MI6, as well as the two agencies themselves, over their torture and rendition.[19] This too was good press for the erstwhile LIFG, as it reinforced the general perception that they were not terrorists but Mandela-like figures, who managed to bury their hatreds for the good of their country and were now channeling their complaints by hiring lawyers and working through the Western legal system.

These lawsuits and the details they revealed about the rendition programs were, needless to say, extremely embarrassing for the West. The United Kingdom paid out over 11 million British pounds in legal fees and 500,000 pounds compensation to Belhaj and his wife. UK Prime Minister Theresa May further issued an apology, which Belhaj's lawyer called "unprecedented," for the United Kingdom's role in his rendition.[20]

Back in Washington, many were starting to look at Libya with serious buyer's remorse. With the potential for yet another failed state following an American military intervention, the Americans were facing the costs of committing to a situation it still only partly understood.

And it is around this time that the media started to look more favorably on the LIFG—at least publicly, and for a range of complex reasons, not least of which was the fact that the Western powers had been caught red-handed. The United States and United Kingdom were undeniably behind the extraordinary renditions, for which there was no adequate apology. There was a certain journalistic glee in this revelation, amplified by a bit of political correctness: one current affairs commentator complained that the LIFG had been unfairly criticized because it "presented the ideal profile of a terrorist."[21]

From Washington and London's perspective, the best that could be hoped for from a public relations standpoint was to take some ownership of the fiasco and hope it all went away. But there was something else going on. It seems that some in London and Washington were still hoping that the LIFG and their allies' conversion was bankable. There may also have been an aspect, particularly in the Obama administration, of following the path of least resistance.

Jacqueline O'Rourke, in her book *Representing Jihad*, describes a Western tendency at this time to switch from "Bad Arab" to "Good Arab" stereotypes to emphasize the idea that the war between the United States and Islam was over.[22] It's also worth noting that there were a couple of outliers within the Libyan Islamists who *didn't* mince words about how they felt about the Americans, and made clear that the *Corrections* were (at least for them) not all they were cracked up to be. One was Abu Sufian Bin Qumu, a former driver for bin Laden, whom the Americans captured in Afghanistan and rendered to Guantanamo Bay before delivering him back to the Gaddafi regime in 2007. Bin Qumu would become one of the most prominent Salafi jihadists in Libya and never concealed his contempt for the United States and anger at his mistreatment. The United States would hear from him again in the coming years.

It is easy to get lost in all these details. But taking a step back, one must marvel at the absurdity of the flip-flopping interactions involving the United States, Britain, Muammar Gaddafi, the LIFG, and the Muslim Brotherhood from the 1980s to the 2011 intervention, and beyond.

One moment dictators like Gaddafi were the sworn enemy and groups like the LIFG were covert allies; then Gaddafi became the ally and the LIFG was the enemy; then they're both allies of a sort to each other and the West. And whose side is the Brotherhood on, exactly? At each turn, the United States made a decision that turned what might otherwise have been a manageable situation worse. Roles change, but the game is constant—a process of trying to gain a short-term advantage by co-opting an adversary, only to realize, once again, that the conversion was only skin-deep.

14

The Ides of February

It had been nearly a year since Ahmed and I had decided to drop everything and look for ways to help Benghazi. In that time, we had enlisted the interest of the emergency medicine departments of three of America's best teaching hospitals and a number of specialist organizations, one of which was focused on screening for diabetic retinopathy (a condition that causes blindness, and which we believed was prevalent in Libya).

But if the early days were challenging, by early 2012, Ahmed's and my trips to Benghazi via Istanbul were becoming more and more fraught. It increasingly felt like we had a small amount of time to accomplish something that might last. And if we failed, it would all be for naught.

During our first year working in Benghazi, Ahmed and I had managed to raise operating expenses (somewhat ironically) by consulting for some of the larger NGOs that had either received substantial US government grants or were hoping to, mainly in the area of democracy-building. We would receive a small grant from the US Embassy, and Benghazi businesses underwrote a training session for Libyan medics.

All in all, we were hopeful. But we were constantly aware of how much more we could be doing had we been able to raise more funds. So while Ahmed made a trip back to Benghazi, I'd go back to Washington to lobby for resources, and vice versa. On one of these trips to D.C., I finally had the chance to speak with Chris Stevens face-to-face.

*   *   *

On February 15, 2012, Chris Stevens and I met at a nondescript café in Foggy Bottom, a couple of blocks from the State Department. Chris's tour in Libya as envoy to the transitional government had ended in November 2011, and he'd been back in Washington, D.C., since then waiting for confirmation as ambassador.

At this point, Chris and I had been corresponding back and forth for seven years about Libya, our impressions of the place, and its prospects—and how much we enjoyed our time there. But due to our crisscrossing schedules, we had never met in person. I wanted to interview him for the book I was writing on the Libyan Revolution.[1]

I also wanted to get his take on pieces of the Libyan Revolution he had witnessed from Benghazi and to update him on Ahmed's and my medical infrastructure efforts in Benghazi. I had no idea then that this would be the first and last time Chris and I would be in the same room. In retrospect, what Chris told me during this meeting would make it much easier for me to understand his motivations for traveling to Benghazi the following September.

I knew what Chris looked like from articles in the State Department magazine; from his portrait in the Foreign Service Institute, when he became number two at the US Embassy in Tripoli in 2007; and from mutual friends' descriptions of him—tall, lanky, a shock of blond hair tinged white. He was dressed in the "State Department uniform," blue jacket, khakis, and a tie. We spotted each other immediately, and the in-person dynamic flowed from our correspondence. Chris hadn't been back to Benghazi since November and was clearly feeling impatient—and concerned. He wanted to know my impressions from our most recent trip.

Chris didn't seem as enthusiastic as I had expected about his pending ambassadorship. Many in the department glowed in his appointment, which was widely seen as a victory for expertise over politics, a win for those who preferred being in the field to working the fluorescent corridors of the C Street "Main State" complex.

After a few minutes, Chris asked if he could speak off the record. He said his absence from Benghazi had been weighing upon him.

"You understand how critical stability in Benghazi is to the revolution and to Libya—we're simply not there. Literally. The United States isn't present."

Chris said that he had been pushing as hard as he could to make the case for deeper US engagement in Benghazi—particularly upgrading the US Mission to a formal consulate—but the State Department wasn't responding as quickly as needed, and time was running out: "If things get any worse, Westerners won't be able to safely travel there without a heavy security contingent," he told me.[2]

At this point Ahmed arrived, in a particularly cheery mood, a contrast to what seemed Chris's somewhat glum—or subdued—vibe. I introduced the two of them, and Ahmed and I gave Chris a rundown of where we thought we were with our medical projects in Benghazi.

We told Chris we had just come from meetings at USAID (United States Agency for International Development) about possible partnerships, as well as funding of our partners' work. Their Libya team came to hear us out and, though very cordial and attentive, were apologetic that USAID had no available budget for medical projects in Libya. I wondered what was going on—nearly a year had passed since the US intervention, and from the perspective of those of us on the ground, it was very hard to see any direct US development impact. The projects that did come to our attention had a surreal air to them: one proposal funded by a major tech company in partnership with USAID proposed to teach Libyan children how to use computers by outfitting buses with computers and Wi-Fi connections and driving them from city to city. Given the proliferation of militias and rise in kidnappings—let alone the very bad Internet connections—this struck us as a miserable idea. Other groups—some American, but mostly French and European— were proposing to build enormous new hospitals. But the problem wasn't hospital buildings; there was plenty of capacity. The bottleneck was expertise, supplies, training, and medications. Some of those NGOs received tens of millions of dollars, of which very little actually made it to Libya, apparently because they had no idea with whom to work, or how. And yet Ahmed and I had managed by being present, on the ground, to seed a number of projects with practically no funding. It was possible. But again, time was running out.

The same week I met with Stevens in Washington, Senator John McCain was back in Tripoli—on his third trip to Libya since the start of the revolution. Though McCain was highly critical of the Obama administration on other issues, he was also one of the few Republican lawmakers who visibly supported Obama's intervention in Libya. McCain saw the Arab Spring revolutions as a defining moment for a region struggling to remove the shackles of authoritarianism, and he decided to support the uprisings in person, taking substantial personal risks to visit with rebel leaders in both Libya and Syria.

McCain's first visit to Libya was in April 2011. He wrote in his 2018 memoir that the Obama administration tried to discourage him from going on the grounds that it was not safe: "my repeated insistence that I be allowed to go was met with repeated resistance until the Qataris offered to fly me into the city [Benghazi]."[3] McCain's advisor and biographer, Mark Salter, would write after the senator's death in 2018 that the administration's objections were "not unreasonable," given the security situation.[4]

It was there, in Benghazi, that McCain met then US Envoy Chris Stevens for the first time.[5] McCain said he felt the Libyans' jubilation in breaking free from the Gaddafi regime. He joined them in Freedom Square (previously Tree Square), in front of the Benghazi courthouse. The senator said that he was touched by the warmth and determination of those he met.

As for Stevens, McCain said he liked him from the moment they met, even though "his politics were decidedly liberal."[6] The two agreed that rebuilding Libya should be an American priority: "We saw Libya the same way," McCain said. "We were both enthusiastic about its prospects . . . We both believed it was essential for the U.S. to be engaged in that project."[7] It was another sign that Stevens wasn't alone in his desire to do more than what the White House script called for in Libya.

Over the years, McCain had emerged as a leading voice of conscience within the Republican party. McCain would return to Libya in September 2011—Tripoli this time—just after the fall of Gaddafi's regime, and then in February 2012. It was on the February trip that the senator came up with an unusual request: he wanted to meet Abdulhakim Belhaj, the former emir of the Libyan Islamic Fighting Group.

It is not completely clear who suggested this meeting. Salter suggests that it was Tom Malinowski—a former diplomat and anti-torture activist who was then the Washington director for the NGO Human Rights Watch (and would be elected to Congress in 2018).[8]

According to Salter, Malinowski flagged to McCain Belhaj's status as one of the LIFG that the United States had captured, tortured, and rendered to Gaddafi in 2004. And Malinowski apparently noted that Belhaj had become a believer in democracy and forgiven the United States for what it had done to him. He also noted that after the fall of Tripoli, Belhaj had helped "calm tensions and lawlessness in Tripoli as various militias roamed the city."[9]

Belhaj's story was bound to resonate with McCain, who as a prisoner of war in Vietnam had been tortured to the point where he nearly took his own life.[10] McCain had supported President George W. Bush's push to invade Iraq in 2003, but once it became clear that the United States was engaged in the torture of what the Bush administration called "enemy combatants"—a legal invention concocted to skirt the letter of conventions covering the humane treatment of prisoners of war—McCain became a vocal opponent of these practices and was one of the sponsors of the Detainee Treatment Act of 2005, which sought to prohibit the "cruel, inhuman or degrading" treatment of prisoners by any US agency, anywhere.[11]

McCain was told of the torture of Belhaj's six-months-pregnant wife and the fact that before turning Belhaj over to the Gaddafi regime,

Belhaj's American captors showed him a picture of her, with duct tape around her face, wrists bound, and naked.[12] For McCain, it was the "degradation of Belhaj's pregnant wife, for the purpose of humiliating her and her husband" that "shocked my conscience, and made me ashamed."[13]

After meeting Belhaj in person, McCain issued a rather remarkable apology: "As an elected representative of my country," he said, "I apologize for what happened, for the way you and your wife were treated, and for all you suffered because of it."[14] McCain told Belhaj that the two might have disagreements about politics and the future of the region, "But as long as you're committed to the democratic process, we can have a good relationship."[15] According to Salter, the CIA station chief in Benghazi expressed his displeasure with McCain's meeting with Belhaj and his subsequent statements, a clear sign that there were differences in how the CIA, NSC, and State Department viewed the LIFG. On the subject of his apology, McCain brushed off the criticism, saying, "I don't care, he was owed one."[16]

That may be true. But the fact that McCain seemed to be unaware of other concerning aspects of the LIFG history (and other salient details of the situation in Libya) is also striking—and presumably at least in part a reflection of the overall poor state of American intelligence on Libya, given that Senator McCain was a ranking member of the Senate Armed Services Committee at the time and as such might have been expected to have had access to better information than many of his legislative colleagues.

The picture that emerges here is one of a degree of American vulnerability in Libya of which senior officials, both Democrats and Republicans, seem to have been completely unaware. And one has to assume that interactions like the one between McCain and Belhaj helped broadcast that vulnerability to others inclined to thwart American interests, not only in Libya but across the region.

15

On the Eve of the Attack

It had been more than a year since I wrote my *Foreign Policy* dispatch from Crete, elaborating on what the Good-Hearted Bookseller had called, simply, the "impending darkness." A year in this kind of situation is an eternity. And Chris Stevens knew that well. After walking into the aftermath of the Younes killing, my next two trips to Benghazi were calm by comparison. That would change.

In the spring and summer of 2012, the number of attacks on foreigners in Benghazi, particularly diplomats, skyrocketed. The convoy of the head of the UN Mission to Libya was attacked, and an improvised explosive device (IED) was lobbed over the US Mission wall in April. The International Committee for the Red Cross headquarters in Benghazi was hit by two RPGs in May. A month later, in June, an IED damaged the front gate of the US Mission, and the British ambassador's convoy was hit by RPGs, which led to the departure of the British from the city. In late July, a team of Iranian medics from the Red Crescent was reported to have been kidnapped.[1]

Stevens had been receiving intelligence reports back at the US Embassy in Tripoli on the evolving situation in Benghazi regularly during the summer. An August 8 cable from the Embassy in Tripoli describes a frightening security situation in Benghazi. Whether Chris Stevens wrote it or not, it's quite possible he added the title, "The Guns of August" (a reference to Barbara Tuchman's classic book on the start of World War I). As with "Die Hard in Derna," Chris was adept at plumbing popular culture for catchy, evocative titles for the internal cables, which had to be sexed up to appeal to a broader audience back in Washington. Tuchman's book has been described as a "spell-binding exploration of the failure of great-power diplomacy to prevent a war no one wanted."[2] The title choice was prescient.

The cable notes that "since the eve of the [July] elections, Benghazi has moved from trepidation to euphoria and back as a series of violent incidents has dominated the political landscape during the Ramadan holiday."[3]

Then on August 16, Stevens signed off on an "Emergency Action" cable requesting an extension of security coverage in Libya to cover the Americans in Tripoli, as well as visits and diplomatic travel in-country (which would have meant, in particular, Benghazi).[4] In that classified cable, he said, "RSO [regional security officer] expressed concerns with the ability to defend Post in the event of a coordinated attack due to limited manpower, security measures, weapons capabilities, host nation support, and the overall size of the compound."[5]

At the time, US diplomats in Libya were protected by a sixteen-member military Site Security Team (SST). But the State Department felt it could be accomplished with the help of local security forces—meaning, in Benghazi, the February 17 Martyrs Brigade (or Feb 17), about which there were ongoing concerns, not only with regard to their loyalty to the Libyan government, but also their friendliness to the United States.[6] Senior management officers at the State Department were aware of the security reports but explicitly told the Embassy not to press the point as their requests would be denied.[7]

The United States Africa Command (AFRICOM) head General Carter Ham, who had a cordial relationship with Stevens, saw the Emergency Action cable sent out under Stevens's name and reached out to Stevens directly with an offer to extend SST coverage for a few months. Stevens has been described as turning these offers down, but his number two, Gregory Hicks, would later testify to the House Committee on Benghazi that "Chris concurred in that decision because he didn't really feel like he had, you know, much leverage other than that."[8] All of this sounds strikingly similar to security concerns I had in Tripoli back in 2005, as well as what Ambassador Bushnell described happened back in 1998 in the lead-up to the East Africa embassy bombings.

The number of State Department security agents assigned to the Embassy in Tripoli dropped suddenly from thirty-four to six. And to top it off, the local security in Benghazi—the forces the State Department wanted the Mission to rely on even more, the February 17 Martyrs Brigade—was in an open dispute with the Mission about pay and contracts. Documents found later at the burned-out mission indicated that the local guards, hired by the British security firm Blue Mountain (many of whom were members of the February 17 Martyrs Brigade), were being paid the equivalent of four dollars an hour.[9] As of September 9, the day before Chris's arrival to Benghazi, the Feb 17 guards had effectively gone on strike, saying they would no longer provide protection for any travel by US personnel outside the Benghazi Mission.

As Hicks described the situation: "On the morning of September 11th, when [David McFarland] flies back to Tripoli . . . [we have] five Diplomatic security special agents protecting the Ambassador and Sean Smith. In Tripoli, we have four[,] we have a Regional Security Officer and three Assistant Regional Security Officers to protect 28 diplomatic personnel."[10]

While the State Department's DS scanned the horizon for any specific, actionable threats against diplomatic personnel, other agencies were more strategic. Some US government officials were aware that Al Qaeda was actively scouting out Benghazi as a node for its expansion within Libya. In August, a report authored by the Library of Congress with a partner in the intelligence community[11] identified Al Qaeda as an emerging threat in Libya, motivated by the interest of Al Qaeda leader Ayman Al-Zawahiri in developing a presence there. Al-Zawahiri and Al Qaeda senior leadership had sent "trusted senior operatives" from Pakistan to Libya to oversee this process. The report explained that Al Qaeda's Libya strategy was to remain low-profile, in order not to draw attention to the underlying strategy, and that it "refrains from using the al-Qaeda name." The report further claimed that Al Qaeda was working through affiliates like Ansar al-Sharia (Supporters of Islamic Law, and the group that would later be identified by the Americans as the lead in the attack) and that Al Qaeda likely had at least 200 members in Libya. It specifically mentioned Wissam Bin Hamid as someone affiliated with Al Qaeda—but likely not the leader of the group in Libya given his visibility. On the other hand, it said Ansar al-Sharia, led by former LIFG member Abu Sufian Bin Qumu, "has increasingly embodied al-Qaeda's presence in Libya . . . and hatred of the West, especially the United States."[12] The report noted that though "some of its former leaders have distanced themselves from al-Qaeda and reiterated their intent to play by the democratic rules of the new Libya, clandestinely, some former members of LIFG may be among those helping to create the al-Qaeda network."

The Library of Congress report is notable for a few reasons. First, it's a remarkably good snapshot of what was happening in Benghazi at the time. Second, it was produced using open-source materials, that is, the Internet. No fancy spy techniques needed here. Just someone capable of reading Arabic and knowing where to look. Third, it wasn't written by core US intelligence assets—so though it did ultimately get circulated within the US government, that came *after* the attack, when everyone could look *it* up on the Internet. In retrospect, it shouldn't really have been that hard to convince people things were spiraling.

When I met Chris Stevens in Washington in February 2012, he mentioned that he was having trouble making his case for more attention to Benghazi. But it seemed in the meanwhile that he had managed to make the case for an upgrade of the Benghazi Mission to a consulate to Secretary Clinton directly. That status change would make the Mission eligible for more services from Washington, not least of which would be security. And that, his colleagues say, produced a kind of catch-22: In order to get the upgrade, which came from unused funds previously earmarked for Iraq, Chris would need to make an inspection of the Mission before the end of September.[13] His desire to upgrade the Mission to Consulate was one of the strongest motivations for his travel, but there were other factors, which couldn't be separated from that objective. This included advance work and reconnaissance for a planned trip by Secretary of State Clinton to Benghazi in October—a perfect opportunity to announce the diplomatic commitment Stevens was working to secure. Hicks would later testify that the secretary's trip would be an opportunity to announce the commitment that Stevens was looking to secure.

As far as the American public and US lawmakers were concerned, Libya could still be described at this point as a success story, despite the subterranean forces that were about to flip over the table. National and local elections had gone remarkably smoothly, without major incidents of violence or fraud. Moderates came out ahead on the party lists. If Clinton were able to travel to Benghazi and announce that the United States hadn't forgotten where the revolution started, and that more assistance was forthcoming, she could end her term on a high note, putting a bracket around both the intervention in Libya and her term as secretary.

Hicks later testified that due to Stevens's contacts in the region, and the trust Stevens had with the local leaders and population, "he was the only person that we felt could go to Benghazi and get a clear picture of the political situation there and the security situation there as well."[14]

In service to these goals, Stevens and Bubaker Habib had arranged to open an "American Corner"—the kind of small library that had been first proposed back in 2005, within an English language school run by Habib.

The RSO in Tripoli, Eric Nordstrom, would say that he was uncomfortable with the idea of Chris traveling to Benghazi then but "knew he was bound and determined to go."[15]

September 9, 2012

In the week before the attack on the US Mission, David McFarland arrived in Benghazi for a ten-day stint as principal officer at the Benghazi Mission. A mid-ranking American diplomat in his thirties, McFarland had only been in Libya for a few months, and this would be his first visit to Benghazi. According to Habib, Stevens's trusted local advisor, McFarland asked Stevens if they could overlap in Benghazi for a few days so McFarland could get to know the eastern region a bit better. Stevens apparently had planned not only to visit Benghazi on this trip but also to travel to several other cities in the east. Stevens said no. He felt McFarland was needed back in Tripoli.

One of McFarland's last meetings before flying back to Tripoli was with the February 17 Martyrs Brigade. McFarland wanted to make sure there weren't any unresolved issues with Feb 17 and its security coverage in advance of Ambassador Stevens's visit. Habib accompanied McFarland to the Feb 17 headquarters, a modern conference facility by the sea.[16] There, the two met with two of the city's most prominent Islamist militia leaders, Wissam Bin Hamid and Mohammed Al Gharabli, while being careful not to reveal that Ambassador Stevens was on his way to Benghazi.

Before the revolution, Bin Hamid had been an auto mechanic. As one of Benghazi's revolutionaries, he learned to command respect, and he had a knack for getting along with difficult characters. After the fall of Tripoli, he was offered a position as commander of the Libya Shield One militia, which technically reported to the Islamist-influenced (if not -controlled) Ministry of Defense. The Shields were directed to stabilize the country and were shifted out to other parts of Libya, including the south. Pictures would later surface of Bin Hamid's Libya Shield One colleagues standing in front of variants of the Al Qaeda flag.[17]

The other militia leader McFarland and Habib met was Mohammed Al Gharabli,[18] who before the revolution ran a sandwich truck. Al Gharabli was head of the Rafallah Sahati Brigade, implicated in the assassination of Abdel Fattah Younes a little over a year before. One of his operatives, Ahmed Abu Khattala, would become the main American suspect in the coming events.[19]

McFarland described the meeting in a draft cable back to Washington that would require Stevens's sign-off before it was transmitted to Washington (and would later be leaked).[20] The two militia leaders said they hoped the United States would help them politically, in the wrangling going on back in Tripoli. They were quite specific: they wanted to see the Muslim Brotherhood candidate for prime minister, Awad al-Barassi (then minister of electricity), win over the "liberal progressivist" candidate, former interim prime minister and foreign minister Mahmoud Jibril. They wanted this, they said, because al-Barassi would appoint Fawzi Bukatif, Feb 17's leader, as Libya's minister of defense. This would then "open the MOD [Ministry of Defense] and other security ministries and offices to plum appointments for his most favored brigade commanders—giving February 17 and Libya Shield tacit control of the armed forces."[21] Then the two said that "if Jibril won . . . they would not continue to guarantee security in Benghazi, a critical function they asserted they were currently providing."[22] As part of their harangue, Bin Hamid urged the United States to pressure US firms to invest in Libya.[23]

As the cable made its way into the diplomatic community following the Benghazi attack, the obvious question was whether what these two militia leaders had said was meant to be a threat. Neither Habib nor McFarland took it that way. Habib said he read these comments as typical bluster, attempts by young militia leaders to inflate their importance to the Americans. He mentioned that Bin Hamid told them that he loved American classic cars, and he hoped to travel to the United States in the future.

McFarland later said that he "did not take that as a threat against U.S. interests, the U.S. compound, U.S. persons, or anything else." According to McFarland's understanding, Libya Shield was "emerging . . . and had numbers to them." He described the meeting as a fascinating opportunity to get to try to learn "which militias they belonged to and who was in control of them and what their ideology was . . . they disagreed on many of those things."[24]

The first the American public heard of the McFarland–Habib meeting with Bin Hamid and Al Gharabli was in 2013, in a *New York Times* piece written by David Kirkpatrick. Kirkpatrick drew a not-so-subtle parallel between the "boyish looking" McFarland and the young, naive US diplomat in Graham Greene's novel *The Quiet American*.[25]

September 10, 2012

Back in Tripoli at the US Embassy, defense attaché Lieutenant Colonel Brian Linvill spoke with Chris Stevens before he left for Benghazi. He said Stevens looked stressed.[26] Linvill recalled that Stevens had been preoccupied with the fallout of the national elections held on July 7—in line with his own belief in their importance, but also Washington's stress on successful elections as an indicator of the overall success of the US-led intervention. On the surface, the elections seemed to have gone very well. But in retrospect, Linvill thought the focus on elections was over-placed—that assuring security in the country should have been the primary objective. That had been the NTC's major worry as well.

The RSO at the Embassy in Tripoli assigned Stevens two additional DS agents for the trip. They were experienced and well trained but, like McFarland and many of those doing temporary duty, had never been to Benghazi before. Two agents who did know the city extremely well, according to Habib, were assigned to duty at the Embassy in Tripoli instead. That would prove to be one fateful decision among many.

In advance of Stevens's arrival and because it was the day before September 11, the Mission had requested an additional ten security cars and twenty-five guards for the compound.

The DS agents had specifically requested support from the CIA Annex in covering the gaps when Stevens went off-compound, and Stevens alerted his staff to the fact that all of them would need to be very careful given the gaps in security.

When he arrived in Benghazi on September 10, Stevens went to the CIA Annex, where he got a thorough briefing on the CIA's understanding of the situation in Benghazi—a "worsening security environment." The diplomatic security agent who briefed Stevens would later testify that Stevens paid close attention: "He took a lot of notes. It struck me a little bit that he was surprised at how fast the situation had deteriorated in eastern Libya . . . He was called in to go to his next appointment [with the Benghazi City Council] several times, and he refused to leave before we finished."[27]

Stevens asked questions about what extremist groups were now operating in Benghazi. He was told Al Qaeda in the Maghreb (AQIM), Al Qaeda in the Arabian Peninsula (AQAP), Al Qaeda Pakistan, Egyptian Islamic Jihad, and Ansar al-Sharia Derna.

Unbeknownst to Stevens or anyone else at the mission, Al Qaeda's leader Ayman Al-Zawahiri posted a message during the day to Al Qaeda's networks, announcing the death of his number two in Al Qaeda, Mohammed Hassan Al Qaid, and calling for revenge: "I proudly announce to the Muslim *ummah* [community] and to the *mujahideen* . . . the news of the martyrdom of the lion of Libya, Sheikh Hassan Mohammed Qaed . . . his blood urges you and incites you to fight and kill the crusaders."[28]

Al-Zawahiri said further: "This liar [Obama] is trying to fool Americans into believing that he will defeat Al Qaeda by killing this person or that person. But he escapes from the fact that he was defeated in Iraq and Afghanistan."[29]

The timing of Al-Zawahiri's statement is curious, and potentially important, as Al Qaid was killed several months before, on June 4, by an American drone in North Waziristan, Pakistan. His death was mentioned in an Al Qaeda statement after the IED attack on the US Mission in Benghazi on June 6. So this was old news, which Al-Zawahiri was recycling, now, just before the attack on the US Embassy in Cairo and on the US Mission in Benghazi, presumably for a purpose: either to place his personal signature on these attacks, or to get the Libyan radicals on deck for an imminent action. Al-Zawahiri had made these kinds of signals before, and they had been linked to American actions against his associates. On August 5, 1998, two days before the bombing of the US embassies in East Africa, the "International Islamic Front for Jihad," a.k.a. Al Qaeda, promised revenge against the United States for a raid in Albania that killed one member of Al-Zawahiri's organization and resulted in the extradition of others to Egypt for torture.[30]

Even before Al-Zawahiri's video message, the US government was on alert for possible 9/11 disturbances. On September 10, President Obama took a call with senior national security staff to review what had been done to protect "U.S. persons and facilities abroad," and according to Defense Secretary Leon Panetta, the US military was "already tracking an inflammatory anti-Muslim video" and was "braced for demonstrations in Cairo and elsewhere across the region."[31] Notably, that didn't include putting military assets in the region on heightened alert.

September 11, 2012

September 11 didn't start well for the US Mission in Benghazi. At 6:43 AM, one of the Mission guards saw someone in a Benghazi police uniform on the upper level of a building across the street taking photos of the Mission. The individual seemed to be part of the police contingent that was supposed to provide supplemental protection.[32]

In the world of diplomatic security, this is a "red flag" event; it suggests that someone may be casing the place for an impending attack.

Diplomatic security briefed Ambassador Stevens on the incident and had letters ready for Stevens to sign informing the Libyan Ministry of Foreign Affairs of the incident and objecting strongly to the government's lack of response to the Mission's requests for supplemental security for the anniversary of 9/11.[33]

Stevens went back to the CIA Annex sometime during the day on September 11. It was almost certainly there that he read and cleared the cable McFarland wrote describing his meeting at the Feb 17 headquarters—and added his own observations about an event with members of the Benghazi City Council and various (threatening) incidents elsewhere in the east, including attacks against Libya's Sufi shrines, which were being perpetrated across the country by Islamic fundamentalists. As for how all of this was affecting Stevens, Habib says he projected his usual air of confidence and nonchalance when he met up with him on the morning of September 11.

"It was a normal day," Habib said. "We spoke about setting up the American corner in my school the next day. Chris didn't mention Cairo—or McFarland and my meeting with Al Gharabli and bin Hamid three days before. If he was thinking about these things, he didn't give any sign of it."[34]

But Stevens *was* clearly thinking about the security at the Mission, as he signed off on a memo drafted later in the day to the Libyan Ministry of Foreign Affairs about the apparent surveillance incident, and the failure to provide more security.[35]

Around 2:00 PM on the afternoon of September 11, I spoke with Stevens on Ahmed's cell and explained where things were with the Benghazi Medical Center project—that both sides were pushing for a Memorandum of Understanding that, if it went forward, would create one of the largest, if not the largest, medical infrastructure programs in post-revolution Libya. It was then that he extended his invitation to come to the Mission for dinner.

Habib said he left Stevens about 5:00 PM to head home.

"That was the last time I saw him alive," he said.

After Habib left, Stevens met with Ali Akin, the Turkish consul general. Stevens had known Akin since he arrived in Benghazi in April 2011. The meeting ended at around 7:40 PM, when Stevens retired to his personal quarters.[36]

That meeting would get some media attention, as it raised the question of whether Stevens's presence in Benghazi might be linked to covert activities, in particular shipments of Libyan weapons to Syrian rebels—via Turkish ports (see Chapter 29). If anyone were to know about that, it was suspected the Turkish diplomat would.[37]

Just prior to the attack, diplomatic security and others were relaxing by the compound pool. Stevens was jotting notes in his diary about a variety of concerns. Particularly chilling was his last entry: "Never ending security threats."[38] For his part, Sean Smith, Stevens's information management officer (the person who manages technical support for embassy communications), seems to have been noticeably on edge, telling friends with whom he was playing an online game that he feared for his life: "Assuming we don't die tonight."[39]

Bubaker Habib is emotional when he speaks of Chris Stevens: The two spent several months working together, and Chris had come to rely on Habib's read on the pulse of Benghazi in his absence. When he got news of the attack, Habib furiously tried to reach Chris on his cell while speeding toward the Mission. One of the first people he thought to call was Wissam Bin Hamid. But he couldn't get through to him either.

"One of the infuriating things about the scandal is that people don't recognize that Chris was a hero," Habib told me several years later. I thought I knew what he meant, but I wanted him to try to elaborate. He points to the fact that Chris was in Benghazi not just on September 11, 2012, but before the fall of Tripoli—because he believed in Libya and knew how important it was to show up so that the people could see evidence of the American presence. For Benghazi natives like

Habib and Omar, the law student we will meet in Chapter 18, Chris's presence meant that the United States was paying attention.

"Chris's presence meant we still had cause for hope," Habib says.

Habib is convinced that this was Chris's primary reason for coming to Benghazi when he did—trying to keep things in Benghazi hanging together just as long as he could, until the cavalry arrived.

Part III

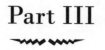

THE ATTACK AND THE SCANDAL

16

The Attack, Part II

What do you want to do?"

Fathi Al-Jehani and I had been sitting across from each other for ten minutes on the oversize black leather couches under a stairwell at the Tibesti Hotel, both of us looking at anything but each other, lost. Finally, Fathi looked at me and posed the question.

What do I want to do? I repeated to myself.

I thought out loud: "So, the Americans are gone, they've left a few hours ago. We're not getting any help there. Are there other embassies whose help we could enlist? Is the airport open?"

Regardless, it was clear we had to move from the Tibesti, where we were exposed. Fathi said what I was thinking: "Let's take you, Ahmed, and Burke to BMC. We plan the next move from there." The hospital had the advantage of being a couple of kilometers closer to the airport. There were also some big problems with going to BMC, which we were about to learn.

Fathi said that while we waited, and perhaps got some sleep, he and Laila would work to get us on the next flight out. Fathi was connected at the highest levels, as was clear when he spoke of phone calls he had during the night with Wanis Bukhamada. Bukhamada was the head of the Al-Saiqa, the Libyan special forces previously under the command of Abdel Fattah Younes, until his assassination. Known as Al Fahd Al Asmar (the Black Panther), he represented the core of the non-Islamist forces in Benghazi and would spend the next few years fighting Ansar al-Sharia.

By this time, it was close to 7:00 AM on September 12. Ahmed came down the stairs, followed a few minutes later by Dr. Thomas Burke. Fathi went out the door to take a call.

I repeated the gist of what Fathi told me.

Before we left the hotel for Fathi's SUV, I collected my passport and brought only what I could easily carry.

At the hospital, the scene was oddly quiet, given the bedlam of the previous fifteen hours—just like the rest of the city.

Dr. Laila Bugaighis came in looking pale but composed—impeccably dressed, as usual.

"Tell Ahmed and Burke to stay here, in the office," she said to me. "It's important. Don't go out."

I asked her why.

"There are a number of people being treated in the ER from last night—some of them are not friendly. We want as few people as possible knowing you're here."

It seemed too late for that, though. I could see a group of ER doctors speaking animatedly with Burke, discussing the condition Chris Stevens had been in when he arrived and their attempts to revive him. By all accounts their efforts had been heroic.

Laila said casualties kept coming in throughout the night, some of them participants in both the attack on the US Mission and the Annex. In the early morning, about the time Fathi was meeting us at the Tibesti, armed men arrived and demanded Stevens's body. BMC refused to release it without official permission. The standoff lasted about thirty minutes. There was shouting and guns drawn. "There was no choice but to cede to their demand," Laila said.

It became clear later that it was Bin Hamid's men, if not Bin Hamid himself, who had the altercation with the BMC staff and subsequently delivered Stevens to the remaining official Americans waiting at the airport.

I tried to call my parents in California, but I couldn't get through. Ahmed managed to reach his wife in the States. I listened as she urged him to come home immediately. It seemed that Ahmed had decided to stay. I felt this was a mistake at first, as he, like the rest of us, had been identified as having connections with senior US diplomats. And I imagined his wife might be relying on me to help change his mind.

Ahmed, Burke, and I spread out over a suite of offices. I found myself at a PC with a working Internet connection. I emailed my parents and told them they'd be seeing some dramatic news about Libya and not to worry. I sat for what seemed like an eternity, browsing US and international news sites for some trace of what the outside world was hearing about what we'd been through. I couldn't find much, which was odd, as certainly the Americans weren't the only ones in Benghazi. Then a story appeared stating the "Consulate" in Benghazi had been attacked and a "consular worker" had been killed.[1]

I looked up at one point to a clock hanging on a sparse white wall and noticed the hour hand nearly at 11:00 AM—the time Stevens was to have met with us here to give an American government push to the program we'd been working on with Laila and Fathi for nearly a year now. Once again, I was overcome with a sense of disbelief at what had happened.

Fathi came into the office I was in, followed by Ahmed and Burke, to confirm what we wanted to do. Did we have his okay to make flight reservations? It seemed a rhetorical question at first, but Burke had continued to insist that he wanted to stay and work with BMC on the agreement. Ahmed and I looked at each other in frustration. It was clear that there was no work to be done anytime soon, and that Fathi wasn't only being extraordinarily helpful, he also didn't want to be responsible for whatever might happen to his three American guests. He wanted us out of BMC. And out of Libya. Safe.

Fathi took me aside. "You all need to get on that flight," he said, with emphasis.

"You don't need to convince me," I said. "Please do what you need to do. I'll try my best to get them to change their minds."

Meanwhile, back at the computer screens, the State Department announced Stevens's death around 7:00 AM Eastern Standard Time—1:00 PM in Benghazi.

Around 4:00 PM, Fathi told me that he'd done it: we had seats on the Turkish flight to Istanbul.

Bravo, Fathi.

Burke by this point had come around to the idea that it was best to leave. Ahmed, however, was fixed in his plan to stay. As a Libyan, he said, he felt an obligation to stay through the immediate crisis and support Fathi and Laila. But he certainly wanted me to go. I sympathized with and respected his position, and knew Ahmed: once he decided on something, there was little use in trying to change his mind.

It was at that moment that Burke mentioned he needed to return to the hotel to get his passport. I was frustrated because it was dangerous for us to split up and we couldn't ask Fathi to make two trips to the airport, so we would have to drive back into the city center—twenty minutes or so if we were lucky—and take one of the circular bypass roads out to the airport. If he wasn't coming with us, Ahmed was taking an unnecessary added risk by joining us. He insisted on coming, though. "I need to know you are both off and okay," he said.

We followed Fathi out to the parking lot, where he cursorily pointed to what he called our "escort"—a group of men in fatigues with long, unruly beards, armed with AK-47s and pistols. Several of them wore patches on their camouflage jackets whose insignia weren't clear.

"Who are these guys?" I asked Fathi in a soft voice.

"Security," he said under his breath. "They're with the hospital."

From all indications these were not members of the official Benghazi security forces. While we didn't know it at the time, over the course of the previous few weeks Ansar al-Sharia had quietly absorbed BMC into the territory it controlled, along with one of the other hospitals in Benghazi, Al Jala. It had become common practice in the escalating fight for Islamist militias to take over public service institutions—hospitals, power stations, etc. And BMC might have had to pay the militias for "protection," under a less voluntary arrangement than the one the US Embassy had struck with the February 17 Martyrs Brigade. Whether they were friendly or not, I assumed Fathi had to have made a deal to get us safe passage to the airport.

The three of us climbed into Fathi's SUV as perhaps half a dozen bearded men, not in the best physical shape, piled into a makeshift tank that looked like something Mussolini's murderous general Rodolfo Graziani might have used in the 1930s, chasing down Omar Al Mukhtar.

When we got to the Tibesti, Burke slipped on a pair of dark sunglasses and jumped out. Our escorts got out of their tank, clutching their Kalashnikovs. One of them came up to the side of Fathi's SUV. We briefly made eye contact.

With Burke back inside the car, we headed to the airport along an empty highway, then a several-mile-long straightaway that ended in a roundabout on which an old Soviet fighter plane was impaled on a pole.

About one thousand feet before the airport, our escort peeled off, and members of another militia enveloped us. The airport at the time was still controlled by friendly forces, answering to Bukhamada. We weren't quite out of the woods yet, but the most dangerous part of the last two days was over. Burke, Fathi, and I were shuttled into a room at the side of the airport. I recognized it as what had been the VIP lounge during the Gaddafi years; the room had been furnished then with baby-blue, brass-beveled armchairs, presumably long since pilfered. We were informed that the regularly scheduled inbound plane from Istanbul was set to arrive at 6:00 PM—an hour late.

A French businessman came up to us to offer his condolences and couldn't stop talking. I later noticed that Fathi had disappeared. When I got a moment, I asked Ahmed how long he planned to stay in Benghazi. He said he wanted to stay until the "immediate crisis" was over— hopefully a couple of days. I told him I'd wait for him at Hotel Ibrahim Pasha in Istanbul, which we had used as our base on our previous trips to Libya.

We waited for the arriving passengers—if there were any—to deplane, and the other departing passengers to board. Fathi had said he would come get us once everyone else was on board, as a precaution. I could see the plane through a side window at the end of the room, and after forty-five minutes, I could tell the plane was fully boarded. There was still no sign of Fathi.

I started to worry.

"Something's wrong," I whispered to Ahmed. "This is taking too long. All the passengers boarded half an hour ago."

Finally, Fathi reappeared, shook Burke and my hands quickly, and wished us a safe flight home. Before I was able to express my gratitude for what he had done for us over the last twenty-four hours, a man came and pushed us out the door of the lounge, onto the tarmac, and into a bus that had come to take us the hundred meters to the movable staircase. I didn't have a chance to say goodbye to Ahmed, who I saw clinging to a chain-link fence, looking forlorn. I wished I had been able to change his mind and was very worried about him, but I was comforted by the fact that there were many looking after him. As Burke and I got on the bus, I shouted out to Ahmed that I'd wait for him in Istanbul and motioned for us to talk by phone. A minute later, we were at the bottom of the movable staircase attached to the plane, where men with guns motioned for us to wait.

As I stood on the tarmac, watching as the light shifted from dusk to darkness, I had a strong feeling that the events we had just witnessed would reverberate far beyond Benghazi. I couldn't, of course, have predicted the domestic political chaos that would unfold; I was thinking more of American policy for the region. Changes were coming; I just didn't know what they would look like.

Months later I got the backstory of the delay. The regular Turkish airline flight had been shifted to new equipment due to a mechanical issue, and a smaller plane had been sent in its stead, not large enough to accommodate everyone who had a ticket. The Turkish Airlines pilot didn't want to spend any more time on the ground than necessary, but Bukhamada's men wouldn't give clearance until we were on board. A standoff ensued. The commander of the Benghazi army instructed his people to board the aircraft with cash to try to convince people to give up their seats. I could imagine that whoever "volunteered" may have felt they had no choice. We got seats. (Admittedly, I'm glad I had no idea what was really happening, though the vast majority of the passengers were Libyan and a good number of those were probably making a regular trip to see relatives or do business in Istanbul.)

As soon as the flight lifted off from Benghazi, heading north out over the Mediterranean Sea, I released a breath that I had been holding for twenty-four hours. I was safe. I thought of Chris. And the fact I'd left Ahmed behind. I wrote some thoughts down on the backs of cocktail napkins. I felt it was important to preserve what happened—we were witnesses, after all. My concerns for my own well-being shifted to concerns for Libya. I was sure there would soon be a push to withdraw all US presence from Benghazi—it felt very important to call that out. And, perhaps most of all, I felt a need to pay tribute to Chris Stevens. I thought back to our conversation in Washington seven months before and felt that I understood what he was trying to do—and realized that Fathi, Burke, and I had been extremely lucky.

We arrived well after midnight in Istanbul, where Fathi's office had, amidst the chaos, managed to book Burke and me a hotel for the night. Exhausted as I was, I couldn't sleep, and I spent the next two hours writing up my notes so I wouldn't forget anything. I sent a draft op-ed

through to my editor at the *New York Times*. The editor got back to
me quickly to say he would like to publish it the next day. It appeared
on September 13 under the title "What Libya Lost." I outlined my
experience over the previous two days and made my case that America
shouldn't back away from Libya because of this tragedy. The punch line
came at the end: "In the West, we can now expect a strong temptation
among governments and private enterprise to declare the Libyan experiment a failure, and to respond by disengaging, retreating or focusing
only on the extirpation of radical elements. That would be a terrible
mistake."[2]

I noticed that Senator John McCain tweeted a link to my op-ed a
couple of days later.[3]

I was eager to get home, but the Benghazi airport closed after our flight
departed and stayed closed for several days. I couldn't reach Ahmed
until September 14. He said it was like the city was under lockdown—
as it was the morning after the attack—except that now the sky was full
of drones, racing across the sky like nails across a chalkboard. "There's
a constant screeching and pinging—it never lets up, night and day."
There were rumors, Ahmed said, that the Americans would either send
cruise missiles or stage a land invasion against the camps of the militias
suspected to have taken part in the attack.

While I was grateful not to have to contend with that, I was unset-
tled. On the hotel's suggestion, I booked a short flight south to the
Antalya coast and found a small hotel on the beach, where I could swim
and wait for Ahmed to confirm that he was on his way. I spent the next
few days in repetitive motion, swimming from one end of a wide bay
to the other, back and forth. On the second day, I swam for so long I
didn't notice that it had gotten dark. As I swam toward the shore, I
noticed five lights streak across the sky. They seemed to be at a high
altitude, moving quickly, in what looked like a missing man formation
(honoring a fallen pilot) at a military parade. There was no sound and
no contrail. A shiver ran through my body. Then the lights were gone. I

pulled myself out of the water onto smooth stones, still warm from the sun. As I walked up a wooden path to the side of the hotel, I wondered if I had imagined what I just saw, even though all of my other senses seemed intact. At that moment, I got a call on my cell.

It was the FBI, asking me to describe what had happened in Benghazi. I have little recollection of what they asked, or what I told them. I assume that I ran through a chronological account of what had happened since the attack started. They wanted to talk to me once I was back in the States.

Finally, a week after the attack, Ahmed texted me to tell me that he had managed to get a flight, so I booked my flight back to California to coincide with his three-hour layover in Istanbul. We met at a café in the transit lounge in the airport. We embraced and sat down at a table, awkwardly placed in the middle of a stream of passengers. We marveled at the insanity of what we'd just been through. The loss of Chris Stevens and the others whose names we didn't then know. We sat there facing one another, in a bubble of gratitude, as scores of people pushed their way around us, heading for their gates.

17

Cairo

While the larger story of Benghazi began in the decades prior—with Gaddafi, the LIFG, Bush, the Libyan Revolution—the immediate background to the September 11, 2012, attack began nearly 800 miles away in Cairo. In the early afternoon, on the eleventh anniversary of 9/11, a crowd began to gather outside the US Embassy in Cairo to protest a video that the vast majority of them hadn't seen.

The video in question was a fourteen-minute movie trailer for a film titled *Innocence of Muslims*, produced by a Los Angeles–based Coptic Christian from Egypt named Nakoula Basseley Nakoula (who uploaded the video under the alias "Sam Bacile"). Nakoula had a criminal history and an abiding hatred for Muslims.[1] Filmed on a Hollywood set over the course of the previous year, the film portrayed the Muslim prophet Mohammed as a pedophile and an adulterer. In one scene, the prophet points to a donkey and says, "This shall be the first Muslim animal."

The actors in the film claim Bacile had told them the movie was about a desert warrior named, implausibly, "George."[2] In post-production, Nakoula dubbed the name "Mohammed" over George. Many of the characters speak in thick New York accents. "It's just a stupid movie!" screamed a later headline in the *New York Post*.[3] And that was very true—but in the right context, and as an object with which to inflame popular anger, it was almost ideally calibrated.[4]

Two months before the Cairo Embassy protest, in the early days of July, Nakoula uploaded the video to YouTube, where it remained mostly unnoticed until September 4 when the short was dubbed into Arabic and posted to YouTube.[5] The following day, another "radical Coptic activist" in the United States posted an announcement in Arabic to his blog promoting the video along with an event by Florida pastor Terry Jones,[6] infamous for his public burning of the Koran in 2011, which was cited as the cause for a mob attack on a UN compound in Mazar-i-Sharif, Afghanistan, that killed seven UN employees.[7]

On September 8, the popular Egyptian TV channel Al Nas aired the video.[8] The leader of an Islamist political party denounced the clip as backed by "vengeful Copts, and the extremist [American] priest Terry Jones." How the film first came to the attention of the Islamists, and whether it was they who discovered and instrumentalized it, is still not clear.

On September 11, hundreds of protestors gradually gathered in front of the US Embassy not far from Tahrir Square, the focal point of the Egyptian Revolution, chanting "Down, Down America! Obama, Obama, We Are All Osama!" At one point, several in the crowd scaled the meters-high retaining wall, pulled down an American flag, set it alight, and hoisted a black Islamist flag in its place. Over the coming hours, the crowd would grow to more than 2,000.

In a later account, CNN journalist Mohamed Fahmy wrote: "I couldn't believe what I was witnessing: radical Islamists not only breaching the grounds of the US embassy, but publicly gloating about it."[9] Fahmy noticed among the protestors several prominent members of the Muslim Brotherhood and Egyptian "Salafis."[10] Also noticeable among the protestors were members of a gang of young vigilante soccer fans called the Ultras, formed in 2007, who had showed up in many of the anti-regime protests since 2011.[11]

As the protests grew, Fahmy made a call to an Islamist contact to confirm what he was seeing. His contact was no ordinary source; it was Muhammed Al-Zawahiri, the brother of then Al Qaeda leader Ayman Al-Zawahiri. Muhammed Al-Zawahiri had been jailed by Hosni Mubarak but released by the new administration of the Muslim

Brotherhood's Mohamed Morsi, who had won Egypt's presidential election in June 2012, three months earlier, by a thin margin.[12] Muhammed Al-Zawahiri confirmed that he had called for a "peaceful protest"[13] joined by different Islamist factions including the Egyptian Islamic Jihad[14] (the organization formerly led by Ayman Al-Zawahiri, which merged with Al Qaeda in 1998 but kept its Egyptian brand) and the Hazem Salah Abu Ismail movement—both hard-core Salafist groups. A couple of months later, the Islamist Al Farooq Media congratulated Muhammed Al-Zawahiri for his role in planning the US Embassy attack.[15]

At the time of the attack, the US Embassy was unaware of much of this information. It simply knew it was facing a growing mob, which it understood to be motivated by anger toward the video. Fearing for the safety of Embassy personnel and further escalation of violence, the Embassy issued a public statement:

> The Embassy of the United States in Cairo condemns the continuing efforts by misguided individuals to hurt the religious feelings of Muslims . . . We firmly reject the actions by those who abuse the universal right of free speech to hurt the religious beliefs of others.[16]

The Embassy also tweeted the message later, despite the fact that the State Department had expressed objections to the wording.[17]

Anne Patterson was the US ambassador to Egypt at this time. But she was in Washington, D.C., for consultations on September 11, and thus only saw the protest on television later. "If you look carefully at the images of protestors," she told me, "these were soccer thugs, small-time criminals, young kids with mohawks—not the kind of image typically associated with Salafis . . . and we were in dialogue with the Salafis!"[18] Patterson clearly meant that she didn't see the Islamists as being a major organizing force behind the demonstration and attack. But this begs a bigger question: What exactly was the United States in dialogue with the Salafis about—and how was this connected to the *Corrections* process in Libya?[19] And how, if at all, was it connected to Presidential Study Directive 11 (PSD-11) on the Muslim Brotherhood?

Not long after the Cairo protest morphed into an assault on the US Embassy, Deputy Chief of Mission Gregory Hicks texted Chris Stevens to ask him if he knew about the Cairo protests and storming of the Embassy. Chris replied "no" and thanked Hicks for telling him. As dusk turned to night, Hicks allowed himself to relax a bit, thinking US diplomats had made it through a 9/11 without incident.[20] He was about to get a rude jolt.

18

"We Were Drinking Tea"

The only people other than the attackers themselves to have a full, unimpeded view of how the attack started were four Libyan guards, who were patrolling the interior perimeter of the mission compound.

The Feb 17 guards say they were warned about strange activity at the Tibesti Hotel—where Ahmed, Burke, and I were staying—about an hour before the attack, but that otherwise there was nothing to report. Then, suddenly, a police car that had been parked in front of the Mission drove off minutes before the attack.

According to the guards, theirs started as just another boring night shift. They were discussing a soccer game beside the high walls that separated the Mission from the luxury houses in the posh neighborhood where it was located. "We were at the main gate, [post] Charlie 1, talking and drinking tea. Things were normal," one of them said.[1] Suddenly, around 9:40 PM, they saw a group of men coming toward them along a dirt path,[2] led by two men carrying RPGs. Some were masked. Some had machine guns, some hand grenades. There were eight men at the front of the group, of which four appeared to be leaders. "Some of them were wearing 'jalabib' and Afghan clothes"—a common practice among Arab veterans of the Afghan wars.[3] The guards said the attackers came from the spaces between the Mission and the other villas.

Here their accounts intersect with those of the agents that made up Chris Stevens's security detail—they maintain that the attackers advanced "unimpeded" into the compound (i.e., the Feb 17 guards had

fled), showing a "blend of tactical planning, perhaps based on reconnaissance, and opportunistic rampage."[4] The attackers found fuel can-
isters just past the main gate and used them to set fire to the complex.
As diplomatic security (DS) scrambled to get their gear, Agent Scott
Wickland, Stevens's personal "body man,"[5] took the ambassador and
Sean Smith to the Mission's safe haven. Meanwhile, the four other DS
agents maintained their positions in other parts of the complex. Stevens
furiously called his own contacts within the Feb 17, trying to get help.
One militia leader he *didn't* call was Wissam Bin Hamid. Whether that
had anything to do with the account he had just read from McFarland
about his meeting with Bin Hamid is unclear.

As acrid, black smoke from the diesel fuel filled the ambassador's
residence in what was called Villa C, Wickland returned to fetch Stevens and Smith. He tried to lead them to a window in a bathroom
through which they could escape. But when he looked back, they had
disappeared. Wickland found Smith's body but not Stevens. He reen-
tered the building several times in search of Stevens, to no avail.

Hearing news of the attack from across town, Bubaker Habib tried
to reach Stevens on his cell phone while driving as quickly as he could
toward the Mission. When he didn't get a response, he then called Wissam Bin Hamid—the head of Libya Shield One—who said he was on
the way to the compound.

The CIA Annex, a mile away from the Mission, had been alerted
to the attack within minutes. But its base leader faced a dilemma—by
sending Annex security to help the Mission, he'd be leaving his own
people vulnerable to attack. He preferred initially to try to get Feb 17 to
help while telling the Annex security team to wait.

"If you don't get here soon," one of the DS agents at the besieged
mission radioed, "we're all going to die!"[6]

After over twenty excruciating minutes of waiting, listening to their
colleagues' increasingly desperate communications, CIA's quick-reaction
team left for the Mission without the base leader's permission, arriving
about forty-five minutes after the start of the attack. They tried once

more to find Stevens, but the search was unsuccessful, and they were forced to retreat with the survivors back to the Annex around midnight.

About half an hour after the attack began, at around 10:06 PM Benghazi time, the State Department Operations Center sent out an email to the White House, Pentagon, FBI, and intelligence community, relaying the regional security officer's message that the Benghazi Mission was under attack: "Embassy Tripoli reports approximately 20 armed people fired shots; explosions have been heard as well. Ambassador Stevens, who is currently in Benghazi, and four COM [Chief of Mission] personnel are in the compound's safe haven. The 17th of February militia is providing security support."[7] Almost an hour later, another email noted that the "firing at the U.S. Diplomatic Mission in Benghazi had stopped and the compound had been cleared," adding that a "response team" was on-site.[8] A third message went out afterward, reporting that a local Islamist group called Ansar al-Sharia had claimed responsibility on Facebook and Twitter.[9]

At 11:10 PM local time, an American surveillance drone arrived over the Mission after being directed from a position about an hour away, having picked up evidence of roadblocks set up to the east of the Mission—further suggestive of a planned, intentional attack.[10]

On the ground, surveillance cameras that worked captured grainy images of the melee around the Mission—individuals later identified as being affiliated with Ansar al-Sharia and the Rafallah Sahati Brigade—including Ahmed Abu Khattala, at alternate times (or in parallel) a member of both the Rafallah Sahati Brigade and Ansar al-Sharia. Americans would later single out Abu Khattala as a possible leader of the attack, after he bragged openly about his role in the following days to *New York Times* reporter David Kirkpatrick while incongruously sipping a strawberry frappé.[11]

Some of those who arrived at the Mission after the attack were friendly—civilians who knew and admired Chris Stevens and were concerned for him. One of these was a law student, "Omar." He said he'd been studying at his house a mile away when he heard the RPGs and machine-gun fire. He initially thought the noise was indicative of one of the frequent firefights between militias in the area, but because he had heard that Ambassador Stevens was in town, he wanted to be sure. Walking near the compound, he saw fires and groups of people looting the compound. He said he heard armed militants with Dernawi accents mentioning "the mountain," which was generally understood to mean the town of Derna. He immediately surmised that at least some of the militants on-site were affiliated with Abu Sufian Bin Qumu, the former LIFG member and Guantanamo detainee who set up Ansar al-Sharia's Derna branch in the spring of 2011, a few years after his release from prison.[12]

Sometime after the Annex security team left the Mission, someone stumbled upon Stevens in the compound, unconscious and covered in soot, and brought him outside. On a cell phone video, voices can be heard saying *"Allahu Akbar* (God is Great)." The person who shot the video said they were frustrated that there was no ambulance and that they had to take Stevens to the hospital in a private car. "There was not a single ambulance to carry him," the videographer said.[13] Someone took Stevens to the Benghazi Medical Center, where doctors worked for around an hour to try to revive him.

Someone at the hospital called numbers on Stevens's phone, reaching staff in Tripoli, and informed them that Stevens had been killed and was at the hospital. Embassy personnel were concerned that it might be a trap to lure Americans to the hospital.

Just after midnight Benghazi time on September 12—over two hours after the attack began—a team of six US security personnel left the Embassy for the Tripoli airport and managed to hire a plane to fly them to Benghazi. Four more DS agents had asked to join the team but were instructed to remain to protect the Embassy. This incident would later become the basis for part of what Republicans would allege were US government-issued orders not to provide assistance to the stricken Mission and, later, the CIA Annex (i.e., "stand-down" orders).[14]

The Libyan government in Tripoli called one of the militias

nominally under the direction of the Ministry of Defense to help. This was none other than Libya Shield One, headed by Wissam Bin Hamid. Libya Shield One had originally been established under the Ministry of Defense, which was already under the influence of more radical Islamists.

Bin Hamid's men met the security personnel from Tripoli when their plane landed around 2:00 AM local time. But they delayed the Americans at the airport for nearly half an hour, eventually offering to let two of them go to the Annex. The Americans refused to be separated, and ultimately permission was given for them all to leave in Toyota Land Cruisers, with approximately fifteen members of Libya Shield One accompanying them.

Minutes after the Tripoli team's arrival, the Annex came under attack. Mortar shells rained down on the roof. In a period of heavy fire, former Navy SEAL commandos Tyrone Woods and Glen Doherty were killed, bringing the US casualties to four.

About half an hour after the attack on the Annex started, about one hundred February 17 Martyrs Brigade members arrived to help fend off the attackers, secure the area, and take the remaining Annex personnel to the airport.

The plane sent from Tripoli departed at 7:30 AM with survivors.[15] A couple of security agents remained behind, waiting to try to recover Stevens. Wissam Bin Hamid's men, apparently at the instructions of the interim government back in Tripoli, went to the hospital. There, they took Stevens's body at gunpoint and delivered him to the airport, where a C-130 transport plane was waiting. It departed with the casualties and remaining American officials around 10:00 AM.

Within a day, Ansar al-Sharia rephrased (but did not retract, as some in the administration would say) its previous claim of responsibility, saying that it "didn't participate in this popular uprising as a separate entity . . . rather, it was a spontaneous popular uprising in response to what happened by the West."[16] That ambiguity would cause problems in the United States in the coming days, weeks, and even years.

19

Witnesses Huddle

As the attack on the US Mission was underway, one of Washington's stated priorities was the security and safety of its officials on the ground. But even before the dust settled, an effective response was predicated on understanding who the attackers were and what motivated them.

Libya and Egypt weren't the only countries that experienced violent anti-Western disturbances around this time. There were reports of protests linked to the *Innocence of Muslims* video in dozens of separate locations in the region—and outside it, as far away as Pakistan, Indonesia, India, and Australia. Many of them took place outside US embassies and consulates. A few involved significant violence, in Tunisia, Egypt, Yemen, Sudan, Greece, Indonesia, and India.[1] NSC spokesman Tommy Vietor described the protests in Pakistan, for example, as "terrifying."[2] One can see how the first impression of Benghazi from London or Washington might be one of a single band within a rapidly expanding circle of protests and violence emanating from the film and the original protest at the US Embassy in Cairo.

But while Washington was struggling to make sense of the video and its connection to the Benghazi attack, as well as the early claim of responsibility by the Islamist militia Ansar al-Sharia, groups of Westerners and Libyans who were in the vicinity of the attack started speaking among themselves, comparing notes. Some spoke cautiously to the media.

The moment I landed back in the States, on September 20, I got a call from Jay Solomon of the *Wall Street Journal*, whom I had first met in Libya back in 2005. He wanted to know what I had to say about the attack, and specifically the video—which still hadn't registered with me as a relevant issue, as at no time during our time in Benghazi did anyone we interacted with ever mention either a protest or a video, let alone a specific video, as being a factor in the attack.

The article, which appeared on the cover of the *Journal* the next day under the lead "Miscues Before Libya Assault," reported that "the ambassador told [Chorin] there was 'no indication of trouble' following the protests in Egypt."[3] To me, this phrasing implied that both Stevens and I knew about the protest outside the US Embassy in Cairo at that time (I didn't, though when he texted me, Stevens may have just learned of it from his deputy, Hicks, back in Tripoli) and that we were worried about it. Solomon didn't seem to see my concern—"it's not an issue," he told me—but from this limited exchange, I could see that these kinds of seemingly insignificant elisions could be problematic.

I had already started to reach out to my own contacts in Benghazi—Libyans and Westerners—and discovered quickly that there were others who, like Ahmed and I, had seen or been exposed to part of the attack. One of these was Italian consul general Guido De Sanctis—who had met Chris Stevens on his arrival in Benghazi in April of the previous year. De Sanctis was eating at the Venezia restaurant on the backside of the US Mission as the attack began. He, too, had been looking forward to meeting Stevens the following day. De Sanctis summarized for me what he told Italian news aggregator ADN Kronos on the morning of September 12, i.e., that he felt he had enough information to confirm that the attack was planned, not "a degenerated protest against the film."[4]

A few more inquiries led me to the country manager of a major European energy concern, "John."[5] John told me that he was eating dinner with a colleague at the same Venezia restaurant when he heard a window-rattling explosion, followed by machine-gun fire: "It startled the heck out of me, but everyone else in the restaurant seemed to want to ignore it—gradually calm turned into pandemonium, as people started flowing in from the neighborhood to see what was happening."

John and his dinner companion, who worked for Blue Mountain, the British contractor responsible for supplementing security at the US Mission, sped back to the Blue Mountain base. As they were heading away from the compound area, John saw a Land Cruiser with its hood popped open.

"Poor souls," he said he thought to himself, "they've broken down in the middle of this pandemonium." But as they reached the next intersection, he saw another truck with its hood popped and armed men huddled around it. "It struck me then," he said, "this was no breakdown—it was a militia cordon to keep people out of the area." Impromptu protests, of course, don't usually involve military cordons.

There were others monitoring the situation in Benghazi. Colonel Wolfgang Pusztai, who had been based in Tripoli as Austrian defense attaché for five years, told the *New York Times* on September 12 that he believed the attack was "deliberately planned and executed" by a core group of thirty to forty assailants who were "well trained and organized."[6] Pusztai would later tell me that it took him, from his post in Tripoli, "a matter of a few hours" to feel he had a good sense of the circumstances around the attack, and that he was baffled by the confusion in Washington.[7] He didn't understand how, with all the resources at the US president's disposal, uncertainty over the most basic details of the attack could persist beyond a day at most.

This was just the start of a litany of eyewitness accounts that confirmed that there was no protest before the attack.

When interviewed later by the House Benghazi Committee, Stevens's number two, Gregory Hicks, would say that the *Innocence of Muslims* video wasn't an issue in Benghazi at the time of the attack.[8] Several DS agents corroborated what Hicks and other DS agents had said. In response to a question about whether there was any suspicious activity outside the Mission just before the attack, one testified, "No. There was nothing out there up until, well, up until there was. I had been out of the gate at 8:30 that night. We had had personnel leaving the compound, and they drove away from our compound and didn't report anything, and I spoke with them subsequently, there was nothing out there."[9]

Even with all the information available to those determined to find it, the idea of a video-induced protest morphing into an attack on the US Mission was not going away anytime soon. But for those looking beyond it, from the beginning, even before the attack, there were anomalies that suggested the situation might be more complex than it seemed. First, there was the matter of the timing of the release of the video in Arabic—which couldn't have been better, if someone or some group wanted to generate mass protests to coincide with the anniversary of 9/11.

Second was the fact that Ayman Al-Zawahiri posted a statement on September 10, the day before the attack, encouraging his followers to avenge the death of one the most prominent of the Afghan Libyans, and his number two within Al Qaeda, Abu Yahya Al Libi, who was killed in Pakistan three months earlier by an American drone. Al-Zawahiri (and the Egyptian Islamic Jihad) had a history of releasing revenge statements prior to attacks; days before the 1998 embassy bombings, a statement by the group, published in an Arabic newspaper, threatened retaliation against America.

Third, there are multiple indications that the Cairo protests were themselves planned in advance, with the help of Al-Zawahiri's brother Muhammed, following the release of the Arabic version of the *Innocence of Muslims* film on September 4. And fourth were the strange signs of impending trouble in Benghazi preceding the attack, including the surveillance event outside the Mission early in the morning on September 11.

The various coincidences led some to ask whether the video and the Cairo protest and attack might not have been a spontaneous explosion of popular anger but rather a purposeful cover or a window of opportunity for attacks elsewhere. There were many protests around the world, but only a handful of organized, violent attacks on US Missions in the Islamic world. And in a number of those cases, branches of Ansar Al-Sharia were implicated. What wasn't widely appreciated at the time was the fact that Ansar Al-Sharia was a product of Al Qaeda: Al Qaeda in the Arabian Peninsula (the group that launched the 2009 Underwear Bomber attack) created a blueprint for community outreach and social services (*da'wa*) under that brand in 2011. Soon after, other groups calling themselves "Ansar Al Sharia" popped up across the region, notably in Egypt, Tunisia, Sudan, and Libya—all countries that experienced violent attacks on or around September 11, 2012.[10] In Libya, ex-Guantanamo prisoner and bin Laden's former driver in Sudan, Abu Sufian Bin Qumu, set up a branch of Ansar al-Sharia in Derna while Muhammed Al-Zawahiri operated a group under that name in Benghazi.

Ansar al-Sharia has been described as a kind of Al Qaeda advance operator, a networked brand that would build support for Al Qaeda but lacked a centralized command-and-control infrastructure. In other words, it has a very general shared strategy that serves Al Qaeda's broader goals, but it doesn't take orders from Al Qaeda leadership.[11] But even if there wasn't a formalized command structure, there is ample evidence that the principals were well known to one another. The head of Ansar al-Sharia in Libya, Mohammed al-Zahawi, was seen to have strong connections with Al Qaeda.[12] There are signs of coordination between Ansars in Libya and Tunisia, and between these Ansars and Al Qaeda in the Islamic Maghreb (AQIM), just as there had long been ties and communication between the various Al Qaeda affiliates in North Africa, i.e., the LIFG, AQIM, the Moroccan Islamic Combatant Group (MICG), and the Armed Islamic Group of Algeria.

On October 4, 2012—less than a month after the Benghazi attack—the State Department added Ansar al-Sharia (in Yemen, along with its various affiliates) to its list of designated terrorist organizations, noting that it was essentially an alias for Al Qaeda in the Arabian Peninsula.[13] The State Department would later confirm its belief that both Ansar al-Sharia branches in Libya—Ansar al-Sharia Benghazi and Ansar al-Sharia Derna—coordinated the Benghazi attack.[14] Further, there is evidence that other Al Qaeda branches were present in Benghazi during the attack.[15]

If the role of Ansar al-Sharia wasn't immediately clear in the Benghazi attack, it was in other attacks around the same time. On Wednesday, September 12, there was a limited attack on the US Embassy in the Tunisian capital of Tunis. Two days later, on Friday, September 14, hundreds of militants staged a much larger attack on the Embassy and an American school nearby. As in Egypt, the attackers jumped the walls, used petrol bombs, tore down the American flag, and replaced it with an Islamic flag. The slogans chanted at these events were the same as well: "Obama, Obama, we are all Osama [bin Laden]."[16] The following day, protests near the Embassy resulted in at least four deaths and forty-six injured. Ambassador Jacob Walles called the attack on the Embassy "a very well-organized event, not a spontaneous demonstration." He concluded, "The attack on Wednesday [in Tunis] was clearly to test how the Tunisian security responded—and how we [the Embassy] would respond . . . We knew immediately it was the Tunisian branch of Ansar Al Sharia."[17]

Ambassador Walles had been US consul general in Jerusalem just prior to the Arab Spring, and Chris Stevens was his political section chief. Both men had their first ambassadorial confirmation hearings at the same time in mid-2012. Walles said he was shocked to hear of Stevens's death but didn't have a chance to process it or what happened in Benghazi because his embassy was hit shortly thereafter. As to how their fates diverged, "Our Embassy structure was far better protected than the Benghazi Mission," Walles elaborated.[18]

Back in Washington, the US government was far clearer in its condemnation of the Ansar al-Sharia attack in Tunisia than of the attack in Benghazi. Both American and Tunisian officials declared it a planned, coordinated attack. Walles took an immediate hard line with the Islamist government, calling the country's foreign minister to tell him he was on "severe notice."[19] Clinton told the Tunisian leadership to "push back hard on the assailants."[20]

Other protests in those days looked equally conspicuous. On September 13, a day after the end of the Benghazi attack, an angry crowd of more than a hundred people appeared outside the US Embassy in the Yemeni capital of Sana'a, laying siege to the building and setting fire to cars. Five people were killed in the surrounding violence. Abdul Majid Al-Zindani, head of the Yemeni al-Islah party (Muslim Brotherhood) and a former mentor to Osama bin Laden, called on his supporters to emulate what happened in Libya and Egypt.[21] Gerald Feierstein, US ambassador to Yemen at the time, described the attack in Sana'a as a "copycat" incident, modeled on those in Cairo and Benghazi. In Feierstein's view, the attack had nothing to do with Ansar al-Sharia but was coordinated by the Houthis, a local Shia-flavored movement that had been waging a long war against the central government. Sheila Carapico, a prominent Western scholar of Yemen, says she believes this cannot have been a spontaneous event, as armed protestors converged on the site in an SUV convoy.[22]

The US Embassy in Sudan was attacked on September 14. Protestors broke through the outer wall and clashed with Embassy guards, leaving three people dead.[23] The Sudanese government deployed riot police, and the United States sent additional marines to help. There were also clashes at the British and German Embassies.

Taken together, the combination of eyewitness reports from Benghazi, details from other attacks triggered by the *Innocence of Muslims* video, and statements from those who participated in those attacks suggest that Benghazi may have been part of a larger, loosely-coordinated set of commando-style actions that occurred in the shadow of the video, and which were encouraged, if not directed, by the highest levels of Al Qaeda. Though this is only one possibility, what's apparent is the lack of any deeper effort to collect and process information with this hypothesis in mind. My interviews with the US ambassadors and/or principal officers posted to the region at the time of the attacks suggest that each had his or her own interpretation of what was going on, locally and regionally. The FBI never brought them together to compare notes. In 2017, Obama's former deputy national security advisor for communications Ben Rhodes told me that I was the first person he'd spoken with who had been in Benghazi at the time of the attack. Was that due to the administration's broad Benghazi-induced risk aversion, or the result of a desire not to influence the outcome of an ongoing investigation? Or did the opportunity just never present itself? It's not clear. What is broadly clear, however, is that many of Obama's senior staff kept a distance from events on the ground.

20

Romney's Lunge

The Benghazi attack would have been a headline grabber regardless of when it occurred, but there were several things about its nature and timing that elevated its potential to cause political trouble. It involved terrorism. An American ambassador was killed. It occurred on the anniversary of 9/11. And it occurred just eight weeks before the general election that would decide whether Obama would get his second term, or whether the Republican challenger, former Massachussetts governor Mitt Romney, would become president.

Both the Romney and Obama campaigns had agreed to observe a moratorium on negative political attacks all day September 11, 2012, out of respect for those killed in the Al Qaeda attacks of 2001.

However, the announcement made by the US Embassy in Cairo as the protestors were gathering outside in greater and greater numbers (the one that condemned the "efforts by misguided individuals to hurt the religious feelings of Muslims") looked to Romney's staff to be too good an opportunity to pass up.[1] It looked like yet another Obama apology, to a campaign that had taken as its slogan the "No Apology Tour"—after what Republicans had labeled the president's "apologies for America" in the "New Beginning" speech the president delivered in Cairo in 2009. It's interesting that the candidate himself, Mitt Romney, seemed to be a passive participant in this process. Using the Cairo Embassy statement to attack Obama wasn't his idea. But he approved it.[2] And so Romney's campaign drafted an attack statement that it sent to the media just after 10:00 PM on September 11. In order to comply with the letter of the Obama–Romney campaigns' moratorium on negative campaigning on September 11, that statement was embargoed until midnight, September 12.[3]

"I'm outraged by the attacks on American diplomatic missions in Libya and Egypt and by the death of an American consulate worker in Benghazi," Romney's statement began. "It's disgraceful that the Obama administration's first response was not to condemn attacks on our diplomatic missions but to sympathize with those who waged the attacks."[4]

But the damage the Romney campaign hoped to inflict on Obama backfired, as details about the two attacks became clearer. The US Embassy in Cairo had released its statement at noon Cairo time, long before the Benghazi attack. The language about the video didn't come from the president or the Obama administration, it came from Embassy staff trying to calm rapidly escalating tensions outside the compound. The Romney campaign seemed to have conflated both the Cairo and Benghazi attacks. And Romney's statement came as the Benghazi attack was still underway and Americans were fighting for their lives. It looked like the rawest form of political opportunism.[5]

Secretary Clinton would tell me in 2022 that though she had a lot of experience with attacks from the Right, the instantaneous politicization of Benghazi took her aback. "In similar past incidents, there was at least a semblance of bipartisanship and solidarity. Look at the USS *Cole* bombing in Yemen, and the Embassy attacks in Africa. We dealt with that on a bipartisan basis. Here, no."[6]

Writing a few years later, Ben Rhodes described in detail his feelings of intense anger at Romney's response. Rhodes had "grown accustomed to ugly Republican attacks," he wrote, "but this felt different. Some threshold had been crossed." It was a part of a "new, uglier reality," which he linked to an "ugly conspiracy theory to delegitimize Obama and Clinton, destroy any concern for facts that didn't fit the theory, and dehumanize a small group of people, including me."[7]

The next day, September 12, the president issued a statement: "The United States condemns in the strongest terms this outrageous and shocking attack," it began. In subsequent paragraphs, Obama referenced the *Innocence of Muslims* video and the local reaction to it, saying, "there is absolutely no justification to this type of senseless violence."[8] In a separate statement the same day, Secretary Clinton echoed the president, condemning the attack and indirectly referencing the video: "But let me be clear—there is no justification for this [violence], none."[9]

For the first few days following the attack, Obama's and Clinton's public remarks tracked one another. But privately, Clinton's were a bit more direct, as her emails would later reveal. In one email to her daughter, Chelsea, on September 11, she wrote, "Two of our officers were killed in Benghazi by an al Qaeda-like group: The Ambassador, whom I handpicked, and a young communications officer on temporary duty [with] a wife and two young children." And in a call with the Egyptian prime minister on September 12, the day after the attack, the secretary writes, "We know the attack in Libya had nothing to do with the film. It was a planned attack—not a protest."[10] The Republicans would later make hay of this during the Benghazi Committee hearing, claiming it proved Clinton was aware from the start that this was not a protest, and that there was an Al Qaeda connection.[11] If there was something to this charge, Clinton wasn't about to confirm it.

On October 1, Sidney Blumenthal, one of Clinton's informal advisors—whom the House Committee on Benghazi would soon make an actor in the Benghazi controversy—sent Clinton a copy of a piece he helped place in *Salon*, warning that Romney planned to use Benghazi as part of a strategy to present Obama as weak on terrorism during the upcoming presidential debates.[12] Clinton pushed it to her policy advisor Jake Sullivan: "Be sure Ben [Rhodes] knows they need to be ready for this line of attack," she wrote. But, as *New York Times* correspondent Mark Landler writes about this exchange in his book on Obama and Clinton, *Alter Egos*: "Ben Rhodes . . . didn't need Blumenthal to warn him; the political team was already devising ways for Obama to parry the issue."[13]

Obama's clash with Romney over Benghazi and Obama's "apologies" came to a crescendo three weeks later on October 16, during the second presidential debate, in which Romney confronted Obama for not calling the Benghazi attack an act of terrorism in the days and weeks after it happened. "It's very clear. This was not a demonstration. This was an attack by terrorists," Romney said, appearing confident he had cornered the president for an omission.[14]

Clearly, Obama had been waiting for Romney to strike again. And he was prepared: "The day after the attack, governor, I stood in the Rose Garden and I told the American people and the world that we were going to find out exactly what happened, that this was an act of terror, and also said that we're going to hunt down those that committed this crime." Obama was ready with this rebuttal—which again illustrates a kind of almost preprogrammed dance going on between Republicans and Democrats, where each side was trying to predict and trap the other at each step.[15]

"You said in the Rose Garden the day after the attack it was an act of terror?" Romney asked, sensing an opportunity to move in for the kill. "I want to make sure we get that for the record because it took the President 14 days before he called the attack in Benghazi an act of terror."

"Get the transcript," the president said.

Romney looked incredulous as the moderator, Candy Crowley, confirmed Obama's statement. "Can you say that a little louder, Candy?" Obama asked with clear satisfaction.[16]

The event was widely seen as a humiliation for Romney. And indeed, had the candidate or his campaign done its homework before the debate, and read the transcripts of the president's remarks before trying to corner him, Romney presumably wouldn't have been caught in a trap of his own making.

No matter that many liberal-leaning media outlets, like *60 Minutes* and the *Washington Post*, partially agreed with Romney. The latter noted that Romney could be partially forgiven for believing that Obama had not called the attackers terrorists—because the president spoke in vaguer terms than that, referring to the attack as an "act of terror" rather than a terrorist act.[17] Just after Obama's Rose Garden speech, the president spoke with a correspondent from *60 Minutes*, who asked him why he had gone out of his way to avoid using the word "terrorism" in the context of the Benghazi attack.

"Well, it's too early to know exactly how this came about, what group was involved, but obviously it was an attack on Americans," Obama responded. To which the *Washington Post* later observed: "A president does not simply utter virtually the same phrase three times in two days about a major international incident without careful thought about the implications of each word." The *Post* concluded that the president had, when given repeated opportunities to forthrightly declare this was an "act of terrorism," for whatever reason, "ducked the question."[18]

Romney's attack may have seemed politically unseemly at the time, but it and Obama's not completely transparent counterpunch didn't cause the Benghazi controversy. They are best seen as scene setters, notice given by both sides of how they were going to play the game that was about to unfold.

21

The Talking Points Debacle

Five days after the attack, confusion reigned in the media sphere about the basics of what had happened in Benghazi. There had been an attack following a protest and attack in Cairo, linked to an anti-Islamic video produced in the States; the United States lost an ambassador much admired by Libyans. The lack of certainty about anything beyond this skeletal framework, combined with the initial partisan sparring, was starting to generate a broad sense of anticipation, and not a few conspiracy theories. Why was the ambassador in Benghazi? Why wasn't he protected? Who were the perpetrators? What was the connection between the Benghazi attack and the video that was linked to the Cairo Embassy incident and other protests that were mushrooming across the region?

Members of Congress requested guidance from the White House in explaining the attack to their constituents and the media. The Obama administration obliged, asking the CIA to prepare a draft of talking points, which the White House could recycle to script appearances by a senior official on the upcoming Sunday news talk shows.

A draft of the talking points dated September 15 stated that "the currently available information suggests that the demonstrations in Benghazi were spontaneously inspired by the protests at the US Embassy in Cairo and evolved into a direct assault against the US diplomatic post in Benghazi and subsequently its annex. There are indications that extremists participated in the violent demonstrations."[1]

The White House reached out first to Secretary Clinton to ask if she would do the shows. Clinton declined, or was simply unavailable. She knew a trap when she saw one.[2] The request then went to Susan Rice, US ambassador to the United Nations. Armed with the CIA talking points, Rice did five network interviews across the Sunday talk shows on September 16.

On CNN's *State of the Union* that day, Rice described the situation:

> There was a hateful video that was disseminated on the Internet. It had nothing to do with the United States government and it's one that we find disgusting and reprehensible. It's been offensive to many, many people around the world.[3]

And on NBC's *Meet the Press*, she continued:

> But putting together the best information that we have available to us today, our current assessment is that what happened in Benghazi was in fact initially a spontaneous reaction to what had just transpired hours before in Cairo—almost a copycat of—of the demonstrations against our facility in Cairo, which were prompted, of course, by the video.[4]

As the country would learn soon enough, there were factual errors in the talking points. The most egregious was the statement that protests "evolved" into the attack. Some Democrats also accused Rice of bending the talking points, specifically by linking the attack to the video, which was not mentioned directly in the CIA talking points.[5]

Within days of Rice's interviews, the intelligence community consensus swung back, this time seemingly decisively, to the notion that the attack was indeed an act of premeditated terrorism, and that there was no protest. On September 19, Matthew G. Olsen, director of the National Counterterrorism Center, called the events in Benghazi "a terrorist attack" and said that the US government was pursuing connections with Al Qaeda affiliates.[6]

Rice's appearance on the talk shows marked an inflection point in the quickly evolving (and escalating) partisan row over Benghazi. The gap between the talking points delivered on September 15 and the changed assessments on September 19 put the talking points at the center of a Republican focus on what they alleged to be Democrats misleading the public. Why, they asked, did Rice deliver those statements if the intelligence community knew otherwise?

A long list of questions began to emerge out of the confusion following Rice's TV appearances. By this point, Republicans and journalists began asking the question that Romney would bring to the presidential debate: Why would the administration want to avoid saying that the attack on the mission in Benghazi looked to be a deliberate act of terrorism? And why didn't the United States understand what was happening, in a country where, the media quickly revealed, we had a relatively large CIA presence?[7]

It's in this morass that the talking points fiasco packed an after-punch. Republicans began to openly suggest that the White House had spun a false story (i.e., that the attack was the result of local anger at *Innocence of Muslims*) to avoid conjuring up Al Qaeda in the lead-up to the 2012 election. Reince Priebus, chairman of the Republican National Committee, wrote in *RealClearPolitics* on September 27: "Amid Middle East turmoil and six weeks before the election, President Obama refuses to have an honest conversation with the American people. The country deserves honesty, not obfuscation, from our president."[8]

In May 2013, in response to increasing media and congressional pressure, the White House released one hundred pages of emails related to the drafting of the talking points used by Susan Rice, in hopes of finally putting the talking points controversy to bed. The public and pundit reaction was mixed.

The released emails do show the CIA taking the lead on the talking points process. The central element of Rice's exposition was present from the start—the erroneous idea that the attack was "spontaneously" inspired by the protests at the US Embassy in Cairo. State Department spokeswoman Victoria Nuland complained that including CIA warnings "could be used by Members [of Congress] to beat the State Department for not paying attention to Agency warnings so why do we want to feed that?"[9] Nuland also referred to the fact that the interests of her "leadership" (i.e., the leadership of the State Department, which can be inferred to mean, mainly, Hillary Clinton) would not be served by leaving the talking points in the form the CIA proposed. And the general discussion was adjourned to an in-person deputies meeting the following morning, which added a layer of secrecy to subsequent discussions on the final talking points.[10] According to Rhodes, it was after this meeting that the CIA made further edits, and the reference to Ansar al-Sharia as well as the CIA's general warnings about security threats in Benghazi in the months leading up to the attack were removed.[11] But it is worth noting that the lead bullet point on the original CIA draft and the final copy remained the same (referencing the protest in Cairo), which suggests that the CIA originated the idea about the attack resulting spontaneously from a protest against the video. As the author of a piece in *Politico* noted, the tranche of emails "does not really conflict with the overall narrative we are familiar with, although it does suggest that the White House was more involved in shaping Rice's TV remarks than it has let on."[12] The fact that the talking points were altered and that CIA references to prior cautions were removed, including those related to Al Qaeda, enabled Republican claims of an administration cover-up—of something.

In retrospect, if the White House wanted to be sure what it was saying was accurate, it would have been better not to speculate at all, but to wait until facts could be confirmed. And indeed, two days after the end of the attack, on September 14, Nuland announced that the State Department (not the White House) wasn't taking any more questions on the topic for the time being: "It is now something that you need to talk to the FBI about, not to us about, because it's their investigation."[13] But the first draft of the talking points was received that same day, and the White House apparently felt differently.

Another option at this point could have been to try to speed up the process of getting information from the various agencies involved by speaking directly to those officials returning from Benghazi and other witnesses. Clinton would later testify that this wasn't done because the State Department didn't want to interfere with an ongoing investigation. It may not have been her call.

The talking points controversy hovered in this place for another year following the release of the emails, when on April 17, 2014, the State Department released another series of emails, this one related to a Freedom of Information (FOIA) request filed by conservative watchdog Judicial Watch. These included an email sent by Ben Rhodes, on Friday, September 14, with the subject line: "RE: PREP CALL with Susan: Saturday at 4:00pm ET."[14] The reference was to a meeting the following day with Rice to prepare her for the Sunday morning talk shows. Under the header "Goals," Rhodes's memo urged NSC staff in public communications "to underscore that these protests are rooted in an Internet video, and not a broader failure of policy."[15]

Republicans seized on this revelation. Judicial Watch released a statement: "JW Finds Benghazi Smoking Gun!"[16] Representative Darrell Issa, chairman of the House Oversight Committee, scheduled yet another hearing in response. The *Village Voice* countered with "Right-bloggers: Had Enough Benghazi? Too Bad!"[17]

Was Rhodes's memo really a smoking gun? In other words, did it prove what the previous email release didn't, that the White House was trying to use the video to distract attention from what it knew to be a terrorist attack? Not exactly. As *Politico* noted, "it reflects the natural desire of any administration spinmeister—Rhodes was head of communications—to put the best possible face on the government's handling of things."[18] But it more or less solves the mystery of why Rice stressed the video on the talk shows when the CIA's talking points did not. Rice herself says she relied "solely and squarely" on the CIA talking points. Consciously or not, she was clearly relying on two sets of talking points: the CIA's and Rhodes's.[19]

Though Rhodes's emails don't prove that he or anyone else was putting forth a story they knew to be false, the net effect of the early, heavy focus on the *Innocence of Muslims* video was to push the White House's narrative beyond the point of return, once it became clear to everyone that it was incorrect.

In trying to figure out what senior Obama administration officials were really thinking in the days and weeks after Benghazi, it's worth recalling reactions to the near-miss Underwear Bomber attack over Detroit in 2009. At first, the president tried to stay above the fray and deny Al Qaeda any attention for the attempt and its failure. But Dick Cheney and the Neocons relentlessly criticized the administration for letting the AQAP plot advance as far as it did.

The Obama administration seemed to have taken two lessons from this: First, the Republicans would stop at nothing to make it look soft on terror. Second, the best way to avoid falling into that trap when and if the next attack came was to lead the narrative, lest the Republicans fill the void. And then, when it happened, the Romney campaign delivered a stark reminder of the Republican playbook. It seems unlikely that the Obama administration was so caught up in events that it was blind to either of these things.

There's another relevant atmospheric factor here, which adds to the picture of the political pressures the Obama administration felt in the lead-up to Benghazi. As Craig Whitlock argues in his 2021 book *The Afghanistan Papers*, the 2011 Obama-ordered raid that killed Osama bin Laden "also raised the public's expectations and intensified pressure" on Obama to show that his policies were working elsewhere, particularly in Afghanistan: "Obama had promised to turn around the war when he first ran for the White House. He would face the judgement of the voters the following year," Whitlock writes. And to cope with these pressures, Whitlock continues, the administration resorted to an extended campaign of "upbeat, reassuring rhetoric (that) obscured the truth: Despite massive investments, Obama's war strategy was failing."[20] This suggests that the White House had already recognized that it was vulnerable to

Republican pre-election bashing on 9/11-related issues and was changing its narrative to stem the tide.

So, you could say that when Benghazi hit, the White House was
already holding its breath on multiple fronts, many of which were somehow connected to 9/11 and terrorism. And though deeply cynical, given
their own role in pushing the administration into a corner, the Republicans' subsequent charges that Obama's emphasis on the *Innocence of
Muslims* video was a way to deflect criticism and lead the narrative—
away from Al Qaeda—struck many as plausible, given the circumstances. But regardless, the Sunday talk shows didn't mean that the
Obama administration was out of options for defusing a partisan war.

22

Stuck with the Story

As the public was digesting the growing controversy over Rice's remarks, President Obama spoke to the United Nations General Assembly about the wave of unrest sweeping the Middle East in reaction to the *Innocence of Muslims* video.

It was September 25, two weeks after the Benghazi attack. Washington's bureaucrats now knew much more about the attack than it had a week before.

On September 19, the director of the National Counterterrorism Center, Matthew Olsen, told the Senate Homeland Security Committee that Stevens and three other Americans "were killed in the course of a terrorist attack on our embassy."[1] It was the first time an Obama official used the phrase "terrorist attack" to describe what happened. The next day White House press secretary Jay Carney said that it was "self-evident" that Benghazi was a terrorist attack.[2]

The day after that, September 21, Clinton followed with even clearer language: "What happened in Benghazi was a terrorist attack, and we will not rest until we have tracked down and brought to justice the terrorists who murdered four Americans."[3]

And by September 20, the FBI finally shared the results of the various interviews it had done with witnesses.[4] James Clapper, director of national intelligence, delivered a brief to closed House and Senate sessions, in which he said Benghazi had "all the earmarks of a premeditated attack."[5] At the same meeting, Clinton is said to have clearly suggested that the attack was the result of a terrorist attack.[6] After Clapper's presentation, Senator McCain allegedly swore and stormed out while other senators erupted, yelling, "Why did Susan [Rice] lie?" An administration official characterized this incident as a "turning point . . . [Senators] just snapped . . . Susan was done,"[7] referring to Rice's candidacy for the position of secretary of state.

But in a speech to the UN General Assembly on September 25, the president's messages were almost unchanged from the beginning of the crisis, particularly with respect to the *Innocence of Muslims* video:

> This is what we saw play out in the last two weeks, as a crude and disgusting video sparked outrage throughout the Muslim world. Now, I have made it clear that the United States government had nothing to do with this video, and I believe its message must be rejected by all who respect our common humanity. It is an insult not only to Muslims, but to America as well—for as the city outside these walls makes clear, we are a country that has welcomed people of every race and every faith.[8]

The theme of the video's offensiveness is once again front and center, without any direct comment about the fact that Benghazi was an attack on the United States. What was jarring here was the president's conflation of all the region's protests with the attack on the US Mission in Benghazi, in other words, the suggestion that they all were the result of the regrettably timed release of an offensive video.

Embedded prominently within Obama's address was a short eulogy for Ambassador Stevens:

> Chris Stevens loved his work. He took pride in the country he served, and he saw dignity in the people that he met. And two weeks ago, he traveled to Benghazi to review plans to establish a new cultural center and *modernize a hospital*. That's when America's compound came under attack. Along with three of

his colleagues, Chris was killed in the city that he helped to save. He was 52 years old.[9] (The emphasis is mine.)

This passage included a detail that only a handful of people would recognize or have an opinion about: Chris didn't come to Benghazi to "modernize a hospital." This was a reference to the project that Ahmed and I had been working on for a year. And I only told Chris about the signing of a Memorandum of Understanding to proceed with the project on the morning of September 11. Once again, Benghazi was colliding with something that looked like an issue of phrasing or semantics—but for me and others who were in Libya and in contact with Chris, it was jarring because it wasn't strictly true. The meeting at BMC, set for 11:00 AM on September 12, didn't even make it onto Chris's official schedule before the attack that evening. It occurred to me that the reference might actually have come from me and my *New York Times* op-ed the day after the attack, in which I mentioned my call with Chris, the meeting planned for September 12, and the fact that it was the kind of initiative that Stevens liked. Or it might have come from Dr. Burke's TV interviews right after the attack, in which he also mentioned the project.

Regardless, the "modernizing a hospital" reference in Obama's UN General Assembly speech jelled my sense of obfuscation in the White House language. I knew the government well enough to understand that the standards of efficiency and speed are not what the general public expects them to be: the chaos of the first days, or even weeks, might conceivably have thrown the White House off track. But Obama's UN General Assembly speech marked two weeks since the attack. The expert consensus had moved well past the video hypothesis. Secretary Clinton had moved past any initial hesitance in linking the attack to terrorism. Someone had made the risky decision to live in the gray area between truth and falsehood, and that determined the party line.[10]

In retrospect, the UN General Assembly speech may have been the administration's last chance to change gears on Benghazi, to clearly acknowledge what the intelligence community had now confirmed: Benghazi was a premeditated terrorist attack. But it may have been a few days too late, given Senator McCain's explosive reaction to the brief on September 20. The senator and many of his colleagues were already in attack position.

In this light, the UN General Assembly speech can really only be seen as a decision not to make a decision (i.e., to continue with the same messaging on Benghazi) or a decision based on the assumption that correcting the narrative would only invite more conflict with the Republicans. And it's very possible that Susan Rice wasn't the only one who felt that the Benghazi controversy would quickly die down—that certainly we'd not still be talking about Benghazi after the election.

Just as I started to think that I was perhaps paying undue attention to what were semantic details, I had a call with a senior US government official who had worked directly with Ambassador Stevens in Tripoli. It was her job to know what development projects were underway and under consideration by American organizations in Libya. She knew about Ahmed's and my work but also knew that this wasn't why Stevens was in Benghazi. She asked if I knew how this idea of Stevens's traveling to Benghazi to modernize a hospital got into the president's speech. I told her I didn't know. But I found her response reassuring, a sign that I wasn't losing my mind. In the months that followed, many associates and colleagues would relate similar experiences, of feeling that there were some details about the Benghazi story that just didn't quite make sense. And that dissonance was a precursor of what was to come.

23

Collateral Damage

The talking points fiasco was the irritant around which the Benghazi scandal oyster would form a pearl. If there was any lingering sense among Republicans that Romney had gone too far in the immediate aftermath of the attack, it was eviscerated by Rice's tour of the Sunday talk shows. Republican leaders started to feel that Romney had been onto something—and that the administration was hiding something.

Rice was the obvious initial target for right-wing anger because she was the administration's messenger for the talking points, which was its first formal accounting of what happened. She was also close to Obama and expected to be nominated as secretary of state for Obama's second term, to replace Hillary Clinton. The fact that Rice had been an active participant in making the case for the Libya intervention (she had been credited as US ambassador to the United Nations with getting the body to pass the resolution authorizing "all necessary measures") may have also been a factor in the Republicans' desire for retribution, to the extent that the Republicans held it against Obama that he didn't go to Congress for authorization, as required by the War Powers Resolution, either before or after the intervention.

There is little reason to believe that Rice did anything but repeat the talking points she was given, and faithfully so. But she would be the first to take the fall for their flaws.

Senator John McCain became one of the leaders of the campaign to deny Rice the position of secretary of state after Clinton stepped down

at the end of 2012. In his 2018 memoir, McCain wrote that in the early
days after the attack, he hadn't been one of those blaming the Obama
administration for Benghazi:

> I was just terribly saddened by it. I wasn't angry with the
> administration. I remember listening to Secretary Clinton's
> memorial remarks about him [Stevens], and being very moved
> by them, and I asked Chris Brose [McCain's political staffer]
> to send her a note of thanks. I started to get angry when it
> appeared administration officials were knowingly misleading us
> about the attack.[1]

Despite the tense moments caused by Benghazi, it became reasonably clear in the two weeks before the election that the Obama campaign had weathered the immediate crisis, and that he was going to win
a second term. What no one seemed to anticipate—certainly not in the
Democratic Party—was that the Benghazi scandal was far from over.
Rather, it was just beginning.

This is when McCain started to characterize the administration's
response as "either willful ignorance or abysmal intelligence"[2] and
"either a massive cover-up or incompetence."[3] His words were a hint
that even if the election was over, he—and other Republicans—
weren't going to leave Benghazi alone. McCain's feelings of personal
betrayal, linked no doubt to his affection for Chris Stevens, as well
as his own emotional connection to the Libyan Revolution, may have
driven his declaration around this time to thwart Rice's confirmation
hearings.

When it became clear that Rice wasn't going to be confirmed by the
Senate because Republicans blamed her for the talking points controversy, she withdrew on December 13, 2012. "If my nomination meant
that the odds of getting comprehensive immigration reform passed
or any other major priority were substantially reduced, I couldn't live
with myself," she said.[4] As it would turn out, Benghazi would cost a

lot more than that. And with that, the Republicans claimed their first Benghazi-linked political victory.

Rice held her peace until long after Obama's second term. In 2019, she released her own memoir of service to the Obama administration, *Tough Love*, which, like many other Obama-era memoirs, devotes a single chapter to Benghazi. In it, Rice argues that she didn't make a link between the attack and the *Innocence of Muslims* video, rather that the press had "elided" her words; what she was trying to say was that "the video was the precipitating factor in Cairo, and events in Cairo inspired Benghazi."

"I did not," Rice wrote, "mean that the Intelligence Community had said that the video itself was the proximate spark in Benghazi."[5]

Rice doesn't blame either Obama or Rhodes explicitly for what happened to her but seems to imply that she was the administration's sacrificial lamb on a highly explosive topic. And she doesn't deliver that message directly, but by quoting her mother—a well-known figure in Washington who clearly had strong political instincts:

"Why do you have to go on the shows? Where is Hillary?" Rice says her mother asked her. To which Rice responded, "I think that Hillary is wiped after a brutal week."

"I smell a rat," her mother responded.[6]

The question of what Rice thinks her mother meant when she said "I smell a rat" is left just vague enough: from the text, her mother appears to be reacting to the fact that Clinton is absent during a highly politically sensitive moment, thus leaving Rice to take the flak. But from what follows, Rice suggests the "rat" refers not to the administration's maneuvering of her, but the brewing Republican attacks, which she says she didn't understand: "I was a comparatively bit player in the actual Benghazi drama," she protested. "Why not White House spokesperson Jay Carney? . . . [He] spoke about the Benghazi attacks almost daily from September 11 onward. . . . Why not Secretary of State Hillary Clinton (until later)? CIA director David Petraeus, whose agency had produced the talking points to begin with?"[7] And even if she accepted the response to her appearances, "Still, I wasn't prepared for the attacks on me escalating after the election."[8]

Rice wrote that she needed to ask a friend at Fox News to explain the Republican motivations in pursuing her, and was told that it was because by going on the talk shows, she had provided Fox "'an opportunity to introduce a new villain,' plus tons of video which provided 'tremendous fodder' they could play over and over."[9] It's a bit difficult to believe that Rice was as politically green as that, particularly after a term in the Obama White House, constantly under attack from the Right. But if Rice's surprise about the longevity of the Benghazi controversy is genuine, it may help explain the assumptions driving the White House's decision on messaging, one of which may have been that there would be plenty of time after the election in which to manage any lingering political fallout. If that was the case, the Democrats hugely underestimated the political winds, and what their right-wing adversaries were willing to do to gain the advantage.

Secretary Clinton escaped the first round of fire, by declining the White House request to appear on the Sunday talk shows the week after the attack. But as the controversy continued, she was inevitably next in line for the Republican firing squad. As head of the State Department, she was far more involved in Libya policy than Rice, and like Rice, she was a visible part of a White House Benghazi narrative that, for many, just didn't add up. But most relevant, she was the presumptive Democratic nominee for the presidential election in 2016. And for nearly two decades, she had been a symbol of pretty much everything the Right detested about the Left.

Clinton says that despite her long experience of being demonized by the Right, she didn't expect the intensity of the Republican attacks over Benghazi, which, she says "started almost immediately." But it didn't take long for her to catch on that things were "qualitatively different this time." In a 2022 interview, she told me:

I didn't foresee the political implications of the [Benghazi] Attack. I felt regret and shock. This was very different from what happened after the 1983 Beirut barracks bombings, or the attack on the USS *Cole* in Yemen. Those tragedies brought Americans together. In normal times, most of the politics would wash out. Not in this case. The politicization of Benghazi was unprecedented.[10]

Shortly after the attack, Secretary Clinton reached out to Republican lawmaker Darrell Issa, chairman of the House Oversight and Government Reform Committee, to urge a bipartisan approach to Benghazi. She told Issa: "I want to cooperate. I will give you as much as I can. But I want to underscore that this should not be politicized."[11] After her initial shock at the speed with which Benghazi had gone completely political, Clinton clearly understood that there was a strong chance this issue would grow into something bigger. How big? And how long would it last? Those were the questions.

24

Investigations Galore

The talking points fiasco weaponized Benghazi. And the initial investigations didn't help to dispel controversy—indeed, each investigation seemed to create more questions that then became part of the overall scandal that later investigations either felt they had to (or chose to) address.

The first official read on what went wrong in Benghazi came with the report of the Accountability Review Board (ARB), a tool the secretary of state normally convenes after any major crisis or issue involving a diplomatic post abroad. Within weeks of the attack, Clinton named career diplomat Thomas Pickering (who, incidentally, had been a mentor to Ambassador Stevens) as chair board and Admiral Michael Mullen as vice chair. The results, released in December 2012, were commonsensical: it put Congress on the spot for more security-related funding for diplomacy, called for more training for diplomats in high-risk posts, and called for better and more language training in Arabic. The most tangible recommendation was to create a position at the State Department with specific ownership of security at high-risk posts—so less-formalized US missions like Benghazi didn't get caught in the cracks between bureaus.[1]

But many felt the ARB raised more questions than it answered—although not everyone agreed on the questions.

The Left didn't criticize the report directly, but many diplomats had questions of their own. The report observed, for example, that "there was little understanding of militias in Benghazi and the threat they posed to U.S. interests." One reason for this, it said, was the fact that the militias kept dissolving, splitting apart, and reforming. Another was that fighters were often members of many militias, and Feb 17 was an "umbrella organization, made up of many different militias with differing ideologies, some of which are extremist in nature."[2] But nowhere in the report is there an explanation for why the US government would conceivably rely on this kind of a setup—an amorphous mixture of so-called moderate and extremist Islamist militias, many of whom had open grudges against the conditions of their employment and their employers, too—to protect American diplomats and high-level officials. Nor was there any explicit attention drawn to the fact that the State Department's plan prior to the attack was not to reduce this dependence but rather to increase it. The document simply noted that there hadn't been any problems with Feb 17 in the past.

The ARB also implicitly put much of the blame on Stevens, who it said failed to "see a direct threat of an attack of this nature and scale on the US Mission." Similarly, "Embassy Tripoli [read: Stevens, in his capacity as ambassador] did not demonstrate strong and sustained advocacy with Washington for increased security for Special Mission Benghazi."[3] The ARB came to this conclusion despite knowing that Stevens and the Embassy's RSO had requested security upgrades multiple times—only to be told to rely on the local security forces. It also can't have escaped the ARB's attention that one of Stevens's objectives in traveling to Benghazi was to get the Mission's status upgraded to that of a consulate so that it could qualify for more security. One wonders, further, if the security deficiencies that had dogged the US presence in Libya since 2004 had been brought to the ARB's attention. The ARB also revealed a major contradiction when it noted that Stevens's "status as the leading U.S. government advocate on Libya policy, and his expertise on Benghazi in particular, caused Washington to give unusual deference to his judgments."[4] Except, of course, when it didn't. What the ARB didn't own here was the fact that Chris Stevens had become, really, the only US government expert on the situation in Libya, and yet wasn't given the tools to do his job properly.

A number of senior diplomats told me off record that they felt the ARB was both palliative and superficial. They objected in particular to the blame of Stevens, and they pointed to the fact that many of the ARB's recommendations had been seen before—specifically, in the ARB that followed the East Africa bombings in 1998.

Though the Right didn't like the ARB report any more than some insiders on the Left, Republicans did find it significantly more useful. With the presidential election now over, they seized on its weakness as a target of their political grappling hook with which they hoped to attack Clinton.

One of the first public "gotcha" moments occurred during a voluntary briefing by Secretary Clinton with the Senate Foreign Relations Committee on January 23, 2013. Republican Senator Ron Johnson asked why the State Department didn't immediately ask some of the official witnesses what was going on before the attack. "Do you disagree with me that a simple phone call to those evacuees to determine what happened would have ascertained immediately that there was no protest?" he asked. "That was a piece of information that could have been easily, easily obtained."[5] Clinton says, "I've spoken to one of them, but I waited until after the ARB had done its investigation because I did not want there to be anybody raising any issue that I had spoken to anyone before the ARB conducted its investigation."[6]

Clinton then strongly rebuked the senator, probably because she knew he had a point and was simultaneously a political enemy: "With all due respect, the fact is we had four dead Americans. Was it because of a protest or was it because of guys out for a walk one night who decided that they'd go kill some Americans? What difference at this point does it make? It is our job to figure out what happened and do everything we can to prevent it from ever happening again, Senator."[7] That simple question—"What difference does it make?"—taken out of its larger context, became one of the most recognized and repeated Benghazi memes, and solidified Hillary Clinton as the main target of Republican ire over Benghazi.

If you listen to the whole exchange carefully, it offers quite a bit of information. First, while Johnson badgers Clinton, his question isn't as patently ridiculous as the Democrats (and Clinton) suggested. And Clinton answers part of it, seemingly directly, indicating that she does see his point. To me, listening to this and reading the transcript, it feels like Clinton is doing her very best to handle a highly volatile situation in which she's caught between Republicans looking to trip her up and a post-attack response she knows makes little sense. Later investigations would recommend that "intelligence analysts should more aggressively request and integrate eyewitness reporting . . . in the aftermath of a crisis."[8]

A year after the attack, the House Committee on Oversight and Government Reform, led by Republican Congressman Darrell Issa (the same Republican congressman to whom Clinton reached out after the attack), completed a review that spelled out what the Republicans found wrong with the ARB, including the Democrats' failure to answer questions about not only why security was denied but also why a military response was not forthcoming during the attack, and failure to do its duty to find and discipline "any U.S. government employee . . . [who] breached her or his duty."[9] The Republicans further claimed that Clinton helped water down the ARB report, and complained that her own actions were not covered by the review. A Fox News report screamed, "A 'Rigorous and Unsparing' Review? ARB Benghazi Report Full of Gaps, Unanswered Questions."[10]

In early 2014, just over a year after the readout of the ARB, the Senate Select Committee on Intelligence, chaired by Democratic Senator Dianne Feinstein and co-chaired by Republican Senator Saxby Chambliss, issued the unclassified version of *its* Benghazi report—which addressed not only the attack but also a story that was occupying an increasingly central role in American political life: the evolution of the scandal that followed.

This report was well-needed fresh air; it was both rigorous and bipartisan, and set down a benchmark against which some of the wilder claims about Benghazi could be measured. The report established that there was no protest prior to the attack; that the attack *was* planned, if perhaps not extensively; that members of several groups directly tied to Al Qaeda participated in the attack; and that several of those groups had been placed on the US and UN terror lists since.[11] It also names a veritable Who's Who of extremists present at, or in the vicinity of, the US Mission during the attack, including members of Al Qaeda in the Arabian Peninsula, the group behind the 2009 Underwear Bomber plot; the Muhammad Jamal network, which was based in Egypt and terrorized the Sinai Peninsula; and the infamous Mokhtar Belmokhtar, who had been a leader of Al Qaeda in the Islamic Maghreb (AQIM), started his own terrorist group Al Mourabitoun in 2012 and, four months after the Benghazi attack, staged a major attack on an Algerian gas plant across the Libyan–Algerian border.[12]

The report also found that the intelligence community as a whole had "provided ample strategic warning that the security situation in eastern Libya was deteriorating," and that "militias and terrorist and affiliated groups had the capability and intent to strike U.S. and Western facilities and personnel in Libya."[13] The report called the talking points "flawed but mostly accurate," noting that "omissions and wording choices contributed to significant controversy and confusion, as did an erroneous reference to 'demonstrations.'"[14]

The Senate report implicated the Benghazi-based franchise of Ansar al-Sharia, but also the Derna-based Ansar al-Sharia franchise, headed by Abu Sufian Bin Qumu. This provides the most direct linkage between the attack and members of the allegedly now-defunct LIFG. Overall, the Senate document quietly made the case that George W. Bush's policy fiasco in Libya had come home to roost in Benghazi.

In a portion of the report that has been widely overlooked by the media, the Senate committee explained part of the initial confusion around the talking points, and why the core CIA talking points themselves were so poor. The intelligence agencies and the FBI actually had in their possession much more information than was registered in the talking points, but it took an inordinately long time to collect, process, and send that information up the chain. In a more startling revelation, the talking points upon which Susan Rice based her talk show interviews were not based on the "most recent information" collected by the CIA and the FBI, as advertised; they were "based on *open source* reports and intelligence"[15] (the emphasis is mine). Meanwhile, the FBI was still working on processing the known Benghazi witnessses' statements.

The report also noted that the CIA analysts referenced statements made by Ansar al-Sharia—the group later identified as one of the main perpetrators of the attack—that the attack resulted from a "spontaneous and popular uprising." And that statement was reflected by Abdul-hakim Belhaj, who, when asked whether the attack was premeditated or spontaneous, said, "The information we have received is that it was spontaneous at first—people gathered outside the consulate then there was an exchange of fire between the two sides, between the guards of the Consulate and the demonstrators, some of whom came armed."[16] In other words, misleading statements by one of the early suspected parties, Ansar al-Sharia, were incorporated directly into the administration's official explanation—akin to allowing bank robbers to write their own police report.

The talking points issue would come to hound the Democrats, but the Senate report made clear that, at the very least, the broader intelligence community was partly responsible for the lack of clarity. In a lot of ways, the Senate report answered many of the questions that under other circumstances might have put Benghazi to bed, at least as far as the public was concerned. Of course, it did not.

*   *   *

The Senate report wasn't the only major addition to the Benghazi narratives that winter. On December 28, 2013, more than fifteen months
after the attack, and with much fanfare, the *New York Times* published
an article written by its Cairo-based correspondent David Kirkpatrick,
under the title "A Deadly Mix in Benghazi." The *New York Times* sold
the piece as a major, even definitive, breakthrough in analysis of what
actually happened in Benghazi.[17]

In the piece, Kirkpatrick made two startling claims: First, there was
no evidence of Al Qaeda involvement in the attack, and second, the
Innocence of Muslims video *did* play a role in motivating the attackers.
Kirkpatrick wrote that "contrary to claims by some members of Congress [by which he presumably meant the various committee members
who agreed there was no evidence of a protest sparked by a video], it
was fueled in large part by anger at an America-made video denigrating
Islam."[18]

Its conclusions flew directly in the face of the already well-solidified
intelligence community consensus on both points. Kirkpatrick's claims
were immediately disputed by two members of the House Permanent
Select Committee on Intelligence, Adam Schiff, a Democrat, and Mike
Rogers, a Republican.[19] As *The Atlantic* noted, whether Kirkpatrick's
article was correct or not largely rested on one's assumptions about who
Al Qaeda was.[20] Kirkpatrick's view was clearly that Ansar al-Sharia was
not Al Qaeda, but Ansar al-Sharia has long and deep demonstrated connections to Al Qaeda, whose proliferation strategy in Libya used it and
groups like it to provide cover. The question of whether the video played
a role is also more complex. Kirkpatrick didn't define what he thought
the role of the video was: Whether it was, as the Obama administration
initially suggested, a more or less random external event that sparked an
emotional response that got out of hand, or whether the video was used
as cover by Benghazi militants to launch a preplanned attack, which had
become the intelligence community's position months before the article's
publication. Kirkpatrick's implication was that it was a bit of both.

The Kirkpatrick piece wouldn't have been such a big deal if the controversy weren't still alive, and if the *New York Times* hadn't presented it as the most informed read to date. And it allowed the Obama administration to say, basically, "we weren't wrong." It also gave the two people in the administration who were most affected by the Obama narrative and took the most flack for it—Susan Rice and Hillary Clinton—some degree of protection. Clinton wrote in her 2014 memoir, *Hard Choices*, that the *New York Times* piece was "the most comprehensive account to date of what happened in Benghazi."[21] Similarly, Rice wrote in 2019 that it "revealed that, contrary to what we thought at the time, the video did appear to have been a catalyst for the attack on the Benghazi diplomatic facility."[22] What's so striking here is the idea that the *New York Times* could launch an investigation more comprehensive than whatever the US government could—or wanted to—come up with.[23]

Some of Kirkpatrick's emphases were spot on, particularly the lessons that the attack had for American policy writ large. "A fuller accounting of the attacks suggests lessons for the United States that go well beyond Libya," he wrote. "It shows the risks of expecting American aid in a time of desperation to buy durable loyalty, and the difficulty of discerning friends from allies of convenience."[24]

Ultimately, the fact that the *New York Times* felt that there was a need to clarify the underlying Benghazi media narrative over a year after the attack says a lot about how much partisan warfare over Benghazi did to confuse the American public and sow distrust in public leadership. But more to the point, it may have made the problem worse. By 2014, enough about the attack was clear that it should have been time for Americans to put this event behind us and begin to apply its valuable lessons about diplomacy, foreign service, and intelligence.

25

Stand-Down Orders

The bipartisan conclusions of the Senate Select Committee on Intelligence's report suggested that there were sufficient grounds for both parties to agree on a shared version of reality on Benghazi. And had the attack taken place five years, or even five months, earlier, well out of the path of the 2012 presidential election, perhaps scandal would have been curtailed. But in 2014, with an ever-widening gulf between the two political parties, Benghazi offered a formidable weapon, one that risked dealing a death blow to any spirit of bipartisanship that remained.

While the Left was trying to pour cold water on the controversy, the Right was honing its messaging for maximum political effect. In the fall of 2014, Fox News seemed to have begun a new chapter of Benghazi, with what became known as the "stand-down orders" controversy. On October 26, the right-wing network aired a story alleging that CIA operatives at the Annex were denied permission to help the Mission during the initial attack, and that the Annex's requests for outside military assistance were also denied by senior members in the chain of command back in Washington. The Fox News report, which contained a number of factual errors, was repeated by the *New York Post*, the *Daily Mail*, and more.[1]

None of the committees and hearings assembled to look into Benghazi before or after this report found evidence to support the claims that Clinton—or any other senior US official—issued orders to deny military assistance to the US Mission (what would be called "stand-down orders"). The ARB concluded there "simply was not enough time given the speed of the attacks for armed U.S. military assets to have made a difference."[2] And the 2014 Senate Select Committee concurred.

But the ARB did flesh out the picture of a thick and clumsy bureaucracy—the same bureaucracy that couldn't think its way through the illogic of the security stance at the Mission. Gaps in protocol, fuzzy lines of authority, and slow response times forced commanders on the ground to make gut-wrenching calls themselves, without guidance from Washington. It couldn't have been easy for the CIA Annex head to weigh the safety of the Mission against that of the larger number of people at the Annex; just as it must have been agonizing for the rapid response team not to have a clear path to help Ambassador Stevens and the others. And that sense of impotence offered yet another source of fodder for those looking to incite political warfare.

Despite the fact that President Obama told Secretary of Defense Leon Panetta to "do whatever you need to do to be able to protect our people,"[3] things back in Washington took time. A lot of time. It took time to ascertain what was going on at the Mission, and then to make the decision about what kind of response was appropriate. In circumstances like Benghazi, the Department of Defense typically activates a Foreign Emergency Support Team (FEST), an "interagency, on-call, short-notice team poised to respond to terrorist incidents worldwide"; the FEST is meant to be dispatched within four hours of deployment orders, "providing the fastest assistance possible."[4] FESTs had responded to the 1998 East Africa bombings and the 2000 USS *Cole* attack, among others. Another option was something called a Fleet Anti-Terrorism Security Team (FAST), which has more direct tactical hit capacity. There's also the Commander's In-extremis Force (CIF), a group trained to provide quick logistical solutions in crises, including rescuing US personnel under threat. All of these options have different functions, and each could have been some help if the circumstances had been different. But there wasn't: a CIF had been based in Croatia but was off-site at the time of the attack; and a FAST or FEST wouldn't have been able to arrive until well past noon the following day.

As it was, Panetta authorized the dispatch of two FAST platoons stationed in Rota, Spain, somewhere between 6:00 PM and 8:00 PM Washington time (two to four hours after the attack on the Mission started) and ordered the positioning of a CIF in southern Europe near to, but not inside, Libya, to await further instructions. The NSC seemed to have been confused about the capabilities of the FEST and determined not to send it. But in retrospect, that was a moot point because of the amount of time it would have taken the FEST to get there. One of the FASTs was delayed for reasons that sounded absurd but were a function of bureaucracy: members of the team said they were ordered to change in and out of their uniforms four times, and had to make a stop en route, as there were conflicting assessments of whether arriving in uniform might rile Libyan hosts.[5] Meanwhile, it was patently obvious to everyone with an eye on the FASTs that, even under the best of circumstances, they would arrive well after the emergency was over. Ultimately, the first FAST, which had been diverted to Tripoli because the last official Americans had left Benghazi many hours before, arrived in Tripoli at 8:56 PM local time on September 12, twenty-four hours after the start of the attack.[6]

This leaves the last possibility: some form of air support. The options here were limited—there were no C-130 gunships anywhere in range that could provide firepower support to repel the attack on the Annex. But many military analysts, and Stevens's number two, Hicks, in later testimony insisted that a show of force, such as a low-altitude flyover, might have been effective—not in the case of the Mission attack, which would have been long over, but in stopping the mortar attacks on the CIA Annex and preventing the deaths of Tyrone Woods and Glen Doherty. This was also a question many of my Benghazi contacts asked repeatedly—why no flyover?

There were three military bases of US forces near Benghazi—350 miles north at Souda Bay in Crete, Greece; 470 miles away at Sigonella in southern Italy, from which thousands of sorties were flown during Operation Odyssey Dawn; and 1,040 miles away at Aviano in northern Italy (where the 510th and 555th Fighter Squadrons were posted, both of which fly F-16s). Sigonella was out, as apparently there were no US fighters based there at the time. The other two facilities would have required refueling services to get to Benghazi and back. And that required tankers, which apparently weren't available. So, as far as the Pentagon was concerned, there were no options. This has been challenged subsequently by reports suggesting there were F-16 fighters fueled and at Aviano, and that there was refueling capacity available either at Aviano or in Sicily. Though the Defense Department hasn't commented directly on those arguments, military officials note that a pit-stop landing in Italy[7] at a facility that had no on-call trained technicians to perform the refueling under dangerous conditions, without a clear authorization from the Libyan government for an overflight, would administratively and diplomatically have been no simple task, and could have taken many hours.

"There's a lot of Monday-morning quarterbacking going on here," Secretary Panetta told reporters at the Pentagon the day Fox News released its story alleging CIA stand-down orders.[8] He added that "the basic principle is that you don't deploy forces into harm's way without knowing what's going on, without having some real-time information about what's taking place."[9] Panetta said that he, General Martin Dempsey, the chair of the Joint Chiefs of Staff, and General Carter Ham of AFRICOM, which was responsible for American military operations in Africa, felt that the risk was too great. Again, whether it was correct or not, risk aversion played a major role in the decision-making. (Not long afterward, conservative blogs floated a rumor linking General Ham's subsequent reassignment from AFRICOM to an alleged attempted override of orders from Panetta.[10] There is no evidence for this.)

It's possible that either Panetta or President Obama was thinking of the possibility of the consequences of another jet downed over Libya—as happened at the start of Operation Odyssey Dawn. And this is very much in keeping with the fact that the US government was unwilling to authorize an FBI mission to Benghazi for two weeks after the attack.

What emerges from all of this is not a dark conspiracy on the part of the Obama administration to deny help to Americans under siege, as many Republicans have alleged, but a *system* that was unprepared—and in many ways incapable—of reacting quickly to a crisis in Libya, which had, from Washington's perspective, reverted, once again, to a marginal piece of real estate in the Middle East. Because the Obama administration wanted to pass off the entire Libyan clean-up operation to the Europeans and our Arab allies, there were no US military assets on alert in the immediate vicinity, even at Souda Bay, Crete. The United States' overall readiness posture was nothing like it had been during the Cold War, when military assets could be scrambled on a moment's notice. That odd mixture of risk-taking and the illusion that one could micromanage risk was a hallmark of the Libya intervention and what came after.

The Right, however, was less worried about the operational details of the slow response than about finding a way to tie the idea of a "stand-down order" to Clinton personally. It was about finding a hook with which to attack Clinton's character. On February 17, 2013, Congressman Darrell Issa told attendees at a Republican political fundraiser that "I have my suspicions, which is Secretary Clinton told Leon [Panetta] to stand down."[11] Yet there is no evidence that Clinton was involved in the military decision-making, or that she spoke with Panetta on the night of September 11. After all of the uproar, Republicans on the House Armed Services Committee would eventually attest that "there was no 'stand down' order issued to U.S. military personnel in Tripoli who sought to join the fight in Benghazi."[12]

Frederick Hill, a spokesman for the House Oversight Committee, explained away Issa's comments about Clinton as a means of putting faces on bureaucracies—but the effect would have been the same: tying

Clinton specifically to hypothetical "stand-down orders." The attachment to Clinton is ironic, however, as most of Clinton's actions with respect to Libya, for better or worse, erred on the risk-tolerant side rather than the opposite.

Even though Secretary Clinton was nowhere in the chain of command to issue such orders, and hadn't had contact with Secretary Panetta to urge him to do so, the idea that Clinton was *personally* connected to potential stand-down orders was powerful. The Right presented it as a supreme marker of her flawed character, which could then be linked to decades of conspiracy theories that associated Clinton and former President Bill Clinton with absurd claims of political assassinations. The Right used these insinuations to come up with more memes and epithets for Clinton that were laughable, but memorable and effective, like "Hillary Clinton: The Butcher of Benghazi?"[13]

As the scandal progressed, the crux of the Benghazi attack once again revealed itself: Republican lawmakers and the media were right to ask such questions about the military response. But by making it about scoring political points rather than trying to fix a broken system, they only perpetuated a controversy that was further tearing apart the country. And with public understanding still muddled and politicians continuing to make hay of it all through 2014, the following year was only going to get worse.

26

Paired Controversies:
Benghazi and the Emails

When Clinton stepped down as secretary of state four months after the attack in Libya, her favorability ratings were high. A late December *USA Today*/Gallup poll had named her the most admired woman in America—making her the longest-running "most admired woman" in Gallup's history.[1] Approval ratings for the job she did as secretary of state remained high through 2014, when a Pew poll found that 67 percent of Americans approved of her performance as secretary of state—despite Benghazi.[2]

But over the course of 2014, Clinton's poll numbers started to drop. It was likely in some part due to an effect seen in previous presidential elections where public officials transitioned into candidates. But some of it was surely due to the near constant drone of Benghazi material, aired by the various hearings and Republican counter-hearings, and the success that Republicans had in transferring suspicion and blame from the Obama administration to her personally. In May 2014, *Politico* referenced the *National Journal*, which cited social media analytics firm Topsy, claiming someone was tweeting about Benghazi every twelve seconds.[3] Fox News, meanwhile, had "made Benghazi a permanent part of its programming," citing "Benghazi" in at least 1,101 programs from 2013 to 2014.[4] "Benghazi has, in effect, become Hillary's social-media twin," announced *Politico* national editor Michael Hirsh, coining it the "Benghazi-Industrial Complex."[5] In 2013, 43 percent of likely voters in one conservative poll believed that Benghazi would hurt Clinton if she ran in 2016; that number crept up to 46 percent in the same poll in January 2014.[6]

This was the political backdrop for what would become the most impactful Benghazi investigation yet. On May 2, 2014, Speaker of the House John Boehner called for the formation of a House Select Committee on Benghazi, soon to be known as the "Benghazi Committee." According to an aide, Boehner had originally been opposed to a Benghazi Committee, on the grounds that it would only repeat what multiple other committees were covering—but he became one of the main forces pushing for it.[7] The aide said the FOIA revelations of Ben Rhodes's involvement in prepping Susan Rice on the talking points was the factor that changed Boehner's mind.[8] This may have been a factor, but even more likely was the fact that, politically, Benghazi was becoming a Republican lodestone.

At first, Democrats were not sure how to handle the committee—whether they would boycott or participate, and if so, to what extent? Chairman Trey Gowdy, a Republican congressman from South Carolina, insisted that his aim was to go much deeper than the previous investigations. Dianne Feinstein, the California Democratic senator who headed the Senate Intelligence Committee and who oversaw its report on Benghazi, called Gowdy out, describing the House committee as "ridiculous . . . a hunting mission for a lynch mob." As she put it, "There have been four major reports, we spent a year and a half on a report. We held hearings, thousands of pages were reviewed, the staff spent hours and weeks on it."[9]

Democrats considered distancing themselves, naming a sole member only to keep tabs on what the committee was doing. Ultimately, they decided to participate fully, so as not to give the Right further reasons to attack Clinton. The committee was formed with seven Republicans in the majority and five Democrats in the minority.

Politically, Republicans seem to have had a few goals with the Benghazi Committee: first, to keep Benghazi alive as a political issue relevant to the November 2016 presidential election; second, to the extent possible, to use the committee to uncover new information that might sway public opinion against Clinton; and third, to keep "an already energized GOP base fired up as voters head to the polls" in the midterm elections.[10] And, in fact, in 2014 the Republicans flipped the Senate and gained thirteen seats in the House—the largest House majority since 1928.[11] This was a disaster for the Obama administration and the Democrats, though its linkages to the Benghazi attack had not been deeply commented on (certainly not to the extent it would be in the 2016 presidential election).

By early 2015, another problem was brewing in the background— a building awareness of Clinton's use of a private server for her State Department work and personal email. This would quickly eclipse Benghazi proper as a focus of national attention, even if the former had helped create the latter.

The email story had its origins in 2012, when a nonprofit called Citizens for Responsibility and Ethics in Washington, ironically established as a counterweight to conservative watchdog groups like Judicial Watch, submitted a FOIA request for information about Clinton's emails, and in mid-2013 it was told that there were no records on file at the State Department—which of course raised some eyebrows, as surely Clinton would be sending and receiving emails as secretary of state. Then in 2013, a Romanian hacker by the name of Marcel Lazar Lehel, with the handle "Guccifer," hacked the emails of Sidney Blumenthal. At the time, Blumenthal was an active, if informal, advisor to Hillary Clinton. In early March 2013, Lehel distributed to members of Congress, conservative politicians, and the media a series of briefings on Libya and Benghazi that had been sent to Clinton by Blumenthal, most of which were allegedly written by a former CIA officer, Tyler Drumheller. The hacked content revealed that Clinton and Blumenthal were corresponding via private email accounts—and that Clinton had a private server on which she was being sent information relevant to the Benghazi attack.

The hacked Blumenthal emails may have given the committee

cause to look into Clinton's email records more deeply, but it was State Department lawyers who may have accelerated the public revelation of Clinton's private server, when it requested past secretaries to return any work correspondence on private email accounts—a move some interpreted as providing cover for the imminent news on the Clinton server. On March 2, 2015, the *New York Times* ran the story.[12] Soon after, the House Select Committee on Benghazi subpoenaed Clinton's emails to, as a spokesman put it, "ensure the public record with respect to Libya and Benghazi is complete."[13] Judicial Watch, Associated Press, and Vice News all sued to gain access to copies of her records.[14]

And quickly the controversy around Clinton's emails, now dubbed "Servergate," surpassed interest in Benghazi. It was a blooming controversy, which had an odd bulldog: the decidedly liberal *New York Times*. According to the *Columbia Journalism Review*, "In just six days, *The New York Times* ran as many cover stories about Hillary Clinton's emails as they did about all policy issues combined in the 69 days leading up to the election."[15]

The Clinton campaign thought it had dodged the worst of the issue with a March 10 press conference on the emails. They also thought its linkage with Benghazi would be useful, as they saw the public getting sick of Benghazi. Clinton advisor Podesta wrote in an email to the head of a Washington think tank, "They will go after the server but that takes us back to Benghazi, which is good for us."[16] Yet the press conference only worsened the email controversy while keeping Benghazi in the news. In the months that followed, there was a "drip drip" of Benghazi-related emails and rampant public speculation as to whether those emails contained anything that would elevate Benghazi once again to the headlines.

It wasn't until late summer that the Clinton campaign caught a break, when on September 29, House Majority Leader Kevin McCarthy told Fox News, "Everybody thought Hillary Clinton was unbeatable, right? But we put together a Benghazi special committee, a select committee. What are her numbers today? Her numbers are dropping."[17]

McCarthy added that it was part of a strategy to "fight and win."[18] There was immediate outcry from the Democrats, who pointed to this as the smoking gun that proved the Republicans' intent was malevolent from the start, and that the Benghazi Committee was purely political—which, of course, it was. The tide turned further against the Benghazi Committee, with an NBC/*Wall Street Journal* poll finding that more Americans considered the Benghazi probe "unfair and too partisan" rather than "fair and impartial."[19]

But Republicans didn't seem too perturbed. The committee had served its purpose, helping to find its replacement strategy in her emails at exactly the right time. And a second NBC/*Wall Street Journal* poll found that by a margin of nearly two to one Americans were (still) unsatisfied with Clinton's response to the Benghazi attack.[20] At a higher level, polls also showed that Americans were unhappy with the GOP and Clinton both.[21]

The play had moved on to the next act: Clinton's testimony before the committee. Her appearance offered the possibility of a misstep by Clinton that the Right could weaponize, and a further opportunity to grill her on the emails. The circus around Clinton's testimony made crystal clear the degree to which Benghazi and the emails had become fused.

Clinton addressed the Benghazi Committee on October 22, 2015. It was undoubtedly the major highlight of the committee activity. It was expected to be a grueling affair—a full day of testimony. Ultimately, she spent 500 minutes in the testifying chair. The entire session, including breaks, was an impressive eleven hours.[22]

The Clinton hearing started off with sparring between Gowdy and Democrat Elijah Cummings over the purpose and fairness of the hearings. Gowdy insisted that the previous investigations weren't thorough, and Cummings said that the select committee was squandering millions of taxpayer dollars on an abusive effort to derail Secretary Clinton's presidential campaign. "Madam Secretary, I understand there are

people frankly in both parties who have suggested that this investigation is about you," Gowdy addressed Clinton. "Let me assure you it is
not. And let me assure you why it is not."[23]

Gowdy apologized to Clinton for the delays in her testimony and
got in a dig about the email controversy, saying the delay was not due
to the Republicans wanting to hurt Clinton politically, but her private
email account, which made it so difficult to request her records from the
State Department—which, indeed, it had.

Though Clinton's day-long testimony before the committee was a
source of major national attention, one of the most interesting parts of
the day—and indeed of the whole operation—was one that received
little attention. At the time, almost no one imagined that Representative Mike Pompeo from Kansas would soon become secretary of
state, under an administration of Donald Trump, not Hillary Clinton.
During his questioning, Pompeo produced a picture of Mohammed
al-Zahawi, leader of Ansar al-Sharia in Benghazi, sitting next to Wissam Bin Hamid.

"Were you aware that your folks in Benghazi, Libya, met with [Bin
Hamid] within 48 hours before the attack?" Pompeo asked Clinton.

Clinton said she knew "nothing about any meeting with him," nor
the cable that Stevens sent back to Washington the same day, describing
that meeting.

Pompeo didn't do himself any favors by being apparently unaware of
the conditions of the meeting about which he asked, or of McFarland's
name or position, or the fact that al-Zahawi was the head of Ansar
al-Sharia in Benghazi—or his connections to Al Qaeda.

This allowed Clinton to dismiss the meeting as something trivial
and Pompeo as foolish for expecting her to know about it. But questions about the role of Bin Hamid in the attack had been circulating for
some time, in part due to David Kirkpatrick's *New York Times Magazine* feature, which Clinton cited directly in her memoir of the period.
If she had read the first few pages of the article, which no doubt she
did, she would certainly have recalled the exposition of the McFarland

meeting with Bin Hamid in Benghazi, and its possibly very troubling implications.

For anyone paying attention, it was a fascinating moment: Clinton's pass and Pompeo's lack of follow-up was highlighted by *Business Insider* as the "biggest issue the Benghazi committee didn't ask Clinton about."[24] But through Pompeo, the committee did ask—it just didn't prepare and had no follow-up. Otherwise, *Business Insider* was right: the exchange between Clinton and Pompeo was highly symbolic of the degree to which the political showmanship around Benghazi distracted Republicans and Democrats from actual substance. And so the committee, once again, did what all the other committees had done—skirted the question of how we wound up trusting the goodwill of individuals we had no business trusting.

A number of publications proclaimed that Clinton—in the words of *Time*—"won the Benghazi hearing."[25] The *New Yorker* called it "Hillary's moment."[26] And in the following days and weeks, Clinton's favorability rating skyrocketed among swing voters, from 6 percent to 23 percent, indicating that her testimony allayed many voters' concerns about Clinton and Benghazi. And Democrats were rallying to her, with a rise in favorability from 58 percent to 72 percent.[27]

Clinton, of course, was not out of the woods yet. On May 25, 2016, the office of the State Department's inspector general issued a report "sharply critical" of Clinton's handling of the emails,[28] and on July 5 the FBI announced that it had found no evidence of criminal intent on Clinton's part, with respect to the sending of classified material.[29] But within this statement, FBI Director James Comey added that he believed that Clinton had been "extremely careless," a qualification the Clinton campaign charged was inappropriate and prejudicial to her campaign. And it *was* prejudicial: in a subsequent ABC/*Washington Post* poll, 56 percent of national respondents said that they disapproved of Comey's decision not to charge Clinton over the emails, 57 percent said it made them worried about her judgment if elected, and 28 percent said it made them less likely to vote for her.[30]

But then, on October 28, eleven days before the election, Comey launched a bigger bomb, announcing that the FBI would reopen the investigation into the Clinton emails, following the discovery of more of them on the personal computer of Clinton's aide Huma Abedin—who shared the device with her husband, former Congressman Anthony Weiner, the subject of a separate FBI investigation.[31]

With Comey's second announcement coming just days before the election, it cast the specter of a president-elect with a criminal investigation hanging over her head. In her election postmortem, *What Happened*, Clinton focused on the October 28 Comey statement as the largest single factor in her loss to Trump.[32]

Though the full reasoning behind Clinton's loss has been endlessly debated, it's indisputable that Trump relied on Benghazi (and of course the emails) as a kind of prodding stick for the rest of the campaign. During the primaries, he rented a movie theater in Iowa to screen the movie *13 Hours*, based on the commando-eye "docudrama" of the book by the same name. (The book, written by Mitchell Zuckoff, with the help of the Annex security team, was fairly restrained in terms of its political content. But the movie, directed by Michael Bay, of the action film series *Transformers* fame, flaunted its right-wing sympathies, focusing on the alleged stand-down orders and portraying Chris Stevens as a clueless diplomat and all of Benghazi as a warren of terrorists.)

Over the course of the final months of the campaign, Benghazi was no longer in the headlines, but Trump and his surrogates made sure it remained alive, inserting it strategically into venues in which his base—and Clinton—would notice. Trump's team brought the distraught mother of Sean Smith, the information management officer slain in Benghazi, to speak in a prime-time slot on the first night of the Republican National Convention, where she insisted that she "blame[s] Hillary Clinton personally for the death of [her] son."[33] A few days later, she told FOX Business Network that "there's a special place in hell for people like [Clinton], and I hope she enjoys it there!"[34] Trump then invited Smith to the final presidential debate on October 19, clearly with the intention of trying to intimidate or unnerve Clinton (as he did before the second debate, appearing at a panel with three women who had accused Bill Clinton of inappropriate sexual behavior).[35] Stevens's mother, for her part, begged Trump—and the whole GOP—to stop using her son's name for politics.

The Benghazi Committee adjourned on December 12, though Republicans had already released an 800-page report months earlier on June 28, which Chairman Gowdy declared would "fundamentally change the way you view Benghazi."[36] (The Democrats issued their own report shortly before the Republicans, intending to debunk what they saw as false claims.[37]) When it was all done, the committee cost 7 million dollars and lasted 782 days, outlasting congressional inquiries into Pearl Harbor, the Kennedy assassination, the Iran–Contra scandal, and Hurricane Katrina.[38]

And once the Right had connected Clinton, in the minds of Republicans, to the nonexistent stand-down orders and other failures around Benghazi, the path was cut for a series of ever-more outrageous conspiracy theories, including what was perhaps the most outlandish of them all: the idea that Clinton was running a child pedophilia ring out of a Washington, D.C., pizza restaurant—a scandal that came to be known as Pizzagate—which became Exhibit A for believers in QAnon. This was a case study in the evolution of fake news: start with something false but plausible, and then escalate into conspiracies without any connection to reality whatsoever.

While there's no denying that the Benghazi Committee had an underlying, divisive, and destructive political purpose, it wasn't an unredeemable exercise.[39] If nothing else, because its interviews were made public, and could be read by anyone wanting to make up their own mind about aspects of the controversy, it remains a valuable resource for historians.

The House committee's conclusions, however, were decidedly anticlimactic. It blamed the State Department for failing to protect diplomats and accurately assess risks but, after all of its bark, put no new responsibility on Hillary Clinton. It blamed the CIA for its failure to grasp how dangerous Libya was; it blamed the Obama administration for subverting the investigation through what it argued was intentional, coordinated, and shameful stonewalling; it blamed Clinton for hiding her emails; it blamed the ARB for being subject to Clinton's influence.[40] It made the odd observation that Americans were taken to the airport by a "Kaddafi [sic] loyalist." The final committee emphasis, however, was unusual for a Republican-led panel: it blamed the military for not having responded to the attack in time, to some degree reversing at the eleventh hour their insinuations that Clinton had been connected in some way to stand-down orders.

There's a lot that was unsatisfying about the American military response to Benghazi. Few in America who followed Benghazi and were aware of the timeline failed to wonder why, over a period of eight hours, let alone a full day, the United States couldn't respond to American citizens who were fighting for their lives. It's the kind of thing that just sounds implausible to the public, whose overall impression is that America can do just about anything it wants to. But though there were some real constraints, the Obama administration's failure to respond— or as some analysts have pointed out, to try to respond—was the sign of a broken system and a broken Libya policy, which, among other things, didn't foresee such circumstances and plan ahead, either by programming coverage at a nearby base like Souda Bay, or making arrangements with our NATO allies in the region to provide needed services. Even if there was no scandal here, a flyover of the Annex, had it been able to be secured, might well have saved Woods and Doherty at the Annex; and had the rapid reaction force left the Annex twenty-nine minutes earlier, there's a reasonable chance it might have been able to save Stevens and Smith.

While the Left seemed to expect Gowdy to feel ashamed for having found very little in over two years of leading the House committee, it is unlikely Gowdy or the other Republican members of the committee felt anything other than satisfaction that the Benghazi Committee had done its job very well, grafting Benghazi to a mainstream issue that upset a lot of Democrats—the email controversy—and laying the foundation for outrageous conspiracy theories, including Pizzagate.

The Clinton campaign issued its own statement, blasting the committee for failing to find anything beyond the conclusions of the earlier investigations, and in the same breath decried Kevin McCarthy's behavior. "This Committee's chief goal," the statement read, "is to politicize the deaths of four brave Americans in order to try to attack the Obama administration and hurt Hillary Clinton's campaign."[41]

The fact that so many investigations resulted in so few answers is its own tragedy. From the edges of the five-ring political circus that was Benghazi, some voices shouted out important questions, none of which were answered. The Benghazi Committee might have been able to break new ground and do the country a service if it had focused on them.

For one, the committee never touched the sensitive questions around arms transfers: the Obama administration's authorizations to arm the Libyan rebels prior to and leading up to the attack, directly and through proxies. It also never addressed the alleged indirect participation in shipping Libyan arms to Syrian rebels, even as publicly Clinton, Panetta, and Petraeus were pushing to arm what they believed were the last of the moderate rebels, just before the Benghazi attack. Thus we still don't know if any of the weapons transferred from Qatar to former LIFG members were ultimately used in the attack against the Mission (given that Ansar al-Sharia Derna and ex-LIFG member Bin Qumu were implicated in the attack, this is within the realm of possibility). However, the lack of insight into these topics wasn't completely, or even primarily, the committee's fault, as according to the report, the NSC apparently denied its requests to see information related to possible US covert operations in Libya leading up to the attack.[42] It does beg the question, though: Had the Republicans been even somewhat cooperative with Democrats, perhaps would more information have been forthcoming?

There was also no probe of why, exactly, the United States was relying on the February 17 Martyrs Brigade for its security when its connections to extremist groups were well known. Nor was there any investigation of the connections in Libya between the Muslim Brotherhood and the various extremist groups. And there was no investigation into the role of Turkey and Qatar in promoting and supporting hard-core jihadist groups in Libya, in direct opposition to US and Libyan interests.

There were no questions from the Benghazi Committee about the possible linkage between these actions and the Obama administration's policy toward political Islam. Was there a strategy? What was contained in the Presidential Study Directive PSD-11, the one that allegedly specified an engagement strategy for political Islam? This might have shed light on possible past and current conflicts of interest in dealing with groups across the spectrum of political Islam, from those the West categorizes as "moderate" to "extreme," and helped shine a light on the need for new policy approaches and tools.

Working back from here, we might have learned more about what went wrong with the intervention, and how institutional failures led to a situation in which few had much idea of what was happening on the ground, and regionally. We might have gotten deeper insight into why Stevens felt he had to be in Benghazi, a subject that has remained outside serious consideration, and clouded by red herrings.

Nor was there any comment from the committee on the status of attempts to identify attackers and bring them to justice. In 2014, the United States captured in Libya whom it charged was the mastermind of the attack, Ahmed Abu Khattala, whom the *New York Times*' David Kirkpatrick interviewed in Benghazi and described as the Libyan government's key suspect.[43] But a number of Libyans with knowledge of the militia situation on the ground in Benghazi at that time disagree, and say that Abu Khattala was "a talker" and suffered from serious mental illness. In November 2017 an American jury acquitted Abu Khattala of murder in the deaths of Ambassador Stevens and Sean Smith. He was sentenced to twenty-two years in jail on lesser terrorism charges.[44]

On October 29, 2017, the United States apprehended a second suspect in the Benghazi attack, Mustafa al-Imam, in Libya and brought him to the United States for trial.[45] In January 2020, al-Imam received a similar, if slightly lesser, verdict and sentence: acquittal on charges of murder and nineteen years in jail on charges related to the Benghazi attack. So though the Obama administration promised to bring the Benghazi perpetrators to justice, a decade later the trail seems to have gone cold. In part this may be due to the fact that many potential suspects were killed in the battle between the Libyan National Army and the jihadists in eastern Libya. But politically, there has also been little appetite to open the Benghazi door again.

In early spring of 2016, I received a call from "L"—the State Department's legal bureau—telling me that I would likely soon be called to testify before the House Benghazi Committee. "L" offered me some guidance, as I was a former foreign service officer, but said I would have to get my own counsel if I felt that was necessary. And it wasn't clear to me why it would be necessary—unless I refused to testify. I wasn't keen, but I wasn't going to say no. My main worry was whether I risked getting stuck within the scandal in some way. Could whatever I said be used to harm the Clinton campaign? Of course it could, but was anything I had to say easy to use in that way? I didn't have a smoking gun; what I had was a whole lot of context.

When I got the notice, I happened to be in Europe on an assignment. I assumed that I would have to fly back to Washington but was told that wasn't necessary—the interview could be done by phone. *Perhaps I was being used to up their witness count*, I thought. There had been an argument over the numbers of "new" witnesses claimed by the committee. Gowdy claimed fifty, but twenty had already been interviewed by the ARB. I would make one of the thirty that hadn't been called in any other context.

So I took the call late at night, from the balcony of my hotel room in Florence, overlooking a sparsely lit piazza.

It was a nearly two-hour call that consisted of the same kind of interview the FBI did right after the attack. I was asked to give a recitation of what I heard and saw from the night of the attack to the following day. This was followed by a series of questions from the "Minority detailee," that is, the representative of the Democratic side. These were the smoking-gun questions: Did I know for a fact that Secretary Clinton gave a stand-down order? These were easy. I didn't. The questioning was friendly and straightforward. At one point, I was asked if I wanted to add anything—and I chose simply to reiterate what I felt was Chris Stevens's very strong interest in keeping American eyes on Benghazi as long as possible, so we, the United States, didn't help lose the city, and the country. There was no drama. No questions that would have required any speculation on my part. I was relieved.

But while my experience was not the ordeal that other witnesses—most of all Clinton—went through, the process of anticipating what could go wrong and the two-hour interview gave me some additional appreciation for Secretary Clinton's position. The secretary's actions during and after the crisis suggest someone who was working to support the president as best she could, while trying to avoid being pinned down. She knew to avoid the Sunday talk shows, she reached out across the aisle to try to tamp down a crisis she saw as a threat, and she said enough to enough professional colleagues and family members to suggest she understood where the attack came from—at least generally—but wasn't going to go beyond the boundaries set by the administration. It wasn't her place. Then, when opportunities presented themselves, she was among the first to join the professional consensus in calling Benghazi an act of terrorism, even as the president did not. Susan Rice was much less strategic—but it's also apparent she didn't feel she had that leeway. It is in this context that Kirkpatrick's 2013 *New York Times* piece "A Deadly Mix in Benghazi" took on extra relevance, as its implicit (and visible) argument that the Obama administration wasn't wrong in its initial read of Benghazi allowed those who were impacted by that position a modest lifeline. Clinton and Rice both took that line in their autobiographies. Obama never did. But he wasn't running for another office.

The fact that the Republicans chose to attack first Rice, and then Clinton, for what they believed was—and what may have been—a deliberate shift in emphasis away from an attack narrative speaks to the political nature of those attacks. If this is what the Right really thought was going on, the criticism should have been aimed at Obama.

Part IV

~~~

THE WORLD
BENGHAZI MADE

27

Benghazi and the 2016 Election

Assisted by the Obama administration's highly confusing response to the attack on the US Mission, the American Right was able to weaponize Benghazi, though not quite in time to upset Obama in the 2012 presidential election. But the scandal was cultivated in such a way to project turbulence well into the future. The basic strategy was to attach Benghazi to Clinton personally as a marker of poor character, underpinned by long-term Republican narratives about the Clintons.

The instrument of this long reach was the House Benghazi Committee, whose main purpose was to keep Benghazi in the public eye as long as possible while serving as a platform from which to search for other material relevant to the 2016 election. The committee hit the jackpot in the form of Clinton's emails, which quickly outpaced Benghazi in terms of public interest—and forced the Republicans to pull back on Benghazi, lest they be accused of overreach. Though the House committee didn't turn up much in the way of real answers, the emails became a constant refrain of right-wing media and lawmakers (and then-candidate Trump).

When all was said and done, Hillary Clinton won the popular vote by nearly 2.9 million votes and lost the electoral college to Donald Trump, 227 to 304. About 80,000 votes stood between Clinton and enough electoral college votes to win the election, across the Rust Belt states of Michigan, Pennsylvania, and Wisconsin—all of which went to Obama in 2012.[1]

In the days before the election, Clinton appeared to be comfortably ahead of Trump, leading by one to seven percentage points, according to various polls, and was expected to win the electoral college handily.[2] "Clinton has 90 percent chance of winning," a Reuters/Ipsos poll proclaimed on the eve of the election.[3] A *New York Times* forecast predicted Clinton's chance of *losing* was equivalent to the odds "that an NFL kicker misses a 37-yard field goal" (about 15 percent).[4]

Predictably, in the aftermath, many pundits' first reactions were to look for a single, unexpected event that disturbed the status quo. The eleventh-hour Comey announcement ripped the scab off of the endless email scandal, and conjured up the prospect of a criminal investigation hanging over a Clinton first term as president. Though many Americans saw Clinton's handling of her emails as disqualifying, many undoubtedly just wanted the whole thing to be over. Benghazi may not have played a major role in postmortem conversations around the election, but the controversy it spawned remained central.

On top of the emails, interest quickly swung to a second, and equally dramatic, plot twist: mounting evidence of unprecedented Russian interference in the election, through a series of cyberattacks on Democratic Party institutions and candidates. The Obama administration had known about the Russian cyberattacks in the weeks leading up to the election but chose not to call them out publicly.[5]

Though it would have been satisfying to identify a single cause or misstep that could be blamed for Clinton's defeat, the idea that such a factor existed is predicated on the persistent idea that Clinton was ahead by a much greater margin than she was in the weeks and months before the election. But as was quickly apparent, the polls were off in ways that they hadn't been in the past, consistently underestimating support for Trump.

Over the following months and years, it became clearer that the factors that influenced who voted and who didn't, and how they voted, were quite complex and intertwined. As Ezra Klein argues in his 2020 book, *Why We're Polarized*, a more productive approach to analyzing

Clinton's loss would be to ask "How did a candidate like Trump . . . get within a few thousand votes of the presidency in the first place?"[6]

As (mostly liberal) pundits started to widen their inquiries around the Trump win, election numbers provided strong clues. The largest demographic voting for Trump was suburban and rural lower and middle-class white males, who also voted in record numbers. Clinton, on the other hand, failed to capture the volume of Black and minority votes that Obama did in the 2008 and 2012 elections. How did Trump manage to excite this base to vote in such numbers, and why didn't minority voters turn out as strongly for Clinton as they did for Obama?

The next phase of liberal reflection focused on Trump's base and their disaffections. Conversations touched on rising inequality in America's heartland, the role of so-called identity politics and political correctness, and the ways in which many whites—particularly poorer whites—began to feel overlooked (a fear ripe for political exploitation by the Right and Trump). And Trump's victory forced a renewed focus on what all of these things and more had to do with the ever-increasing ways in which American politics has become supercharged and super polarized in recent years.

Looking at the election in that context, Benghazi takes on a much bigger role.

Even though the Benghazi attack has been conspicuously absent from debates over what factors and what trends influenced the 2016 election, its presence can be seen practically everywhere.

Even if the issue of Clinton's emails had nothing directly to do with Benghazi, it was inextricably connected to it. Various Benghazi touch-points framed the discovery of the emails—from the leaked Blumenthal correspondence (which alerted members of Congress to the existence of Clinton's private email account) to the various frustrated FOIA requests for copies of her official emails (which intensified various media attempts to investigate Benghazi). The House Benghazi Committee's subpoena of Clinton's emails led the State Department to request former secretaries return copies of their private emails, which then led to the *New York Times* breaking the story of the existence of the private server in early March 2015. That led to the FBI investigation into whether or not Clinton had released classified information, which, of course, then led to the two Comey statements, both of which were damaging to Clinton's prospects. The first statement, whose "extremely careless" qualification infuriated Clinton and the Democrats, has been credited for driving Republicans to the polls to vote against her. The second, announcing the reopening of the FBI investigation into the emails, has been seen as potentially discouraging those who otherwise would have voted for her from voting at all.

But Benghazi's impact on American public opinion and polarization didn't stop there. The Russians used the controversy and its derivative scandals as feedstock to power its Right-riling fake news campaigns. Kathleen Hall Jamieson, in her book *Cyberwar*, documents how Russian bots and trolls inserted Benghazi-related memes and phrases, like "Killary," "Remember Benghazi," "Lock her up," and "the Butcher of Benghazi," into their social media campaigns.[7] The Russians clearly understood the potential to use social media platforms like Facebook and Twitter to destabilize American society before the American political classes did, or could mount an effective defense. They also understood how well-suited Benghazi was to their objectives. There was even one incident during the campaign in which Trump seemingly quoted a false, Kremlin-funded news report about Benghazi.[8]

And this is clear to many of those in the Obama administration who were watching this unfold.

When I asked Ben Rhodes in 2017 whether he thought Benghazi affected the 2016 election, he responded, "Of course Benghazi had an effect on the election—just start with the email server and move on down the line."[9]

And despite Clinton's focus on the email issue and Comey's role, she acknowledges Benghazi's pernicious and pervasive influence as well. In her election memoir, *What Happened*, she writes: "The press agreed that the committee was a bust for the Republicans. But I was experienced enough in the ways of Washington scandals to know that some damage had already been done. Accusations repeated often enough have a way of sticking, or at least leaving behind a residue of slime you can never wipe off."[10]

But a deeper question needs to be asked: Was Benghazi just one (albeit visible) factor among many that led to a dramatic increase in American political polarization, or was it truly a game changer? Did the extended brawl over Benghazi fundamentally alter the normal rules of American politics? And if so, what was it about Benghazi that was capable of triggering such transformation?

It's hard to imagine creating a controversy with more potential to divide the American electorate than Benghazi. First, for Americans, the setting was a complete blank slate. Even the name—Benghazi—was distinctively foreign to American ears. Yet it also had all the latent negative associations that came with being part of a war-torn region of the Middle East and in a country in which the United States had intervened militarily.

Second, the nature of the attack touched on a large number of hot-button issues that defined the fight between Democrats and Republicans over the previous two decades—and overlapped uncannily well with Trump's "America first" campaign platform, with its anti-terrorist, anti-immigrant, protectionist themes. Without much effort, the Right could link Obama—and then Clinton—to any of these issues through Benghazi, and then package it as a narrative of abandonment, in which Democrats allowed "terrorists" to take advantage of their negligence and left American heroes to die on the field.

Add to this the plausibility of the Democrats' trying to shape the story to dodge attacks they knew were coming (and which Romney confirmed), and a subsequent blowout over what constituted "truth" was almost inevitable. What the Obama administration might have seen as justifiable little white lies may have pushed the campaign past the finish line, but they enabled a relentless stream of far bolder lies by the Right afterward. Obama may have saved himself with this strategy, but the story handicapped many of the Democrats who would follow in his wake, and would hollow out both the domestic and international legacy he aspired to leave.

None of these developments, however, quite explain the full explosive nature of Benghazi. There's one additional ingredient of interest here, and that's the development trajectory of social media.

Walter Quattrociocchi, who researches the polarizing effects of social media on elections and teaches computer science at Sapienza University in Rome, says 2012 was a watershed moment in both the ability and exploitation of social media to polarize political contests—not just in the United States, but also in Europe.[11] "Had Benghazi occurred a year before it did," Quattrociocchi says, "the technology and revenue models could not likely have been weaponized to the same degree."[12] As is entirely evident now, for conspiracy theories and misinformation, social media is a force multiplier the like of which has never been seen—a reality that just so happened to coincide with Benghazi.

This coincidence may have been a necessary but insufficient condition for an explosion of self-referential, echo-chamber, and silo-grown hate in America and around the world.[13] And it may have given Benghazi its ultimate power in finally convincing each side of the aisle that the "other" was simply awful and irredeemable.

And indeed, in late August 2013, the media started associating Benghazi with the rising trend of fake news.[14] The lack of prior information about the place or the conditions, so few witnesses, and the foggy conditions around the attack made Benghazi perfect for fake news. Who could tell what was fake news when members of Congress didn't seem to really know what happened? And in response, there was a remarkable proliferation of fact-checking feeds. PolitiFact, founded in 2007, published ninety-six fact-checking pieces on various aspects of the Benghazi attack alone.[15]

President Obama could insist that with respect to "phony scandals" like Benghazi, "Washington has taken its eye off the ball, and I'm here to say this needs to stop."[16] But much as the Democrats might have wanted it to stop, it looked like they really didn't understand the dynamics at play, especially not in the way Republicans did. Clinton, like most of the rest of the country and despite all she'd been through with Benghazi, probably still didn't fully understand the roots of the rage Benghazi had help awaken on the Right. She thus stumbled into an unexpected trap when she made the following remarks at a private fundraiser, just before the election:

> You know, to just be grossly generalistic, you could put half of Trump's supporters into what I call the basket of deplorables. Right? The racist, sexist, homophobic, xenophobic, Islamophobic—you name it . . . He [Trump] tweets and retweets offensive, hateful, mean-spirited rhetoric. Now some of those folks, they are irredeemable, but thankfully they are not America.[17]

It was exactly the kind of comment that could motivate white, suburban middle-class males to get out and vote, as it spoke to many of Trump's followers' deep-rooted fears of being marginalized in a multi-cultural, multi-ethnic society.[18] But it was ironically also an opportunity for the Right to ridicule what it saw as the Left's embrace of extreme political correctness.

Clinton seemed to take the election results deeply personally—and she may have been right to do so. "There was a fundamental mismatch between how I approach politics and what a lot of the country wanted to hear in 2016," she wrote in her 2017 memoir *What Happened*.[19] But there was so much about this election that had nothing to do with her, and everything to do with forces over which she had no control. Looking back to the rationale Clinton gave for initially rejecting Obama's offer of the secretaryship—that some event might arrive that constrained her ability to act—one has to say that her worst fear had been realized.

Trump's win in 2016 was undeniably a product of America's extreme polarization. Though it's impossible to prove how much of this transformation was due to what, the more one digs into the dynamics of Benghazi—what it resulted from and what it produced—the more it's clear that Benghazi was a part of that process, not just a reflection of it.

28

The Damage Done to Libya

One of the first casualties of the Benghazi attack was the city of Benghazi itself. In his 2018 memoir, Ben Rhodes describes passing a candlelight vigil for Chris Stevens held by a group of Libyans outside the White House in the week after the attack. One of them expressed his hope that the attack didn't mean that the United States would leave Benghazi.

"I hope not," Rhodes says he replied, but he knew that it did.[1]

Rhodes seems to have felt that Benghazi conformed to that unwritten rule that once the political costs approached a certain level, the United States would withdraw—regardless of any countervailing logic. And that's what happened. Further, once the United States left Benghazi, other countries followed.

The Italian Consulate was one of the few Western diplomatic missions that remained open after the Benghazi attack. Consul General Guido De Sanctis, who had been with Stevens in Al Bayda back in early April 2011 and witnessed the attack on the US Mission, said that despite the ever-growing violence and the attack on the US Mission, he and other Italians felt that they enjoyed some degree of immunity against attack, in part due to the fact that theirs was the only consulate left that could supply visas to Europe.

"For a time, we tried to carry on," De Sanctis said, "somewhat as normal."[2]

That would be a mistake. De Sanctis said Libya had been "lucky" for him, helping him secure a follow-on ambassadorship to Qatar. But on

January 12, 2013, a couple of weeks before departing his post, his luck nearly ran out. De Sanctis and his security detail had just taken a drive through the city: "Dusk was already over town when we got back home at 5:40 PM. While we were entering the car parking, another car came out of the closest corner and opened fire. They were waiting for us."[3] Thanks to armor plating on the cars, De Sanctis and his security team managed to escape.

"Anyway, the message was clear," De Sanctis said. The Italian Consulate closed, for the time being, leaving the city nearly devoid of any Western diplomatic presence and inviting more of the darkness predicted by the Good-Hearted Bookseller.

While the Benghazi scandal took time to leave its full mark on US domestic politics, it had an immediate impact on American foreign policy, which largely went unnoticed by the American public—in large part due to the political fireworks at home. These impacts sprang from a huge uptick in risk aversion on the part of the Obama administration— and his successors. Obama didn't begin his term quite so risk averse. Despite trying to shift the focal point of American foreign policy away from the Middle East, toward Asia, he took some major risks with respect to policy in the Middle East—the Libya intervention, the raid that killed Osama bin Laden, the troop surge in Afghanistan. Yet after Benghazi, the desire to control and limit risks froze US intelligence and diplomatic assets in place.

A couple of weeks after the attack, author and former Middle East CIA field officer Robert Baer wrote in *Time* that Benghazi would be "disastrous for U.S. intelligence-gathering capabilities in the Middle East," and predicted that "the resultant siege mentality in Washington creates an imperative to pull American spies and diplomats back into fortresses, heavily defended U.S. sanctuaries from which it's almost impossible to collect good human intelligence."[4] And he was right. American officials were already subject to severe restrictions in movement in Afghanistan and Iraq and would be further constrained across the region, from Libya to Yemen. This was consistent with past American reactions to terrorist attacks, like the 1983 bombing of the US Marine barracks in Beirut by an Iranian-backed Islamist militia that killed 241 service members. In the wake of that disaster, the United States left Lebanon. Much of the rest of the international community left as well, prolonging the Lebanese civil war by nearly a decade and facilitating Iran's stranglehold over the country through the local Shi'a militia, Hezbollah. A similar dynamic played out after the Battle of Mogadishu led to the downing of two American combat helicopters and eighteen American dead during Bill Clinton's 1993 humanitarian intervention in Somalia (depicted in the movie *Black Hawk Down*).

But Benghazi was different, as the chill on American diplomacy abroad was diffuse and wide-ranging. And Washington's reaction was more extreme than it was to any of those earlier events. There are a number of likely reasons for this—first, the fact that Libya had become the unexpected focal point of America's reaction to the Arab Spring; second, the impact Stevens had on the US decision to intervene; and third, the visibility this afforded Stevens in Washington—where ambassadors are often a dime a dozen. Stevens had become, within the halls of Congress, a bit of a legend—the scrappy, unflappable diplomat willing to travel into the maw of danger on a Greek freighter to help assure America's intervention in Libya turned out well. Younger diplomats looked up to him as a role model—and an example of what they might aspire to. So Chris's death was not just a shock; for many in Washington, it was deeply personal. After the reception at Andrews Air Force Base for the returning coffins, Secretary of State Clinton felt the need to hold a session at the State Department to console those who knew Stevens and interacted with Stevens personally.

Analysts and officials who had direct contact with White House and NSC staff in the weeks and months that followed described a NSC shell-shocked by the attack, how it could have happened, what they

missed. Emile Hokayem, a senior fellow for Middle East security at the
International Institute for Strategic Studies, then writing a book on the
origins of the Syrian civil war, says that Benghazi came up in discussions with White House and NSC staff "repeatedly, incessantly, even in
contexts where there was no direct connection."[5] While bad things do
happen around the world, for the NSC and others at the White House,
Benghazi felt deeply personal. And that pain and sense of offense only
got worse as the event turned into a scandal.

In 2018, Anne Patterson, who served as ambassador in Egypt during the Arab Spring and went on to become assistant secretary for
Near Eastern affairs, summarized Benghazi's effects on American diplomacy: "After Benghazi, what we could do in the Middle East was
nothing short of catastrophic . . . [the attack] made it impossible to
take risks, we withdrew from the Middle East, but most importantly,
we are now blind in areas of the world where we need to know what
is going on."[6] Expeditionary diplomacy was predicated on the idea
that diplomacy required a certain degree of risk-taking. And in one of
Benghazi's ironies, the attack that killed Stevens also killed both one
of expeditionary diplomacy's best exemplars and the ethos behind the
approach.

The attack on the US Mission occurred at a critical point in Libya's
political transition. This was almost certainly part of the plan. Two
months before, on July 7, Libya held its first national election, in which
60 percent of registered voters participated. For a country with no
experience with democracy in forty-two years, it was an impressive
performance.[7] Jibril's National Forces Alliance (NFA), a coalition of
"progressive," non-Islamist parties, won a plurality of votes; the Islamist
parties did relatively poorly. Abdulhakim Belhaj's Al Watan (Homeland) party did not win a seat.[8] September 12—the day after the attack
on the US Mission—was to be the date that Libya's new parliament
chose a prime minister, whose first order of business would be to try to
form a government.

During a Democratic primary debate with Bernie Sanders in 2015, Hillary Clinton referenced this period with some nostalgia: "The Libyan people had a free election for the first time since 1951. And you know what, they voted for moderates, they voted with the hope of democracy."[9] Before a television audience of tens of millions of Americans, Clinton was clearly arguing that the Libya intervention, the main foreign policy initiative of her tenure as secretary of state, was not doomed from the start. There had been promise.

But Clinton may not have been aware of just how deeply US actions over the previous years, dating back to both the Bush-era extraordinary renditions of the LIFG leadership and the subsequent *Corrections*, had damaged the so-called progressives' longer-term viability. Had the Obama administration understood the dynamics on the ground better, and had it had a clear policy on political Islam, it might have done better in responding to the Arab Spring in general. Clinton says that she was not nearly as optimistic as some about the outcome of the Arab Spring. "From the fall of Mubarak," she said, "it was clear this was not going to be a smooth transition."[10]

But America's intentions with respect to political Islam, and the Brotherhood, soon became an issue within Libya. The issue of the Islamists' political legitimacy was a topic on which Bubaker Habib says he and Chris Stevens debated frequently. "Chris thought that the Brotherhood had a place in Libyan politics," Habib said. "They were Libyan, after all, and as such had a right to participate in determining the country's political future."

"Others," Habib said, "felt that the Brotherhood had an unfair advantage. They were a minority and had external support and organization. Their political goal of turning Libya into an Islamic state was foreign to most Libyans. I mean, what does an Islamic State really mean in this context? Were they trying to tell us we Libyans weren't already sufficiently Muslim?"[11]

But if his cables were any indication, Stevens's feelings for the Islamists and their political relevance were informed, if not heavily influenced, by his understanding of the injustices Gaddafi and the United States had committed toward Libyans—as well as an underestimation of their access to abundant resources. Mahmoud Jibril described a meeting with Stevens and the ambassadors of France and the United Kingdom, just before the 2012 election. "The Europeans were convinced the Muslim Brotherhood would win by a landslide," Jibril told me. "Stevens was a bit less sure."[12] The results of the election favored Stevens's caution against a Brotherhood landslide, but he also understood that the public results masked the fact that the true affiliations of many of the candidates who ran as independents were unknown, both to the foreign diplomats and to the majority of voters. Stevens may have been right about the Brotherhood's grip on the country, but not for long.

Jibril lost the September 12 contest for prime minister back in Tripoli, and the Brotherhood-backed candidate Mustafa Abushagur was tasked with forming a government, taking over from interim prime minister Abdurrahim El Keib. Abushagur provoked a backlash by proposing a cabinet that did not include any of Jibril's NFA party members (despite the party having won a plurality of the popular vote). His government did not receive enough votes to remain standing, and so human rights lawyer Ali Zeidan was given the chance to form a government, which he did successfully on October 14, 2012, becoming Libya's first non-interim prime minister.

Zeidan was not an Islamist, but he was immediately subject to immense pressures to bring more Islamists into the government and give them more powers. The Islamists had tremendous leverage, especially because of the Gaddafi weapons depots that the United States failed to destroy during Operation Odyssey Dawn and the weapons deliveries it had green-lighted from Qatar, in lieu of direct oversight. As part of the political bargaining process, former LIFG members obtained key roles in the government, many at deputy-minister level, and were appointed to senior military posts in eastern Libya. Though some blamed Zeidan for caving to the militias, others saw him as someone who tried to manage an impossible situation, only to be rewarded with the indignity of being kidnapped in 2013 and in 2017 and held for several days by one of the militias.

Ibrahim Dabbashi, Libya's former representative to the UN, was one of many who insisted that the core post-revolution need was for a swift, well-organized disarmament, demobilization, and reintegration campaign that took the guns out of the hands of the regional militias and the Islamist groups, and created jobs for young people.

This approach is highlighted in one of the foundational texts on the aspirational Responsibility to Protect (R2P) norm, published in 2001 by the International Commission on Intervention and State Sovereignty (ICISS). The ICISS report was drafted in response to UN Secretary-General Kofi Annan's 1999 call for an international consensus around what R2P interventions would look like in practice. The ICISS report stressed the need for "sustainable reconstruction and rehabilitation" and noted that this often requires commitment of sufficient funds, resources, cooperation, and time.[13] Chapter 5 of the report is dedicated to a key corollary of R2P, something called the Responsibility to Rebuild (R2R). Ignoring this, the ICISS warned, comes at a heavy cost:

> Too often in the past the responsibility to rebuild has been insufficiently recognized, the exit of the interveners has been poorly managed, the commitment to help with reconstruction has been inadequate, and countries have found themselves at the end of the day still wrestling with the underlying problems that produced the original intervention action.[14]

The Obama administration and its assembled coalition framed Libya as a model implementation of R2P, so how could the R2R component have been left out? Yes, the Bush administration also couched American wars in Iraq and Afghanistan as humanitarian operations, but their core military operation was undeniable—and certainly affected both their credibility as R2P operations as well as those operations' attention paid to the associated recommendations.

President Obama would famously tell *New York Times* columnist Thomas Friedman that one of his biggest regrets was the failure to plan for what came next in Benghazi.[15] Secretary Clinton says she feels strongly, to this day, that Libya was a missed opportunity, and that the United States "could have done much more for the country."[16]

So why didn't we? The short answer is politics.

In addition to the political pressures Obama felt to shape the intervention to accomplish a good end, but not at his (and America's) expense, there were related, practical constraints, almost all of them imposed by the United States. The Libyans, for one, were expected to foot the bill for their own reconstruction, at a time when they had no access to funding (due to the fact that the government wasn't yet recognized as the legitimate representative of the Libyan people, and Libya's assets abroad were frozen). This made them dependent on grants from Qatar and Turkey, without which the revolution would have collapsed. Obama administration officials insisted that the United States was always ready to help, even after Benghazi—but that the Libyans failed to engage or clarify what they needed. Ben Fishman, who coordinated Libya policy at the NSC, attributed the Libyans' failure to engage to what they saw as "neo-colonial implications."[17] Liberal members of Parliament say that the Islamists used terms like this to keep the Americans at bay while they built up their own militia networks and took control of the few quasi-functioning institutions that remained from the Gaddafi government, such as the Central Bank and the Libyan Investment Fund. The Americans took certain Libyans at their word without a larger understanding of the whole situation. In other words, the Americans had no clue what was happening.

During El Keib's year as interim prime minister, the militias successfully pressured the government to put in place a pension system that channeled hundreds of millions of dollars a year in automatic payments to those who registered (themselves or others, some deceased) as *thuwar* (revolutionaries). And once the West unfroze Gaddafi-era assets, the lack of proper infrastructure and safeguards allowed the vast majority of it to be looted, as those with influence siphoned off huge amounts of money for things like cars and elective surgeries abroad. While the United States remained in a state of paralysis, waiting for Libyans to explain what they wanted America to do, those most determined to control the political process went ahead unimpeded.

Fishman noted that the United States had tried—after the Benghazi attack—to set up a General Purpose Force (GPF) of about 7,000 Libyans to help with stabilization and security, but that they couldn't find enough recruits willing to participate. Monem Alyaser, the head of the Libyan Security Committee within the General National Congress (the elected Parliament), says that the program was hopelessly mismanaged and under-resourced, and remained plagued by the same persistent issue: the Americans had no idea about the militia dynamics on the ground and whose loyalties were with whom.

This, Alyaser says, was certainly connected to the Benghazi attack, and America's resultant reduced ground capacity and intelligence.[18] Sarah Carlson, a CIA threat assessment officer based in Tripoli from 2013 to 2014, describes the impact that the Benghazi attack had on US operations in Tripoli in 2013: "[The US government] had even less information, especially because there was no longer a US presence in Benghazi, which meant we'd have even less warning about Ansar al-Sharia plans and intentions throughout the entire region."[19] Further, the security restrictions imposed on all US embassies in the region, let alone Tripoli, made it impossible to get out and talk to anyone. Meetings with contacts were held at the Embassy, which typically created a heavy disincentive for locals to share information.

It took nearly eight months for the United States to name an ambassador to succeed Stevens. Not many diplomats were keen to take the job, for somewhat obvious reasons: few senior US Foreign Service officers had exposure to the country, the administration clearly had an extremely limited appetite to engage with Libya, and the physical dangers were very real. Senator Dianne Feinstein formally nominated me for the position, and I was told by a reliable source that Senator McCain seconded her nomination. But it was very clear to me that this was going to be a punishing position for whomever filled it.[20] The mood in Washington didn't appear to be one of doubling down and getting things right, but of avoiding the possibility of making new mistakes (which, of course, meant it would be hard to get anything done at all).

Ambassador Deborah Jones, who had previously served as US ambassador to Kuwait, was confirmed in the summer of 2013. The United States would return to Libya (to Tripoli, not Benghazi), with an uncertain mission, and one eye on the exit: the Embassy now had a bare-bones staff, much more security, and huge restrictions on diplomats' movement.

Libyan progressives were struck that Benghazi failed to provoke any fundamental review of US policy toward Libya and the lopsided influence of the Islamists. To many senior liberal Libyan politicians, it appeared that the United States was not only still speaking with the Islamists but actually prioritizing talks with them—even as their popularity in Libya fell dramatically, with more evidence of the groups' draconian political agenda.[21]

Over the course of the months since the attack, the Islamist militias had consolidated their hold over Benghazi. And the city's residents continued to resist. On June 8, 2013, popular anger against the militants boiled over once more, as protestors converged on the Benghazi headquarters of Libya Shield One—the militia led by Wissam Bin Hamid, which had been absent when the attack was underway, but ubiquitous in the aftermath. Bin Hamid's men opened fire on the crowd, killing more than thirty, and leaving dozens injured, in an incident known as Black Saturday.[22]

If there was one lesson the US government should have learned immediately from Benghazi, it was that the line between radical and moderate Islamists—whether Muslim Brotherhood, LIFG, Ansar al-Sharia, or other groups—was paper thin. There was no effective way of divorcing the Libyan Brotherhood from the international Brotherhood, or from their more extreme associates in Libya (for whom the Brotherhood had played the role of intermediary with the West). There was no firewall here. But the State Department stuck to its policy of engagement across Libya's political spectrum, even as the CIA, which had felt burned by the department over Benghazi, and other agencies voiced their objections.

Tensions between the CIA and the State Department over Libya policy bubbled up once again during Ambassador Jones's tenure as ambassador.

Jones's approach to the job was far blunter than Stevens's. Using the Twitter handle @SafiraDeborah (Arabic for Ambassador Deborah), she quickly generated controversy, with a number of senior progressives accusing her of taking sides in favor of the Brotherhood—in the same way that Anne Patterson was seen by Egyptians to be taking the side of the Brotherhood under President Morsi. Jones insists that "there was no US relationship with the LIFG nor the Libyan MB [Brotherhood] *per se*."[23] She attributed discussions with former LIFG members to the United States' desire to support the peace-making efforts of the United Nations, which saw these groups as essential to long-term peace. As for any potential threat posed by the ostensibly disbanded LIFG, Jones noted simply that by the time she arrived, the group had been taken off the State Department's list of foreign terrorist organizations (December 2015).[24]

Concerning the progressives, Jones felt that they were exaggerating their own importance in Libya, and downplaying the influence of the Brotherhood. "When I first arrived in the country I was told that there were 'fewer than 5 percent' of Libyans one might consider to be MB [Muslim Brotherhood]," Jones wrote in October 2018. "Of course by the time I departed, they were seen to be coming out of the closet every-where . . . In reality, there is no such thing as a Libyan secularist."[25] But Jones's willingness to equate social conservatism with sympathy for the Muslim Brotherhood was perhaps ill-informed, or of necessity aligned with Washington's continuing belief that the key to stability in the Middle East went through an incarnation of moderate political Islam, which may or may not exist. Benghazi doesn't seem to have forced a reconsideration or rephrasing of that position.

In 2013 and 2014, there was insufficient will in Washington even to help Libyans fight back against the more radical forces that were known to be responsible for the Benghazi attack. Wanis Bukhamada's "Thunderbolt" forces requested American help fighting Ansar al-Sharia in Benghazi, but the United States deferred to the objections of the Libyan Ministry of Defense, which was now heavily under the control of former LIFG and Brotherhood elements.[26]

Sarah Carlson's descriptions of the CIA's interaction with the State Department in Libya in 2014 suggest that the two agencies remained in disagreement over what needed to be done in Libya, to combat Ansar al-Sharia, and with respect to the motives and threat posed by the supposedly disbanded LIFG.[27] With respect to helping fight Ansar al-Sharia, "The US military agreed [to support forces in Libya]," she wrote. "The CIA was ready. The State Department weighed options. Ultimately bureaucracy kept the administration from providing the needed assistance."[28]

One of the things that was so striking in the wake of the Benghazi attack, but rarely mentioned, was the fact that the Islamist militias had done exactly what Wissam Bin Hamid and Mohammed Al Gharabli had requested the Americans help them do, back when they met David McFarland and Bubaker Habib on September 9, 2012. They opened up the defense and security ministries to Islamists, many of whom were party to the *Corrections*.

Khalid al-Sherif was the LIFG's number two. He had been arrested in Pakistan, then turned over to the Americans, who tortured him and rendered him to Libya in 2005. He became deputy defense minister.[29] Abdel Wahab Al Qaid, the LIFG's political counselor and the brother of Al Qaeda's former number two, became head of the Parliamentary Committee for National Security. Belhaj had already been named head of the Tripoli Military Council, following his disputed role in the liberation of Tripoli. And throughout this process, the former LIFG members maintained that they remained committed to the moderate positions they took on as part of the *Corrections* process. And the Western media, to the extent it was paying attention, took most of this at face value, partly because there were so few journalists on the ground in Libya, and outlets like Al Jazeera filled the void.

In the following months, Abdel Wahab Al Qaid spearheaded a controversial piece of legislation that aimed to disqualify all those who had served in positions of influence under Gaddafi from serving in government and military positions.[30] Enacted in May 2013, the Political Isolation Law knocked out of contention many of the most visible of the liberals and technocrats, including the former liberal interim prime minister Mahmoud Jibril. The Islamist militias and their allies further enforced the law by laying siege to noncompliant government ministries, until they conceded.[31] Meanwhile, Islamist militias fanned out to destroy buildings and pieces of art they deemed offensive to Islamic morals, including prominent Sufi shrines. Ambassador Stevens had described similar acts committed in Benghazi in the cable he sent back to Washington just before his death.

Over the following years, when I heard stories from the post-Benghazi period, I couldn't help thinking of Defense Secretary Robert Gates's articulation of his opposition to US intervention in Libya. It wasn't that he was opposed to humanitarian interventions; it was that the United States was overstretched in Iraq and Afghanistan, and further, neither of those conflicts had demonstrated a positive record of post-intervention state-building, for all the insane amounts of resources thrown at them. Implicit in this warning seemed to be his belief that this wasn't a capacity that the US government could realistically develop overnight, even if the will was there—which it didn't seem to be. Hillary Clinton and Robert Gates had often been on the same side of important issues. But on Libya, they diverged. Clinton believed that change in Libya, and the American bureaucracies, was difficult but possible—and that it was better to get caught trying and failing, than not trying.

In light of this, for a time I was somewhat baffled that Libya didn't get more attention from the bureau Clinton set up, CSO. The reasons for this were explained to me later by those who headed the group:

"When it came down to it, we had some great people and ideas and just too few resources available," said Dr. Jerry White, who served as the deputy assistant secretary for the CSO. "Chris Stevens was grateful for our suggestions," White said, "because he felt other agencies just weren't paying attention. But there was a limit to what we could do under the circumstances."

Of course, even if the Benghazi attack hadn't happened, Libya would have faced an uphill battle, barring a much more active intervention, not only by the United States, but also Europe, whose interests were far more immediately impacted by what happened in Libya than the United States' were. But the attack accelerated its unraveling. As Marc Lynch, a D.C.-based professor and blogger on the Arab Spring, observed, "For Libya, the Benghazi attack helped to push its delicate transitional process into a death spiral."[32] According to former assistant secretary of state for Near Eastern affairs (and now CIA chief) William Burns, "The Benghazi tragedy and the endless political circus around it substantially lessened the administration's appetite for deeper involvement in Libya."[33] Whether the timing was intentional or not, Benghazi pushed the United States off the chessboard just as Libyans needed us most.

But the aftershocks of the attack on the US Mission in Benghazi weren't limited to Libya. The attack and the political scandal affected how the Obama administration responded to other regional conflicts, in ways that were often hard to quantify. One of these was the revolution raging in Syria, whose evolution had been linked to Libya from the start.

29

Killing the Whispers
(of a Strong Syria Policy)

On March 6, 2011, the regime of Syrian President Bashar al-Assad arrested fifteen schoolboys for painting slogans on the walls of buildings in the southern Syrian city of Dera'a, including "the people demand the fall of the regime," a revolutionary phrase that was spreading across the Middle East.[1] Protestors called for the children's release. The regime responded with violence, sparking further clashes, which ultimately led to mass defections from the Syrian army and more regime reprisals. On August 18, 2011, President Obama joined various European leaders in calling for Assad to step down.[2]

The Syrian and Libyan Revolutions both started around the same time. Through the first year, Assad was faring much better than his Libyan counterpart in holding on to power. In the absence of an intervention like the one that toppled Gaddafi, Assad had maintained the upper hand over the rebel movement, whose organizational focal point had become the Istanbul-based Syrian National Council (somewhat analogous to Libya's NTC) and various militias fighting as the Free Syrian Army.

But by the summer of 2012, the tide had turned, and Assad was facing significant losses. On July 18, a rebel attack in Damascus killed several high-level regime officers, including Assad's minister of defense and his brother-in-law. President Obama and other Western leaders started to believe that Assad's days were numbered.[3]

A month later, at a White House press briefing on August 20, the president was asked about the US response to any use of chemical weapons in Syria. Obama replied that if the Assad regime were to use chemical weapons on civilians, this would be a "red line" that would "change my calculus" with respect to military intervention in the Syrian conflict.[4] The US intelligence community had been relaying unconfirmed reports of small-scale usage of chemical weapons to the White House over the first half of 2012.[5] One wonders if the president's remark was a warning to Assad that Obama knew about these violations, and they better stop, or if it was, as many suggested, an "off-the-cuff" response that Obama may later have regretted.[6]

Regardless of what (or to whom) Obama might have been trying to communicate, the remark had tangible consequences on the ground. Pro-Western members of the Syrian opposition interpreted Obama's "red line" to mean that the United States had ruled out a repeat of the kind of intervention that the United States had made in Libya—a no-fly zone, for example, to prevent Assad from using airpower on the rebels and civilians.[7] The Arabian Gulf states, divided among themselves on other issues (including the nature and threat posed by the Muslim Brotherhood), were uniformly hostile to the Assad regime. They seemed to have interpreted Obama's remarks similarly and escalated lethal aid to the rebels, much of which wound up in the hands of hard-core, battle-hardened Islamist radicals.

It was at this apparent tipping point—when Assad looked to be hanging by a thread, but before the opposition had been irredeemably radicalized—that the Benghazi attack hit. And a few months later, the situation in Syria had flipped once again: Assad was back in a position of relative strength, and simultaneously the opposition had become further radicalized. What effect, if any, did Benghazi have on these dynamics and Assad's reversal of fortune? Of the few attempts to get more information out of the Obama administration, most seemed to have been stymied by presidential privilege and top-secret classification.[8] Thus any attempt to answer these essential questions requires a wide-ranging analysis and some degree of speculation.

Secretary Clinton spent the summer of 2012 advocating for a more decisive US intervention in Syria. In late July, she approached CIA Director David Petraeus about the feasibility of pulling together a "carefully vetted and trained force of moderate rebels" to fight Assad.[9] Clinton and Petraeus made common cause with Defense Secretary Leon Panetta to push the case with Obama, and they were joined by the Joint Chiefs of Staff and the director of national intelligence.[10] In his book on the rise of ISIS, Joby Warrick describes their view of "the notion of arming Syria's moderate rebels as undesirable yet necessary—the least objectionable out of a list of exceedingly bad options."[11]

The president's NSC and White House advisors were largely opposed to this idea, however. It was a striking reversal of roles compared to the debate over intervention in Libya, where the gray-hairs were against intervention and Obama's younger advisors were strongly in favor. Meanwhile, the president had challenged his NSC advisors to come up with a single example where the United States had supported an insurgency and it had been successful. When a counterexample wasn't forthcoming, he declared the idea "half baked."[12]

Later in the summer, Petraeus, backed by Clinton and Panetta, made a more formal case to the president for armed assistance to the Syrian rebels. The presentation took place in the White House Situation Room. What became known as the "Petraeus-Clinton argument" held that while arming the rebels would not necessarily—or even likely—topple Assad at that point, it might give the United States and its allies leverage in pursuit of a negotiated solution while increasing American visibility on what was going on on the ground. Clinton called it having "skin in the game."[13] Obama polled the room: Vice President Biden called it a "stupid idea"; Susan Rice insisted it would destroy Obama's second-term agenda. The president left the room without making a decision.[14]

Obama gave many signs of his reluctance to get involved in Syria militarily, but there was one that doesn't seem to have been mentioned at the Petraeus meeting: the 2012 election. Syria wasn't even going to get the chance to wreck his second term, as Rice worried, if he didn't get one. In his book *Alter Egos*, *New York Times* correspondent Mark Landler highlights Obama's concern: "If Obama was reluctant on the merits to get drawn into Syria, he was certainly not going to do it just before he faced the voters."[15] As is, he was already fending off the first round of Benghazi-related attacks from the right.

Another discussion about the potential arming of Syrian opposition took place in December (after Obama won the election), with Mike Morrell in the place of Petraeus, who had been ousted as head of the CIA in a somewhat bizarre and oddly timed sex scandal involving his biographer Paula Broadwell. (A month before Petraeus's resignation, Broadwell had caused a momentary stir when she claimed in a speech that the Benghazi attack was an attempt by Libyan radicals to retrieve prisoners being held in Libya by the CIA.[16]) Morrell strongly re-pitched the Petraeus–Clinton plan but added stricter controls on the end recipients.[17] Ultimately, decisions were made to support the Free Syrian Army with lethal and nonlethal aid. It was seemingly all for naught: the debate over how much of what to send the Syrian opposition was still going on a year later, and there's no evidence that the United States ever directly did much to help, officially at least.

The Benghazi attack added some unexplained wrinkles to this high-level, quasi-public hand-wringing about whether to arm the Syrian opposition, mainly by shining some light on a piece of a Syrian–Libyan arms supply chain. One part, it seems, went through Benghazi. The day after the attack on the US Mission, a cargo ship, *Al Intisar* (*Victory*), departed Benghazi for Turkey and Syria, presumed to be loaded with weapons. Libyan Islamists claimed that they were destined for the Free Syrian Army.[18] And later, a leaked US Defense Department cable revealed that the United States had been monitoring arms shipments leaving Benghazi for Turkey in late August, just weeks before the Benghazi attack.[19] That cable indicates that whatever else might have been going on, at the very least, the United States didn't seem to be making any effort to *stop* the shipments.[20]

Over time, increasing evidence would emerge that the arms leaving Benghazi for Syria were a relatively minor part of the whole movement of military, cash, and human aid to Syria via Tripoli. Arabian Gulf authority Kristian Ulrichsen supports widespread speculation inside and outside Libya that, in March 2012, Qatar "may have provided a covert $100 million 'donation' to the rebel cause sent through Libyan coffers."[21]

Several of my Libyan political contacts told me that Benghazi was a side road. They explained that the weapons freeway ran from Tripoli to Ankara, and the large transfers of money went from Libyan banks to Syrian fighters via Turkish financial institutions. Another technique for transferring money from Libya to Syria is thought to have been via fake letters of credit opened through Turkish banks.[22] A UN Panel of Experts on Libya report issued in March 2013 further confirmed these activities, which seemed to be ongoing: "Since 2012, the Panel has reported several transfers of weapons from Libya to Syria or seized en route . . . The [network] included Libyans holding official positions in the Ministry of the Interior and the Ministry of Defense."[23]

Already by April 2011 (just after the US–NATO intervention in Libya), the Obama administration was growing concerned that Qatar was diverting weapons earmarked for Libya's NTC to veterans of such groups as the LIFG.[24] And yet, in the case of Libya, Qatar's military support for these groups—including RPGs and assault rifles—only increased up to the fall of Tripoli, by which point LIFG allies like Mahdi Harati were helping set up groups like Liwa al Ummah in Syria to fight Assad.[25]

Certainly, there seems to be a disconnect between the high-level urgings of Clinton, Panetta, and Petraeus to the president to act in Syria and the fact that US proxies were actually already acting, but via channels that were more radical than Obama professed to be comfortable supporting. Was this conversation all something of a show, that is, the United States was *already* intentionally arming the Syrian rebels through proxies, and the president and his administration just didn't want to be publicly connected to it? (Petraeus as director of the CIA would presumably have known about covert assistance, but Clinton and Panetta might not have.) Or was the question about whether the United States would publicly support the Syrian opposition, if there was more control over who got that support?

Those questions, though tantalizing and full of significance for the broader US strategy in the Middle East, don't resolve the question of Benghazi's influence upon the course of the Syrian Revolution. But evidence suggests that the Benghazi attack (combined with Obama's "red line" speech) accelerated the flow of arms, money, and training going from Libya and the Arabian Gulf states to the hard-core Islamists in Syria. And it may have effectively stopped in its tracks any effort by the United States to target its assistance to what it believed were more moderate groups. And in that sense, as *Black Wave* author Kim Ghattas suggested to me, "Benghazi may have killed the whispers of a strong US Syria policy."[26]

There's still far too much we don't know about this period of the Arab Spring—which was critical to the course of the Libyan Revolution and was likely critical to the course of the Syrian Revolution. For its part, the Obama administration has downplayed the idea that it missed a window of opportunity to intervene productively in Syria in the fall of 2012, following the Benghazi attack. In a 2014 interview with the *New York Times*'s Thomas Friedman, Obama described any initial hopes of steering the Syrian conflict in a positive direction by arming the moderate rebels as a "fantasy."[27] He continued:

> This idea that we could provide some light arms or even more
> sophisticated arms to what was essentially an opposition made
> up of former doctors, farmers, pharmacists and so forth, and

that they were going to be able to battle not only a well-armed state but also a well-armed state backed by Russia, backed by Iran, a battle-hardened Hezbollah, that was never in the cards.[28]

And Ben Rhodes supported the president's claim in his memoir *The World as It Is*, in which he wrote that the 2012 Clinton–Petraeus initiative had achieved "mythical status" as a missed opportunity: "it was a small-scale recommendation to engage a portion of the opposition," not something meant to change the course of the war.[29] When I asked Jake Sullivan, former director of policy planning at the State Department, if he saw any connection between the Benghazi attack and Obama's position on Syria, he replied, as have many others in government at the time: "Did Libya as a whole influence the President's attitude towards Syria? Yes. Did Benghazi? I don't see it."[30]

Despite all the unanswered questions, at least a few things remain clear. But given the White House's demonstrated extreme caution with respect to Republican criticisms on its handling of Islamic terrorism, one can safely assume that in the last lap of the 2012 election, the last thing the Obama administration wanted was to encourage the idea that the CIA was running arms to Syria via Libya (not only because it smacked of past American arms scandals [i.e., the Reagan-era Iran-Contra affair] but because it might have invited further questions about the lack of US oversight of arms shipped to Libyan rebels—some of which could conceivably have been used in the attack itself). There were, in other words, many overlapping and strong motives for the Obama administration to find something other than Al Qaeda to talk about in the immediate wake of the Benghazi attack.

The way in which American policy toward Syria impacted the evolution of the Benghazi scandal remains one of the most obscure, least explored, and yet potentially most illuminating aspects of the Benghazi story.

Few have argued that a "Syria effect" shaped the Obama administration's communications around Benghazi. But given that we know that the US defense and intelligence agencies knew about third-party arms transfers from Benghazi to Syria at the time, as well as the president's spring 2011 concern about the misdirection to Libyan radicals of weapons (arms that could conceivably have been used later in the Benghazi attack), it's hard to imagine that there weren't a few people in the Obama administration hoping to tamp down mentions of Syria and Benghazi in the same sentence. And though none of the Benghazi investigations managed to get far with the Syria–Benghazi connection, these are the kinds of questions that need to be asked and answered, even if it's a decade after the fact, just so we can understand what went wrong and learn from it.

30

Back to Libya

Three months after the United States evacuated the last of its diplomats from Libya, and three years after the US intervention that helped
liberate the country from the forty-two-year reign of Muammar Gaddafi, I had an opportunity, if not exactly to "meet" President Obama, at
least to shake his hand.

The occasion had nothing to do with me, or anything I had done.
My father, a professor of mathematics, had been awarded, along with
eleven other American scientists, the National Medal of Science.

During the October 2014 ceremony, the president used my father as
an example of America's promise for immigrants who have talent and
who work hard. In a background statement prepared for the event, my
father said he was grateful that America took him in and gave him the
opportunity to achieve a life that would have been much more difficult
elsewhere. He said he felt he belonged in this country.

Taking my father's words as his cue, President Obama responded:

> You *do* belong—because this is America, and we welcome
> people from all around the world who have that same striving
> spirit. We're not defined by tribe or bloodlines. We're defined by
> a creed, idea. And we want that tradition to continue.[1]

The ceremony was, in a word, presidential. Obama was poised and unflappable. There was an air of adoration in the audience. I tried to focus on the ceremony and my father, of whom I was very proud.

But I couldn't shake a feeling of cognitive dissonance, as if I were living in two parallel universes. In one, I was playing the role of admiring son. In another, I was an extra playing multiple side roles in the evolution of the president's relationship with Libya: apparently the lone Libya contributor to then Senator Obama's 250-odd-person foreign policy advisory group back in 2007; a former colleague of Ambassador Stevens; a witness to the Benghazi attack itself. Obama's speech connected these two universes when he used my father's remarks as a lead-in to the wishful idea that there were no tribes and bloodlines in America—while outside the White House, America's tribalism seemed to be growing deeper, stoked by continuing partisan conflict over the Benghazi attack. Standing there in the White House, I felt distinctively voiceless. When I shook the president's hand, I imagined saying something like, "It's not too late, Libya's not lost"—but I was well aware this was both a platitude and a fantasy. I had written op-eds, given interviews, even given congressional testimony, without changing anyone's mind. It was then that I first recognized the solution to how I felt might be back in Benghazi, more than in Washington.

The year 2014 was the year Libya split, and a new drama began—one that continues to this day. The elected government was in deadlock, under constant pressure from the Tripoli militias, which had the capital in a vise grip. Corruption was out of control.

In this atmosphere, the General National Congress (GNC) declared in early 2014 that it was going to extend its mandate—unconstitutionally—past the date set for national elections the coming summer. This move was hugely unpopular, and it compounded Libyans' pervasive awareness that Benghazi was inescapably sinking into a darkness that threatened to envelop the whole country. Large protests broke out in Tripoli.[2] All this paved the way for the return of General

Khalifa Heftar, the defected Gaddafi general whom the United States had recruited in the late 1980s and cultivated as a Plan B for getting rid of Libya's dictator. During the early days of the revolution, Heftar had been recruited by some of the Libyan opposition to return to the country but had lost out to General Abdel Fattah Younes. Here was Heftar's opportunity for a comeback. He assembled his own forces, bringing in many of his past associates from Gaddafi's Libyan National Army.

Heftar called on the GNC to dissolve itself—an action that some GNC members called an attempted coup. Nothing much happened. And a few months later, on May 16, Heftar announced the creation of Karama (Dignity), a national campaign to fight the Islamist militias and their allies, as well as to kick ISIS and Al Qaeda out of eastern Libya. Over the previous months, US and NATO jets had been pummeling the Islamic State in Syria and Iraq, prompting Libyan fighters—many of whom came from Derna (the town Stevens surreptitiously visited in 2007)—to return to Derna, where under the banner of Katibat al-Battar al-Libi (the al-Battar Brigade), they had recently helped establish the first official ISIS emirate outside Syria and Iraq.

Under these clouds, Libya's second national legislative elections were held in July. Turnout was much lower than in 2012, which might have been expected to benefit the much better organized Islamists. But the Islamist parties did even worse than the first time, allowing the more liberal elements to form the House of Representatives (HOR). The new government had intended to escape the extortive power of the Tripoli militias by relocating to Benghazi, but given the Islamist takeover of the city, it set up shop in the far eastern town of Tobruk. Its cabinet, led by Abdullah Al-Thinni, set up in Al Bayda—a town of about 250,000 people, about 120 miles northeast of Benghazi, about an hour from General Heftar's military headquarters.

As the international community looked around for someone capable of uniting the country and putting a stop to the war, it tepidly recognized the House of Representatives as the legitimate representative of the Libyan people, a policy that some called, tellingly, "recognition without support."[3]

Meanwhile, clashes spread through Tripoli between militias allied to the city of Misrata, on one hand, and Zintan, on the other. Misrata had an illustrious history as a trading city, and after the revolution their fighters had allied with various Islamist groups. Zintan was a town in the western mountains, and its fighters were aligned with Heftar's Karama movement. One of the bigger battles took place at the Tripoli airport, where several commercial jets were torched before violence spilled over into the capital proper. Facing a firefight at the US Embassy's front door and having no viable contingency plan, Ambassador Deborah Jones decided on July 26 to evacuate US personnel. It was a move one of Jones's ambassador colleagues called "the worst thing we [the United States] could have done for Libya's stability."[4] But given Washington's extreme sensitivity to risk following the Benghazi attack, it's hard to see how Jones had any other choice. A lack of foresight and planning once again produced an emergency that couldn't be overcome. The Americans' departure would mark the full US withdrawal from Libya.

While the Americans were evacuating the Embassy in Tripoli, Ansar al-Sharia—the group that had become infamous for orchestrating the attack on the US Mission—attacked the headquarters of Colonel Bukhamada's Heftar-allied Thunderbolt forces in Benghazi, driving the last organized resistance to the militias out of Benghazi's city limits.

"We will not stop until we establish the rule of God," Wissam Bin Hamid proclaimed in a video of him and Ansar al-Sharia's leader Mohammed al-Zahawi, touring the ransacked special forces headquarters.[5] A couple days later, on July 30, al-Zahawi declared Benghazi as an Islamic emirate, at the head of a coalition of Islamist militias, including Ansar al-Sharia, who banded together to fight Heftar.[6]

The United Nations took the lead in trying to put the Libyan Humpty Dumpty back together again, initiating a dialogue that it hoped would create the basis for a fusion of the two dueling governments. Despite the unquestionable goodwill of some of its leadership, this was never going to be more than a dance of expedience. The UN stakeholders, particularly the Europeans, wanted to patch up Libya to avoid the spread of terrorism and an increase in immigration. The United States was no longer interested. The ambition therefore was to create a government that might maintain minimal order—while authorizing foreign strikes against ISIS—and hope things worked out over time.

The result was something called the Libyan Political Agreement (LPA), which aimed to fuse the two governments into a Byzantine structure composed of a High Council of State (mainly members of the Tripoli-based government), a legislature (the House of Representatives), and a nine-member Presidency Council.[7] The new Government of National Accord (GNA) was to take its electoral legitimacy from ratification by the last elected government, the House of Representatives (HOR). The agreement to start the process was signed in December and received public support from early revolutionaries like Libya's former UN representative Ibrahim Dabbashi, who told the BBC that he was endorsing the process because the country simply couldn't take any more division.[8] The negotiations over the LPA quickly degenerated, in particular over a revised article in the agreement that stipulated that the Presidency Council would "assume the functions of the Supreme Commander of the Libyan army." This would prove to be a major sticking point; lacking trust, neither the HOR nor Heftar were willing to give the keys to the Libyan National Army to a Tripoli-based government.

In the absence of an agreement, the international community unilaterally shifted its recognition from the HOR to the Government of National Unity, which hadn't been ratified by the HOR as stipulated in the LPA. Dabbashi had harsh words for the United Nations, which he said "killed" the LPA by failing to follow its own rules.

Meanwhile, Heftar's Libyan National Army, after two years of fighting ISIS and Al Qaeda in Benghazi, was making progress. By late summer 2016, Heftar's forces had pushed the jihadists to the edges of the city. He and the Libyan National Army wouldn't proclaim Benghazi fully liberated for another year, but friends from Benghazi who had been away for three years were starting to go back. And I saw an opportunity to do the same.

There were many reasons I wanted to go back to Benghazi. For one, it was very hard to get reliable information on what was going on in Libya without being there. Having been involved as a consultant in various governmental studies of the situation, I wanted to know more. While the West and the GNA perspective dominated the media, many were speaking for eastern Libya, but few of those people were actually from or in the east. I wanted to know what residents of Benghazi felt about the siege they had been under for four years since the attack on the US Mission. What did they think of the United States and the LPA? If possible, I wanted to meet Heftar and see if I could manage to gain any insight that others who had profiled him in the previous years might have missed.

These were the professional reasons for my return. But there were other forces motivating me, of which at the time I was still thinly aware. The shock of my last experience in Benghazi was calling me back to work through the psychological impressions it made on me. Like America as a whole, part of me was still stuck on the event and having trouble moving forward.

Given the polarized situation in Libya and in the international perception of Libya, I was taking more than a physical risk, as I was sure my trip would be interpreted as a sign that I supported Heftar, which was certainly too strong a characterization. My interest was in the possibility that Libyans could have a chance to express their collective free will, in the face of external interventions—wherever they came from.

I had a few misgivings, though I should have had a lot more. First, of course, was whether the people I trusted could actually assure my safety. Second was whether my *New York Times* article, which the editor had titled "The New Danger in Benghazi" (referring to Heftar), had offended Heftar or any of his people personally.[9] My intent was not to be favorable or unfavorable, but it seemed to have become one of those pieces that people read the way they wanted to. Some in the State Department read it as anti-Heftar while others read it as pro-.

In September 2014, I got a call from a Libyan friend in California who was well connected with the eastern government and Heftar's people. He said he could set up an interview with Heftar and assured me that I would be safe. Though I knew that no one could completely guarantee my safety in Libya, this was the closest I was going to get.

Next, I traveled to Washington to meet with Wafa Bugaighis, Libya's ambassador to the United States. Wafa's sisters were Laila, the Benghazi Medical Center's deputy director general, and Salwa, a prominent progressive Benghazi civil rights activist who was gunned down in Benghazi in 2013.

Wafa, like most of the Bugaighis women, had a formidable presence. She was in a difficult position—her embassy staff was split between the two camps yet somehow had to work together. She had to remain neutral and somehow keep order in Washington. I asked her opinion about the wisdom of what I was doing. She was surprisingly encouraging.

"Go—you'll be okay," Wafa told me. She knew who was making the arrangements. "It's very important that people on the outside understand what's happening there. There are no other Americans in Benghazi now."

I knew that if I thought about it too much, I would have a hard time going, so I compartmentalized.

There were no flights direct from Europe to Libya, and flights hadn't resumed from the region into Benghazi. So, I would have to travel to Cairo, which at the time was still experiencing aftershocks from its own Arab Spring convulsion, and from there to Alexandria, where I would need to take a flight to Labraq Airport, a few miles from the seat of the cabinet of the eastern government, in Al Bayda.

I arrived in Alexandria by car in the late afternoon. The airport was an imposing structure with large glass windows that seemed to leap from the flatness. Luckily I had arrived several hours before the nominal departure to make sure I didn't miss the flight, as their airport was tied up by a desultory line of hundreds of passengers. I got into the line and followed it to the front, which took over an hour. At that point, the airport worker waved me off and said he didn't know when the flight would leave.

"Try later."

I repeated this exercise twice, and on the third time, they let me in. The plane was already boarding. Eventually I was admitted to the boarding area, where I stood among a collection of Libyan families, many with small children.

I was anxious. But not nearly as much as I probably should have been, given that I was about to plunge myself back into an environment from which I had been lucky to escape four years before.

I examined that anxiety a bit. I found that I could almost look at it from the outside and recognize that this was a normal reaction, and that I still had the power to walk out. Part of me wanted to, very much. Another part of me was almost happy that I'd made it this far without backing out, and was determined to keep going.

I wondered how similar this urge was to the one Chris Stevens expressed to me in Washington, in early 2012. Why was I so determined? I knew it had something to do with the fact that this was the first time I could come back. I knew it had something to do with not wanting my last experience in Benghazi to be the one that overshadowed my previous experiences there. It's easy to understand now that I was seeking some kind of closure.

The interior of the plane looked like it had been torn apart: Seats were worn, and the windows were scratched in places so much that I could barely see out into an already pitch-black sky. The heat rising from the desert created turbulence that kept me and my fellow passengers in our seats for most of the hour-and-a-half flight.

To my left sat a thin Libyan man who looked to be in his fifties. He noticed my discomfort, and, I assume, the fact that I wasn't Libyan. And alone. In typical Libyan fashion he made various discreet remarks in Arabic to try to make me feel at ease: "I assume you're not here to see your uncle."

"No, not this time," I replied, smiling.

He told me his family was returning home after spending time with their relatives in Cairo, after they were forced to leave as war had engulfed eastern Libya.

When the plane landed, while the other passengers scrambled for their bags, I made my way to the front. I had gotten halfway down the movable stairs when suddenly I saw two figures race up the steps past me and disappear into the cabin, asking in Arabic, "Where's the American?"

Subtle, I thought, feeling a need to escape. Someone pointed to me, and the two young men with long hair, in their early twenties at most, raced back down the stairs to catch up with me.

They brought me into a hangar, where a taller, much older man in fatigues put out his hand to shake mine and smiled briefly. The two younger men then led me down an alley to a brand-new white Lexus SUV. They motioned for me to get in as one lit a cigarette. The two spoke to each other in low voices.

Once inside, they maneuvered the car off a dirt path onto the edge of a paved road in a jerky motion, forcing me to brace myself to avoid getting bounced violently from one side of the car to the other.

I asked where we were going—how long it would take to get to Al Marj, the site of Heftar's headquarters.

"The plan has changed," one of them said in Arabic. "We are not going to Al Marj." He didn't say more.

My pulse escalated as I made a concerted effort to remain cool. Had I been kidnapped? And if so, by whom? And for what purpose? I could think of no other ready reason why the two had suddenly become so evasive. I was unnerved by the fact that the roads we were traveling passed very close to towns like Derna, which were not safe. I contemplated bolting from the car at one of the many checkpoints we passed, but I knew better. I had been on these roads before, and though it was dark, I tried to use the names of the smaller towns and exit numbers we passed as a primitive GPS.

After another half hour of driving, I asked again, calmly, where we were going. At that point, the kid driving said we were going to a hotel. And sure enough, I recognized that we were pulling into Al Bayda, home of the eastern cabinet. I recalled that officials visiting the Libyan prime minister were often housed at a guest house in the city center. It looked like this was it. I was led inside, and the two kids handed me off to a receptionist, who asked me to provide a deposit. The kids disappeared only to be replaced by blank-faced, heavy-set men who were similarly tight-lipped. One of them ordered me not to leave the room—for any reason—until someone came for me.

I spent a total of thirty-six hours in the room, a long and lonely time span in which I spoke to no one. Both nights, I could hear the incessant sound of cars racing on the main road, overlain by a soundtrack of occasional machine-gun fire. I kept myself busy by memorizing obscure words from an Arabic dictionary I had brought with me. The anxiety of the situation stifled hunger—but after a day I became ravenous. I had brought along with me six energy bars, and they were quickly history.

Why in the hell was I here? For the second time in as many days, I felt that my judgment had failed me. My guess was that all my communications were being monitored, perhaps by multiple parties, so I refrained from calling or texting anyone for a day. Finally, I relented and texted Wael, the person who helped arrange all this, back in California.

"I'm here alone, no one has come for me."

". . . What??" Wael texted back, alarmed. "Hold on. Stay put. I'll make a call," he wrote.

Almost to the minute an hour later, I heard a knock on the door. I looked through the peephole and was surprised to see two older women in local face coverings. I opened the door and was confronted with two outstretched casserole dishes and tantalizing odors of lamb and stuffed courgettes. I couldn't help but laugh.

"We're friends of your friend," they said. This was the Libyan hospitality I knew.

Later in the day, a member of General Heftar's staff showed up. He introduced himself as S., and he was a refreshing contrast to the kids I had been interacting with so far. He feigned a lack of awareness at how long I had been waiting.

"The commander has been called to the front," he said. "It will be a week before we can arrange a meeting, but we will take you to Benghazi and give you a tour of the front, and of course you will meet him there. It may take ten days."

I did not have that much time—I had given myself a set amount of time for the trip, and I was not going past that time. I knew the longer I stayed, the more risk that things could get out of hand. I realized that unless I wanted to risk myself further, I would not be going to Benghazi on this trip, nor was I going to interview Heftar. And I had taken a major risk for that outcome. But I was also starting to see that the success of my trip didn't depend on either of those objectives.

S. asked me whether I would reconsider. I told him I had to get back for personal reasons. I regretted not being able to do more, but I needed to be on the flight back to Alexandria that night. S. took it in stride.

"Well then, let's make the best of it. We have an hour, what would you like to see?" S. showed me around Al Bayda—a city of about 250,000 people I had visited once before, very briefly, in 2005. Al Bayda in the daytime was gorgeous. It was a stunning day in the foothills, with a deep blue sky shining down on fields of clover. A few large cumulus clouds hung above. We drove past an area where some of the first demonstrations in 2006 and 2011 had taken place.

As we drove, I asked S. to tell me what he thought of the events of the last few years. Why did he stay? What did he think would happen next? What did he, having studied in the States and gone back at least a few times, think of how the conflict was represented outside Libya? S. described the conflict as the inevitability of chaos emerging from a political vacuum. In words that could have been spoken verbatim by the Good-Hearted Bookseller, S. said he had been glad the United States had intervened but deeply regretted that it had left Libya to its own devices. The question journalists loved to ask of people like S. was whether Libya was better or worse off without Gaddafi. He didn't fall for that simple what-if: "There weren't just two options, there were multiple possible outcomes. But unfortunately, we wound up with one of the worst," he said.

We drove past the unfinished facade of an ornate, imposing hotel commissioned by Gaddafi's son Saif just before the revolution. A monument to one of those paths not taken.

S. said more than once that what Libya needed were experts—not corrupt leaders with external agendas: "Libyan experts, who respond to Libyan needs. We keep hearing how there aren't any. Maybe there aren't a lot, but there are enough to make a start of it." I didn't ask him directly what he thought of his boss, Heftar, because I could see nothing to be gained by that question, at that time.

We stopped for a quick lunch at a local restaurant serving hummus and fava beans. After a few minutes, S. motioned that we needed to get to the airport if I was going to make my flight to Alexandria. He asked if I minded if we stopped to pick up his kids. The two boys, ages seven and twelve, spoke Arabic fluently, but they wore Knicks jerseys and high-tops. They spoke English with an American accent. S. explained that he had sent them to a cousin in the United States for most of the war, so actually, they were just as American as I was.

We arrived back to Labraq Airport at 5:00 PM, for a flight that was to leave at 6:00 PM. I had heard that there were no flights after sundown due to generator failures that affected the runway lights. S. went off with my passport to get my ticket while I remained with his two kids. They told me they missed the States and hoped they could go back soon.

S. returned with a pained look on his face and said the flight overbooked. That fact was apparent to everyone, as there looked to be nearly a thousand people milling around. Messages were sent to the army command on my behalf, and we waited. And waited. It dawned on me that the scene around me might turn ugly. Any trip to Libya would not be complete without a story of chaos at an airport. Boarding finally started around 7:30 PM, with the last light of day. So much for the concern about landing lights. A crowd of people denied seats started to gather on the tarmac and were accosting any official-looking person within reach. The pilot had cracked open the cockpit window and was barking orders to the ground crew. By this point, I had given up hope of getting on—S. had disappeared for a few minutes to check on something but seemed to come up empty-handed. The four of us—me, S., and the kids—sat there watching a painful scramble for a scarce resource. I wondered what my disappointing experience here in trying to shed light on current and past events might cost me, given the increasingly unlikely chance I would get a seat.

Then, suddenly, a muscular, bald man wearing a white shirt with black shoulder stripes made a beeline down the movable stairs. I assumed this was the pilot. I wondered what he was doing and saw him head in our direction. About twenty feet away from me, I could see his eyes fixed upon me. *What on earth is happening?* I asked myself.

"Ethan?" he shouted, above the din of the crowd. I nodded. He was now close enough that I could see the color of his eyes.

The man grabbed me by the arm, preempting a goodbye wave to my chaperones. It almost felt like the pilot was willing me up the staircase, trying to get me on before the mob on the tarmac noticed that someone else had broken through the cordon and reacted. And they did.

The pilot motioned me into the cockpit and then pointed at the jump seat behind his chair: "Take that." We sat down, and someone in uniform burst into the cockpit and began screaming in an eastern Libyan dialect: "Captain! There are babies in the overhead compartment and people lying on top of one another! The plane is overweight!" He paused. "If this plane crashes, Captain, *wallahi* (by God), it's on your head!"

I could see that the crowd on the tarmac, those who had not been able to get on board, had not dispersed. Indeed, the crowd, amoeba-like, seemed to be looking for a formation that might prevent the plane from moving forward. The pilot was a blur, directing traffic in the main cabin while barking orders to the ground crew through the tiny open window next to his seat.

I had a direct view of the copilot, who was perhaps twenty years the pilot's junior. It wasn't particularly hot, but I could see beads of sweat dripping down his forehead. He made no effort to wipe them away and said nothing.

And it was clear he would continue to say nothing. Throughout this surreal episode, I sat still. I thought back to a time when I had some fear of flying. From everything I was hearing around me, there was real concern about the airworthiness of this plane. But all I could think was *Damn, let's get going.* The alternatives to flying—trying to make my way overland across the Egyptian–Libyan border by car, for example, were distinctly unappealing.

"Do you have a seat belt back there?" the pilot called out to me, sliding himself once more into his leather seat and flicking dials in front of him. I told him I didn't.

"No?" he said, "This isn't a safe flight anyway. I wouldn't worry too much about it." A bit of impromptu gallows humor. I watched in some awe as he masterfully maneuvered the plane around crowds of people on the tarmac, now scampering to clear the way.

The pilot took the plane down the length of the single-strip runway, which I noticed earlier buckled in the middle—perhaps the result of damage from the Gaddafi regime's bombing sorties during the revolution. The runway lights remained on, for the moment. The next major hurdle was getting the plane into the air.

The pilot pushed down on the thrusters, and the engines roared to life. Everyone in the cockpit took a collective breath. Less than a minute later, the nose lifted up, the plane pivoted, and we were airborne. There was no moon, and I couldn't make out stars. It felt like we were suspended in absolute darkness.

After a couple of minutes, a voice called out through the radio: "Benghazi tower."

The voice surprised me: It was decidedly American. And sounded military. Were the rumors true, that there were now American advisors in Benghazi? Was this yet another sign of the split within the American bureaucracies over what to do about Libya? The tower guided the pilot east, toward the Egyptian border. Clearly the air traffic in and out of Benghazi would have many eyes on it. I looked out the window and could make out the lights of the Benghazi port below.

After the plane climbed for a few minutes, a stunning panorama emerged, a negative image of the coastline from eastern Libya to Alexandria, created by thousands upon thousands of points of light, each of them marking some human settlement. It was a strikingly beautiful sight, enhanced by a kind of infectious giddiness among the crew.

The pilot turned around and explained to me that he did this four times a week. Different destinations, but it was always chaotic. Just as the story of eastern Libya's post-Benghazi takeover by extremists wasn't covered by the international media, neither were scenes like this.

A surprisingly intimate exchange followed, maybe a result of the fact that, contrary to what the pilot said was normal, we had just dodged a bullet. "I feel I'm doing something useful for my people," he said. "These flights are our lifeline to the outside world, for people seeking medical treatment or visiting their families. We get good at pushing the envelope."

The next afternoon, I had a few hours to kill before heading back to Cairo, which I spent lying on a strip of beach, littered with signs reading: No swimming: Jellyfish.

I noticed that I felt lighter. And I thought back to my calm reaction upon realizing that I wasn't going to get to see Benghazi on this trip. I concluded it may have been because Benghazi wasn't the main issue; it was demonstrating to myself that I wasn't afraid to try. As I'd intended to do, I had at least replaced my last images of Libya, of violence, with something at least somewhat more benign.

I booked my return flight through London, with a two-day stop-over, during which I wanted to meet with someone about whom I had heard a lot: a twenty-something tech entrepreneur named Khalid El Mufti, who had a vision for a future Libya. Before the war, he had been lucky to study in the United Kingdom, and he was trying to kick-start Benghazi's reconstruction through a series of projects that mixed urban design and the cultivation of a tech-focused start-up culture. I didn't know the details, but that was enough to make me want to meet him.

I met Khalid at a nondescript communal office space, somewhere in the middle of London. He was tall, about six feet two inches, with close-cropped hair and a lanky gait. He had a wide smile, spoke Arabic with the recognizable eastern Libyan accent, and had the Western polish of a Cambridge-educated management consultant.

Before saying much, he said he wanted to show me a video that his company had made of what they envisioned as the future Benghazi.

The images unfolding before me were striking in their elegance but also their innate faithfulness to their subject. This fictional Benghazi was full of modern glass-faced buildings, interspersed with modern takes on inner courtyards and gardens filled with flame-red bougainvillea. The city's center had been pushed out toward the shore. I could make out the re-engineered contours of Lake Giuliana. Gone were the archaic, slightly ominous Tibesti Hotel and the fetid swamp in front of it. In their place appeared a sprawling café and beach umbrellas on a stretch of white sands and, back off the coast, a fleet of wave-energy power generators.

In this alternate universe, what little remained of the old Italian architecture—the Qureena theater and the courthouse, among them—was integrated into buzzing, modern communal areas, decorated with date palms.

There was an aspect of the Arabian Gulf in this virtual panorama—elements of the supermodern, architectural creativity bordering on excess. But taken as a whole, it was a city at home with its surroundings. It was also a vision at one with Benghazi's past—a city buffeted by the world around it, which rose, and fell, and rose again.

Khalid narrated the video playing on his laptop. Most of what I was looking at was a figment of the imagination of a small team of designers. But not all. In reality, the port area *had* been established as a free zone, and plans were being made, despite the political chaos, to develop it as a transshipment hub. Friends and contacts had sent me pictures of new life in areas of Benghazi that were either spared the worst of the fighting and bombing, or were being reclaimed. Ironically, one of these was Dubai Street, a Libyan-style strip mall, full of restaurants, high-end fashion outlets, and hookah bars, all framed in bright neon—or the electronic equivalent.

I was moved by what I saw—and the assumptions manifest in the video. Apparently, this wasn't a city run by dictatorship of any kind; the concern for sustainability and the environment was obvious in every detail of the design, as if consciously reflecting the realization that Libya had been a country built and destroyed by oil. "Creative destruction" is a term in economics that implies tossing out whole systems and industries to start afresh. It's not meant literally. But I had to ask whether the physical destruction, as devastating as it was, might have a silver lining in making it easier to optimize what came next.

I asked Khalid to explain those assumptions, to make them explicit. His vision went beyond the physical: He said that he took inspiration from countries like Estonia, which had built its post-Soviet identity and economy on investment in e-government, which in his mind was key to managing Libya's transition to democracy. "If a small corner of the former Soviet Union could do it, why can't we? If Norway could insulate its oil wealth from politics, why can't we?" he asked. Khalid was moving forward with his vision on multiple fronts—including by supporting a business-plan competition whose winners happened to be convening in London the following day. He invited me to come along for the presentations, and I was very impressed by what I saw. Young Libyans who had been deprived of any formal education during the recent war had managed to teach themselves how to code and create sophisticated software. Their business plans demonstrated local solutions to complex delivery and logistics problems wrought by years of war.

I couldn't help wondering, as I have so many times, what might Libya look like had the United States and its allies been prepared to help rebuild Libya in the wake of the intervention. The intervention in Libya cost the United States more than a billion dollars—nothing compared to the ultimate two-trillion-dollar price tag for the Iraq War—and yet the United States invested less than a tenth of that in development assistance. Secretary of Defense Robert Gates had argued that the United States wasn't ready for another state-building exercise, saying, "If we did authorize [military intervention], we [would have to] limit both the scale . . . [and] the duration, given that we were already fighting two wars that were consuming all available military resources."[10] But Libya was not Iraq, or Afghanistan, the visible examples of America's state-building failures. The factors that were used to argue for the feasibility of the US intervention in Libya—its low population, great wealth, absence of religious schisms, and general favorable disposition to the West—were the same factors that still could enable people like Khalid to succeed after others had failed. But Western governments were still not thinking about long-term sustainability or stability—only how to stem the unpleasant effects of Libya's disintegration.

A few days later, I was back in Washington, D.C. There, I met Chris Stevens's Benghazi advisor, Bubaker Habib, for the first time. I had wanted to speak with him since I set out to write this book—he was another figure who had been exposed to the long arc of the US involvement in Libya. I was pretty sure that he had worked for the US Mission back in 2005. If so, we would have many common reference points.

And when I saw him, it was clear that, indeed, we had met before. I recognized Habib immediately; I just hadn't matched his name to the face I remembered from my years in Tripoli. We gave each other the summaries of what we had done since we had last seen one another.

Habib had continued with the Embassy in Tripoli for a few years and then moved back to Benghazi with the hopes of setting up a school. The Libyan Revolution presented an opportunity to work again with the US Embassy, this time in support of Chris Stevens. And he continued to work on the school, which Chris had planned to open as the "American Corner" that the United States had been trying to launch since 2004. After the attack, the US Embassy helped him get to safety in the States, and he'd been here ever since.

He said he heard that I had gone back to Benghazi, and that I was writing a book. He looked me straight in the eyes for a minute without saying anything. I wondered what he was thinking, and whether he'd lecture me for taking such a risk—or whether he was asking himself what it was about these eccentric Americans who found Libya so compelling. I wondered if he regretted getting involved with the Americans, as he had paid a heavy price. Life in America had its advantages, certainly, but he was living a life of exile, for who knows how long.

Habib didn't say anything then, and our conversation took us down another course, but as we parted, he said, simply, "Hats off to you, brother," and walked away.

31

The World After Benghazi

Benghazi fundamentally changed America's risk profile in the Middle East, and in the world at large. It was a common denominator in all the factors cited for Trump's election win. It may have been one of the factors that propelled Americans into a state of extended high polarization. For these reasons, the current political and international reality is a world that Benghazi helped create.

It isn't a surprise that in 2022 Libya is still a mess. Heftar announced the liberation of Benghazi in early July 2017. A year later, he retook control of Derna, the last bastion of jihadist fighters in eastern Libya.[1] Some Libyans hoped that Trump might bring America back in to sort things out. But those hopes were quickly dashed. Trump was just as disinterested in Libya as Obama had become, and while America looked away, foreign involvement in the conflict intensified.

Finding little support in the West, Heftar deepened his relationship with Russia and tried to topple the GNA in Tripoli in early April 2019, backed silently by many of the countries that publicly insisted that there was no military solution to the Libyan conflict.[2] Heftar's gambit was cut off at the knees at the last minute by Turkey, which used a UN peace conference as cover to deliver advanced weaponry to the western front, effectively canceling Heftar's airpower advantage and triggering his withdrawal.[3]

Libya's conflict entered a new stage, where foreign powers understood that the United States was out for the count and moved to take advantage. Russia saw an opportunity to expand its influence in eastern Libya while Turkey's prime minister Recep Tayyip Erdogan used the latest Libya crisis not only to anchor Turkey's presence in western Libya but also to conclude economic treaties that laid competing claims to oil-rich zones claimed by Greece, Cyprus, Israel, and Egypt.

For both Russia and Turkey, this was an opportunity for political revenge, in response to past humiliations and what their leaders felt was the West's denial of their historical weight and destiny. As of 2016, the European Union had effectively paused Turkey's bid to join that bloc. Putin, meanwhile, had not forgiven the United States for its "mission creep" in Libya, which he saw as disrespect to him personally and a reckless threat to Russia's broader interests.

The predictable failure of the UN-backed Libya reconciliation process helped hasten the outcomes the Europeans feared most: the spread of terrorism across North Africa and the Sahel, and an acceleration of immigration to Europe at a time when Europe was already swamped by refugees from other conflict zones in the region, especially Syria. Attacks against Europeans escalated, first in neighboring countries like Algeria and Tunisia. But soon enough Libya-supported terrorism spread to Europe proper. A five-pronged assault in Paris in November 2015 killed 130 people and injured 416. Then came the Manchester Arena bombing of 2017, in which Salman Abedi, a twenty-two-year-old British citizen of Libyan descent, blew himself up after an Ariana Grande concert, killing twenty-two others and injuring 1,017. Abedi was the son of Libyan refugees from the Gaddafi regime, and his father was reportedly an active member of, or affiliate of, the LIFG.[4]

Libya's post-Benghazi political spiral boosted African emigration through Libya to Europe, giving smugglers wider berth to send more and more refugees drifting north, packed like sardines on unseaworthy dinghies that often capsized, resulting in hundreds of casualties.[5] Refugees coming from Libya mixed with those from Syria and Iraq, creating public outcry that fed far-right parties in several European countries—and is thought to have been a major factor in the victory of the "Leave" votes in the 2016 British referendum on withdrawal from the European Union, with all of the economic and social consequences of that move.[6]

Consistent with former CIA officer Robert Baer's prediction, the Benghazi attack led to the drawdown of US diplomats and military assets across the region. In Yemen, that contributed to the United States' inability to understand the relative threat posed by Al Qaeda and growing Iranian support for the Houthis.[7] Yemen-focused sources reported that the withdrawal of US forces from Al Anad Air Base in Yemen in March 2015 was the direct result of fear in Washington that exposure to increased Al Qaeda attacks would leave the administration and the military politically exposed.[8] In other words, the fear was of another Benghazi. "It's a very unstable situation in Yemen," a US defense official was quoted as saying at the time. "It was time to bring these guys out of there before it got too bad."[9]

The Iran-backed Houthi rebels had seized the Yemeni capital in September of the previous year, setting off a chain reaction that, in turn, helped create one of the world's largest humanitarian disasters. And the American response was to rely further on remote warfare while Yemen's conflict devolved quickly into an international proxy war—not so different from the situation in Libya.

The next candidate for Benghazi linkage, though more tenuous, is the Obama administration's biggest (or second-biggest, after Libya) regional bet over its two terms: the 2016 Joint Comprehensive Plan of Action (JCPOA), more commonly known as the Iran nuclear deal. Obama's strategy to limit negotiations to the nuclear issue was shrewd, but the administration's keenness to conclude that deal may have limited its willingness to push back on Iran's aggressions elsewhere—in Syria, Iraq, and Yemen.[10] Had the United States been more present in Yemen and Syria—where one can see traces of Benghazi-induced hesitation—many of the United States' ensuing headaches might have been much more manageable.

My aim here is not to say that Benghazi is singularly responsible for all these major developments, only to show where linkages exist, or are possible. One thing is for sure: as the long and winding effects of the Benghazi attack worked their way through America, Europe, and the Middle East, by the end of the decade, the trajectory of global politics had changed, and not necessarily for the better.

In Obama's worldview, the United States had to recognize the limits of its influence in a globalized world; multilateralism was a sign of his caution and disinterest in going in alone. But Trump, thanks to Benghazi, exploded the idea of multilateralism, preferring isolationism punctuated by dramatic unilateralism.

Trump preferred to make decisions with few consultations, so even the NSC was frequently sidelined—dragging presidential decisions even further into the back rooms and away from American foreign policy experts, which were becoming something of an endangered species.[11] Trump greatly accelerated the process of undermining the State Department, leaving many key appointments vacant and marginalizing the department's work while once again bringing in outsiders to provide policy advice. President Biden's Secretary of State–designate Antony Blinken called the exodus of career diplomats under Trump a disaster, the impact of which would "go on for generations, not just a bunch of years" and that "we're going to get into all kinds of conflicts we might have avoided through development [and] through diplomacy."[12]

"Encouraging America's absence" may be the best summary of Benghazi's impact on the wider world. America is no longer there, in places where it has the potential to do good or bad. It does not have the diplomatic tools it needs to manage this new, and more complex, world. And there are many countries that wouldn't have thought to challenge the United States influence directly but are now doing so. One of the largest lurkers is China. Over the last years, China has added more of the Middle East to its global portfolio, peeling the Arabian Gulf states away from their special relationships with the United States and under-cutting Western sanctions on Iran. Some analysts fear that the temptation to become politically and militarily active in the Middle East may be too great for China to resist. A glimpse of how China sees its future in the region might be visible in the 2018 blockbuster Chinese action film *Operation Red Sea*. The movie, which *Variety* called "a patriotic film . . . carried away by its own visceral, pulverizing violence," focuses on a Chinese rescue mission to save its citizens from a collapsing country (ostensibly Yemen) while it foils a terror plot to create a dirty bomb. In the final scenes, the Chinese Navy warns off American ships from its territorial waters.[13]

A theme that emerges from all of this is one in which American foreign policy is greatly—and unreasonably—shaped by what's happening at home politically rather than what is in America's long-term interests, or the interests of global stability. In this context, one administration's politically driven foreign policy blunders invite more blunders down the line and provide an endless, self-reinforcing source of partisan recrimination. What's particularly tragic is that many of the problems America's leaders are persuaded require massive, insanely expensive interventions could be handled far better, with much lower-level, but sustained and informed interventions. As former UK Development Secretary Rory Stewart observed about US (and Western) policy in Afghanistan:

> Having failed to fulfill their fantasies and realize their power as saviors, the United States and its allies now seemed unable to recognize or value the progress that was actually occurring on the ground—in part, because it was slow, unfamiliar, and often not in line with their plans. Political leaders had so overstated their case that once they were revealed to be wrong, they could not return to the moderate position of a light footprint and instead lurched from extreme overreach to denial, isolationism, and withdrawal. In the end, they walked out, blaming the chaos

that followed on the corruption, ingratitude, and the supposed cowardice of their former partners.[14]

What Stewart describes in Afghanistan should sound familiar. Because one can say the same about Libya (and many other Western interventions), though I would argue that there were far fewer variables (at least at the start) to manage for a success in Libya. And we had the added advantage of past experience in Afghanistan and Iraq to inform us. Obama was right when he said at the start of his first term that a strong foreign policy comes from a strong domestic policy. But one just can't simply abandon one to fix the other and not expect things to go haywire. Part of the solution should be obvious: the United States needs to invest far more in people, in developing its foreign policy and national security infrastructure to be more agile and transparent, and in steeling its input from political influence. The alternative is not subtle: the United States will not remain a world superpower for long, and its fall will not likely be quiet.[15]

32

Other Benghazis?

In the years following the Benghazi attack, and particularly into the Trump administration, the media scrutinized a number of events for their political flammability, their potential to become the next Benghazi. In most of these cases, comparisons are weak—a symptom, perhaps, of the culture of hyperbole that Benghazi encouraged. But these comparisons lent support to the idea that there was something qualitatively different about Benghazi; that it had become a standard against which the scandal-worthiness of other events was now being measured—just like Nixon's Watergate, for which the suffix "gate" has been attached to almost every political scandal since (and nonpolitical, i.e., Deflategate), including Servergate and the much more banal Pizzagate.

The first of these comparisons arrived a week after Trump's inauguration, on January 29, 2017, after a botched US military raid on an Al Qaeda safehouse in Yemen. Trump authorized a joint US–United Arab Emirates commando raid in the Yemeni village of al-Ghayil. The raid targeted Al Qaeda in the Arabia Peninsula and its then leader, Qasim al-Raymi, who had apparently been tipped off to the attack and was prepared for a fight. The ensuing fifty-minute clash killed an American Navy SEAL, fourteen Al Qaeda members, and thirty-two Yemeni civilians, including the American-born daughter of Anwar al-Awlaki, the mastermind behind the underwear bombing attempt over Detroit in 2009.

Trump green-lighted the raid during an informal conversation

with advisors, including Defense Secretary James Mattis and National
Security Advisor Michael Flynn, without going through an interagency
review process, as the Obama administration had done in similar situations. The father of the SEAL killed in the attack accused the president
of authorizing a pointless raid and refused to meet with him during a
ceremony at Dover Air Force Base that evoked memories of the reception given to Chris Stevens and the three other American victims of
Benghazi.[1] The *National Interest* asked, "Will the Yemen Raid Become
Trump's Benghazi?" while in *The Atlantic*, former Deputy Assistant Secretary for Defense Andrew Exum begged, "Don't Politicize the Failed
Yemen Raid," a direct reference to Benghazi. Military inquiries were
launched into the circumstances behind the botched raid, but the issue
died out quickly thereafter.[2]

The Yemen raid prompted what may have been one of the first public
uses of the term "Benghazi effect" to describe systemic and exaggerated risk aversion in the wake of the attack on the US Mission. In an
interview on *PBS NewsHour* shortly after Trump's failed raid, Exum,
a Yemen point person in Obama's NSC, objected to criticisms of the
Trump administration on the grounds that it might deepen the risk
aversion that Benghazi produced and hamstring effectiveness of US
forces in the field:

> The reason why I think putting the—putting real blame on the
> Trump administration here is dangerous is because you have
> the Benghazi effect. You remember, when the Republicans used
> Benghazi and what happened there as a cudgel to beat Hillary
> Clinton, and without—you know their effort was successful,
> it must be added, to weaken her as a political candidate. But
> it also had a chilling effect on the bureaucracy. It makes the
> bureaucracy risk-averse. And, quite frankly, that's not something
> that we want from our diplomats. It's not something we want
> from our special operators. We want them to be aggressive. We
> want them to take risks.[3]

Later in the first year of the Trump presidency, the media lobbed the "Benghazi" label at another incident involving the US military, this time on the Niger–Mali border. On October 4, four members of US Special Forces were killed while in pursuit of leaders of an ISIS cell. The soldiers had made an unplanned overnight stop in a dangerous area and were killed in an ambush after a local informant revealed their location to ISIS. A *Newsweek* headline screamed, "Is Niger Trump's Benghazi? Four U.S. Soldiers Died and It Took Him 12 Days to Respond."[4]

Florida Democratic Congresswoman Frederica Wilson was quoted as saying, "This might wind up to be Mr. Trump's Benghazi."[5] As with the Yemen raid, Trump created a side controversy by getting into an argument with the widow of one of the slain soldiers.[6] And again, the media widely criticized the raid for being rash, reckless, and unsupervised. Senior politicians in Washington claimed that they hadn't been informed that US troops were in Niger to begin with.[7]

But the parallels with Benghazi were thin: These were military raids against senior Al Qaeda and ISIS personnel—not so different from hundreds if not thousands of such raids in Iraq and Afghanistan over the previous two decades. They weren't attacks perpetrated on US diplomats and intelligence officers. No senior US diplomat was killed. And there was no protracted contradiction between how the White House described the events and what actually happened. Further, the explosive political jeopardy was missing: Trump wasn't facing reelection in a matter of weeks.

Another key difference was the fact that, in both of the above situations, a Republican was in the White House. Democrats had long shown themselves unwilling and incapable of mounting the kinds of negative media campaigns that the Republicans had long since mastered. (As the Trump years continued through two impeachment proceedings, Democrats would shake some of their hesitation to fight back, but they still couldn't match the Republicans' skill for political warfare, as exhibited in their handling of Benghazi.)

And as far as many on the Right were concerned, Trump could do no wrong. Trying to create a scandal under these conditions was like trying to light a wet log with a match. Even Trump's unseemly interactions with the families of the victims didn't get much attention, which theoretically should have upset his very pro-military base (and he had already insulted a Gold Star family on his way to the White House)—had this been done by a Democratic president, there would have been no end to the controversy.

Two additional events attracted more (and more substantive) comparisons with Benghazi. The first occurred in the last days of the Trump presidency; the second midway through President Biden's first year in office.

After the 2020 election, President Trump continued to insist, without basis, that Biden had "stolen" the November 2 election from him. And on January 6, a mob of between 2,000 and 3,000 people attacked the Capitol with the intent to interrupt the joint session of Congress convened to ratify the electoral college votes confirming Joe Biden as the forty-sixth president. The media variously described the attack as a mob action, an insurrection, and an attempted coup—whatever it was, it was egged on, if not directed by, the president of the United States. For many it was a profane, unthinkable act, a direct attack on the institution, symbol, and process of American democracy.

Speaker of the House Nancy Pelosi proposed the immediate formation of a nonpartisan commission to investigate the events of January 6. The bill passed the House but was blocked by Republicans in the Senate. Democrats made concessions on the shape of the inquiry, which were still not enough to bring Republicans on board for a joint investigation.[8] Whereas Democrats had led the Senate inquiry into Benghazi and participated in a House inquiry that they knew would be political, Republicans felt it more effective to refuse entirely. A House Select Committee, much like the Select Committee on Benghazi, was formed in July by a vote mainly on party lines. The Republican party formally censured its two members who participated. While Democrats have pushed for a Justice Department inquiry into President Trump's role in the January 6 affair, as of this writing, that inquiry has not taken place.[9] However, in March 2022, the department did expand its investigation to cover pro-Trump figures who were more closely tied to the president.[10]

January 6 had aspects of an adaptation of the Benghazi drama on American soil. A spectacle in which the actors were not groups of Afghan-trained jihadists, but home-grown, American extremists. One US Capitol Police officer died from the attack, four other officers subsequently committed suicide, and one Trump supporter died after being shot by Capitol Police. But despite the seriousness of the charges against participants—and Trump—and despite the obvious parallels with Benghazi, it was clearly hard for the Democrats to muster a level of outrage and venom on the level of what the Right elicited through Benghazi.

"Welcome Back, Benghazi" read the first line of a July 2021 op-ed in *Time*—six months later.[11] A big part of the Democrats' response to the Republicans was the charge of hypocrisy: a headline in *Slate* proclaimed, "Republicans Are Tough on Terrorism Until the Terrorists Are Republicans."[12] This was expressed often by pointing out that the Republicans weren't even a fraction as interested in investigating January 6 as they were Benghazi. (Of course they weren't.) Or that they were running the "Benghazi playbook" in reverse, accusing the Democrats of making a mountain out of a molehill. (Of course they did.)

The Democrats' response was a clear indication of why January 6, although a major event in American politics, would never have the power of Benghazi. The Democrats' response was defensive, was fractured, and lacked the relentless repetition of the Republican framing of Benghazi. And this was consistent with the fact that the Democrats failed to hold Trump accountable for a scandal that had a far larger immediate human cost—his administration's politicization of the COVID-19 pandemic. By any measure, Trump's response was both disastrous and incompetent—and has been cited as a contributing factor in a large number of COVID-related deaths.[13]

"Throw the GOP's Benghazi Playbook at Trump's Catastrophic Coronavirus Response," screamed an article in *The Hill*.[14] But it was another cry into the wind. Those whom the Left wanted to be outraged didn't believe the coronavirus was real: another illustration of why the Benghazi playbook continues to work for Republicans, whether forward or in reverse.

The partisan advantage in the creation of scandal tilted to the Right once again when Biden took office on January 20, 2021.

In mid-August 2021, the Biden administration found itself in the middle of a sudden, volatile situation in Afghanistan. In a deal brokered by Qatar, outgoing President Trump had agreed to withdraw American troops from Afghanistan by May 1, 2021. Biden told the American public in a televised address in April that he would begin the withdrawal on May 1 and have the last troops out by the twentieth anniversary of 9/11. He would "end America's longest war."[15] But come August, the orderly evacuation that the Biden administration had envisioned rapidly collapsed as the Afghan army melted away before the advancing Taliban, producing scenes that immediately evoked comparisons with the 1975 fall of Saigon.

Desperate Afghans chased after departing US military transports, some of them clinging to the wheel wells and falling to their deaths as the planes took off. A suicide bombing at Kabul's airport on August 26 killed thirteen US service members, and an unknown number of Afghans who had collaborated with the United States were exposed to Taliban reprisals. The Biden administration pointed retroactively to the fact that 120,000 people were airlifted out, but NGOs and journalists pointed to the carnage that America left in its wake. It was pandemonium.

And within hours, Republicans were drawing comparisons to Benghazi: Senator Joni Ernst said, "Absolutely, I'm afraid of a Benghazi 2.0. I think that this is something that many of us have worried about for weeks now as we have watched this scene deteriorate in Afghanistan."[16]

Once again, a Democratic president faced a fusillade of blame. Not content with "Benghazi 2.0," "Benghazi multiplied by 10" became a right-wing rallying cry.[17] A glaring question, similar to those asked after Benghazi, was how was it possible that Biden and the administration didn't know that the Afghan army would dissolve as quickly as it did, and plan accordingly? Just a few months before, on July 8, Biden claimed "the likelihood there's going to be the Taliban overrunning everything and owning the whole country is highly unlikely."[18] Were the CIA and the State Department unaware of the fragility of the Afghan army? Or did the president and his NSC advisors simply not pay attention? The Right quickly reverted to the familiar tactic of framing the outcome as the result of Biden's poor character. "Hillary slept as Benghazi burned. Joe vacationed as Afghanistan fell," Donald Trump Jr. posted to Instagram.[19] As in Benghazi, they highlighted the theme of American disgrace and abandonment of commitments (even though in this case, it was President Trump who made the deal with the Taliban, and Biden who fulfilled it, to say nothing of whose president started the disastrous war). This time, many of these accusations were also coming from the Left. George Packer, in a January 31, 2022, piece for *The Atlantic*, wrote that America's chaotic withdrawal from Afghanistan "added moral injury to military failure."[20] A Democrat-controlled Congress launched three investigations and the House its own, leading *The Week* to ask, "Are Democrats Going to Benghazi Biden?"[21]

Another alarming element was the seeming ease with which the Republicans were willing to turn against senior military officials to make their political kill. This was an extension of the House committee's focus on the Defense Department's failures at the end of the Benghazi report. One *Politico* report said that Pentagon officials "worry that the military could become just another institution that's dragged into partisan warfare."[22] In September, Republicans brought senior military brass in front of House and Senate committee hearings for an unprecedented grilling on their actions under Biden. In this circus, very reminiscent of the House Benghazi Committee hearings, Republicans accused Trump-appointed Chairman of the Joint Chiefs of Staff Mark Milley of "wasting time giving interviews to Bob Woodward" and "dabbling in Critical Race theory."[23]

"Perhaps we would not have had 13 members and hundreds of Afghans killed and service members wounded and citizens abandoned," Republican Congressman Ronny Jackson railed at Milley, "if you had been focused on duty to this country instead of pandering to the Biden administration's woke social experiment with the U.S. military, doing book interviews and colluding with officials."[24] Jackson's comments were a clear effort to link Afghanistan to the American domestic turmoil over race.

Less attention was paid to the fact that Trump had been warned by a staffer that he was risking another Benghazi by ordering troop levels in Afghanistan down to 2,500 just before the Biden transition.[25] Whether this was Trump's plan is still unclear.[26]

With the Republicans failing to relinquish their narratives, and Trump continuing to poll well—assisted in part by the chaotic Afghanistan withdrawal—Democrats started to worry, particularly after Republicans won key state and local races in 2021.[27] What remains to be seen is whether the Republicans will revive and weaponize Afghanistan as an issue with which to take back control of Congress in the 2022 midterm elections, as they had done in 2014 with Benghazi.[28] Or if they do take control of Congress, whether they might continue hearings on Afghanistan leading up to the 2024 presidential election. But the hearings on Biden's Afghanistan pullout suggest that even if Afghanistan isn't the main focus of the Republican strategy, it's a part of a "broader narrative" on foreign policy that links back to Benghazi.[29]

While the chaotic American withdrawal from Afghanistan and

certainly the January 6 riots were much worthier of comparison with Benghazi than botched raids in Yemen and Niger, in terms of their ability to generate lasting partisan rancor and undermine trust in America. Yet, as of mid 2022, one would still be hard-pressed to say that either of these events had quite the same originality and game-changing impact on both American politics and foreign policy.

Conclusion

Benghazi and the Brink

Ten years on, Benghazi still hasn't received its due. This is ironic, given how much of America's attention Benghazi—the attack *and* the controversy—occupied, and for so long. A blowout, which came out of nowhere, turned into a national obsession, then seemed to be leading toward a major reveal, only to sputter off like a deflating balloon behind its leading derivative, the Clinton email controversy. This is how the majority of the American Left sees it. For the Right, Benghazi can still muster some outrage-on-demand, albeit drained of most of the power it once had. Benghazi is no longer just a scandal; it is an entry in the *lexicon* of scandal, shorthand for any kind of event that can be blown up for partisan advantage. It is a level of scandal by which we measure others.

But as should be clear by now, Benghazi was far more than just an attack or a scandal: It was the product of a long series of decisions dating back to before the George W. Bush administration, and it had consequences beyond four lost lives and a political brawl. Benghazi was both a contributor to and a marker of changes in America's political and social atmosphere. It helped create the political world we live in today: a world in which America remains distracted, divided, and exhausted— and in which its adversaries and competitors exploit its hesitance to advance their own ambitions.

Benghazi can be seen in the tenor of American political discourse: a Left paralyzed by the immutability of the Right. It can be seen in Russia's invasion of Ukraine, to the extent that America's post-Benghazi abandonment of Libya and hesitance in Syria created openings for Russia in both countries, which further emboldened Putin to invade Crimea, and then Ukraine.[1] It can be seen in Assad's gradual return to acceptability on the international stage. It can be seen in the continued conflict in Libya and Yemen, enlistment of Qatar's help in moderating the extremist Taliban, and its search for ways to fix the Iran nuclear deal. It can be seen in the loss of the previously undivided attention of Arabian Gulf states, who are compensating for what they see as America's new unreliability by papering over disputes amongst themselves and hedging their bets with China. Where this is all going is anyone's guess, but the bottom line is that these developments don't bode so well for the United States.

These are unstable times. Democracies appear to be on the wane, and autocracies on the rebound. And domestically, America seems to be treading water before the next internal conflict. If Republicans gain control of the House in 2022, as looks likely, America may be headed off to another intense round of government gridlock. Two steps forward, three steps back.

In 2014, at the height of the Benghazi scandal, an article appeared in *The Onion*, under a photo of a man in a long beard and Afghan clothes, sitting on a couch, watching TV. The headline read: "FBI Uncovers Al-Qaeda Plot to Just Sit Back and Enjoy Collapse of United States."[2] It was *The Onion* doing what it does best: satire that rings perfectly true. The terrorist attacks of 9/11 and the reactions it set off managed to undermine American power and influence in ways that bin Laden probably never anticipated. And eleven years later, Benghazi, itself the result of 9/11's long tail of blowback, marked another phase in that self-deconstruction.

Understanding Benghazi's significance and its kinetic power—not just as an attack or a scandal, but also as a consequence and prime mover in two decades of world history—requires exposing context: domestic context, regional context, historical context. It requires examining the repeating themes of American policy in the Middle East and transitions between American administrations, and the increasingly toxic rhetoric that accompanies these transitions, figuring out why America makes the same mistakes over and over again, and—more to the point—doing something about it.

Obama was right: America's War on Terror was not only a massive, gargantuan waste of resources and a distraction; it also created monsters. And the biggest, most dangerous monster was domestic partisan warfare. America's widespread use of torture confirmed the jihadist narrative of a violent West, hell-bent on destroying Islam, and helped create a dynamic that Arab Spring authority Gilbert Achcar called the "Clash of Barbarisms"—an asymmetrical war in which both sides committed acts that reinforced and perpetuated a cycle of war and terror.[3]

This was a war led by extremes—and extreme minorities. The irony in the Obama administration's response to Bush's wars is that its actions were tempered and shaped more by American extremes than Middle East extremes. The Obama administration started with good intentions—apologies for America's moral lapses, combined with a variety of high-level conflict resolution efforts. But those conflicts were very complicated, and the Obama administration couldn't manage to defuse them with one hand tied behind its back in the form of its constant worry that it was going to upset the Republican opposition.

Obama tried to ignore or avoid the Republican baiting on issues of national security and terrorism, but that approach came back to bite him. It deepened a sense of cynicism within the White House, particularly toward Republican motives, which were often reduced to attempts to prevent Obama from winning a second term. Though this was often true, it was also a simplification. The Republicans weren't *always* laying political traps. And assuming that they were could only deepen the divide, particularly when there were more legitimate concerns at play.

The Obama administration clearly thought that it had bought itself a huge scoop of political cover with the 2011 raid in Pakistan that killed Osama bin Laden. But ironically, though it was hugely popular in the United States, bin Laden's assassination increased political pressure on the White House to resolve all other problems related to 9/11 and, in turn, increased incentives for either making continuing problems look like they were going better than they were (as in Afghanistan) or avoiding public discussions of the consequences of action or inaction (in places like Syria).

The Arab Spring presented the Obama administration with a number of simultaneous crises—of which an intervention in Libya looked, for a time, like it could be America's lucky number: a chance to repair America's international image, save a city from a dictator's wrath, score a win for democracy, and help create an international humanitarian norm (R2P). But the only way any of that could become reality was if the Obama White House had been able to shed the fear of its own shadow and absorb the implications of America's intervention in Libya under the Bush administration—the extraordinary rendition and "correction" of Libyan radicals. By allowing domestic battles to shape foreign policy, American policymakers failed to consider local Libyan political and social dynamics, and how they determined the path to success. So it's not so surprising that President Obama wound up repeating the same fundamental mistake George W. Bush made in Iraq—failing to fill the political vacuum in a strongman's wake. The motives may have been very different, but the outcome was very similar.

Had America's foreign policy and national security institutions not been so demoralized, weakened, defunded, and separated from decision-making, much of the collateral damage of the Benghazi attack could have been avoided. Just as with the original 9/11, the 1998 embassy bombings, the 2000 USS *Cole* bombing, and the failed Underwear Bomber, there were experts within the US government who had critical pieces of the puzzle, but the system couldn't put them together in time. Same with the Benghazi attack: Pockets within the intelligence community that knew what was coming weren't in the loop. Those who had observed the follies of the Bush administration in Libya didn't have a voice. The diplomats in the field had no effective way of getting critical messages up the ladder. In this hollow environment, narratives became the first line of attack and, in the Obama administration, of defense. Narratives are an essential political tool, but to make good policy, they have to be built from the ground up, based on expertise. And they have to be repeated with belief and conviction.

If there was an individual whose experience embodied the collision between America's awesome capabilities and its supreme dysfunction, it was Chris Stevens. He believed in the real possibility of change in Libya but came to realize, too late, that he knew both too much and too little. He'd helped launch the US intervention, and he had a vision for how to achieve it, but he (and many others with whom he worked directly) had no means to stop it from going over the cliff. The attack in Benghazi that killed him and three other official Americans was a long time in coming, the result of nine-plus years of inconsistent, bipartisan, and uninformed policy toward Libya that left the United States relying on groups and allies that did not share America's interests.

There's no indication that the Benghazi attackers understood that targeting the US Mission would set off a political firestorm back in the States. In all likelihood, they were taking advantage of Libya's chaos to advance Al Qaeda's stated goal of creating a bulwark in North Africa, and Libya specifically, against losses suffered in the Sunni Arab heartland. But just as 9/11 could have been managed in such a way to lessen the appeal of Al Qaeda and protect American interests—as Middle East authority Robert Springborg has so perfectly phrased, "treating it like [the] criminal act it was, not the pretext for a religious war"[4]—the two American political parties immediately made it about themselves, playing their traditional roles: the Republicans on offense and the Democrats playing defense.

Romney's precipitous claim that the Obama administration was accommodating extremists in the wake of the Cairo Embassy's response to protests on September 11, 2012, was an immediate confirmation of the likely Republican strategy—but it wasn't built on nothing. Obama had set the overall post–War on Terror narrative and tone, and there was certainly no shortage of Muslims in the region who also thought White House communications toward violence committed in the name of Islam was unhelpful—or worse. The White House's focus on defensive narrative sealed the dynamic. The fact that it's still difficult to pin down what the Obama administration knew, when, about the Benghazi attack says less about the motives of Obama's staff than it does about the dismal state of American intelligence as a whole. Had the system been working properly, there would have been no opportunity for confusion to persist as long as it did. Memoirs from the Obama White House give good-enough hints as to what the administration was thinking at this time: manage the incoming missiles, get past the election, and the whole thing would blow over. This was additional misjudgment, compounded umpteen times by a subtle but revolutionary change in the media environment as apps like Facebook and Twitter were suddenly capable of taking an incident like Benghazi and using it to catapult public discord to an entirely new level.

Susan Rice's candidacy for secretary of state was the first political casualty of these maladaptive strategies. Once the election was over, the Right went into high gear to attach personal blame for Benghazi to Hillary Clinton, who saw this coming in slow motion. There were shades of Colin Powell, when he was asked to address the United Nations in support of the Iraq War, which he later acknowledged was a permanent "blot" on his record.[5] Clinton had agreed to the job of secretary of state. The president's job was decider-in-chief; her job was to be loyal.

As Americans became consumed with the growing Benghazi-linked scandals, the resulting fog blocked out the impact the attack was having on the Obama administration's policy in the Middle East—and the deeper, insidious effects partisan warfare was having on American political dynamics. Benghazi exacerbated an already pathological aversion to certain kinds of risk-taking in the region, which percolated through the bureaucracies, where the name of the game was to avoid being blamed or having to testify before another Congressional committee to explain another American official's death abroad.

Benghazi decisively ended the US experiment in Libya and

condemned Libya to a proxy war between militias answering to more than ten countries. It also indicated to leaders like Russia's Putin that America was reckless, indecisive, and self-absorbed all at the same time. Though the exact mechanism and direction of influence is still unclear, Benghazi clearly made the decision-making process relative to the evolving disaster in Syria more fraught and complicated, either accelerating aid to radicals or preventing aid to the more moderate opposition—or both. And though this, too, has its speculative elements, it seems to have strengthened the Obama administration's resolve to conclude a nuclear deal with Iran—which had some smart elements but didn't push back nearly enough on Iran's aggression in the Arab Middle East. All this certainly contributed to the growth of the Houthis and Al Qaeda in Yemen, which further entrenched Obama's preference for intervention at arm's length, that is, through drone warfare. And slowly but surely, the moral distinctions that Obama so much wanted to reassert and preserve eroded.

Meanwhile, the relentless Republican attacks on Hillary Clinton during Obama's second term turned a hairline fracture in American public political discourse into an aortic tear, one of the symptoms of which was the election of Donald Trump, which shifted America's attitude toward the world from muted multilateralism to one of capriciousness, xenophobia, and self-centeredness. America's absence from the Middle East has benefited virtually all our adversaries and competitors—from China to Russia to radical Islam. It killed four years of American leadership on climate change and invited an incompetent and deadly response to the COVID pandemic.

Of course, it's possible to overstate the impact of Benghazi. It was one factor in a series of others that contributed to the present state of America and the Middle East. But understating its impact is a far more relevant problem: America hasn't yet admitted to itself that Benghazi had any influence at all, or that it offers a treasure trove of lessons about the greater consequences of the polarization of American politics, the politicization of American foreign policy and security, and the fact that our once exemplary professional bureaucracies have been hemorrhaging talent and resources for decades. Had there been an automatic trigger that produced a single expert, nonpartisan, apolitical committee to investigate the Benghazi attack rather than a series of committees each with their own biases, there might have been no scandal. We might today know exactly who perpetrated the attacks—a question that disappeared following the embarrassing acquittal of murder of the two suspects kidnapped and brought to trial in the United States.[6] And we might be sitting now with lessons learned and a world that's more secure because of America's leadership.

Though I would love to be able to end this book with a comprehensive solution to all the problems I've highlighted, that's of course not possible. These problems are far too vast and complex. Most Americans know that the United States must somehow find a way to heal its internal divisions, secure its democracy, and grow and protect the institutions essential to sound decision-making, or within decades—or years—it will have lost its edge in favor of much more ominous ideologies, which will not care about the issues on which the world should be focusing its efforts (particularly, addressing climate change). America must find a way to recalibrate a system that rewards extreme voices and opinions. There is no shortage of expert ideas on how to do this, whether ranked-choice voting, a third political party, further controls on social media, etc. The real problem is political will.

It may seem like a minor aside in the face of such immense problems, but based on my own experience, and those of many people I have known (Ambassador Stevens is an obvious example), there is one investment that will always produce strong returns for society, and the US government: programs for study or service abroad (or in a different community within the United States). I personally benefited enormously from programs like the Fulbright and Fulbright–Hays fellowships, which afforded me the opportunity to live and study in places like Yemen and Jordan while I was a student. This is how I learned Arabic and ultimately got the idea to join the State Department, which introduced me to Libya and the United Arab Emirates, and taught me Farsi. Chris Stevens was an alumnus of another venerable US institution, the Peace Corps, which was a stepping-stone to his distinguished career in the Foreign Service. These programs—like the State Department itself—are constantly under threat of budget cuts, which is no coincidence.

Time in another culture grows one's tolerance and curiosity, and interest in government, like no other. Experiences like these get people out of their usual frames of reference, their silos, ruts, and bubbles, and teach skills of communication, conflict resolution, and resilience. Whatever our collective future, these are some of the skills that can help us get out of our current predicament.[7]

In addition to our dividedness, the other core problem revealed by Benghazi is that American foreign policy has become a proxy battleground for American domestic warfare, where momentous decisions of life and death are made based on political optics at home rather than the merits—and morality—of a given policy. And this is extraordinarily dangerous. One cannot separate foreign policy from politics, nor would one want to. But for America to retain its exceptionality— something the likes of Putin are out to disprove—certain core functions must remain fully funded and apolitical, serving the American people. Full stop. This assures that policy advice will be the best it can be and insulates the president from the political pressure of unpopular, but necessary, decisions.

The foreign affairs bureaucracies have been battered by the last twenty years' worth of political manipulation. They are obsolete in many ways, in process and technology, and having been pit against one another, so that they don't play well together. Further, the needs of twenty-first-century diplomacy have changed and require new skills and new approaches. This costs money. But it's clear that the United States has wasted trillions of dollars on military actions that have only led to chaos and more war, which have enriched the military-industrial complex, tarnished America's reputation abroad, and added instability to the world while deepening inequality in America. Cost isn't the issue.

The deaths of Chris Stevens, Sean Smith, Glen Doherty, and Tyrone Woods were a tragedy. But it was a tragedy only further compounded by what followed. For both political parties, anyone unfortunate enough to have been involved, and most American voters, Benghazi has become exactly what Hillary Clinton called it: a stain. On democracy, on credibility, on America's role in the world. Most of us would rather continue walking away from it, recalling it as an odd historical footnote, using it only as a cudgel to beat the other party or a crystal ball to look for the next scandal. But if, at long last, Benghazi can help draw attention to America's national deficiencies and motivate changes, then the American lives lost in the process will not have been in vain.

Acknowledgments

This book would not have seen the light of day without the efforts of several people. My agent Julia Lord was a champion for the book from the time I pitched the idea to her in 2017, through to its completion. She became a dear friend in the process. My editor at Hachette Books, Sam Raim, believed this was a story that needed to be told; I'm deeply grateful for his expert editorial steerage. Robert Springborg's friendship, encouragement, and feedback on several drafts were invaluable. I'm deeply grateful for my parents' encouragement and support throughout.

Thanks to the larger team at Hachette Books: Fred Francis (production editor), who along with Sam Raim was essential in getting everything done in time, Niyati Patel (editorial assistant), Sharon Kunz (publicist), Julianne Lewis (marketing), Monica Oluwek (managing editor), Mary Ann Naples (publisher), Michelle Aielli (publicity director), and Michael Barrs (marketing director). Thanks to Amanda Kain for a striking cover and Charlotte Byrnes for the copyedit. I'm grateful also to Elaine Duffy and her team at Open Boat Editing: Anna Fiorino and Liz Provencher assisted with fact-checks, while Ben Gambuzza spent many months in the trenches with me as a sounding board, fact-checker, and sous-editor. I valued his quick mind, enthusiasm, and millennial reminders for self-care. Thanks to Dana Kaye and her team at Kaye Publicity, including Katelynn Dreyer, Hailey Dezort, and Eleanor Imbody. Any errors in the book are ultimately mine alone.

My thanks for additional comments and feedback to Azza Maghur, Lidija Canovic, Aya Burweila, Hassan Bouhadi, Professor Christopher Taylor, Najat Rizk, Philip Bejjaly, Dr. Monem Alyaser, Sherif Dhaimish,

Ghassan Fergiani, Ashley Christiani, Sohail Nakhooda, Leyla Sharabi, Bubaker Habib, Judy Schalick, Sara Ackermann, and Professor Marie Brown. My thesis advisor Peter Berck passed while I was writing this book. Brilliant and kind, he saw what direction I was headed and encouraged it.

Additional appreciation to the Evan, Kit, Harry and Monica Dobelle, Claude Ghez, the Volks, Esther Brass-Chorin, Leyla Sharabi, Amy Bouchard, Marcia Masse, Dr. Diana Pickworth, the Sadeghi family, and Ambassador and Mrs. Murphy. Many more friends and relatives listened to my stories about my time in Libya and Benghazi with interest, and often indulgence. Some who helped a great deal (or were critical to the story) would prefer not to see their names in print. You know who you are.

I'd like to thank the literally hundreds of people who took the time to be interviewed (or helped with referrals) for this book, on both sides of the aisle, including Senator Dianne Feinstein, Secretary Hillary Clinton, Ben Rhodes, Jake Sullivan, Ambassador William J. Burns, Lt. Col. Brian Linvill, DAS Jerry White, Sir John Jenkins, Sir Graham Boyce, Rory Stewart OBE, DAS Karin Von Hippel, Michael Lewis, AS Richard Barton, DAS David McFarland, Ambassador Frederic Hof, Dr. Steven Heydeman, Ambassador Prudence Bushnell, Lara Logan, Ambassador Ryan Crocker, Ambassador Gene Cretz, Ambassador Robert Ford, Anne O'Leary, Ambassador Deborah Jones, Ambassador Anne Patterson, Professor Sheila Carapico, Ambassador Joseph Stafford III, Kim Ghattas, Ambassador Ibrahim Dabbashi, Ambassador Guido De Sanctis, Scott Shane, Bubaker Habib, Derek Chollet, and Anne Stevens, H.E. Dr. Aref Nayed, H.E. Salah El-Marghani, H.E. Mahmoud Jibril, H.E. Ibrahim Al Dabbashi, Professor Dirk Vandewalle, Professor Gilbert Achcar, Cheryl Mills, Ambassador Lange Schermerhorn, Dana Remus, Col. Wolfgang Pusztai, Professor Marie Brown, Hassan Bouhadi, Khalid El Mufti, Abdelmoula Lenghi, Eric Hansen, Dr. Peter Cole, Professor Eric Alterman, Professor Bernard Haykel, Dr. Peter Bartu, Emile Hokayem, Karim Sadjadpour, Ambassador Wafa Bugaighis, Professor

Walter Quattrociocchi, Ahmed Ibrahim Al-Fagih, Mohammed Bin Lamin, and Jalel Harchaoui.

Last, but never least, my gratitude to Newton, "sag-e-nevisande." By my side through all the turbulence wrought by Benghazi, he whispered the words when they escaped me.

Bibliography

Books, Pamphlets, and Government Documents

Achcar, Gilbert. *The Clash of Barbarisms: The Making of the New World Disorder*. London: Saqi Books, 2006.

Ahmad, Muhammad Idrees. *The Road to Iraq: The Making of a Neoconservative War*. Edinburgh: Edinburgh University Press, 2014.

Al Hateita, Abdelsitar. *Hurub Al Militiaat: Libiyya ma ba'd Al-Gaddafi*. Cairo: Kenouz Publishers, 2015.

Al-Houni, Mohammed Al Mutallab. *Saif Al-Gaddafi*. Self-published, n.d.

Allen, Jonathan, and Amie Parnes. *HRC: State Secrets and the Rebirth of Hillary Clinton*. New York: Broadway Books, 2014.

———. *Shattered: Inside Hillary Clinton's Doomed Campaign*. New York: Crown, 2017.

Alterman, Eric, *Lying in State: Why Presidents Lie—and Why Trump Is Worse*. New York, Basic Books, 2020.

Bandeira, Luiz Alberto Moniz. *The Second Cold War: Geopolitics and the Strategic Dimensions of the USA*. Cham: Springer, 2017.

Baryin, Gaël. *Dans les mâchoires du chacal: Mes amis Touaregs en guerre au Nord-Mali*. Paris: Le Passager Clandestin, 2013.

Başkan, Birol. *Turkey and Qatar in the Tangled Geopolitics of the Middle East*. London: Palgrave Pivot, 2016.

Belhaj, Abdulhakim, Sami al-Saadi, Khalid al-Sherif, Abdel Wahab Al Qaid, Mitfah al-Duwdi, and Mustafa Qanaifid. *Corrective Studies in Understanding Jihad, Accountability, and the Judgment of the People*. LIFG recantations document, September 2009.

Ben-Halim, Mustafa Ahmad (trans. Leslie J. McLoughlin). *Libya: The Years of Hope—The Memoirs of Mustafa Ahmed Ben-Halim*. Surrey: AAS Media Publishers, 1998.

Biden, Joseph. "Remarks by President Biden on the Drawdown of U.S. Forces in Afghanistan." The White House. July 8, 2021. https://www.whitehouse.gov/briefing-room/speeches-remarks/2021/07/08/remarks-by-president-biden-on-the-drawdown-of-u-s-forces-in-afghanistan/.

———. "Remarks by President Biden on the Way Forward in Afghanistan." The White House. April 14, 2021. https://www.whitehouse.gov/briefing-room/speeches-remarks/2021/04/14/remarks-by-president-biden-on-the-way-forward-in-afghanistan/.

Bloomfield, Lincoln P. *The Foreign Policy Process: A Modern Primer*. Englewood Cliffs, NJ: Prentice-Hall, 1982.

Buhite, Russell D. *Lives at Risk: Hostages and Victims in American Foreign Policy.* Wilmington, DE: Scholarly Resources, Inc., 1995.

Bullington, James R., and Tuy-Cam Bullington. *Expeditionary Diplomacy in Action: Supporting the Casamance Peace Initiative.* Self-published, 2015.

Burns, William J. *The Back Channel: A Memoir of American Diplomacy and the Case for Its Renewal.* New York: Random House, 2019.

Burton, Fred, and Samuel M. Katz. *Under Fire: The Untold Story of the Attack in Benghazi.* New York: St. Martin's Press, 2013.

Bushnell, Prudence. *Terrorism, Betrayal, and Resilience: My Story of the 1998 U.S. Embassy Bombings.* Lincoln, NE: Potomac Books, 2018.

Carlson, Sarah M. *In the Dark of War: A CIA Officer's Inside Account of the U.S. Evacuation from Libya.* New York: Fidelis Books, 2020.

Cheney, Dick, and Tim Russert. "The Vice President Appears on Meet the Press with Tim Russert." The White House. September 16, 2001. https://georgewbush-whitehouse.archives.gov/vicepresident/news-speeches/speeches/vp20010916.html.

Chesnot, Christian, and Georges Malbrunot. *Qatar: Les secrets du coffre-fort.* Paris: Michel Lafon Publishing, 2013.

Chollet, Derek. *The Long Game: How Obama Defied Washington and Redefined America's Role in the World.* New York: PublicAffairs, 2016.

Chorin, Ethan. *Exit the Colonel: The Hidden History of the Libyan Revolution.* New York: PublicAffairs, 2012.

———. *Translating Libya: In Search of the Libyan Short Story.* London: Darf Publishers, 2015.

Clinton, Hillary Rodham. *Hard Choices: A Memoir.* New York: Simon & Schuster, 2014.

———. "Remarks on the Deaths of American Personnel in Benghazi, Libya." US Department of State. September 12, 2012. https://2009-2017.state.gov/secretary/20092013clinton/rm/2012/09/197654.htm.

———. *What Happened.* New York: Simon & Schuster, 2017.

Coates, Ta-Nehisi. *We Were Eight Years in Power: An American Tragedy.* New York: One World, 2017.

Cole, Peter, and Brian McQuinn, eds. *The Libyan Revolution and Its Aftermath.* New York: Oxford University Press, 2016.

Cooley, John. *Unholy Wars: Afghanistan, America and International Terrorism.* London: Pluto Press, 2002.

Department of Defense, Freedom of Information Division, Office of Litigation Support. Response to Freedom of Information Act (FOIA) request. Case no. 14-L-0552. April 8, 2015. http://www.judicialwatch.org/wp-content/uploads/2015/05/JW-v-DOD-and-State-14-812-DOD-Release-2015-04-10-final-version.pdf.

———. Case no. F-2012-38774. April 17, 2014. https://foia.state.gov/_docs/WhatsNew/JW8%20RD4%20Package.pdf.

David, Charles-Philippe. *Au sien de la Maison-Blanche: De Truman à Obama, la formulation (imprévisible) de la politique étrangère des États-Unis.* 3rd edition. Paris: Presses de Sciences-Po, 2015.

Draper, Robert. *To Start A War: How the Bush Administration Took America into Iraq*. New York: Penguin Press, 2020.

Embassy of the United States Cairo, Egypt. "U.S. Embassy Condemns Religious Incitement." Press Release. September 11, 2012. http://web.archive.org /web/20120912155134/https://egypt.usembassy.gov/pr091112.html.

Executive Office of the President. "Blocking Property and Prohibiting Transactions with Persons Who Commit, Threaten to Commit, or Support Terrorism." Executive Order 13224. September 23, 2001. *Code of Federal Regulations*, title 3 (2001): 49079–49083. https://www.federalregister.gov/documents/2001/09/25/01-24205/blocking-property -and-prohibiting-transactions-with-persons-who-commit-threaten-to-commit-or -support.

Fahmy, Mohamed, and Carol Shaben. *The Marriott Cell: An Epic Journey from Cairo's Scorpion Prison to Freedom*. Toronto: Random House Canada, 2016.

FBI National Press Office. "Statement by FBI Director James B. Comey on the Investigation of Secretary Hillary Clinton's Use of a Personal E-Mail System." FBI. July 5, 2016. https://www.fbi.gov/news/pressrel/press-releases/statement-by-fbi-director-james -b-comey-on-the-investigation-of-secretary-hillary-clinton2019s-use-of-a-personal -e-mail-system.

Federal Research Division, Library of Congress. *Al-Qaeda in Libya: A Profile*. August 2012. https://irp.fas.org/world/para/aq-libya-loc.pdf.

Fishman, Brian, and Joseph Felter. *Al-Qa'ida's Foreign Fighters in Iraq: A First Look at the Sinjar Records*. West Point, NY: Combating Terrorism Center, 2007. https://ctc.usma .edu/al-qaidas-foreign-fighters-in-iraq-a-first-look-at-the-sinjar-records/.

Gates, Robert. *Duty: Memoirs of a Secretary at War*. New York: Knopf, 2014.

Gates, Robert. *Exercise of Power: American Failures, Successes, and a New Path Forward in the Post–Cold War World*. New York: Vintage, 2020.

Gertler, Jeremiah. "Operation Odyssey Dawn (Libya): Background and Issues for Congress." Report R41725. Congressional Research Service. March 30, 2011. https://sgp.fas .org/crs/natsec/R41725.pdf.

Ghattas, Kim. *Black Wave: Saudi Arabia, Iran, and the Forty-Year Rivalry That Unraveled Culture, Religion, and Collective Memory in the Middle East*. New York: Picador, 2020.

Giles, Keir. *The Turning Point for Russian Foreign Policy*. Carlisle, PA: Army War College Press, 2017.

Halliday, Fred. *Political Journeys: The openDemocracy Essays*. New Haven, CT: Yale University Press, 2012.

Hegghammer, Thomas. *The Caravan: Abdallah Azzam and the Rise of Global Jihad*. Cambridge, UK: Cambridge University Press, 2020.

Hersh, Seymour M. *The Killing of Osama bin Laden*. Brooklyn: Verso Books, 2016.

International Commission on Intervention and State Sovereignty. *The Responsibility to Protect*. Ottawa: International Development Research Centre, 2001. (Available at https:// walterdorn.net/pdf/Responsibility-to-Protect_ICISS-Report_Dec2001.pdf.)

Jamieson, Kathleen Hall. *Cyberwar: How Russian Hackers and Trolls Helped Elect a President— Why We Don't, Can't, and Do Know*. New York: Oxford University Press, 2018.

Kandil, Hazem. *Soldiers, Spies, and Statesmen: Egypt's Road to Revolt*. London: Verso Books, 2012.

Klein, Ezra. *Why We're Polarized*. New York: Avid Reader Press, 2020.

Labat, Séverine. *Les islamistes tunisiens. Entre l'Etat et la Mosquée*. Paris: Editions Demopolis, 2013.

Lakoff, George. *Moral Politics: What Conservatives Know That Liberals Don't*. Chicago: University of Chicago Press, 1996.

Landler, Mark. *Alter Egos: Hillary Clinton, Barack Obama, and the Twilight Struggle over American Power*. New York: Random House, 2016.

Laurent, Samuel. *Sahelistan: De la Libye au Mali au cœur du nouveau Jihad*. Paris: Éditions du Seuil, 2013.

Lieberman, Joseph I., and Susan M. Collins. *Flashing Red: A Special Report on the Terrorist Attack at Benghazi*. United States Senate Committee on Homeland Security and Governmental Affairs. December 30, 2012. https://irp.fas.org/congress/2012_rpt/benghazi.pdf.

Lister, Charles R. *The Syrian Jihad: Al-Qaeda, the Islamic State and the Evolution of an Insurgency*. New York: Oxford University Press, 2016.

Lynch, Marc. *The New Arab Wars: Uprisings and Anarchy in the Middle East*. New York: PublicAffairs, 2016.

Machon, Annie. *Spies, Lies and Whistleblowers: M15, M16 and the Shayler Affair*. Harborough: Book Guild Ltd., 2005.

Mandraud, Isabelle. *Du djihad aux urnes: Le parcours singulier d'Abdelhakim Belhadj*. Paris: Éditions Stock, 2013.

Mayer, Jane. *The Dark Side: The Inside Story of How the War on Terror Turned into a War on American Ideals*. New York: Doubleday, 2008.

McCain, John, and Mark Salter. *The Restless Wave: Good Times, Just Causes, Great Fights, and Other Appreciations*. New York: Simon & Schuster, 2018.

Mufti, Mohammed. *Thakirat al Nar*. Tripoli: Dar Al Fergiani, 2012.

Neihoum, Sadiq. *Qisas Atfal*. Beirut: Tala Books, 2002.

Obama, Barack. "Remarks by the President at the Acceptance of the Nobel Peace Prize." The White House. December 10, 2009. https://obamawhitehouse.archives.gov/the-press-office/remarks-president-acceptance-nobel-peace-prize.

———. "Remarks by the President at Cairo University, 6-04-09." The White House. June 4, 2009. https://obamawhitehouse.archives.gov/the-press-office/remarks-president-cairo-university-6-04-09.

———. "Remarks by the President at National Medals of Science and National Medals of Technology and Innovation Award Ceremony." The White House. November 20, 2014. https://obamawhitehouse.archives.gov/the-press-office/2014/11/20/remarks-president-national-medals-science-and-national-medals-technology.

———. "Remarks by the President on the Deaths of U.S. Embassy Staff in Libya." The White House. September 12, 2012. https://obamawhitehouse.archives.gov/the-press-office/2012/09/12/remarks-president-deaths-us-embassy-staff-libya.

———. "Remarks by the President to the UN General Assembly." The White House. September 25, 2012. https://obamawhitehouse.archives.gov/the-press-office/2012/09/25/remarks-president-un-general-assembly.

———. "Remarks by the President to the White House Press Corps." The White House. August 20, 2012. https://obamawhitehouse.archives.gov/the-press-office/2012/08/20/remarks-president-white-house-press-corps.

O'Rourke, Jacqueline. *Representing Jihad: The Appearing and Disappearing Radical*. London: Zed Books, 2012.

Ouannes, Moncef. *Révolte et reconstruction en Libye: Le Roi et le Rebelle*. Paris: Éditions L'Harmattan, 2014.

Paglen, Trevor, and A.C. Thompson. *Torture Taxi: On the Trail of the CIA's Rendition Flights*. Brooklyn: Melville House, 2006.

Pargeter, Alison. *Return to the Shadows: The Muslim Brotherhood and An-Nahda Since the Arab Spring*. London: Saqi Books, 2016.

Rabasa, Angel, Stacie L. Pettyjohn, Jeremy J. Ghez, and Christopher Boucek. *Deradicalizing Islamist Extremists*. Santa Monica, CA: RAND National Security Research Division, 2010. https://www.rand.org/content/dam/rand/pubs/monographs/2010/RAND_MG1053.pdf.

Rhodes, Ben. *The World as It Is: A Memoir of the Obama White House*. New York: Random House, 2018.

Rice, Condoleezza. *No Higher Honor: A Memoir of My Years in Washington*. New York: Crown, 2011.

Rice, Susan. *Tough Love: My Story of the Things Worth Fighting For*. New York: Simon & Schuster, 2019.

Richter, Paul. *The Ambassadors: America's Diplomats on the Front Lines*. New York: Simon & Schuster, 2019.

Rogers, Mike, and Dutch Ruppersberger. *Investigative Report on the Terrorist Attacks on U.S. Facilities in Benghazi, Libya, September 11–12, 2012*. November 21, 2014. https://irp.fas.org/congress/2014_rpt/benghazi-hpsci.pdf.

Rosenthal, John. *The Jihadist Plot: The Untold Story of Al-Qaeda and the Libyan Rebellion*. New York: Encounter Books, 2013.

Rothkopf, David. *Running the World: The Inside Story of the National Security Council and the Architects of American Power*. New York: PublicAffairs, 2009.

Salter, Mark. *The Luckiest Man: Life with John McCain*. New York: Simon & Schuster, 2020.

Shane, Scott. *Objective Troy: A Terrorist, a President, and the Rise of the Drone*. New York: Tim Duggan Books, 2015.

Shipman, Tim. *All Out War: The Full Story of How Brexit Sank Britain's Political Class*. London: William Collins, 2016.

Solomon, Jay. *The Iran Wars: Spy Games, Bank Battles and the Secret Deals That Reshaped the Middle East*. New York: Random House, 2016.

Stevens, Christopher. "Die Hard in Derna." US State Department cable, ID 08TRIP-OLI430. February 6, 2008. (Released by WikiLeaks at and published by *The Daily*

Telegraph on January 31, 2011, https://www.telegraph.co.uk/news/wikileaks-files/libya-wikileaks/8294818/DIE-HARD-IN-DERNA.html.)

Tawil, Camille. *The Al Qaeda Organization in the Islamic Maghreb: Expansion in the Sahel and Challenges from Within Jihadist Circles.* New York: The Jamestown Foundation, April 2010. (Available at https://gisf.ngo/wp-content/uploads/2020/02/0905-Tawil-2009-AQMI-in-the-Islamic-Maghreb.pdf.)

———. *Brothers in Arms: The Story of al-Qai'da and the Arab Jihadists.* London: Saqi Books, 2011.

Thompson, Hunter S. *Fear and Loathing in Las Vegas: A Savage Journey to the Heart of the American Dream.* New York: Random House, 1972.

Timmerman, Kenneth. *Dark Forces: The Truth About What Happened in Benghazi.* New York: Broadside Books, 2014.

Ulrichsen, Kristian Coates. *Qatar and the Arab Spring.* New York: Oxford University Press, 2014.

UN Security Council. "Final Report of the Panel of Experts Established Pursuant to Resolution 1973 (2011) Concerning Libya." UN Report S/2013/99. March 9, 2013. https://www.securitycouncilreport.org/atf/cf/%7B65BFCF9B-6D27-4E9C-8CD3-CF6E4FF96FF9%7D/s_2013_99.pdf.

UN Support Mission in Libya. *Libyan Political Agreement.* December 17, 2015. https://unsmil.unmissions.org/sites/default/files/Libyan%20Political%20Agreement%20-%20ENG%20.pdf.

US Department of State. "Accountability Review Board (ARB) Report (Unclassified)." Accessed March 23, 2022. https://2009-2017.state.gov/documents/organization/202446.pdf. (The unclassified report is undated, but the classified report was delivered to Congress on December 18, 2012.)

———. "Benghazi Weekly Report, September 11, 2012." Message reference number 12 TRIPOLI 1098. September 11, 2012. https://web.archive.org/web/20121010215243/http://oversight.house.gov/wp-content/uploads/2012/10/9-11-12-Memo.pdf.

———. "Briefing on the State Department Inspector General's Report, Office of the Secretary: Evaluation of Email Records Management and Cybersecurity Requirements." May 25, 2016. https://2009-2017.state.gov/r/pa/prs/ps/2016/05/257733.htm.

———. "Foreign Emergency Support Team (FEST)." https://2001-2009.state.gov/s/ct/about/c16664.htm.

———. "Report of the Accountability Review Boards on the Embassy Bombings in Nairobi and Dar es Salaam on August 7, 1998." US Department of Justice. January 1999. https://www.ojp.gov/ncjrs/virtual-library/abstracts/report-accountability-review-boards-embassy-bombings-nairobi-and.

US House of Representatives. "Benghazi: Exposing Failure and Recognizing Courage." Hearing Before the Committee on Oversight and Government Reform, no. 113-30. May 8, 2013. https://www.govinfo.gov/content/pkg/CHRG-113hhrg81563/html/CHRG-113hhrg81563.htm.

———. *Documents Provided to the Select Committee on the Events Surrounding the 2012 Terrorist Attack in Benghazi,* vol. 2. Washington, D.C.: US Government Publishing

Office, 2016. (Available at https://www.congress.gov/114/cprt/HPRT23149/CPRT-114 HPRT23149.pdf.)

———. *Final Report of the Select Committee on the Events Surrounding the 2012 Terrorist Attack in Benghazi.* House Report 114-848. December 7, 2016. https://www.govinfo .gov/content/pkg/CRPT-114hrpt848/html/CRPT-114hrpt848.htm.

———. "Hearing 4 Before the Select Committee on the Events Surrounding the 2012 Terrorist Attack in Benghazi." US Government Publishing Office. October 22, 2015. https://www.govinfo.gov/content/pkg/CHRG-114hhrg98884/html/CHRG-114 hhrg98884.htm.

———. *Honoring Courage, Improving Security, and Fighting the Exploitation of a Tragedy.* Report of the Democratic Members of the Select Committee on the Events Surrounding the 2012 Terrorist Attack in Benghazi. June 27, 2016. http://web.archive .org/web/20160627233619/http://democrats-benghazi.house.gov/sites/democrats .benghazi.house.gov/files/documents/Report_of_the_Benghazi_Select_Commit tee_Democratic_Members-Honoring_Courage_Improving_Security_and_Fight ing_the_Exploitation_of_a_Tragedy.pdf.

———*Identifying The Enemy: Radical Islamist Terror.* Hearing Before the Subcommittee on Oversight and Management Efficiency of the Committee on Homeland Security. September 22, 2016. https://www.govinfo.gov/content/pkg/CHRG-114hhrg25270 /html/CHRG-114hhrg25270.htm.

———*Reforming the National Security Council: Efficiency and Accountability.* Hearing Before the Committee on Foreign Affairs, House of Representatives, September 8, 2016. Washington, D.C.: US Government Publishing Office, 2016. https://www.gov info.gov/content/pkg/CHRG-114hhrg21460/pdf/CHRG-114hhrg21460.pdf.

US House of Representatives Committee on Armed Services. *Majority Interim Report: Benghazi Investigation Update.* February 2014. https://www.hsdl.org/?view&did=749488.

US Office of the Spokesperson. "U.S. Department of State Launches Bureau of Conflict and Stabilization Operations." US Department of State Press Release 2011/1993. November 22, 2011. https://2009-2017.state.gov/r/pa/prs/ps/2011/11/177636.htm.

US Senate. "Homeland Threats and Agency Responses: Hearing Before the Committee on Homeland Security and Governmental Affairs." Senate Hearing 112-639. September 19, 2012. https://www.govinfo.gov/content/pkg/CHRG-112shrg76070/html /CHRG-112shrg76070.htm.

US Senate Select Committee on Intelligence. *Review of the Terrorist Attacks on U.S. Facilities in Benghazi, Libya, September 11–12, 2012 Together with Additional Views.* Senate Report 113–134. January 15, 2014. https://www.intelligence.senate.gov/sites/default /files/publications/113134.pdf.

Vaïsse, Justin. *Barack Obama et sa politique étrangère (2008–2012).* Paris: Odile Jacob, 2012.

Vandewalle, Dirk. *Libya Since Independence: Oil and State-Building.* Ithaca, NY: Cornell University Press, 1998.

Warrick, Joby. *Black Flags: The Rise of ISIS.* New York: Anchor, 2015.

Whitlock, Craig. *The Afghanistan Papers: A Secret History of the War.* New York: Simon & Schuster, 2021.

Woodward, Bob. *Obama's Wars*. New York: Simon & Schuster, 2010.

Woodward, Bob, and Robert Costa. *Peril*. New York: Simon & Schuster, 2021.

Yassin-Kassab, Robin, and Leila Al-Shami. *Burning Country: Syrians in Revolution and War*. London: Pluto Press, 2016.

Zuckoff, Mitchell. *13 Hours: The Inside Account of What Really Happened in Benghazi*. New York: Twelve Books, 2015.

Articles

"46% Think Benghazi Will Hurt Hillary Clinton in 2016." *Rasmussen Reports*. January 20, 2014. https://www.rasmussenreports.com/public_content/politics/general_politics/january_2014/46_think_benghazi_will_hurt_hillary_clinton_in_2016.

"Abu Sufyan Bin Qumu." Counter Extremism Project. Accessed January 5, 2022. https://www.counterextremism.com/extremists/abu-sufyan-bin-qumu.

Ackerman, Spencer. "Frappe-Sipping Libyan Militant Laughs at U.S. Manhunt for Benghazi Killers." *Wired*. October 19, 2012. https://www.wired.com/2012/10/frappe-libya-attack/.

Addley, Esther, Nazia Parveen, Jamie Grierson, and Steven Morris. "Salman Abedi: From Hot-Headed Party Lover to Suicide Bomber." *The Guardian*. May 26, 2017. https://www.theguardian.com/uk-news/2017/may/26/salman-abedi-manchester-arena-attack-partying-suicide-bomber.

Adraoui, Mohamed-Ali. "The Unfinished History Between America and the Muslim Brotherhood." Hudson Institute. July 12, 2019. https://www.hudson.org/research/15136-the-unfinished-history-between-america-and-the-muslim-brotherhood.

Al Hateita, Abdelsitar. "Asharq Al Awsat Obtains the Accounts of the Guards Who Spoke with Those Who Attacked the American Consulate in Benghazi." *Asharq Al-Awsat*, October 7, 2011.

Al Mahmoud, Abdelaziz. "Al-Ikhwan al-Muslimun fi Qatar . . . Man hum?" (The Muslim Brotherhood in Qatar . . . Who Are They?). *Al-Arab*. August 1, 2012. https://gulfpolicies.org/2019-05-18-07-14-32/93-2019-06-26-10-11-31/870-2019-06-26-12-04-48.

Al Shalchi, Hadeel, and Marie-Louise Gumuchian. "Libya's Jibril in Election Landslide over Islamists." Reuters. July 12, 2012. https://www.reuters.com/article/ozatp-libya-elections-20120713-idAFJOE86C00H20120713.

Al-Warfalli, Ayman. "Haftar's Forces Say They Have Captured Libyan City of Derna." Reuters. June 28, 2018. https://www.reuters.com/article/us-libya-security-derna/haftars-forces-say-they-have-captured-libyan-city-of-derna-idUSKBN1JO339.

Amoore, Miles. "Storming Tripoli." *The Sunday Times*. August 28, 2011. https://web.archive.org/web/20131111083614/http://www.thesundaytimes.co.uk/sto/news/focus/article763308.ece.

Ashour, Omar. "Between ISIS and a Failed State: The Saga of Libyan Islamists." Working paper. The Brookings Institution. August 2015. https://www.brookings.edu/wp-content/uploads/2016/07/Libya_Ashour_FINALv.pdf.

Ashour, Omar. "De-radicalizing Jihadists the Libyan Way." Carnegie Endowment for International Peace. April 7, 2010. https://carnegieendowment.org/sada/40531.

Associated Press. "Benghazi Report: Systematic Failures." *Politico*. December 18, 2012. https://www.politico.com/story/2012/12/benghazi-report-systematic-failures-085290.

———. "New Video Appears to Show Libyans Trying to Rescue US Ambassador." *Times of Israel*. September 18, 2012. https://www.timesofisrael.com/new-video-shows-libyans -trying-to-rescue-killed-us-ambassador/.

———. "U.S. Embassy in Tripoli, Libya Attacked." Encyclopedia.com. December 3, 1979. https://www.encyclopedia.com/politics/energy-government-and-defense-magazines /us-embassy-tripoli-libya-attacked.

Attkisson, Sharyl. "Officials on Benghazi: 'We Made Mistakes, but Without Malice.'" CBS News. May 17, 2013. https://www.cbsnews.com/news/officials-on-benghazi-we -made-mistakes-but-without-malice/.

Ayad, Christophe. "'We Are Simply Muslim': Libyan Rebel Chief Denies Al-Qaeda Ties." *Time*. September 4, 2011. http://content.time.com/time/world/article/0,8599,2091 744,00.html.

Bade, Rachael. "Weapons trafficking questions remain unanswered in Benghazi report." *Politico*. June 28, 2016. https://www.politico.com/blogs/benghazi-report-findings-2016 /2016/06/benghazi-report-weapons-trafficking-224869.

Baer, Robert. "Why the Benghazi Consulate Attack Will Blind the U.S." *Time*. September 25, 2012. https://world.time.com/2012/09/25/why-the-benghazi-consulate-at tack-will-blind-the-u-s/.

Baker, Graeme. "Mark Allen, the Spy Who Wrote Too Much." *Middle East Eye*. January 17, 2017. https://www.middleeasteye.net/news/mark-allen-spy-who-wrote-too-much.

Baker, Peter. "Obama's Turn in Bush's Bind." *New York Times*. February 9, 2013. https://www.nytimes.com/2013/02/10/world/obamas-turn-in-bushs-bind-with -defense-policies.html.

Baker, Peter, Anne Barnard, Mark Landler, and David E. Sanger. "Off-the-Cuff Obama Line Put U.S. in Bind on Syria." *New York Times*. May 4, 2013. https://www .nytimes.com/2013/05/05/world/middleeast/obamas-vow-on-chemical-weapons-puts -him-in-tough-spot.html.

Baker, Peter, Mujib Mashal, and Michael Crowley. "How Trump's Plan to Secretly Meet with the Taliban Came Together, and Fell Apart." *New York Times*. September 8, 2019. https://www.nytimes.com/2019/09/08/world/asia/afghanistan-trump-camp-david -taliban.html.

Balanche, Fabrice. "Syrie: De la revolution laïque et démocratique à Daech." *Hérodote* 160–161 (2016): 123–142. (English translation available at https://www.cairn-int.info /journal-herodote-2016-1-page-123.htm.)

Beauchamp, Scott. "Why Clinton's Iraq Apology Still Isn't Enough." *The Atlantic*. September 8, 2016. https://www.theatlantic.com/international/archive/2016/09/clinton -iraq-bush-war-hussein-wmd-senate/499160/.

Becker, Jo, and Scott Shane. "The Libya Gamble: Hillary Clinton, 'Smart Power' and a Dictator's Fall." *New York Times*. February 27, 2016. https://www.nytimes.com/2016 /02/28/us/politics/hillary-clinton-libya.html.

Beckhusen, Robert. "Diplomat Killed in Libya Told Fellow Gamers: Hope I 'Don't Die Tonight.'" *Wired.* September 12, 2012. https://www.wired.com/2012/09/vilerat/.

"Benghazi Mission Attack Fast Facts." CNN. October 3, 2021. https://www.cnn.com /2013/09/10/world/benghazi-consulate-attack-fast-facts/index.html.

Benner, Katie, Alan Feuer, and Maggie Haberman. "Justice Dept. Widens Jan. 6 Inquiry to Range of Pro-Trump Figures." *New York Times.* March 30, 2022. https://www.nytimes .com/2022/03/30/us/politics/justice-dept-widens-jan-6-inquiry.html.

Bennett, Jessica. "Paula Broadwell, David Petraeus and the Afterlife of a Scandal." *New York Times.* May 28, 2016. https://www.nytimes.com/2016/05/29/fashion/david-petraeus -paula-broadwell-scandal-affair.html.

Berman, Russell. "Boehner to Appoint Panel on Benghazi." *The Hill.* May 2, 2014. https:// thehill.com/homenews/house/205046-boehner-close-to-forming-select-committee -on-benghazi/.

Bin-Ladin, Shaykh Usamah Bin-Muhammad, Ayman al-Zawahiri, Abu-Yasir Rifa'i Ahmad Taha, Shaykh Mir Hamzah, and Fazlur Rahman. "Jihad Against Jews and Crusaders: World Islamic Front Statement." *Al-Quds al-Arabi.* February 23, 1998. https://irp.fas.org/world/para/docs/980223-fatwa.htm.

Black, Ian. "Barack Obama Offers Iran 'New Beginning' with Video Message." *The Guardian.* March 20, 2009. https://www.theguardian.com/world/2009/mar/20/barack-obama -video-iran.

Black, Ian, Chris McGreal, and Harriet Sherwood. "Barack Obama: Qatar Crucial to Coalition's Success in Libya." *The Guardian.* April 14, 2011. https://www.theguardian .com/world/2011/apr/15/barack-obama-qatar-libya-gaddafi.

Blake, Aaron. "The GOP Pushed Benghazi Probes for Years. It's Already Done with Jan. 6." *Washington Post.* August 5, 2021. https://www.washingtonpost.com/politics /2021/08/05/gop-pushed-benghazi-probes-years-its-already-done-with-jan-6/.

Boucek, Christopher. "Dangerous Fallout from Libya's Implosion." Carnegie Endowment for International Peace. March 9, 2011. https://carnegieendowment.org/2011/03/09 /dangerous-fallout-from-libya-s-implosion-pub-42940.

Bouckaert, Peter. "The Gaddafi Files." *Foreign Policy.* October 20, 2011. https://foreign policy.com/2011/10/20/the-qaddafi-files-2/.

Boukhars, Anouar. "What's Next for Mali and Algeria?" Carnegie Endowment for International Peace. January 23, 2013. https://carnegieendowment.org/2013/01/23/what-s -next-for-mali-and-algeria-pub-50736.

Bowcott, Owen. "Abdel Hakim Belhaj Wins Right to Sue UK Government over His Kidnap." *The Guardian.* October 30, 2014. https://www.theguardian.com/world/2014 /oct/30/abdel-hakim-belhaj-court-kidnap-mi6-cia-torture.

Bruton, F. Brinley. "Analysis: Turkey Coup Attempt Sees Erdogan Tighten Grip on Power." NBC News. July 18, 2016. https://www.nbcnews.com/storyline/turkey-military-coup /turkey-coup-erdogan-tightens-grip-power-after-failed-putsch-n611496.

Bumiller, Elisabeth. "Panetta Says Risk Impeded Deployment to Benghazi." *New York Times.* October 25, 2012. https://www.nytimes.com/2012/10/26/world/africa/panetta -tells-of-monitoring-situation-in-benghazi.html.

Bump, Philip. "Donald Trump Will Be President Thanks to 80,000 People in Three States." *Washington Post*. December 1, 2016. https://www.washingtonpost.com/news /the-fix/wp/2016/12/01/donald-trump-will-be-president-thanks-to-80000-people -in-three-states/.

Burns, Robert, Lolita C. Baldor, and Howard Altman. "US Down to 2,500 Troops Each in Afghanistan and Iraq, as Ordered by Trump." *Military Times*. January 15, 2021. https:// www.militarytimes.com/news/your-military/2021/01/15/us-down-to-2500-troops-in -afghanistan-as-ordered-by-trump/.

Caldwell, Leigh Ann. "McCain: Libya Either a 'Cover Up' or 'Incompetence.'" CBS News. October 28, 2012. https://www.cbsnews.com/news/mccain-libya-either-a-cover -up-or-incompetence/.

Caputo, Marc, and Lara Seligman. "'Benghazi Multiplied by 10': Afghanistan Becomes Rallying Cry for Republicans." *Politico*. September 30, 2021. https://www.politico .com/news/2021/09/30/afghanistan-withdrawal-pentagon-republicans-514779.

Carrell, Severin. "Tony Blair Kept Colleagues in the Dark over Megrahi Deal, Claims Alex Salmond." *The Guardian*. January 12, 2010. https://www.theguardian.com /world/2010/jan/12/alex-salmond-tony-blair-megrahi.

Carroll, Rory. "Film-Maker Behind Anti-Islam Trailer Stays Silent amid Media Siege." *The Guardian*. September 13, 2012. https://www.theguardian.com/world/2012/sep/13 /anti-islam-trailer-police-california.

Chorin, Ethan. "Benghazi Blues." *Foreign Policy*. August 5, 2011. https://foreignpolicy .com/2011/08/05/benghazi-blues-2/.

———. "Benghazi's Karmic Revenge." *Forbes*. November 20, 2016. https://www.forbes .com/sites/ethanchorin/2016/11/20/benghazis-karmic-revenge/?sh=53b817ac6396.

———. "The New Danger in Benghazi." *New York Times*. May 27, 2014. https://www .nytimes.com/2014/05/28/opinion/the-new-danger-in-benghazi.html.

———. "What Libya Lost." *New York Times*. September 13, 2012. https://www .nytimes.com/2012/09/14/opinion/what-libya-lost-when-ambassador-stevens-died .html.

Chotiner, Isaac. "The Both Side–ism of Amy Chua." *Slate*. February 28, 2018. https:// slate.com/news-and-politics/2018/02/amy-chua-thinks-identity-politics-on-both -sides-are-to-blame.html.

"Chris Stevens." AllGov. Accessed March 14, 2022. http://www.allgov.com/officials /stevens-chris?officialid=29554.

Chulov, Martin. "Gaddafi's Last Moments: 'I Saw the Hand Holding the Gun and I Saw It Fire.'" *The Guardian*. October 20, 2012. https://www.theguardian.com/world/2012 /oct/20/muammar-gaddafi-killing-witnesses.

CNN Wire Staff. "U.S. Vows to Hunt Down Perpetrators of Benghazi Attack." CNN. September 12, 2012. https://www.cnn.com/2012/09/12/world/africa/libya-us-ambas sador-killed/index.html.

Cobain, Ian, and Owen Bowcott. "Settlement in Abdel Hakim Belhaj Rendition Case to Be Announced." *The Guardian*. May 9, 2018. https://www.theguardian.com/world/2018 /may/09/settlement-in-abdul-hakim-belhaj-rendition-case-to-be-announced.

Cobain, Ian, Owen Bowcott, Pippa Crerar, and Kareem Shaheen. "Britain Apologises for 'Appalling Treatment' of Abdel Hakim Belhaj." *The Guardian.* May 10, 2018. https://www.theguardian.com/world/2018/may/10/britain-apologises-for-appalling-treatment-of-abdel-hakim-belhaj.

Coker, Margaret, Adam Entous, Jay Solomon, and Siobhan Gorman. "Miscues Before Libya Assault." *Wall Street Journal.* September 21, 2012. https://www.wsj.com/articles/SB10000872396390444165804578008411144721162.

Collins, David. "Gangsters Linked to Manchester Arena Bomb." *The Times.* May 16, 2021. https://www.thetimes.co.uk/article/gangsters-linked-to-manchester-arena-bomb-2p2hvlmh2.

Connor, Phillip. "At Least a Million Sub-Saharan Africans Moved to Europe Since 2010." Pew Research Center. March 22, 2018. https://www.pewresearch.org/global/2018/03/22/at-least-a-million-sub-saharan-africans-moved-to-europe-since-2010.

Cooper, Ryan. "Are Democrats Going to Benghazi Biden?" *The Week.* August 19, 2021. https://theweek.com/politics/1003871/are-democrats-going-to-benghazi-biden.

Crowley, Michael. "Clinton Ties Her Record to Obama's." *Politico.* October 13, 2015. https://www.politico.com/story/2015/10/hillary-clinton-foreign-policy-democratic-debates-214761.

Cruickshank, Paul. "LIFG Revisions Posing Critical Challenge to Al-Qa'ida." *CTC Sentinel* 2, no. 12 (December 2009): 5–8.

D'Addario, Daniel. "'The Newsroom' Takes on Fake News and Benghazi." *Salon.* August 26, 2013. https://www.salon.com/2013/08/26/the_newsroom_takes_on_fake_news_and_benghazi/.

Daly, Corbett. "Clinton on Qaddafi: 'We Came, We Saw, He Died.'" CBS News. October 20, 2011. https://www.cbsnews.com/news/clinton-on-qaddafi-we-came-we-saw-he-died/.

Daragahi, Borzou. "Libya Helps Bankroll Syrian Opposition." *Financial Times.* November 5, 2012. https://www.ft.com/content/0897f0d0-2748-11e2-9863-00144feabdc0.

Davis, Charles R. "Afghanistan: Former Advisor to Mike Pence Warned in 2020 That Trump Was Setting Up Another 'Benghazi.'" *Business Insider.* August 26, 2021. https://www.businessinsider.com/kabul-ex-pence-adviser-warned-trump-setting-up-another-benghazi-2021-8.

Davis, Julie Hirschfeld, and Jonathan Martin. "Obama Endorses Hillary Clinton, and Urges Democrats to Unite." *New York Times.* June 9, 2016. https://www.nytimes.com/2016/06/10/us/politics/obama-hillary-clinton-endorsement.html.

Del Vicario, Michela, Sabrina Gaito, Walter Quattrociocchi, Matteo Zignani, and Fabiana Zollo. "News consumption during the Italian Referendum: A cross-platform analysis on Facebook and Twitter." *2017 IEEE International Conference on Data Science and Advanced Analytics (DSAA),* 2017, pp. 648-657, doi: 10.1109/DSAA.2017.33.

Department of Public Information. "Security Council Approves 'No-Fly Zone' over Libya, Authorizing 'All Necessary Measures' to Protect Civilians, by Vote of 10 in Favour with 5 Abstentions." United Nations. March 17, 2011. https://www.un.org/press/en/2011/sc10200.doc.htm.

DeYoung, Karen, and Anne Gearan. "Susan Rice Withdraws as Candidate for Secretary of State." *Washington Post.* December 13, 2012. https://www.washingtonpost.com /world/national-security/susan-rice-withdraws-as-candidate-for-secretary-of-state/20 12/12/13/17ad344e-4567-11e2-8e70-e1993528222d_story.html.

Diaz, Daniella. "Key Senators Say They Didn't Know the US Had Troops in Niger." CNN. October 23, 2017. https://www.cnn.com/2017/10/23/politics/niger-troops-law makers/index.html.

Dionne, E. J., Jr. "Kevin McCarthy's Truthful Gaffe on Benghazi." *Washington Post.* September 30, 2015. https://www.washingtonpost.com/opinions/kevin-mccarthys-truth ful-gaffe/2015/09/30/f12a9fac-67a8-11e5-8325-a42b5a459b1e_story.html.

Donati, Jessica, Ghaith Shennib, and Firas Bosalum. "The Adventures of a Libyan Weapons Dealer in Syria." Reuters. June 18, 2013. https://www.reuters.com/article/us-libya-syria /the-adventures-of-a-libyan-weapons-dealer-in-syria-idUSBRE95H0WC20130618.

Doornbos, Harald, and Jenan Moussa. "'Troubling' Surveillance Before Benghazi Attack." *Foreign Policy.* November 1, 2012. https://foreignpolicy.com/2012/11/01/troubling-sur veillance-before-benghazi-attack.

Eastwood, Basil, and Richard Murphy. "Talk to Political Islamists in the Arab World." *Daily Star* (Beirut). May 4, 2005.

Ebadolahi, Mitra. "The Border Patrol Was Monstrous Under Obama. Imagine How Bad It Is Under Trump." ACLU Blog. May 23, 2018. https://www.aclu.org/blog /immigrants-rights/ice-and-border-patrol-abuses/border-patrol-was-monstrous -under-obama-imagine.

Edroso, Roy. "Rightbloggers: Had Enough Benghazi? Too Bad!" *Village Voice.* May 4, 2014. https://www.villagevoice.com/2014/05/04/rightbloggers-had-enough-benghazi -too-bad/.

"Egyptian Islamic Jihad." Center of International Security and Cooperation. October 2015. https://cisac.fsi.stanford.edu/mappingmilitants/profiles/egyptian-islamic-jihad.

Elliott, Philip. "By Making the Jan. 6 Probe Political, Republicans Stand to Re-Run Benghazi Playbook." *Time.* July 14, 2021. https://time.com/6080349/capitol-attack-probe-pelosi -mccarthy/.

Elyan, Tamim. "Egyptians Angry at Film Scale U.S. Embassy Walls." Reuters. September 11, 2012. https://www.reuters.com/article/us-egypt-usa-protest/egyptians-angry-at -film-scale-u-s-embassy-walls-idUSBRE88A11N20120911.

Emery, C. Eugene, Jr. "Hillary Clinton's Approval Ratings as Secretary of State Were High, but They're Not Now." PolitiFact. May 22, 2016. https://www.politifact .com/factchecks/2016/may/22/hillary-clinton/hillary-clintons-approval-rating -secretary-state-w/.

Erlanger, Steven. "'Brexit' Proved to Be Sign of Things to Come in U.S." *New York Times.* November 9, 2016. https://www.nytimes.com/2016/11/10/world/europe/for-us -brexit-was-a-sign-of-things-to-come.html.

———. "By His Own Reckoning, One Man Made Libya a French Cause." *New York Times.* April 1, 2011. https://www.nytimes.com/2011/04/02/world/africa/02levy.html.

Etzioni, Amitai. "Will the Yemen Raid Become Trump's Benghazi?" *National Interest.* February 12, 2017. https://nationalinterest.org/feature/will-the-yemen-raid-become -trumps-benghazi-19404.

"Ex-Foreign Minister Says Libya Behind 1989 Airline Attack." Al Arabiya News. July 18, 2011. https://web.archive.org/web/20110718133408/http://english.alarabiya.net/arti cles/2011/07/18/158145.html.

Exum, Andrew. "Don't Politicize the Failed Yemen Raid." *The Atlantic.* February 3, 2017. https://www.theatlantic.com/politics/archive/2017/02/dont-blame-trump-for-the -failed-raid-in-yemen/515496/.

Farrow, Ronan. "Can Biden Reverse Trump's Damage to the State Department?" *New Yorker.* June 17, 2021. https://www.newyorker.com/books/page-turner/can-biden -reverse-trumps-damage-to-the-state-department.

"FBI Uncovers Al-Qaeda Plot to Just Sit Back and Enjoy Collapse of United States." *The Onion.* April 15, 2014. https://www.theonion.com/fbi-uncovers-al-qaeda-plot-to-just -sit-back-and-enjoy-c-1819576375.

Fishman, Ben. "United States: Reluctant Engagement." In *Foreign Actors in Libya's Crisis,* edited by Karim Mezran and Arturo Varvelli, 91–109. Milan: Ledizioni, 2017.

Friedersdorf, Conor. "How Obama Ignored Congress, and Misled America, on War in Libya." *The Atlantic.* September 13, 2012. https://www.theatlantic.com/politics /archive/2012/09/how-obama-ignored-congress-and-misled-america-on-war-in-libya /262299/.

Friedman, Thomas L. "Obama on the World." *New York Times.* August 8, 2014. https://www.nytimes.com/2014/08/09/opinion/president-obama-thomas-l-friedman -iraq-and-world-affairs.html.

Frizell, Sam. "How Hillary Clinton Won the Benghazi Hearing." *Time.* October 23, 2015. https://time.com/4084578/benghazi-hearing-hillary-clinton-analysis/.

"Gaddafi Case: The Prosecutor v. Saif Al-Islam Gaddafi." International Criminal Court. June 27, 2011. https://www.icc-cpi.int/libya/gaddafi.

Gearan, Anne. "State Dept. Acknowledges Rejecting Requests for More Security in Beng-hazi." *Washington Post.* October 10, 2012. https://www.washingtonpost.com/world /national-security/state-dept-downgraded-security-in-libya-before-deadly-attack-ex -officer-claims/2012/10/10/d7195faa-12e6-11e2-a16b-2c110031514a_story.html.

Glass, Andrew. "This Day In Politics: U.S. Planes Bomb Libya, April 15, 1986." *Politico.* April 15, 2019. https://www.politico.com/story/2019/04/15/reagan-bomb-libya-april -15-1986-1272788.

Glenn, Cameron. "Libya's Islamists: Who They Are—and What They Want." Wilson Cen-ter. August 8, 2017. https://www.wilsoncenter.org/article/libyas-islamists-who-they-are -and-what-they-want.

Golby, Jim. "Trump Makes a Bad Situation Worse in Afghanistan." *The Atlantic.* Novem-ber 30, 2020. https://www.theatlantic.com/ideas/archive/2020/11/trump-leaving-biden -mess-afghanistan/617229/.

Gold, Hadas. "Benghazi, Benghazi, Benghazi." *Politico.* May 5, 2014. https://www.poli tico.com/blogs/media/2014/05/benghazi-benghazi-benghazi-187963.

Goldberg, Jeffrey. "Hillary Clinton: 'Failure' to Help Syrian Rebels Led to the Rise of ISIS." *The Atlantic*. August 10, 2014. https://www.theatlantic.com/international/archive/2014/08/hillary-clinton-failure-to-help-syrian-rebels-led-to-the-rise-of-isis/375832/.

Goldman, Adam, and Charlie Savage. "2nd Benghazi Suspect Is Convicted on 2 Counts Amid Signs of Deadlock on Others." *New York Times*. June 13, 2019. https://www.nytimes.com/2019/06/13/us/politics/mustafa-al-imam-convicted-benghazi.html.

Gordon, Michael, and Jeff Zeleny. "Interview with Barack Obama." *New York Times*. November 1, 2007. https://www.nytimes.com/2007/11/01/us/politics/02obama-transcript.html.

Graetz, Michael J. "Energy Policy: Past or Prologue?" *Daedalus* 141, no. 2 (Spring 2012): 31–44.

Gramer, Robbie, Dan De Luce, and Colum Lynch. "How the Trump Administration Broke the State Department." *Foreign Policy*. July 31, 2017. https://foreignpolicy.com/2017/07/31/how-the-trump-administration-broke-the-state-department/.

Greenblatt, Alan. "Leaders of the Libyan Opposition Emerge." NPR. March 14, 2011. https://www.npr.org/2011/03/15/134452475/leaders-of-the-libyan-opposition-emerge.

Greg. "Benghazi—the Mystery of the Missing Air Support." *Passion for Liberty*. June 16, 2013. http://www.passionforliberty.com/2013/06/16/benghazi-the-mystery-of-the-missing-air-support/.

Haddad, Said. "Order et disorder milicien en Libya" (Order and Military Disorder in Libya). *Moyen Orient* 25 (January–March 2015): 24–26.

Haltiwanger, John. "Is Niger Trump's Benghazi? Four U.S. Soldiers Died and It Took Him 12 Days to Respond." *Newsweek*. October 18, 2017. https://www.newsweek.com/niger-trumps-benghazi-four-us-soldiers-died-and-it-took-him-12-days-respond-688082.

Hart Research Associates. NBC News/*Wall Street Journal* Survey, Study #15463. https://www.wsj.com/public/resources/documents/NBCWSJLateOctoberPoll.pdf.

Hastings, Michael. "Inside Obama's War Room." *Rolling Stone*. October 13, 2011. https://www.rollingstone.com/politics/politics-news/inside-obamas-war-room-238074/.

Hauslohner, Abigail. "Libya's Central Government Exercises Little Authority Outside Capital." *Washington Post*. September 19, 2012. https://www.washingtonpost.com/world/middle_east/libyas-central-government-exercises-little-authority-outside-capital/2012/09/19/d8f46610-0280-11e2-91e7-2962c74e7738_story.html.

Helsel, Phil. "Mother of Chris Stevens, Ambassador Killed in Benghazi, Tells GOP: Stop Using Son's Death." NBC News. July 23, 2016. https://www.nbcnews.com/politics/2016-election/mother-ambassador-killed-benghazi-tells-trump-gop-stop-invoking-son-n615591.

"Hillary Clinton's Strengths: Record at State, Toughness, Honesty." Pew Research Center. March 4, 2014. https://www.pewresearch.org/politics/2014/03/04/hillary-clintons-strengths-record-at-state-toughness-honesty/.

Hirsh, Michael. "The Benghazi-Industrial Complex." *Politico*. May 4, 2014. https://www.politico.com/magazine/story/2014/05/hillarys-nightmare-the-benghazi-industrial-complex-106332/.

Holpuch, Amanda. "US Could Have Averted 40% of Covid Deaths, Says Panel Examining Trump's Policies." *The Guardian*. February 11, 2021.

Holyk, Gregory. "Majority Disapprove of Decision Not to Charge Clinton on Emails (Poll)." ABC News. July 11, 2016. https://abcnews.go.com/Politics/majority-disapproves-decision-charge-clinton-emails-poll/story?id=40445344.

Hook, Janet. "Clinton's Explanations on Benghazi Attacks Winning Over Voters—WSJ/NBC Poll." *Wall Street Journal*. November 3, 2015. https://www.wsj.com/articles/BL-WB-58991.

Hosenball, Mark. "Clinton: Facebook Post About Benghazi Attack Not Hard 'Evidence.'" Reuters. October 24, 2012. https://www.reuters.com/article/us-usa-benghazi-emails-idUSBRE89N12020121024.

Hughes, Dana, and Kirit Radia. "'Underwear Bomber's' Alarming Last Phone Call." ABC News. December 31, 2009. https://abcnews.go.com/WN/bombers-phone-call-father/story?id=9457361.

Huntington, Samuel. "The Clash of Civilizations?" *Foreign Affairs* 72, no. 3 (Summer 1993): 22–49. https://www.foreignaffairs.com/articles/united-states/1993-06-01/clash-civilizations.

Hussein, Tam. "Mahdi al-Harati: A Libyan Force Multiplier." *Syria Comment*. September 26, 2017. https://www.joshualandis.com/blog/mahdi-al-harati-a-libyan-force-multiplier/.

Hutcheson, Ron. "President Admits Personal Grudge Against Saddam." *Orlando Sentinel*. September 28, 2002. https://www.orlandosentinel.com/news/os-xpm-2002-09-28-0209280145-story.html.

Isikoff, Michael. "U.S. May Be Softening Stance on Muslim Brotherhood." *Newsweek*. April 22, 2007. https://www.newsweek.com/us-may-be-softening-stance-muslim-brotherhood-97847.

"It's Just a Stupid Movie! Film Leads to Muslim Attack on US." *New York Post*. Cover story. September 12, 2012. https://nypost.com/cover/post-covers-on-september-12th-2012/.

Jacinto, Leela. "Gaddafi's Gutted Edifice of Power Draws Gaping Crowds." France 24. April 28, 2011. https://www.france24.com/en/20110428-reporters-notebook-gaddafis-gutted-edifice-power-draws-gaping-crowds-benghazi-libya.

Jackson, Brooks. "Romney Gets It Backward." FactCheck.org. September 12, 2012. https://www.factcheck.org/2012/09/romney-gets-it-backward/.

Joscelyn, Thomas. "Al Qaeda's Expansion into Egypt." *FDD's Long War Journal*. February 11, 2014. https://www.longwarjournal.org/archives/2014/02/al_qaedas_expansion.php.

———. "Al Qaeda Often Agitated for Omar Abdel Rahman's Release from US Prison." *FDD's Long War Journal*. February 19, 2017. https://www.longwarjournal.org/archives/2017/02/al-qaeda-calls-for-revenge-after-omar-abdel-rahman-dies-in-us-prison.php.

———. "State Department: Ansar al Sharia an Alias for AQAP." *FDD's Long War Journal*. October 4, 2012. https://www.longwarjournal.org/archives/2012/10/state_department_ans.php.

Judicial Watch. "JW Finds Benghazi Smoking Gun!" May 2, 2014. https://web.archive.org/web/20140506061522/http://www.judicialwatch.org/press-room/weekly-updates/weekly-update-jw-finds-benghazi-smoking-gun.

Karl, Jonathan. "Exclusive: Benghazi Talking Points Underwent 12 Revisions, Scrubbed of Terror Reference." ABC News. May 10, 2013. https://abcnews.go.com/blogs/politics /2013/05/exclusive-benghazi-talking-points-underwent-12-revisions-scrubbed-of -terror-references.

Katz, Josh. "Who Will Be President?" *New York Times*. November 8, 2016. https:// www.nytimes.com/interactive/2016/upshot/presidential-polls-forecast.html.

Kellogg, Tom, and Hossam el-Hamalawy. "Bad Precedent: The 1995 and 1998 Renditions." Part V of "Black Hole: The Fate of Islamists Rendered to Egypt." Human Rights Watch. May 2005. https://www.hrw.org/reports/2005/egypt0505/5.htm.

Kelly, Morgan. "Like a Natural System, Democracy Faces Collapse as Polarization Leads to Loss of Diversity." High Meadows Environmental Institute. December 6, 2021. https://environment.princeton.edu/news/like-a-natural-system-democracy-faces-col lapse-as-polarization-leads-to-loss-of-diversity/.

Kersten, Mark. "Libya's Political Isolation Law: Politics and Justice or the Politics of Justice?" Middle East Institute. February 5, 2014. https://www.mei.edu/publications /libyas-political-isolation-law-politics-and-justice-or-politics-justice.

Kertscher, Tom. "In Context: Hillary Clinton's 'What Difference Does It Make' Comment." PolitiFact. May 8, 2013. https://www.politifact.com/article/2013/may/08 /context-hillary-clintons-what-difference-does-it-m/.

Kessler, Glenn. "Hillary Clinton and the Aug. 16 Cable on Benghazi Security." *Washington Post*. April 10, 2013. https://www.washingtonpost.com/blogs/fact-checker/post /hillary-clinton-and-the-aug-16-cable-on-benghazi-security/2013/04/09/675de8f8 -a179-11e2-9c03-6952ff305f35_blog.html.

———. "Issa's 'Suspicions' That Hillary Clinton Told Panetta to 'Stand Down' on Benghazi." *Washington Post*. February 21, 2014. https://www.washingtonpost .com/news/fact-checker/wp/2014/02/21/issas-suspicions-that-hillary-clinton-told -panetta-to-stand-down-on-benghazi/.

———. "Obama's Claim He Called Benghazi an 'Act of Terrorism.'" *Washington Post*. May 14, 2013. https://www.washingtonpost.com/blogs/fact-checker/post/obamas-claim-he-call ed-benghazi-an-act-of-terrorism/2013/05/13/7b65b83e-bc14-11e2-97d4-a479289a31 f9_blog.html.

Kiely, Eugene. "The Benghazi Timeline, Clinton Edition." FactCheck.org. June 30, 2016. https://www.factcheck.org/2016/06/the-benghazi-timeline-clinton-edition/.

Kirkpatrick, David D. "Brazen Figure May Hold Key to Mysteries." *New York Times*. June 17, 2014. https://www.nytimes.com/2014/06/18/world/middleeast/apprehension-of-ahmed -abu-khattala-may-begin-to-answer-questions-on-assault.html.

———. "A Deadly Mix in Benghazi." *New York Times*. December 28, 2013. https://www .nytimes.com/projects/2013/benghazi/index.html.

Kirkpatrick, David D., and Steven Lee Myers. "Libya Attack Brings Challenges for U.S." *New York Times*. September 12, 2012. https://www.nytimes.com/2012/09/13 /world/middleeast/us-envoy-to-libya-is-reported-killed.html.

Kliegman, Julie. "Cokie Roberts: Susan Rice Didn't Put the Whole Benghazi Attack 'on the Video.'" PolitiFact. May 4, 2014. https://www.politifact.com/factchecks/2014 /may/04/cokie-roberts/cokie-roberts-susan-rice-didnt-put-whole-benghazi-/.

Krayewski, Ed. "President Obama Had One Conversation with Leon Panetta on the Day of the Benghazi Attack." *Reason.* February 7, 2013. https://reason.com/2013/02/07/president-obama-had-one-conversation-wit/.

Kristof, Nicholas. "Obama: Man of the World." *New York Times.* March 6, 2007. https://www.nytimes.com/2007/03/06/opinion/06kristof.html.

Lake, Eli. "Why Obama Let Iran's Green Revolution Fail." *Bloomberg.* August 24, 2016. https://www.bloomberg.com/opinion/articles/2016-08-24/why-obama-let-iran-s-green-revolution-fail.

———. "Yes, There IS Evidence Linking al Qaeda to Benghazi." *Daily Beast.* December 29, 2013. https://www.thedailybeast.com/yes-there-is-evidence-linking-al-qaeda-to-benghazi.

Landler, Mark. "Ambassador Becomes Focus of Egyptians' Mistrust of U.S." *New York Times.* July 3, 2013. https://www.nytimes.com/2013/07/04/world/middleeast/ambassador-becomes-focus-of-egyptians-mistrust-of-us.html.

———. "Secret Report Ordered by Obama Identified Potential Uprisings." *New York Times.* February 16, 2011. https://www.nytimes.com/2011/02/17/world/middleeast/17diplomacy.html.

Lee, Maggie. "Film Review: 'Operation Red Sea.'" *Variety.* March 2, 2018. https://variety.com/2018/film/asia/operation-red-sea-review-1202710157/.

Leigh, David. "WikiLeaks Cables: Muammar Gaddafi and the 'Voluptuous Blonde.'" *The Guardian.* December 7, 2010. https://www.theguardian.com/world/2010/dec/07/wikileaks-cables-gaddafi-voluptuous-blonde.

Lerer, Lisa. "Clinton Wins Popular Vote by Nearly 2.9 Million." AP News. December 22, 2016. https://apnews.com/article/electoral-college-donald-trump-us-news-ap-top-news-elections-2c7a5afc13824161a25d8574e10ff4e7.

Lewis, Bernard. "The Roots of Muslim Rage." *The Atlantic.* September 1990. https://www.theatlantic.com/magazine/archive/1990/09/the-roots-of-muslim-rage/304643/.

Lewis, Michael. "Obama's Way." *Vanity Fair.* September 11, 2012. https://www.vanityfair.com/news/2012/10/michael-lewis-profile-barack-obama.

"Libya: 202 Prisoners Released but Hundreds Still Held Arbitrarily." Human Rights Watch. March 25, 2010. https://www.hrw.org/news/2010/03/25/libya-202-prisoners-released-hundreds-still-held-arbitrarily.

"Libya Eastern Commander Haftar Declares Benghazi 'Liberated.'" *BBC News.* July 6, 2017. https://www.bbc.com/news/world-africa-40515325.

"Libya: No Impunity for 'Black Saturday' Benghazi Deaths." Human Rights Watch. June 13, 2013. https://www.hrw.org/news/2013/06/13/libya-no-impunity-black-saturday-benghazi-deaths.

"Libyan Dissident, Long Imprisoned, Is Dead." Human Rights Watch. May 21, 2009. https://www.hrw.org/news/2009/05/21/libya-libyan-dissident-long-imprisoned-dead.

Lipton, Eric, Noam Scheiber, and Michael S. Schmidt. "Clinton Emails Became the New Focus of Benghazi Inquiry." *New York Times.* October 11, 2015. https://www.nytimes.com/2015/10/12/us/politics/clinton-emails-became-the-new-focus-of-benghazi-inquiry.html.

Lipton, Eric, Brooke Williams, and Nicholas Confessore. "Foreign Powers Buy Influence at Think Tanks." *New York Times.* September 6, 2014. https://www.nytimes .com/2014/09/07/us/politics/foreign-powers-buy-influence-at-think-tanks.html.

Lizza, Ryan. "The Consequentialist: How the Arab Spring Remade Obama's Foreign Policy." *New Yorker.* May 2, 2011. https://www.newyorker.com/magazine/2011/05/02 /the-consequentialist.

Lynch, Marc. "Islam Divided Between Salafi-jihad and the Ikhwan." *Studies in Conflict and Terrorism* 33, no. 6 (2010): 467–487.

MacAskill, Ewen, and Suzanne Goldenberg. "Obama Aide Resigns After Calling Clinton a 'Monster.'" *The Guardian.* March 6, 2008. https://www.theguardian.com /world/2008/mar/07/barackobama.hillaryclinton.

Mackey, Robert, and Liam Stack. "Obscure Film Mocking Muslim Prophet Sparks Anti-U.S. Protests in Egypt and Libya." *New York Times.* September 11, 2012. https://thelede.blogs.nytimes.com/2012/09/11/obscure-film-mocking-muslim -prophet-sparks-anti-u-s-protests-in-egypt-and-libya/.

Manchester, Julia. "Analyst Says US Is Most Divided Since Civil War." *The Hill.* October 3, 2018. https://thehill.com/hilltv/what-americas-thinking/409718-analyst-says -the-us-is-the-most-divided-since-the-civl-war.

Markey, Patrick, and Ghaith Shennib. "In Standoff, Libyans Protest over Parliament Extension." Reuters. February 7, 2014. https://www.reuters.com/article/us-libya-crisis /in-standoff-libyans-protest-over-parliament-extension-idUSBREA161MH2014 0207.

Martin, Jonathan, and Alexander Burns. "Reeling from Surprise Losses, Democrats Sound the Alarm for 2022." *New York Times.* November 6, 2021. https://www .nytimes.com/2021/11/03/us/politics/democrat-losses-2022.html.

Masterson, Julia, and Leanne Quinn. "Timeline of Syrian Chemical Weapons Activity, 2012–2022." Arms Control Association. May 2021. https://www.armscontrol.org /factsheets/Timeline-of-Syrian-Chemical-Weapons-Activity.

Mastrangelo, Dominick. "Ernst 'Afraid of a Benghazi 2.0' in Afghanistan." *The Hill.* August 16, 2021. https://thehill.com/homenews/senate/568010-ernst-afraid-of-a-ben ghazi-20-in-afghanistan.

Mayer, Jane. "Outsourcing Torture: The Secret History of America's 'Extraordinary Rendition' Program." *New Yorker.* February 14, 2005. https://www.newyorker.com/magazine /2005/02/14/outsourcing-torture.

"McCain Calls for More Military Support to Anti-Qaddafi Forces During Libya Visit." Fox News. December 23, 2015. https://www.foxnews.com/politics/mccain-calls-for-more -military-support-to-anti-qaddafi-forces-during-libya-visit.

McGreal, Chris. "Obama Deflects Romney's Challenge on Benghazi Attack During Hofstra Debate." *The Guardian.* October 17, 2012. https://www.theguardian.com /world/2012/oct/17/romney-obama-benghazi-defeated-debate.

McGregor, Andrew. "Libya's Ansar al-Shari'a Declares the Islamic Emirate of Benghazi." Jamestown Foundation. August 8, 2014. https://jamestown.org/program /libyas-ansar-al-sharia-declares-the-islamic-emirate-of-benghazi/.

Mercer, Andrew, Claudia Deane, and Kyley McGeeney. "Why 2016 Election Polls Missed Their Mark." Pew Research Center. November 9, 2016. https://www.pewresearch.org/fact-tank/2016/11/09/why-2016-election-polls-missed-their-mark/.

Mikkelson, David. "Attack on the U.S. Diplomatic Mission in Benghazi." Snopes. November 1, 2012. https://www.snopes.com/fact-check/benghazi-bungle/.

Miller, Leila. "Facing a Russian Cyber Attack, Obama Officials Struggled to Respond." *Frontline*. October 31, 2017. https://www.pbs.org/wgbh/frontline/article/facing-a-russian-cyber-attack-obama-officials-struggled-to-respond/.

Monitor's Editorial Board. "McCain's Mutiny Against War Bitterness." *Christian Science Monitor*. August 27, 2018. https://www.csmonitor.com/Commentary/the-monitors-view/2018/0827/McCain-s-mutiny-against-war-bitterness.

Montanaro, Domenico. "Hillary Clinton's 'Basket of Deplorables,' in Full Context of This Ugly Campaign." NPR. September 10, 2016. https://www.npr.org/2016/09/10/493427601/hillary-clintons-basket-of-deplorables-in-full-context-of-this-ugly-campaign.

Montoya, Mario. "Mission to a Revolution." *State* 562 (December 2011): 18–23. https://play.google.com/books/reader?id=VIRNAQAAMAAJ&pg=GBS.RA4-PA18&printsec=frontcover.

Munsil, Leigh. "Feinstein: House Benghazi Committee 'Ridiculous.'" *Politico NOW Blog*. May 18, 2014. https://www.politico.com/blogs/politico-now/2014/05/feinstein-house-benghazi-committee-ridiculous-188727.

Murray, Patrick. "National: America Tired of Clinton Email Story." Monmouth University Poll. October 21, 2015. https://www.monmouth.edu/polling-institute/documents/monmouthpoll_us_102115.pdf/.

Mustafa, Ahmed, Jamal Gerges Al-Muzahem, Muhammad Hajjaj, Muhammad Reda, and Muhammad Al-Sayed. "سياسيون أقباط المهجر يشعلون الفتن .. بينتاج فيلم مسيء للرسول للفيلم.. الءقانوني أويطالبون بالملاحق «يهاجمون العقس الءأمريكي تيري جونز و«صادق» و«زقلم رضوان: المسيحيون المصريون قبل المسلمين ضد العفيلم (*Aqbat Al-Muhajir Yashiloon Al-Fitna bi-Intaj Film Musi' LilRasool*, Expatriate Copts Ignite Chaos with Production of Film Insulting the Prophet)." *Youm7*. September 9, 2012.

Myers, Steven Lee. "Amid Impasse in Peace Negotiations, America's Chief Middle East Envoy Resigns." *New York Times*. May 13, 2011. https://www.nytimes.com/2011/05/14/world/middleeast/14mitchell.html.

———. "Clinton Meets in Paris with Libyan Rebel Leader." *New York Times*. March 14, 2011. https://www.nytimes.com/2011/03/15/world/africa/15clinton.html.

———. "In Tripoli, Clinton Pledges U.S. Help to a 'Free Libya.'" *New York Times*. October 18, 2011. https://www.nytimes.com/2011/10/19/world/africa/clinton-in-libya-to-meet-leaders-and-offer-aid-package.html.

Myers, Steven Lee, and Eric Lichtblau. "Hillary Clinton Is Criticized for Private Emails in State Dept. Review." *New York Times*. May 25, 2016. https://www.nytimes.com/2016/05/26/us/politics/state-department-hillary-clinton-emails.html.

Naylor, Brian. "Trump Apparently Quotes Russian Propaganda to Slam Clinton on Benghazi." NPR. October 11, 2016. https://www.npr.org/2016/10/11/497520017/trump-apparently-quotes-russian-propaganda-to-slam-clinton-on-benghazi.

NBC News Staff and Wire Services. "Susan Rice: 'I Relied Solely and Squarely' on Intel Given to Me for Benghazi Comments." NBC News. November 21, 2012. https://www.nbcnews.com/news/world/susan-rice-i-relied-solely-squarely-intel-given-me-benghazi-flna1c7210498.

Newhauser, Daniel. "As Midterms Approach, House GOP Puts Spotlight Back on IRS, Benghazi." *Roll Call.* May 5, 2014. https://rollcall.com/2014/05/05/as-midterms-approach-house-gop-puts-spotlight-back-on-irs-benghazi/.

Newport, Frank. "Hillary Clinton, Barack Obama Most Admired in 2012." Gallup. December 31, 2012. https://news.gallup.com/poll/159587/hillary-clinton-barack-obama-admired-2012.aspx.

Nissenbaum, Dion. "U.S. Confirms Military Withdrawal from Yemen." *Wall Street Journal.* March 22, 2015. https://www.wsj.com/articles/u-s-confirms-special-operations-forces-withdrawal-from-yemen-1427046997.

"The Nobel Peace Prize for 2009." Nobel Prize. October 9, 2009. https://www.nobelprize.org/prizes/peace/2009/press-release/.

Nordland, Rod. "In Libya, Former Enemy Is Recast in Role of Ally." *New York Times.* September 1, 2011. https://www.nytimes.com/2011/09/02/world/africa/02islamist.html.

Oliphant, James, and David Morgan. "Panel's Report Reignites Debate over Clinton and Benghazi." Reuters. June 28, 2016. https://www.reuters.com/article/us-usa-congress-benghazi/panels-report-reignites-debate-over-clinton-and-benghazi-idUSKCN0ZE1RC.

Ottaway, David B., and Laura Parker. "CIA Confident Iran Behind Jet Bombing." *Washington Post.* May 11, 1989. https://www.washingtonpost.com/wp-srv/inatl/longterm/panam103/stories/cia0589.htm.

Packer, George. "The Betrayal." *The Atlantic.* January 31, 2022. https://www.theatlantic.com/magazine/archive/2022/03/biden-afghanistan-exit-american-allies-abandoned/621307/.

Paisley, Laura. "Political Polarization at Its Worst Since the Civil War." USC News. November 8, 2016. https://news.usc.edu/110124/political-polarization-at-its-worst-since-the-civil-war-2/.

Patteson, Callie. "Gen. Milley Says Biden Ignored Request to Keep Some Troops in Afghanistan, Contradicting Earlier Biden Claim." *New York Post.* September 28, 2021. https://nypost.com/2021/09/28/gen-milley-faces-congress-over-afghanistan-withdrawal/.

Pearson, Michael. "What the Obama Administration Has Said About the Libya Attack." CNN. May 9, 2013. https://www.cnn.com/2013/05/08/politics/libya-attack-statements-2013/index.html.

Peraino, Kevin. "Cover: The Jihadist Riddle." *Newsweek.* April 19, 2008. https://www.newsweek.com/cover-jihadist-riddle-85605.

Peralta, Eyder. "What We Know About 'Sam Bacile,' the Man Behind the Muhammad Movie." NPR. September 12, 2012. https://www.npr.org/sections/thetwo-way/2012/09/12/161003427/what-we-know-about-sam-bacile-the-man-behind-the-muhammad-movie.

Phillips, Amber. "The 5 Most Serious Accusations from Republicans' Benghazi Report." *Washington Post.* June 28, 2016. https://www.washingtonpost.com/news/the

-fix/wp/2016/06/28/the-5-most-serious-accusations-from-republicans-benghazi
-report/.

Phillips, Chris. "Libya's Golden Boy Is No Black Sheep." *The Guardian*. August 30, 2008.
https://www.theguardian.com/commentisfree/2008/aug/30/libya.middleeast.

Pilkington, Ed. "UN General Assembly: 100 Minutes in the Life of Muammar Gaddafi." *The Guardian*. September 23, 2009. https://www.theguardian.com/world/2009
/sep/23/gaddafi-un-speech.

Pitter, Laura. "Delivered into Enemy Hands: US-Led Abuse and Rendition of Opponents
to Gaddafi's Libya." Human Rights Watch. September 5, 2012. https://www.hrw
.org/report/2012/09/05/delivered-enemy-hands/us-led-abuse-and-rendition-oppo
nents-gaddafis-libya.

Preston, Andrew. "The Little State Department: McGeorge Bundy and the National
Security Council Staff, 1961–65." *Presidential Studies Quarterly* 31, no. 4 (December
2001): 635–659.

Priebus, Reince. "Why Won't Obama Call It Terrorism?" *RealClearPolitics*. September 27,
2012. https://www.realclearpolitics.com/articles/2012/09/27/why_wont_obama_call
_it_terrorism_115599.html.

"Qasem Soleimani: US Kills Top Iranian General in Baghdad Air Strike." BBC News.
January 3, 2020. https://www.bbc.com/news/world-middle-east-50979463.

Quattrociocchi, Walter. "Inside the Echo Chamber." *Scientific American* 316, no. 4 (April
2017): 60–63.

Rayment, Sean. "How the Special Forces Helped Bring Gaddafi to His Knees." *Telegraph*. August 28, 2011. https://www.telegraph.co.uk/news/worldnews/africaandindian
ocean/libya/8727076/How-the-special-forces-helped-bring-Gaddafi-to-his-knees
.html.

Reuters Staff. "Al Qaeda Confirms Death of bin Laden Confidant Libi." Reuters. September 11, 2012. https://www.reuters.com/article/cnews-us-security-qaeda-idCABRE88
A04L20120911.

———. "Gaddafi Son Says Revolt Will Be Over in 48 Hours." Reuters. March 16, 2011. https://
www.reuters.com/article/us-libya-saif/gaddafi-son-says-revolt-will-be-over-in-48
-hours-idUSTRE72F2SP20110316.

———. "Qatar Says Only Libyans Can Decide Their Future." Reuters. March 31, 2011.
https://www.reuters.com/article/libya-qatar/qatar-says-only-libyans-can-decide-their
-future-idUSLDE72U0ES20110331.

———. "Timeline: Libya's Uprising Against Muammar Gaddafi." Reuters. August 22,
2011. https://www.reuters.com/article/us-libya-events/timeline-libyas-uprising-against
-muammar-gaddafi-idUSTRE77K2QH20110822.

Richter, Greg. "Mother of Benghazi Victim: 'Special Place in Hell' for Hillary." Newsmax. March 10, 2016. https://www.newsmax.com/newsfront/benghazi-hillary-clinton
-patricia-smith/2016/03/10/id/718546/.

Risen, James, and Benjamin Weiser. "Before Bombings, Omens and Fears." *New York
Times*. January 9, 1999. https://www.nytimes.com/1999/01/09/world/unheeded
-warnings-a-special-report-before-bombings-omens-and-fears.html.

Risen, James, Mark Mazzetti, and Michael S. Schmidt. "U.S.-Approved Arms for Libya Rebels Fell into Jihadis' Hands." *New York Times*. December 5, 2012. https://www.nytimes.com/2012/12/06/world/africa/weapons-sent-to-libyan-rebels-with-us-approval-fell-into-islamist-hands.html.

Roberts, Dan, Megan Carpentier, Paul Lewis, Jon Swaine, Ed Pilkington, and Rory Carroll. "Republicans Win Majority in US Senate, Giving Party Full Control of Congress." *The Guardian*. November 5, 2014. https://www.theguardian.com/us-news/2014/nov/04/us-midterm-elections-republican-wins-senate-takeover.

Roggio, Bill. "Ansar al Shariah Issues Statement on US Consulate Assault in Libya." *FDD's Long War Journal*. September 12, 2012. https://www.longwarjournal.org/archives/2012/09/ansar_al_shariah_issues_statem.php.

———. "Libyan Islamic Fighting Group Joins al Qaeda." *FDD's Long War Journal*. November 3, 2007. https://www.longwarjournal.org/archives/2007/11/libyan_islamic_fight.php.

Rogin, Josh. "Inside the Public Relations Disaster at the Cairo Embassy." *Foreign Policy*. September 12, 2012. https://foreignpolicy.com/2012/09/12/inside-the-public-relations-disaster-at-the-cairo-embassy/.

Rohde, David, and Warren Strobel. "Special Report: How Syria Policy Stalled Under the 'Analyst in Chief.'" Reuters. October 28, 2014. https://www.reuters.com/article/us-usa-diplomacy-obama-specialreport/special-report-how-syria-policy-stalled-under-the-analyst-in-chief-idUKKBN0IH28L20141030.

Rosen, Armin. "Here's the Biggest Issue the Benghazi Committee Didn't Ask Hillary Clinton About." *Business Insider*. October 25, 2015. https://www.businessinsider.com/hillary-clinton-benghazi-testimony-militia-groups-2015-10.

Rothkopf, David. "Obama's 'Don't Do Stupid Shit' Foreign Policy." *Foreign Policy*. June 4, 2014. https://foreignpolicy.com/2014/06/04/obamas-dont-do-stupid-shit-foreign-policy/.

"Saif Gaddafi's Speech Translated." *The Times*. February 21, 2011. https://www.thetimes.co.uk/article/saif-gaddafis-speech-translated-xz0x90fdllk.

Saletan, William. "Republicans Are Tough on Terrorism Until the Terrorists Are Republicans." *Slate*. January 13, 2021. https://slate.com/news-and-politics/2021/01/benghazi-capitol-attack-republicans-cruz-jordan.html.

Samuels, David. "The Aspiring Novelist Who Became Obama's Foreign Policy Guru." *New York Times*. May 5, 2016. https://www.nytimes.com/2016/05/08/magazine/the-aspiring-novelist-who-became-obamas-foreign-policy-guru.html.

Sargent, Greg. "Morning Plum: Clinton May Be Changing Minds on Benghazi, E-mails." *Washington Post*. November 3, 2015. https://www.washingtonpost.com/blogs/plum-line/wp/2015/11/03/morning-plum-hillary-may-be-changing-minds-on-benghazi-emails/.

Savillo, Rob, and Hannah Groch-Begley. "Report: Fox's Benghazi Obsession by the Numbers." Media Matters for America. September 9, 2014. https://www.mediamatters.org/sean-hannity/report-foxs-benghazi-obsession-numbers.

Schama, Simon. "Onward Christian Soldiers." *The Guardian*. November 5, 2004. https://www.theguardian.com/world/2004/nov/05/usa.uselections2004.

Schleifer, Theodore. "Benghazi Committee Runs Its Course and Ends Operations." CNN. December 12, 2016. https://www.cnn.com/2016/12/12/politics/benghazi-committee -ends-hillary-clinton/index.html.

Schmidt, Michael S. "Hillary Clinton Used Personal Email Account of State Dept., Possibly Breaking Rules." *New York Times.* March 2, 2015. https://www.nytimes .com/2015/03/03/us/politics/hillary-clintons-use-of-private-email-at-state-department -raises-flags.html.

Schmitt, Eric. "Father of Commando Killed in Yemen Refused to Meet Trump." *New York Times.* February 26, 2017. https://www.nytimes.com/2017/02/26/us/politics /father-of-commando-killed-in-yemen-refused-to-meet-trump.html.

Schogol, Jeff. "Marines Responding to Benghazi Were Held Up by Debate on Weapons and Uniforms, Commander Says." *Marine Corps Times.* June 28, 2016. https:// www.marinecorpstimes.com/news/your-marine-corps/2016/06/28/marines-respond ing-to-benghazi-were-held-up-by-debate-on-weapons-and-uniforms-commander- says/.

Sedarat, Firouz, and Lin Noueihed. "Obama Says Ready to Talk to Iran." Reuters. January 27, 2009. https://www.reuters.com/article/us-obama-arabiya/obama-says-ready-to -talk-to-iran-idUSTRE50Q23220090127.

Shachtman, Noah. "U.S. Paid Guards $4 per Hour at Threatened Benghazi Consulate." *Wired.* October 3, 2012. https://www.wired.com/2012/10/benghazi-guards/.

Sheridan, Mary Beth. "Libya Declares Liberation with an Islamic Tone." *Washington Post.* October 23, 2011. https://www.washingtonpost.com/world/middle_east/libya -declares-liberation-with-an-islamic-tone/2011/10/23/gIQA4VsbAM_story.html.

Sherlock, Ruth. "Leading Libyan Islamist Met Free Syrian Army Opposition Group." *Telegraph.* November 27, 2011. https://www.telegraph.co.uk/news/worldnews/africa andindianocean/libya/8919057/Leading-Libyan-Islamist-met-Free-Syrian-Army -opposition-group.html.

Sherwood, Harriet. "Gaddafi Violence Against Libya Civilians Exaggerated, Says British Group." *The Guardian.* April 19, 2011. https://www.theguardian.com/world/2011 /apr/19/gaddafi-violence-exaggerated-british-group.

Sieff, Kevin. "Florida Pastor Terry Jones's Koran Burning Has Far-Reaching Effect." *Washington Post.* April 2, 2011. https://www.washingtonpost.com/local/education /florida-pastor-terry-joness-koran-burning-has-far-reaching-effect/2011/04/02/AFpi FoQC_story.html.

Silverstein, Ken. "How Kadafi Went from Foe to Ally." *Los Angeles Times.* September 4, 2005. https://www.latimes.com/archives/la-xpm-2005-sep-04-fg-uslibya4-story .html.

Sorkin, Amy Davidson. "The Hillary Hearing." *New Yorker.* October 23, 2015. https:// www.newyorker.com/magazine/2015/11/02/hillarys-moment-at-the-benghazi-hearing.

Sotloff, Steven. "The Other 9/11: Libyan Guards Recount What Happened in Benghazi." *Time.* October 21, 2012. https://world.time.com/2012/10/21/the-other-911-libyan -guards-recount-what-happened-in-benghazi/.

Stack, Liam. "Donald Trump Featured Paula Jones and 2 Other Women Who Accused Bill Clinton of Sexual Assault." *New York Times.* October 9, 2016. https://www .nytimes.com/2016/10/10/us/politics/bill-clinton-accusers.html.

Stacher, Joshua, and Samer Shehata. "Hear Out the Muslim Brotherhood." *New York Times.* March 26, 2007. https://www.nytimes.com/2007/03/26/opinion/26iht -edstach.1.5028488.html.

Staff Writer. "Clinton Can Thank Obama for Her Benghazi Headache." *Herald Democrat.* October 7, 2015. https://www.heralddemocrat.com/story/opinion/columns/gu est/2015/10/07/clinton-can-thank-obama-her-benghazi-headache/27180933007/.

Stewart, Rory. "The Last Days of Intervention: Afghanistan and the Delusions of Maximalism." *Foreign Affairs* 100, no. 6 (November/December 2021). https://www.for eignaffairs.com/articles/afghanistan/2021-10-08/last-days-intervention.

Tamman, Maurice. "Clinton Has 90 Percent Chance of Winning: Reuters/Ipsos States of the Nation." Reuters. November 7, 2016. https://www.reuters.com/article/us-usa -election-poll/clinton-has-90-percent-chance-of-winning-reuters-ipsos-states-of-the -nation-idUSKBN1322J1.

Tapper, Jake. "Documents Back Up Claims of Requests for Greater Security in Benghazi." ABC News. October 19, 2012. https://abcnews.go.com/blogs/politics/2012/10 /documents-back-up-claims-of-requests-for-greater-security-in-benghazi.

Tau, Byron. "U.S. Embassy in Cairo Condemns Muhammed Video." *Politico.* September 11, 2012. https://www.politico.com/blogs/politico44/2012/09/us-embassy-in-cairo -condemns-muhammed-video-135222.

Temple-Raston, Dina. "New Terrorism Adviser Takes a 'Broad Tent' Approach." NPR. January 24, 2011. https://www.npr.org/2011/01/24/133125267/new-terrorism-adviser -takes-a-broad-tent-approach.

Timmerman, Kenneth R. "The Iranian Connection to the Benghazi Attacks." *Washington Times.* March 20, 2016. https://www.washingtontimes.com/news/2016 /mar/20/kenneth-timmerman-the-iranian-connection-to-the-be/.

Toaldo, Mattia. "Europe: Carving Out a New Role." In *Foreign Actors in Libya's Crisis,* edited by Karim Mezran and Arturo Varvelli, 57–72. Milan: Ledizioni, 2017.

Travis, Alan, and Randeep Ramesh. "Muslim Brotherhood Are Possible Extremists, David Cameron Says." *The Guardian.* December 17, 2015. https://www.theguardian.com /world/2015/dec/17/uk-will-not-ban-muslim-brotherhood-david-cameron-says.

Tucker, Eric. "Militant Convicted in Fatal Benghazi Attack Seeks New Trial." AP News. November 24, 2020. https://apnews.com/article/trials-terrorism-ahmed-abu -khattala-c0f3e737bdb3ac2efddbf13482c6cd66.

Tures, John A. "Investigating Benghazi but Ignoring the Jan. 6 Insurrection." *Ohio Capital Journal.* June 9, 2021. https://ohiocapitaljournal.com/2021/06/09/investi gating-benghazi-but-ignoring-the-jan-6-insurrection/.

Tyler, Patrick E. "Two Said to Tell of Libyan Plot Against Saudi." *New York Times.* June 10, 2004. https://www.nytimes.com/2004/06/10/world/two-said-to-tell-of-lib yan-plot-against-saudi.html.

"UAE Charges 'Plotters Linked to Muslim Brotherhood.'" BBC News. January 28, 2013. https://www.bbc.com/news/world-middle-east-21226174.

Unger, Craig. "GOP's October Surprise?" *Salon*. October 1, 2012. https://www.salon.com/2012/10/01/gops_october_surprise/.

"US Official Dies in Libya Consulate Attack in Benghazi." BBC News. September 12, 2012. https://www.bbc.com/news/world-africa-19562692.

"US/UK: Documents Reveal Libya Rendition Details." Human Rights Watch. September 8, 2011. https://www.hrw.org/news/2011/09/08/us/uk-documents-reveal-libya-rendition-details.

Vasilogambros, Matt, and *National Journal*. "Officials: Cairo Embassy Staffer Ignored Instructions Not to Release Statement." *The Atlantic*. September 13, 2012. https://www.theatlantic.com/politics/archive/2012/09/officials-cairo-embassy-staffer-ignored-instructions-not-to-release-statement/437349/.

Von Rennenkampff, Marik. "Throw the GOP's Benghazi Playbook at Trump's Catastrophic Coronavirus Response." *The Hill*. April 21, 2020. https://thehill.com/opinion/white-house/493774-throw-the-gops-benghazi-playbook-at-trumps-catastrophic-coronavirus.

Warren, James A. "Barbara Tuchman's 'The Guns of August' Is Still WWI's Peerless Chronicle." *The Daily Beast*. April 14, 2017. https://www.thedailybeast.com/barbara-tuchmans-the-guns-of-august-is-still-wwis-peerless-chronicle.

Washington Post Staff. "The CNN Democratic Debate Transcript, Annotated." *Washington Post*. October 13, 2015. https://www.washingtonpost.com/news/the-fix/wp/2015/10/13/the-oct-13-democratic-debate-who-said-what-and-what-it-means/

———. "Full Text: Clinton Testifies Before House Committee on Benghazi." *Washington Post*. October 22, 2015. https://www.washingtonpost.com/news/post-politics/wp/2015/10/22/transcript-clinton-testifies-before-house-committee-on-benghazi/.

Watts, Duncan J., and David M. Rothschild. "Don't Blame the Election on Fake News. Blame It on the Media." *Columbia Journalism Review*. December 5, 2017. https://www.cjr.org/analysis/fake-news-media-election-trump.php.

Wehrey, Frederic, and Peter Cole. "Building Libya's Security Sector." Carnegie Endowment for International Peace. August 6, 2013. https://carnegieendowment.org/2013/08/06/building-libya-s-security-sector-pub-52603.

Weisman, Steven R. "Powell Calls His U.N. Speech a Lasting Blot on His Record." *New York Times*. September 9, 2005. https://www.nytimes.com/2005/09/09/politics/powell-calls-his-un-speech-a-lasting-blot-on-his-record.html.

Whitlock, Craig. "Drone Strikes Killing More Civilians Than U.S. Admits, Human Rights Groups Say." *Washington Post*. October 22, 2013. https://www.washingtonpost.com/world/national-security/drone-strikes-killing-more-civilians-than-us-admits-human-rights-groups-say/2013/10/21/a99cbe78-3a81-11e3-b7ba-503fb5822c3e_story.html.

Wiener-Bronner, Danielle. "Who Attacked Benghazi Depends on Who You Think Is in al-Qaeda." *The Atlantic*. December 30, 2013. https://www.theatlantic.com/national/archive/2013/12/benghazi-story-now-dispute-about-who-exactly-al-qaeda/356561/.

Williams, Jennifer. "'Benghazi Mom' Patricia Smith, and How the Trump Campaign Is Exploiting Her, Explained." *Vox*. October 19, 2016. https://www.vox.com /debates/2016/10/19/13331182/benghazi-mom-patricia-smith-trump-debate.

Willon, Phil, and Rebecca Keegan. "'Innocence of Muslims' Unrest." *Los Angeles Times*. September 13, 2012. https://timelines.latimes.com/unrest-timeline/.

Wilson, Scott, and Jon Cohen. "Poll Finds Broad Support for Obama's Counterterrorism Policies." *Washington Post*. February 8, 2012. https://www.washingtonpost.com /politics/poll-finds-broad-support-for-obamas-counterterrorism-policies/2012/02/07 /gIQAFrSEyQ_story.html.

Wilson, Scott, and Joby Warrick. "Assad Must Go, Obama Says." *Washington Post*. August 18, 2011. https://www.washingtonpost.com/politics/assad-must-go-obama -says/2011/08/18/gIQAelheOJ_story.html.

Woodward, Bob. "Gadhafi Target of Secret U.S. Deception Plan." *Washington Post*. October 2, 1986. https://www.washingtonpost.com/archive/politics/1986/10/02/gad hafi-target-of-secret-us-deception-plan/f185d0b5-81e6-4019-ae42-1a631e4abb01/.

Wu, Nicholas, and Kyle Cheney. "Dems Push DOJ to Look at Trump After Jan. 6 Panel's Blockbuster." *Politico*. March 3, 2022. https://www.politico.com/news/2022/03/03 /democrats-justice-department-trump-jan-6-00013847.

"Yemen Crisis: US Troops Withdraw from Air Base." BBC News. March 22, 2015. https:// www.bbc.com/news/world-middle-east-32000970.

York, Byron. "Why Don't Liberal Syria Intervention Critics Talk About Libya?" *Washington Examiner*. September 7, 2013. https://www.washingtonexaminer.com/why-dont -liberal-syria-intervention-critics-talk-about-libya.

Zapotosky, Matt, Josh Dawsey, Tom Hamburger, and Rachel Weiner. "The Justice Dept. Alleged Jan. 6 Was a Seditious Conspiracy. Now Will It Investigate Trump?" *Washington Post*. January 15, 2022. https://www.washingtonpost.com /national-security/trump-jan-6-investigation-garland/2022/01/15/e55a3ca2-7555 -11ec-b202-b9b92330d4fa_story.html.

Zelin, Aaron Y. "Know Your Ansar al-Sharia." *Foreign Policy*. September 21, 2012. https:// foreignpolicy.com/2012/09/21/know-your-ansar-al-sharia/.

Zenko, Micah. "Obama's Embrace of Drone Strikes Will Be a Lasting Legacy." *New York Times*. January 12, 2016. https://www.nytimes.com/roomforde bate/2016/01/12/reflecting-on-obamas-presidency/obamas-embrace-of-drone -strikes-will-be-a-lasting-legacy.

Zurcher, Anthony. "Myeshia Johnson: Soldier's Widow Says Trump Made Me Cry." BBC News. October 23, 2017. https://www.bbc.com/news/world-us-canada-41724827.

Zway, Suliman Ali, and Rick Gladstone. "In Libya, Chaos Was Followed by Organized Ambush, Official Says." *New York Times*. September 13, 2012. https://www .nytimes.com/2012/09/14/world/africa/libya-attacks-came-in-two-waves-official -says.html.

Other Media

BenghaziRunningClub. "Remember Benghazi." Pinterest board. https://www.pinterest .com/benghazirunning/remember-benghazi/.

Browne, Pamela K., and Catherine Herridge. "Was Syrian Weapons Shipment Factor in Ambassador's Benghazi Visit?" Fox News video and article. December 23, 2015. https://www.foxnews .com/politics/was-syrian-weapons-shipment-factor-in-ambassadors-benghazi-visit.

Clinton, Hillary. "Common Ground Award Address Honoring J. Christopher Stevens." American Rhetoric video and transcript. November 8, 2012. https://www.american rhetoric.com/speeches/hillaryclintonhonoringchrisstevens.htm.

Crocker, Ryan. "Former Syrian Ambassador: U.S. 'Complicit' in Aleppo Brutality." *Takeaway.* Podcast audio. December 21, 2016. https://www.wnycstudios.org/pod casts/takeaway/segments/how-significant-assads-victory-aleppo1. (Interview with John Hockenberry.)

De Jonge, Chad Kiewiet. "Both Clinton and GOP Viewed Negatively on Benghazi (Poll)." ABC News video and article. October 22, 2015. https://abcnews.go.com/Politics /clinton-gop-viewed-negatively-benghazi-poll/story?id=34630314.

"Embassies Under Attack over Anti-Islam Video." Al Jazeera video and article. September 15, 2012. https://www.aljazeera.com/news/2012/9/15/embassies-under-attack-over -anti-islam-video.

Exum, Andrew. Interview with Hari Sreenivasan. *PBS NewShour* video and transcript. March 1, 2017. https://www.pbs.org/newshour/show/yemen-raid-planning-obama-administration -leave-off-trump-pick.

Gadaffi, Muammar. "Muammar Gaddafi at the 64th UN General Assembly in 2009." Speech. September 19, 2017. https://www.africanews.com/2017/09/19/speech -muammar-gaddafi-at-the-64th-un-general-assembly-in-2009.

Griffin, Jennifer. "Exclusive: CIA Operators Were Denied Request for Help During Benghazi Attack, Sources Say." Fox News video and article. January 12, 2017. https://www .foxnews.com/politics/exclusive-cia-operators-were-denied-request-for-help-during -benghazi-attack-sources-say.

"Hillary Clinton's Benghazi Testimony by the Numbers." ABC News video and article. October 22, 2015. https://abcnews.go.com/Politics/hillary-clintons-benghazi-testi mony-numbers/story?id=34667634.

"House Hearing on Benghazi Consulate Attack." C-SPAN video. January 23, 2013. https://www.c-span.org/video/?310545-1/house-hearing-benghazi-consulate-attack.

Karadsheh, Jomana, and Moni Basu. "Libyans Turn Out Big, Then Celebrate Historic Election." CNN video and article. July 8, 2012. https://www.cnn.com/2012/07/07 /world/africa/libya-election/index.html.

Karl, Jonathan, and Chris Good. "The Benghazi Emails: Talking Points Changed at State Dept.'s Request." ABC News video and article. May 15, 2013. https://abc news.go.com/Politics/benghazi-emails-talking-points-changed-state-depts-request /story?id=19187137.

"Killary 'Butcher of Benghazi' Clinton." Facebook community. https://www.facebook .com/Killary-Butcher-of-Benghazi-Clinton-1060309507359407/photos/?_rdr.

McCain, John. Interview by Candy Crowley. *State of the Union*, CNN, September 30, 2012. (Transcript available at https://transcripts.cnn.com/show/sotu/date/2012-09-30/segment/01.)

McCain, John (@SenJohnMcCain). "Ethan Chorin: 'What Libya Lost'—A very important insight into Chris Stevens and Libya." Twitter. September 14, 2012. https://twitter.com/senjohnmccain/status/246600626895720448?lang=cs.

Milley, General Mark. "Matt Gaetz Uses Bob Woodward Book While Grilling Gen. Milley on Afghanistan in Tense Exchange." *Newsweek*, YouTube video, September 29, 2021. https://www.youtube.com/watch?v=bQH72OvSTsg.

Moe, Alex, and Carrie Dann. "McCarthy Links Benghazi Panel, Clinton's Sinking Poll Numbers." NBC News video and article. September 30, 2015. https://www.nbcnews.com/politics/2016-election/mccarthy-links-benghazi-panel-clintons-sinking-poll-numbers-n436151.

Neyfakh, Leon. *Fiasco*. Podcast. Luminary. "Season 4: Benghazi." June–July, 2021.

Obama, Barack. Interview by Steve Kroft. In "Campaign 2012," *60 Minutes*, CBS. September 12, 2012.

Obama, Barack. "Videotaped Remarks by the President in Celebration of Nowruz." The White House. March 20, 2009. https://obamawhitehouse.archives.gov/video/The-Presidents-Message-to-the-Iranian-People#transcript.

"Search Results for 'Benghazi.'" PolitiFact. Accessed April 10, 2022. https://www.politifact.com/search/?q=benghazi.

Al-Senussi, Abdullah. Letter to the Tripoli court, beginning "Fi Bidayat Aqul Innani Waqibl Kul Shei Ana Muwatin Libi" (First off and before anything else, I affirm that I am a Libyan national), published by *Libya Al-Moustaqbal* (date unknown) and later excerpted on Abdullah Senussi's Facebook account July 21, 2020. https://www.facebook.com/112819197121826/posts/159726135764465/, accessed 5/18/22.

SLOBoe. "Muammar Gaddafi Zenga Zenga Speech Translated." YouTube video, February 23, 2011. https://www.youtube.com/watch?v=69wBG6ULNzQ&t=0s.

Sreenivasan, Hari. "On Yemen Raid Planning, Where Did the Obama Administration Leave Off for Trump to Pick Up?" *PBS NewsHour* video and transcript. March 1, 2017. https://www.pbs.org/newshour/show/yemen-raid-planning-obama-administration-leave-off-trump-pick.

Stracqualursi, Veronica, Liz Kreutz, and Paola Chavez. "Hillary Clinton Concludes It's 'Time to Move On' Following Release of Benghazi Committee Final Report." ABC News video and article. June 28, 2016. https://abcnews.go.com/Politics/hillary-clinton-campaign-benghazi-committee-final-report-attempt/story?id=40186044.

"Surviving Torture in a CIA Secret Prison: Khaled al-Sharif of Libya Recounts Horrors." *Democracy Now!* video and transcript. October 13, 2016. https://www.democracynow.org/2016/10/13/surviving_torture_in_a_cia_secret.

Telegraph. "Libya: Saif al-Islam Gaddafi Warns Captors About Islamist Leader in New Video." YouTube video. November 22, 2011. https://www.youtube.com/watch?v=yJ87DR1j_lc.

"Timeline: Haftar's Months-Long Offensive to Seize Tripoli." Al Jazeera video and article. February 19, 2020. https://www.aljazeera.com/news/2020/2/19/timeline-haf tars-months-long-offensive-to-seize-tripoli.

Toensing, Victoria. "A 'Rigorous and Unsparing' Review? ARB Benghazi Report Full of Gaps, Unanswered Questions." Fox News video and article. May 8, 2015. https:// www.foxnews.com/opinion/a-rigorous-and-unsparing-review-arb-benghazi-report -full-of-gaps-unanswered-questions.

TPNN Videos. "Obama Calls Benghazi, FF and IRS Targeting 'Phony Scandals.'" You-Tube video. July 25, 2013. https://www.youtube.com/watch?v=7awZY3dQL-0.

Trump, Donald, Jr. (@donaldjtrumpjr). "You guys noticed a pattern with Democrats and work ethic here?" Instagram photo. August 22, 2021. https://www.instagram.com/p /CS4oHmrrYJc/.

Notes

Prologue: The Attack, Part I
1. Erlanger, "By His Own Reckoning."

Introduction
1. Manchester, "US Is Most Divided Since Civil War"; Paisley, "Political Polarization at Its Worst"; Schama, "Onward Christian Soldiers."
2. Savillo and Groch-Begley, "Fox's Benghazi Obsession."
3. Murray, "America Tired of Clinton Email Story."

Chapter 1: Setting Up Blowback
1. Adraoui, "The Unfinished History."
2. One of the most influential of these was Sayyid Qutb, whose radicalization followed a two-year stay in the United States and a period in Nasser's jails, which pushed him toward the belief in the need for systemic change in the Islamic world, and the need for Muslims to take specific actions to bring about a just Islamic society. Though Qutb never publicly supported the killing of innocents or large-scale terrorist attacks, his approach was radical. And practically all the Afghan Arab leaders, including Osama bin Laden, Ayman Al-Zawahiri, Abdallah Azzam, and many others, have cited Qutb as a key influence in their move toward violent jihad.
3. Cooley, *Unholy Wars*, 69.
4. Hegghammer, *The Caravan*, 157–158.
5. Cooley, *Unholy Wars*, 10.
6. Cooley, *Unholy Wars*, 226.
7. Hegghammer, *The Caravan*, 269.
8. Ben-Halim, *Libya: The Years of Hope*, 124.
9. Author interview with Ahmed Ibrahim al-Figih on November 10, 2017.
10. Though Egypt is arguably the birthplace and epicenter of Political Islam, Libya was not particularly fertile territory for these ideas, mainly because of the uniformity of Libyans' religious beliefs. It was a religious and culturally conservative society, heavily influenced by Sufi traditions, which were considered by Revivalist Islam to be heretical. Though Libya had certainly suffered the stabbing pains of Western colonialism, a more radical interpretation of Islam wasn't seen to be the key to Libya's religious and cultural emancipation.

11. Glass, "U.S. Planes Bomb Libya."
12. Woodward, "Gadhafi Target."
13. Ottaway and Parker, "CIA Confident."
14. "Ex-Foreign Minister Says Libya Behind 1989 Airline Attack."
15. Graetz, "Energy Policy," 32.
16. Halliday, *Political Journeys*, 225.
17. Mandraud, *Du djihad aux urnes*, 17.
18. Mandraud, *Du djihad aux urnes*, 19.
19. Note that Chad was also being backed by France.
20. Mandraud, *Du djihad aux urnes*, 29.
21. Mandraud, *Du djihad aux urnes*, 246.
22. Ayad, " 'We Are Simply Muslim.' "
23. See, for example, Nour Al-Din Al-Saed Al-Tulti, Jam'iyat Omar Al Mukhtar: Watha'iq Markaz Darna, Markaz Al-Nokhba, 2014, Cairo.
24. Cooley, *Unholy Wars*, 73.
25. Bin-Ladin et al., "Jihad Against Jews and Crusaders." For years, Al-Zawahiri had been singularly focused on overthrowing secular Middle East regimes, starting in his home country of Egypt. Early on, he was arrested as a teenager for complicity in the plot to kill Egyptian President Anwar Sadat, but he was later released. Bin Laden, who was far less familiar with Islamic jurisprudence—and saw the struggle with the West in broader, global terms—was attracted to the idea of expanding the jihad beyond the Middle East to countries that supported what he saw as the region's godless dictators.
26. The LIFG was announced in 1995, but many of its members date its creation to the gathering of its principal members in Libya back in the mid-1980s.
27. Mandraud, *Du djihad aux urnes*, 60.
28. Mandraud, *Du djihad aux urnes*, 60.
29. Al Hateita, *Hurub Al Militiaat*, 315.
30. Al Hateita, *Hurub Al Militiaat*, 315.
31. Tawil, *Brothers in Arms*, 65.
32. Bushnell, *Terrorism, Betrayal, and Resilience*.
33. Machon, *Spies, Lies and Whistleblowers*, 166–167.
34. Tawil, *Brothers in Arms*, 138.
35. Tawil, *Brothers in Arms*, 139.
36. Collins, "Gangsters Linked to Manchester Arena Bomb."
37. Pitter, "Delivered into Enemy Hands."
38. Tawil, *Brothers in Arms*, 206–207.
39. Eastwood and Murphy, "Talk to Political Islamists."
40. Isikoff, "U.S. May Be Softening Stance."
41. Kellogg and el-Hamalawy, "Bad Precedent."
42. Bushnell, *Terrorism, Betrayal, and Resilience*, 179.
43. Bushnell, *Terrorism, Betrayal, and Resilience*, 166.
44. The Americans would later kidnap Al-Ruqai'i in Libya in 2013 and fly him back to the US. He died in custody before his scheduled trial in 2015.

45. Bushnell, *Terrorism, Betrayal, and Resilience*, 72.

46. Bushnell, *Terrorism, Betrayal, and Resilience*, 72.

47. Author email correspondence with Ambassador Prudence Bushnell on March 15, 2022.

48. US Department of State. "Report of the Accountability Review Boards."

49. Bushnell, *Terrorism, Betrayal, and Resilience*, 82.

50. Bushnell, *Terrorism, Betrayal, and Resilience*, 151.

51. Bushnell, *Terrorism, Betrayal, and Resilience*, 185.

52. Al Mahmoud, "Al-Ikhwan al-Muslimun fi Qatar."

53. "UAE Charges 'Plotters Linked to Muslim Brotherhood.'"

54. Lipton, Williams, and Confessore, "Foreign Powers."

55. Bushnell, *Terrorism, Betrayal, and Resilience*, 186.

Chapter 2: Flipping a Rogue

1. Hutcheson, "President Admits Personal Grudge."

2. Ahmad, *The Road to Iraq*, 138.

3. Ahmad, *The Road to Iraq*, 10–11.

4. Draper, *To Start a War*, 103.

5. Draper, *To Start a War*, 281.

6. Silverstein, "How Kadafi Went from Foe to Ally."

7. AP, "U.S. Embassy in Tripoli, Libya Attacked."

8. Pitter, "Delivered into Enemy Hands."

9. Chorin, *Exit the Colonel*, 84.

10. "Chris Stevens," AllGov.

11. It was common practice in the State Department to "bid" on posts several years before they began.

12. Burton and Katz, *Under Fire*, 42–43.

Chapter 3: The Dark Side of the Moon

1. Transformational diplomacy was a post-9/11 initiative created by Secretary Condoleezza Rice to refocus and energize the State Department, particularly around democracy-promotion initiatives abroad.

2. Executive Office of the President, "Blocking Property and Prohibiting Transactions."

3. Bouckaert, "The Gaddafi Files."

4. Mandraud, *Du djihad aux urnes*, 94.

5. Mandraud, *Du djihad aux urnes*, 102.

6. Mandraud, *Du djihad aux urnes*, 103.

7. Mandraud, *Du djihad aux urnes*, 106–107.

8. Mandraud, *Du djihad aux urnes*, 115.

9. Mandraud, *Du djihad aux urnes*, 118.

10. Pitter, "Delivered into Enemy Hands."

11. Pitter, "Delivered into Enemy Hands."

12. Rosenthal, *The Jihadist Plot*, 37.

13. Mandraud, *Du djihad aux urnes*, 100.
14. Kandil, *Soldiers, Spies, and Statesmen*, 198.
15. Stacher and Shehata, "Hear out the Muslim Brotherhood."

Chapter 4: City of Light and Darkness

1. Chorin, *Translating Libya*, 29–37.
2. Chorin, *Translating Libya*, 103–113.
3. I later published these stories as *Translating Libya: In Search of the Libyan Short Story*.

Chapter 5: Die Hard in Derna

1. Richter, *The Ambassadors*, 91.
2. Before departing the United States for Libya, as the deputy chief of the Mission, Chris made a point to speak with the families of the Pan Am victims, to assure them that he would continue to press for information on the case.
3. "US/UK: Documents Reveal Libya Rendition Details."
4. Phillips, "Libya's Golden Boy."
5. Rice, *No Higher Honor*, 702–703.
6. Peraino, "The Jihadist Riddle."
7. Fishman and Felter, *Al-Qa'ida's Foreign Fighters in Iraq*, 11.
8. Fishman and Felter, *Al-Qa'ida's Foreign Fighters in Iraq*, 28.
9. Stevens, "Die Hard in Derna." This cable was published by WikiLeaks in 2009 and excerpted in the *Daily Telegraph* in 2011.
10. Stevens, "Die Hard in Derna."
11. Stevens, "Die Hard in Derna."
12. "Libyan Dissident, Long Imprisoned, Is Dead."
13. He knew that he was also making a point to an audience—the State Department—that would be sympathetic to his view.

Chapter 6: The Corrections

1. Phillips, "Libya's Golden Boy."
2. Al-Houni, *Saif Al-Gaddafi*, 119.
3. Roggio, "Libyan Islamic Fighting Group."
4. Belhaj et al., *Corrective Studies*.
5. Mandraud, *Du djihad aux urnes*, 145.
6. Tawil, *The Al Qaeda Organization*, 20.
7. Ashour, "De-radicalizing Jihadists."
8. Tawil, *The Al Qaeda Organization*, 18.
9. Tawil, *The Al Qaeda Organization*, 134.
10. Ashour, "De-radicalizing Jihadists."
11. "Libya: 202 Prisoners Released."
12. Author interview with Ambassador Gene Cretz on March 4, 2019.
13. Tawil, *The Al Qaeda Organization*, 6.

14. Cruickshank, "LIFG Revisions," 5–8.

15. Ashour, "De-radicalizing Jihadists."

16. Boucek, "Dangerous Fallout."

17. Rabasa et al., *Deradicalizing Islamist Extremists.*

Chapter 7: Fear and Loathing in Washington

1. Beauchamp, "Why Clinton's Iraq Apology Still Isn't Enough."

2. Coates, *We Were Eight Years in Power*, 62.

3. Even Obama, later, would muse at one point whether it would have been better for the country that Clinton won in 2008, and he ran in 2016.

4. Kristof, "Obama: Man of the World."

5. Kristof, "Obama: Man of the World."

6. MacAskill and Goldenberg, "Obama Aide Resigns."

7. Woodward, *Obama's Wars*, 29, 28.

8. Davis and Martin, "Obama Endorses Hillary Clinton."

9. Woodward, *Obama's Wars*, 30.

10. Woodward, *Obama's Wars*, 31.

11. Bloomfield, *The Foreign Policy Process*, 47.

12. Rohde and Strobel, "How Syria Policy Stalled."

13. David, *Au sien de la Maison-Blanche*, 999.

14. Preston, "The Little State Department."

15. Rothkopf, *Running the World*, xiv.

16. US House of Representatives, *Reforming the National Security Council.*

17. Samuels, "The Aspiring Novelist."

18. Samuels, "The Aspiring Novelist."

19. Vaïsse, *Barack Obama*, 46–47.

Chapter 8: Goodwill Hunting

1. Gordon and Zeleny, "Interview with Barack Obama."

2. Myers, "Amid Impasse."

3. Sedarat and Noueihed, "Obama Says Ready to Talk to Iran."

4. Black, "Barack Obama Offers Iran 'New Beginning'"; Obama, "Videotaped Remarks in Celebration of Nowruz."

5. Obama administration officials point out that secret negotiations on the nuclear deal didn't progress until after the election of Hassan Rouhani as president in August 2013. Others, including Ambassador Frederic Hof, Clinton's Syria coordinator at the State Department until 2012, and former *Wall Street Journal* foreign correspondent Jay Solomon have argued that the Obama administration was singularly focused on concluding a deal with Iran much earlier. Author interview with Frederic Hof, May 5, 2017; Solomon, *The Iran Wars.*

6. Bruton, "Turkey Coup Attempt."

7. Bruton, "Turkey Coup Attempt."

8. Obama, "Remarks at Cairo University."

9. "The Nobel Peace Prize for 2009."

10. Obama, "Remarks at the Acceptance of the Nobel Peace Prize."

11. Hughes and Radia, " 'Underwear Bomber's' Alarming Last Phone Call."

12. Shane, *Objective Troy*, 9.

13. Shane, *Objective Troy*, 20.

14. Shane, *Objective Troy*, 15.

15. Wilson and Cohen, "Poll Finds Broad Support."

16. Whitlock, "Drone Strikes."

17. Baker, "Obama's Turn."

18. Landler, "Secret Report Ordered by Obama."

19. Remarks by Peter Hoekstra during a congressional hearing. US House of Representatives, *Identifying the Enemy*.

20. Author interview with Peter Mandaville on July 29, 2017.

21. Author email correspondence with Marc Lynch on March 29, 2022.

22. Lynch, "Islam Divided Between."

23. Travis and Ramesh, "Muslim Brotherhood Are Possible Extremists."

Chapter 9: The 51/49 Decision

1. Gates, *Duty: Memoirs of a Secretary at War*, 518; Becker and Shane, "The Libya Gamble."

2. Obama, "Remarks at Cairo University."

3. Pargeter, *Return to the Shadows*, 117.

4. Al-Senussi, Letter to the Tripoli court.

5. Sherwood, "Gaddafi Violence."

6. Author interview with Dr. Tamara Wittes on November 15, 2017.

7. Jacinto, "Gaddafi's Gutted Edifice."

8. "Saif Gaddafi's Speech Translated."

9. Al-Houni, *Saif Al-Gaddafi*, 73.

10. SLOBoe, "Muammar Gaddafi Zenga Zenga Speech Translated."

11. Reuters Staff, "Timeline: Libya's Uprising."

12. Author interview with Secretary of State Hillary Clinton on March 3, 2022.

13. Gates, *Exercise of Power*, 395.

14. Quoted in Rhodes, *The World as It Is*, 113.

15. Becker and Shane, "The Libya Gamble."

16. Richter, *The Ambassadors*, 186.

17. Richter, *The Ambassadors*, 214.

18. Chollet, *The Long Game*, 110. Why Robert Kaplan is cited here is unclear, as his area of expertise is indeed the Middle East, but not Libya; Chollet would also later say that American officials were mainly relying on public domain news for what was happening in Libya.

19. Author interview with Ambassador Gene Cretz on March 4, 2019.

20. Vandewalle, *Libya Since Independence*.

21. Hastings, "Inside Obama's War Room"; Pilkington, "100 Minutes in the Life of Gaddafi."

22. Hastings, "Inside Obama's War Room."

23. Carrell, "Tony Blair Kept Colleagues in the Dark."
24. Gadaffi, "Muammar Gaddafi at the 64th UN General Assembly in 2009."
25. Leigh, "WikiLeaks Cables: Muammar Gaddafi."
26. Hastings, "Inside Obama's War Room."
27. Becker and Shane, "The Libya Gamble."
28. Myers, "Clinton Meets in Paris."
29. Tyler, "Two Said to Tell of Libyan Plot."
30. Friedersdorf, "How Obama Ignored Congress."
31. Greenblatt, "Leaders of the Libyan Opposition Emerge."
32. Author interview with Secretary of State Hillary Clinton on March 3, 2022.
33. Author interview with Mahmoud Jibril on October 14, 2016.
34. Reuters Staff, "Gaddafi Son Says."
35. Reuters Staff, "Qatar Says."
36. Lewis, "Obama's Way."
37. Lewis, "Obama's Way."
38. Lewis, "Obama's Way."

Chapter 10: Expeditionary Diplomat

1. Bullington and Bullington, *Expeditionary Diplomacy in Action.*
2. US Office of the Spokesperson, "U.S. Department of State Launches Bureau."
3. Author interview with Secretary of State Hillary Clinton on March 3, 2022.
4. Author interview with Secretary of State Hillary Clinton on March 3, 2022.
5. Gertler, "Operation Odyssey Dawn."
6. Montoya, "Mission to a Revolution," 20.
7. Baer, "Why the Benghazi Consulate Attack."
8. Montoya, "Mission to a Revolution," 20.
9. Author interview with Ambassador Guido De Sanctis on June 30, 2014.
10. Author interview with Secretary of State Hillary Clinton on March 3, 2022.
11. Author interview with Ambassador Gene Cretz on March 4, 2019.
12. Author interview with Secretary of State Hillary Clinton on March 3, 2022.
13. Richter, *The Ambassadors*, 191.
14. Montoya, "Mission to a Revolution," 23.
15. Richter, *The Ambassadors*, 189.
16. Richter, *The Ambassadors*, 189.
17. Author interview with Ambassador Guido De Sanctis on June 30, 2014.
18. https://www.rememberingchrisstevens.com/page/11
19. Buhite, *Lives at Risk*, 12; Fremont-Barnes, Gregory, *The Wars of the Barbary Pirates* (Oxford, UK: Osprey Publishing, 2006), 41.

Chapter 11: Arming the Radicals

1. Lizza, "The Consequentialist."
2. Heftar had returned from the United States after the US intervention to see if he could challenge Younes as head of the rebel army, who looked like he might be nursing power ambitions of his own.

3. Pargeter, *Return to the Shadows*, 137.

4. Pargeter, *Return to the Shadows*, 137.

5. See Ashour, "Between ISIS and a Failed State."

6. This partnership would ultimately serve as an umbrella for more extreme groups like Ansar al-Sharia. which would play a starring role in the Benghazi attack more than a year later. "Feb 17," as it became known, attracted other LIFG members like Ismail Sallabi (brother of Ali Sallabi, who had negotiated the *Corrections* with Saif Gaddafi).

7. Bin Qumu's comments weren't all inflammatory: he urged the West, and by extension the Americans, to invest in Libya's—and specifically Derna's—reconstruction, to address the inequities that powered despair. We heard that message when Chris Stevens met with residents of Derna back in 2007.

8. Ouannes, *Révolte et reconstruction en Libye*, 52.

9. Ouannes, *Révolte et reconstruction en Libye*, 139.

10. Ouannes, *Révolte et reconstruction en Libye*, 65.

11. Black, McGreal, and Sherwood, "Barack Obama: Qatar Crucial."

12. Chesnot and Malbrunot, *Qatar*, 138.

13. Baryin, *Dans les mâchoires du chacal*, 57.

14. Author interview with Mahmoud Jabril on October 14, 2016.

15. Risen, Mazzetti, and Schmidt, "U.S.-Approved Arms for Libya Rebels."

16. Becker and Shane, "The Libya Gamble."

17. Becker and Shane, "The Libya Gamble."

18. Becker and Shane, "The Libya Gamble."

Chapter 12: The Good-Hearted Bookseller

1. Author interview with Dr. Mahmoud Jibril on October 14, 2016.

2. Author interview with Dr. Aref Nayed on November 29, 2020.

3. Mufti, *Thakirat al Nar*, 469–472.

4. Cole and McQuinn, *The Libyan Revolution and Its Aftermath,* 193.

5. Author email correspondence with Chris Stevens on August 8, 2011.

Chapter 13: The Fall

1. For an excellent description of the complex political and military dynamics within the opposition at this time, see Peter Cole and Umar Khan, "The Fall of Tripoli, Parts I and 2," in Cole and McQuinn, eds., *The Libyan Revolution and Its Aftermath*.

2. Cole and McQuinn, *The Libyan Revolution and Its Aftermath*, 93.

3. Author interview with Mahmoud Jabril on October 14, 2016.

4. Chulov, "Gaddafi's Last Moments."

5. Myers, "In Tripoli, Clinton Pledges.'"

6. Daly, "Clinton on Qaddafi."

7. Sheridan, "Libya Declares Liberation."

8. Abdel Jalil remains a controversial figure—he was a defector from the Gaddafi regime, known to be particularly devout. Some assumed that he was either a member of or affiliated with the Muslim Brotherhood, but he later suggested that the Brotherhood was behind Younes's murder.

9. Sherlock, "Leading Libyan Islamist."

10. Amoore, "Storming Tripoli."

11. Hussein, "Mahdi al-Harati."

12. Lister, *The Syrian Jihad*, 76.

13. Author interview with Sir John Jenkins on November 17, 2017.

14. *Telegraph*, "Libya: Saif al-Islam Gaddafi Warns Captors."

15. "Gaddafi Case."

16. Baker, "Mark Allen, the Spy."

17. Nordland, "In Libya, Former Enemy."

18. Nordland, "In Libya, Former Enemy."

19. Bowcott, "Abdel Hakim Belhaj Wins Right"; Cobain and Bowcott, "Settlement in Belhaj Rendition Case."

20. Cobain et al., "Britain Apologises."

21. Laurent, *Sahelistan*, 33, 39.

22. Laurent, *Sahelistan*, 32.

Chapter 14: *The Ides of February*

1. Published as *Exit the Colonel: The Hidden History of the Libyan Revolution* (New York: PublicAffairs, 2012).

2. Ambassador Cretz would later tell me that both he and Chris "believed strongly that the US should maintain a visible presence in Benghazi and argued for funds to make it viable." Author interview with Ambassador Gene Cretz on March 4, 2019.

3. McCain and Salter, *The Restless Wave*, 169.

4. Salter, *The Luckiest Man*, 458.

5. McCain and Salter, *The Restless Wave*, 177.

6. McCain and Salter, *The Restless Wave*, 177.

7. McCain and Salter, *The Restless Wave*, 177.

8. Salter, *The Luckiest Man*, 462.

9. Salter, *The Luckiest Man*, 462.

10. Monitor's Editorial Board, "McCain's Mutiny."

11. McCain and Salter, *The Restless Wave*, 91.

12. McCain and Salter, *The Restless Wave*, 73.

13. McCain and Salter, *The Restless Wave*, 74.

14. Salter, *The Luckiest Man*, 463.

15. McCain and Salter, *The Restless Wave*, 75.

16. Salter, *The Luckiest Man*, 463.

Chapter 15: **On the Eve of the Attack**

1. The presence of Iranian medics in Benghazi fed a number of conspiracy theories, including that the Iran Revolutionary Guard Corps' Al Quds Force was behind the attack: see Timmerman, *Dark Forces*.

2. Warren, "Barbara Tuchman's 'The Guns of August.'"

3. Tapper, "Documents Back Up Claims."

4. US House of Representatives, *Documents Provided to the Select Committee on Benghazi*, vol. 2, 1015.

5. Kessler, "Hillary Clinton and the Aug. 16 Cable."

6. Lieberman and Collins, *Flashing Red*.

7. Gearan, "State Dept. Acknowledges Rejecting Requests."

8. US House of Representatives, *Final Report of the Select Committee on Benghazi*.

9. Shachtman, "U.S. Paid Guards $4 per Hour."

10. US House of Representatives, *Final Report of the Select Committee on Benghazi*.

11. Federal Research Division, Library of Congress, *Al-Qaeda in Libya*.

12. Federal Research Division, Library of Congress, *Al-Qaeda in Libya*.

13. According to a State Department official familiar with the relevant procedures for upgrading a Mission to a Consulate, a US ambassador is not strictly required to inspect the Mission to initiate authorization for funds. That could be done by someone else. But in this case, it seems once again Chris's expertise and familiarity with the situation in Benghazi were seen to be invaluable (interview conducted on condition of anonymity, February 2, 2015).

14. US House of Representatives, *Final Report of the Select Committee on Benghazi*.

15. US House of Representatives, *Final Report of the Select Committee on Benghazi*.

16. Author interview with Habib Bubaker on November 14, 2021.

17. Rosenthal, *The Jihadist Plot*, 25.

18. The cable sent from Benghazi on September 11 misspells his name "Al Garabi."

19. Kirkpatrick, "Brazen Figure."

20. US Department of State, "Benghazi Weekly Report, September 11, 2012."

21. The State Department cable entitled "Benghazi Weekly Report, September 11, 2012" was originally posted to http://oversight.house.gov/wp-content/uploads/2012/10/9 -11-12-Memo.pdf (and subsequently removed). Kirkpatrick, "A Deadly Mix."

22. US Department of State, "Benghazi Weekly Report, September 11, 2012"; Kirkpatrick, "A Deadly Mix."

23. Kirkpatrick, "A Deadly Mix."

24. US House of Representatives, *Final Report of the Select Committee on Benghazi*.

25. Kirkpatrick, "A Deadly Mix."

26. Author interview with Lieutenant Colonel Brian Linvill on August 17, 2017.

27. US House of Representatives, *Final Report of the Select Committee on Benghazi*.

28. Reuters Staff, "Al Qaeda Confirms Death."

29. Reuters Staff, "Al Qaeda Confirms Death."

30. Mayer, *The Dark Side*, 114; Mayer, "Outsourcing Torture."

31. US House of Representatives, *Final Report of the Select Committee on Benghazi*.

32. Doornbos and Moussa, "'Troubling' Surveillance Before Benghazi Attack."

33. US House of Representatives, *Final Report of the Select Committee on Benghazi*; Doornbos and Moussa, "'Troubling' Surveillance Before Benghazi Attack."

34. Author interview with Habib Bubaker on November 14, 2021.

35. These memos would be found in the ruins of the structure later, unsent. Zuckoff, *13 Hours*, 75; Al Hateita, "Asharq Al Awsat Obtains the Accounts."

36. Zuckoff, *13 Hours*, 81.

37. Browne and Herridge, "Was Syrian Weapons Shipment?"

38. US House of Representatives, *Final Report of the Select Committee on Benghazi*.

39. Beckhusen, "Diplomat Killed in Libya Told."

Chapter 16: The Attack, Part II

1. "US Official Dies in Libya."

2. Chorin, "What Libya Lost."

3. McCain, Tweet on September 14, 2012.

Chapter 17: Cairo

1. Peralta, "What We Know About 'Sam Bacile.'"

2. Carroll, "Film-Maker Behind Anti-Islam Trailer."

3. "It's Just a Stupid Movie!"

4. CNN Wire Staff, "U.S. Vows to Hunt Down."

5. Willon and Keegan, "'Innocence of Muslims' Unrest."

6. Mackey and Stack, "Obscure Film Mocking Muslim Prophet."

7. Sieff, "Florida Pastor Terry Jones's Koran Burning."

8. Willon and Keegan, "'Innocence of Muslims' Unrest"; Mustafa et al., "Aqbat Al-Muhajir Yashiloon Al-Fitna bi-Intaj Film Musi' LilRasool" (Expatriate Copts Ignite Chaos with Production of Film Insulting the Prophet).

9. Fahmy and Shaben, *The Marriott Cell*, 103.

10. A slightly more meaningful term, adopted by the West, to describe the more puritanical of the Islamists, the Al-Salaf al-Salih, meaning those of the first three generations of Muslims, who lived in the manner of the Prophet—but also a category that contains different groups, from violent Salafis to relatively nonviolent Salafis.

11. Elyan, "Egyptians Angry at Film."

12. Fahmy and Shaben, *The Marriott Cell*, 101–102.

13. Fahmy and Shaben, *The Marriott Cell*, 104.

14. "Egyptian Islamic Jihad."

15. Fahmy and Shaben, *The Marriott Cell*, 104.

16. Embassy of the United States Cairo, Egypt, "U.S. Embassy Condemns Religious Incitement."; Tau, "U.S. Embassy in Cairo Condemns."

17. Rogin, "Inside the Public Relations Disaster."

18. Author interview with Ambassador Anne Patterson on November 12, 2017.

19. Patterson, who took up the post of US ambassador in Egypt in 2011, would become a lightning rod for Egyptian criticism of the American handling of demonstrations against Muslim Brotherhood President Mohamed Morsi a year after Benghazi exposed America's sympathies for the Muslim Brotherhood. Middle East expert and former diplomat Vali Nasr defended Patterson, saying "the fact that she's being excoriated instead of the president only represents the fact that the rest of the American administration is absent [from policy-making with respect to Egypt]." Landler, "Ambassador Becomes Focus."

20. Neyfakh, *Fiasco*, Season 4, Episode 4, "Feckless," July 15, 2021.

Chapter 18: "We Were Drinking Tea"

1. Al Hateita, "Asharq Al Awsat Obtains the Accounts."
2. Al Hateita, *Hurub Al Militiaat*, 225.
3. Al Hateita, *Hurub Al Militiaat*, 225. It wasn't uncommon for the Arab veterans of the Afghan wars to wear Afghan dress, as a badge of honor and a signal of their commitment to the cause of armed jihad.
4. Lieberman and Collins, *Flashing Red*; Zuckoff, *13 Hours*, 85.
5. Zuckoff, *13 Hours*, 87.
6. Zuckoff, *13 Hours*, 120.
7. US House of Representatives, *Final Report of the Select Committee on Benghazi*.
8. US House of Representatives, *Final Report of the Select Committee on Benghazi*.
9. Hosenball, "Clinton: Facebook Post About Benghazi."
10. US House of Representatives, *Final Report of the Select Committee on Benghazi*.
11. Ackerman, "Frappe-Sipping Libyan Militant Laughs."
12. "Abu Sufyan Bin Qumu."
13. Associated Press, "New Video Appears to Show."
14. Kessler, "Issa's 'Suspicions.'"
15. Zuckoff, *13 Hours*, 289.
16. Roggio, "Ansar al Shariah Issues Statement."

Chapter 19: Witnesses Huddle

1. Zway and Gladstone, "In Libya, Chaos Was Followed."
2. Hirsh, "The Benghazi-Industrial Complex."
3. Coker et al., "Miscues Before Libya Assault."
4. Chorin, "Benghazi's Karmic Revenge."
5. All "John" quotes are from an interview with the author under the condition of anonymity.
6. Kirkpatrick and Myers, "Libya Attack Brings Challenges."
7. Author interview with Colonel Wolfgang Pusztai on November 5, 2016.
8. US House of Representatives, *Final Report of the Select Committee on Benghazi*.
9. US House of Representatives, *Final Report of the Select Committee on Benghazi*.
10. Joscelyn, "Al Qaeda's Expansion into Egypt."
11. Zelin, "Know Your Ansar al-Sharia."
12. After Muhammad Al-Zawahiri was killed in eastern Libya in 2015 by General Khalifa Heftar's Libya National Army, various Al Qaeda franchises in the region eulogized him.
13. Joscelyn, "State Department: Ansar al Sharia."
14. US House of Representatives, *Final Report of the Select Committee on Benghazi*.
15. Rogers and Ruppersberger, *Investigative Report on the Terrorist Attacks*.
16. Joscelyn, "Al Qaeda Often Agitated."
17. Author interview with Ambassador Jacob Walles on December 11, 2017.
18. Author interview with Ambassador Jacob Walles on December 11, 2017.
19. Rhodes, *The World as It Is*, 148.

20. Labat, *Les islamistes tunisiens*, 146; Rhodes, *The World as It Is*, 183.

21. Zway and Gladstone, "In Libya, Chaos Was Followed."

22. Author interview with Ambassador Gerald Feierstein on October 15, 2018; author interview with Professor Sheila Carapico on August 27, 2017.

23. "Embassies Under Attack," Al Jazeera.

Chapter 20: Romney's Lunge

1. Embassy of the United States Cairo, Egypt, "U.S. Embassy Condemns Religious Incitement"; Jackson, "Romney Gets It Backward."

2. *Fiasco*, "Benghazi" Season 4, Episode 4, July 15, 2021.

3. *Fiasco*, "Benghazi" Season 4, Episode 4, July 15, 2021.

4. Jackson, "Romney Gets It Backward."

5. President Obama quickly backed away from the Embassy's statement, and an unnamed administration official said that it "was not cleared by Washington and does not reflect the views of the United States government." So when the full scope of the damage of the Benghazi attack was known the following morning, the Romney campaign statement looked like an even bigger, and lower, political blow than it was presumably intended to be. Vasilogambros and *National Journal*, "Officials: Cairo Embassy Staffer."

6. Author interview with Secretary of State Hillary Clinton on March 3, 2022.

7. Rhodes, *The World as It Is*, 180–181.

8. Obama, "Remarks by the President on the Deaths."

9. Kiely, "The Benghazi Timeline"; Clinton, "Remarks on the Deaths."

10. Kiely, "The Benghazi Timeline."

11. Clinton responded to Representative Jim Jordan's references to these emails thus: "When I was speaking to the Egyptian prime minister, or in the other two examples you showed, we had been told by Ansar al-Sharia that they took credit for it. It wasn't until about 24 more hours later that they retracted taking credit for it." House of Representatives, "Hearing 4 Before the Select Committee on Benghazi."

12. Unger, "GOP's October Surprise?"

13. Landler, *Alter Egos*, 199.

14. McGreal, "Obama Deflects Romney's Challenge."

15. McGreal, "Obama Deflects Romney's Challenge."

16. McGreal, "Obama Deflects Romney's Challenge."

17. Kessler, "Obama's Claim."

18. Kessler, "Obama's Claim."

Chapter 21: The Talking Points Debacle

1. US Senate Select Committee on Intelligence, *Review of the Terrorist Attacks in Benghazi*, 43.

2. Landler, *Alter Egos*, 200.

3. Pearson, "What the Obama Administration Has Said."

4. Kliegman, "Cokie Roberts: Susan Rice."

5. Allen and Parnes, *HRC*, 306.

6. Hauslohner, "Libya's Central Government."

7. Burke and I assumed that a large CIA presence was one of the reasons we weren't included in the evacuation flights.

8. Priebus, "Why Won't Obama Call It Terrorism?"

9. Karl and Good, "The Benghazi Emails."

10. Allen and Parnes, *HRC*, 304.

11. Karl, "Exclusive: Benghazi Talking Points"; Rhodes, *The World as It Is*, 183.

12. Hirsh, "The Benghazi-Industrial Complex."

13. Kiely, "The Benghazi Timeline."

14. Department of Defense, Freedom of Information Division, Case no. F-2012-38774.

15. Department of Defense, Freedom of Information Division, Case no. F-2012-38774.

16. Judicial Watch. "Weekly Update: JW Finds Benghazi Smoking Gun!"

17. Edroso, "Rightbloggers: Had Enough Benghazi?"

18. Hirsh, "The Benghazi-Industrial Complex."

19. NBC News Staff and Wire Services, "Susan Rice: 'I Relied Solely.'"

20. Whitlock, *The Afghanistan Papers*, 201.

Chapter 22: Stuck with the Story

1. This is not confidence-inspiring either, as the attack was on a mission, not an embassy. US Senate, "Homeland Threats and Agency Responses."

2. Pearson, "What the Obama Administration Has Said"; "Benghazi Mission Attack Fast Facts."

3. Pearson, "What the Obama Administration Has Said."

4. US Senate Select Committee on Intelligence, *Review of the Terrorist Attacks in Benghazi*, 36.

5. Attkisson, "Officials on Benghazi."

6. Allen and Parnes, *HRC*, 308.

7. Attkisson, "Officials on Benghazi."

8. Obama, "Remarks to the UN General Assembly."

9. Obama, "Remarks to the UN General Assembly."

10. Pearson, "What the Obama Administration Has Said."

Chapter 23: Collateral Damage

1. McCain and Salter, *The Restless Wave*, 178–179.

2. McCain, Interview by Candy Crowley.

3. Caldwell, "McCain: Libya Either"; McCain and Salter, *The Restless Wave*, 179.

4. DeYoung and Gearan, "Susan Rice Withdraws."

5. Rice, *Tough Love*, 314.

6. Rice, *Tough Love*, 307.

7. Rice, *Tough Love*, 332.

8. Rice, *Tough Love*, 318.

9. Rice, *Tough Love*, 333.

10. Author interview with Secretary of State Hillary Clinton on March 3, 2022.

11. Allen and Parnes, *HRC*, 334.

Chapter 24: Investigations Galore

1. US Department of State, "Accountability Review Board Report."
2. US Department of State, "Accountability Review Board Report," 39.
3. US Department of State, "Accountability Review Board Report," 6, 4.
4. US Department of State, "Accountability Review Board Report," 6.
5. "House Hearing on Benghazi Consulate Attack"; Kertscher, "In Context."
6. Washington Post Staff, "Full Text: Clinton Testifies."
7. "Hillary Clinton Senate Hearing on Benghazi"; Kertscher, "In Context."
8. US Senate Select Committee on Intelligence, *Review of the Terrorist Attacks in Benghazi*, 35.
9. Toensing, "A 'Rigorous and Unsparing' Review?"
10. Toensing, "A 'Rigorous and Unsparing' Review?"
11. US Senate Select Committee on Intelligence, *Review of the Terrorist Attacks in Benghazi*.
12. Boukhars, "What's Next for Mali and Algeria?"
13. US Senate Select Committee on Intelligence, *Review of the Terrorist Attacks in Benghazi*.
14. US Senate Select Committee on Intelligence, *Review of the Terrorist Attacks in Benghazi*.
15. US Senate Select Committee on Intelligence, *Review of the Terrorist Attacks in Benghazi*.
16. Al Hateita, *Hurub Al Militiaat*, 306.
17. Kirkpatrick, "A Deadly Mix in Benghazi."
18. Kirkpatrick, "A Deadly Mix in Benghazi."
19. Lake, "Yes, There IS Evidence."
20. Wiener-Bronner, "Who Attacked Benghazi."
21. Clinton, *Hard Choices*, 403.
22. Rice, *Tough Love*, 314.
23. I was on a trip abroad when Kirkpatrick's Benghazi investigation piece came out, and it took me a few days to read it. I found several assumptions and statements to be inaccurate. I messaged my *New York Times* editor with a request to write a response piece, but was told this wasn't possible: "the window for replies had closed"—despite the fact that the article was only a few days old. About an hour later, I got a somewhat urgent-sounding message from Kirkpatrick saying he wanted to talk. But he never called back.
24. Kirkpatrick, "A Deadly Mix in Benghazi."

Chapter 25: Stand-Down Orders

1. Griffin, "Exclusive: CIA Operators Were Denied Request."
2. US Department of State, "Accountability Review Board Report."
3. Krayewski, "President Obama Had One Conversation."
4. US Department of State, "Foreign Emergency Support Team."
5. Marines responding to the Benghazi attack were held up by debate on weapons and uniforms as well, a commander says. Schogol, "Marines Responding to Benghazi."
6. US Department of State, "Accountability Review Board Report," 32.
7. Greg, "Benghazi—the Mystery."
8. Bumiller, "Panetta Says Risk."
9. Bumiller, "Panetta Says Risk."

10. Mikkelson, "Attack on the U.S. Diplomatic Mission."
11. Kessler, "Issa's 'Suspicions.'"
12. US House of Representatives Committee on Armed Services, *Majority Interim Report: Benghazi Investigation Update.*
13. Hirsch, "The Benghazi-Industrial Complex."

Chapter 26: Paired Controversies: Benghazi and the Emails

1. Newport, "Hillary Clinton, Barack Obama Most Admired."
2. Emery, "Hillary Clinton's Approval Ratings"; "Hillary Clinton's Strengths."
3. Gold, "Benghazi, Benghazi, Benghazi."
4. Gold, "Benghazi, Benghazi, Benghazi."
5. Hirsch, "The Benghazi-Industrial Complex."
6. "46% Think Benghazi Will Hurt."
7. These forces included the State Department, House Committee on Oversight and Government Reform, House Judiciary Committee, House Foreign Affairs Committee, House Armed Services Committee, House Select Committee on Intelligence, Senate Select Committee on Intelligence, and Senate Committee on Homeland Security and Government Affairs. Berman, "Boehner to Appoint Panel."
8. Staff Writer, "Clinton Can Thank Obama."
9. Munsil, "Feinstein: House Benghazi Committee."
10. Newhauser, "As Midterms Approach."
11. Roberts et al., "Republicans Win Majority."
12. Schmidt, "Hillary Clinton Used Personal Email."
13. Lipton, Scheiber, and Schmidt, "Clinton Emails."
14. Allen and Parnes, *Shattered*, 54.
15. Watts and Rothschild, "Don't Blame the Election."
16. Allen and Parnes, *Shattered*, 57.
17. Dionne, "Kevin McCarthy's Truthful Gaffe"; Moe and Dann, "McCarthy Links Benghazi Panel."
18. Dionne, "Kevin McCarthy's Truthful Gaffe."
19. Sargent, "Morning Plum: Clinton."
20. Hart Research Associates, NBC News/*Wall Street Journal* Survey, Study #15463.
21. De Jonge, "Both Clinton and GOP."
22. "Hillary Clinton's Benghazi Testimony."
23. Washington Post Staff, "Full Text: Clinton Testifies."
24. Rosen, "Here's the Biggest Issue."
25. Frizell, "How Hillary Clinton Won."
26. Sorkin, "The Hillary Hearing."
27. Hook, "Clinton's Explanations."
28. US Department of State, "Briefing: Evaluation of Email Records Management"; Myers and Lichtblau, "Hillary Clinton Is Criticized."
29. FBI National Press Office, "Statement by FBI Director Comey."
30. Holyk, "Majority Disapprove of Decision."

31. The new emails were discovered during a separate FBI investigation into Weiner's sexting with a minor.

32. Clinton, *What Happened*, 403.

33. Williams, " 'Benghazi Mom' Patricia Smith."

34. Richter, "Mother of Benghazi Victim."

35. Stack, "Donald Trump Featured."

36. Schleifer, "Benghazi Committee Runs Its Course"; Phillips, "The 5 Most Serious Accusations."

37. US House of Representatives, *Honoring Courage*.

38. Oliphant and Morgan, "Panel's Report Reignites Debate."

39. Phillips, "The 5 Most Serious Accusations."

40. Phillips, "The 5 Most Serious Accusations."

41. Stracqualursi, Kreutz, and Chavez, "Hillary Clinton Concludes."

42. Bade, "Weapons trafficking questions remain." A portion of the final report reads: "Over the course of nearly a dozen interviews with the State Department, the Defense Department and the CIA personnel witnesses consistently refused to answer questions related to certain allegations with respect to the U.S. activity in Libya even though the House specifically gave the committee access to materials relating to intelligence sources and methods." The report continues: "These refusals meant significant questions raised in public relating to Benghazi could not be answered." One committee interview, in a "classified setting," supported the idea that the United States was overseeing "some sort of weapons shipping."

43. Kirkpatrick, "A Deadly Mix in Benghazi"; Kirkpatrick, "Brazen Figure."

44. Tucker, "Militant Convicted."

45. Helsel, "Libyan Man Sentenced."

Chapter 27: Benghazi and the 2016 Election

1. Bump, "Donald Trump Will Be President"; Lerer, "Clinton Wins Popular Vote."

2. Mercer, Deane, and McGeeney, "Why 2016 Election Polls."

3. Tamman, "Clinton Has 90 Percent Chance."

4. Katz, "Who Will Be President?"

5. Miller, "Facing a Russian Cyber Attack."

6. Klein, *Why We're Polarized*, xi.

7. Jamieson, *Cyberwar*, 91–93; "Killary 'Butcher of Benghazi' Clinton"; BenghaziRunningClub, "Remember Benghazi."

8. Naylor, "Trump Apparently Quotes Russian Propaganda."

9. Author interview with Ben Rhodes on May 11, 2017.

10. Clinton, *What Happened*, 299.

11. Del Vicario, et al., "News consumption during the Italian Referendum." Quattrociocchi and his team studied the impact of fake news on the 2016 Italian Constitutional Referendum and documented the polarizing effect of relevant posts to Facebook and Twitter. One observed effect was that the polarizing action and impact were rarely limited to one side of the political spectrum. In other words, fake news is a mutually reinforcing, multipartisan phenomenon.

12. Author interview with Walter Quattrociocchi on March 16, 2021.

13. Quattrociocchi, "Inside the Echo Chamber."

14. D'Addario, "'The Newsroom' Takes on Fake News."

15. "Search Results for 'Benghazi.'"

16. TPNNVideos, "Obama Calls Benghazi, FF and IRS."

17. Montanaro, "Hillary Clinton's 'Basket of Deplorables.'"

18. Chotiner, "The Both Side–ism of Amy Chua."

19. Clinton, *What Happened*, 398.

Chapter 28: The Damage Done to Libya

1. Rhodes, *The World as It Is*, 183.

2. Author interview with Ambassador Guido De Sanctis on June 30, 2014.

3. Author interview with Ambassador Guido De Sanctis on June 30, 2014.

4. Baer, "Why the Benghazi Consulate Attack."

5. Author interview with Emile Hokayem on November 12, 2018.

6. Author email correspondence with Ambassador Anne Patterson on November 27, 2017.

7. Karadsheh and Basu, "Libyans Turn Out Big."

8. Al Shalchi and Gumuchian, "Libya's Jibril in Election Landslide."

9. Washington Post Staff, "The CNN Democratic Debate." Clinton also stated, "But unless you believe the United States should not send diplomats to any place that is dangerous, which I do not, then when we send them forth, there is always the potential for danger and risk."

10. Author interview with Secretary of State Hillary Clinton on March 3, 2022.

11. Author interview with Bubaker Habib on November 3, 2021.

12. Author interview with Dr. Mahmoud Jibril on October 14, 2016.

13. International Commission on Intervention and State Sovereignty, *The Responsibility to Protect*, 39.

14. International Commission on Intervention and State Sovereignty, *The Responsibility to Protect*, 39.

15. Friedman, "Obama on the World."

16. Author interview with Secretary of State Hillary Clinton on March 3, 2022.

17. Fishman, "United States: Reluctant Engagement," 98.

18. Author interview with Dr. Monem Alyaser on April 7, 2016.

19. Carlson, *In the Dark of War*, 42.

20. I was extremely honored to be put forth for the post, but neither surprised nor wholly disappointed when it went to a senior member of the US diplomatic corps.

21. Glenn, "Libya's Islamists."

22. "Libya: No Impunity."

23. Author email correspondence with Ambassador Deborah Jones on April 27, 2018; italics are hers. By this point the LIFG had been rebranded the Libyan Islamic Movement for Change.

24. Presumably, this was because, formally, it no longer existed pursuant to the *Corrections*.

25. Author email correspondence with Ambassador Deborah Jones on April 27, 2018.

26. Carlson, *In the Dark of War*, 80.

27. Carlson, *In the Dark of War*, 115.

28. Carlson, *In the Dark of War*, 95.

29. "Surviving Torture in CIA Prison."

30. Kersten, "Libya's Political Isolation Law."

31. Haddad, "Order et disorder milicien en Libya."

32. Lynch, *The New Arab Wars*, 179.

33. Burns, *The Back Channel*, 321.

Chapter 29: Killing the Whispers (of a Strong Syria Policy)

1. Yassin-Kassab and Al-Shami, *Burning Country*, 38.

2. Wilson and Warrick, "Assad Must Go."

3. Balanche, "Syrie."

4. Obama, "Remarks to the White House Press Corps."

5. Masterson and Quinn, "Timeline of Syrian Chemical Weapons."

6. Baker et al., "Off-the-Cuff Obama Line."

7. Department of Public Information, "Security Council Approves 'No-Fly Zone.'"

8. US House of Representatives, *Final Report of the Select Committee on Benghazi.*

9. Warrick, *Black Flags*, 278.

10. Gates, *Exercise of Power*, 306–307.

11. Warrick, *Black Flags*, 277.

12. Crowley, "Clinton Ties Her Record to Obama's."

13. Goldberg, "Hillary Clinton: 'Failure' to Help."

14. Gates, *Exercise of Power*, 306; Landler, *Alter Egos*, 218–219.

15. Landler, *Alter Egos*, 220.

16. Bennett, "Paula Broadwell."

17. Landler, *Alter Egos*, 221.

18. Donati, Shennib, and Bosalum, "The Adventures of a Libyan."

19. Department of Defense, Freedom of Information Division, Case no. 14-L-0552.

20. In his 2016 book, *The Killing of Osama Bin Laden*, journalist Seymour Hersh claims sources told him that the CIA in early 2012 set up what in the intelligence business is known as a "rat line"—a third-party operation—to transfer weapons from Libya to Syria. Hersh claims that the Benghazi attack, by forcing the withdrawal of CIA personnel from Benghazi, disrupted the operation, allowing the rat line to continue without American supervision toward more radical groups in Syria. Hersh quotes a former intelligence officer as summarizing the situation: "The United States was no longer in control of what the Turks were relaying to the jihadists." Syria experts remain divided on the accuracy of Hersh's claims.

21. Ulrichsen, *Qatar and the Arab Spring*, 137. Even before the election in 2012, Islamist members of Libya's National Transitional Council allegedly gave the Syrian opposition a "gift" of 100 million US dollars, before President Mustafa Abdel Jalil told Abdulhakim Belhaj to give it back.

22. Daragahi, "Libya Helps Bankroll Syrian Opposition."
23. UN Security Council, "Final Report of the Panel of Experts."
24. Risen, Mazzetti, and Schmidt, "U.S.-Approved Arms for Libya Rebels."
25. Chesnot and Malbrunot, *Qatar*, 184.
26. Author interview with Kim Ghattas on November 20, 2018.
27. Friedman, "Obama on the World."
28. Friedman, "Obama on the World."
29. Rhodes, *The World as It Is*, 197.
30. Author interview with Jake Sullivan on November 30, 2017.

Chapter 30: Back to Libya

1. Obama, "Remarks at National Medals of Science Ceremony."
2. On February 7, 2014, protests across Libya demanded that the GNC get out. Markey and Shennib, "In Standoff, Libyans Protest."
3. Toaldo, "Europe: Carving Out a New Role," 62.
4. Carlson, *In the Dark of War*, 205.
5. McGregor, "Libya's Ansar al-Shari'a Declares."
6. McGregor, "Libya's Ansar al-Shari'a Declares."
7. UN Support Mission in Libya, *Libyan Political Agreement*.
8. Ibrahim Dabbashi, correspondence with the author, August 8, 2015.
9. Chorin, "The New Danger in Benghazi."
10. Gates, *Exercise of Power*, 299.

Chapter 31: The World After Benghazi

1. "Libya Eastern Commander Haftar Declares"; Al-Warfalli, "Haftar's Forces Say."
2. "Timeline: Haftar's Months-Long Offensive."
3. Ruth Michaelson, "Turkey and UAE openly flouting UN arms embargo to fuel war in Libya," *The Guardian*, October 7, 2020. https://www.theguardian.com/global-development/2020/oct/07/turkey-and-uae-openly-flouting-un-arms-embargo-to-fuel-war-in-libya.
4. Addley et al., "Salman Abedi."
5. Connor, "At Least a Million Sub-Saharan Africans."
6. Shipman, *All Out War*, 15.
7. As of the Benghazi attack, the Houthis (who had participated in the 2011 Yemeni revolution against the regime of Ali Abdullah Saleh) still hadn't received much tangible support from Iran. A senior Indian diplomat with visibility on these issues told me that the Houthis had sent a delegation to Tehran in late 2011/early 2012 to try to elicit support, but were initially turned down. For one, the Houthis followed a different Shi'a doctrinal lineage as the rulers in Iran, and second, Yemeni operations posed logistical impediments for the Iranian regime. That would quickly change.
8. "Yemen Crisis: US Troops Withdraw."
9. Nissenbaum, "U.S. Confirms Military Withdrawal."
10. Ambassador Frederic Hof, who was until late 2012 Secretary Clinton's coordinator for the hoped-for Syria transition (away from Assad), said the administration had "stovepiped" (prioritized) everything in support of the Iran deal—long before such a deal

was even formally on the table. Author interview with Ambassador Frederic Hof on November 16, 2018.

11. Baker, Mashal, and Crowley, "How Trump's Plan."
12. Farrow, "Can Biden Reverse Trump's Damage?"
13. Lee, "Film Review: 'Operation Red Sea.'"
14. Stewart, "The Last Days of Intervention."
15. Rothkopf, "Obama's 'Don't Do Stupid Shit.'"

Chapter 32: Other Benghazis?

1. Schmitt, "Father of Commando."
2. Etzioni, "Will the Yemen Raid"; Exum, "Don't Politicize the Failed Yemen Raid."
3. Sreenivasan, "On Yemen Raid Planning."
4. Haltiwanger, "Is Niger Trump's Benghazi?"
5. Haltiwanger, "Is Niger Trump's Benghazi?"
6. Zurcher, "Myeshia Johnson."
7. Diaz, "Key Senators Say."
8. Blake, "The GOP Pushed"; Tures, "Investigating Benghazi."
9. Wu and Cheney, "Dems Push DOJ."
10. Zaptosky et al., "The Justice Dept. Alleged"; Benner, Feuer, and Haberman, "Justice Dept. Widens."
11. Elliott, "By Making the Jan. 6 Probe Political."
12. Saletan, "Republicans Are Tough on Terrorism."
13. Holpuch, "US Could Have Averted."
14. Von Rennenkampff, "Throw the GOP's Benghazi Playbook."
15. Biden, "Remarks on the Way Forward."
16. Mastrangelo, "Ernst 'Afraid of a Benghazi 2.0.'"
17. Caputo and Seligman, "'Benghazi Multiplied by 10.'"
18. Biden, "Remarks on the Drawdown of U.S. Forces."
19. Trump, "You Guys Noticed a Pattern?"
20. Packer, "The Betrayal."
21. Cooper, "Are Democrats Going to Benghazi Biden?"
22. Caputo and Seligman, "'Benghazi Multiplied by 10.'"
23. Milley, "Matt Gaetz Uses Bob Woodward Book."
24. Caputo and Seligman, "'Benghazi Multiplied by 10.'"
25. Davis, "Afghanistan"; Burns, Baldor, and Altman, "US Down to 2,500 Troops."
26. Golby, "Trump Makes a Bad Situation Worse."
27. Martin and Burns, "Reeling from Surprise Losses."
28. Newhauser, "As Midterms Approach."
29. Caputo and Seligman, "'Benghazi Multiplied by 10.'"

Conclusion: Benghazi and the Brink

1. Giles, *The Turning Point*, 25–26.
2. "FBI Uncovers Al-Qaeda Plot."
3. See Achcar, *The Clash of Barbarisms*.

4. Author interview with Robert Springborg on November 8, 2021.

5. Weisman, "Powell Calls His U.N. Speech."

6. It's widely suspected that many of these individuals were killed in clashes with Khalifa Heftar in the battles for Benghazi. Goldman and Savage, "2nd Benghazi Suspect Is Convicted."

7. As you might expect, there is evidence that just increasing the number of sources and kinds of interpersonal interactions in a person's day is a strong antidote to political polarization. See, for example, Kelly, "Like a Natural System."

Index